The Greek Military Dictatorship

THE GREEK MILITARY DICTATORSHIP

Revisiting a Troubled Past, 1967–1974

Edited by
Othon Anastasakis and Katerina Lagos

berghahn
NEW YORK • OXFORD
www.berghahnbooks.com

First published in 2021 by
Berghahn Books
www.berghahnbooks.com

© 2021, 2024 Othon Anastasakis and Katerina Lagos
First paperback edition published in 2024

All rights reserved. Except for the quotation of short passages for the purposes of criticism and review, no part of this book may be reproduced in any form or by any means, electronic or mechanical, including photocopying, recording, or any information storage and retrieval system now known or to be invented, without written permission of the publisher.

Library of Congress Cataloging-in-Publication Data

Names: Anastasakis, Othon, editor. | Lagos, Katerina, editor.
Title: The Greek Military Dictatorship: Revisiting a Troubled Past, 1967–1974 / edited by Othon Anastasakis, and Katerina Lagos.
Description: New York: Berghahn Books, 2021. | Includes bibliographical references and index.
Identifiers: LCCN 2021032954 (print) | LCCN 2021032955 (ebook) | ISBN 9781800731745 (hardback) | ISBN 9781800731752 (ebook)
Subjects: LCSH: Greece—Politics and government—1967–1974. | Greece—Foreign relations—1967–1974.
Classification: LCC DF853 .G745 2021 (print) | LCC DF853 (ebook) | DDC 949.507/5—dc23
LC record available at https://lccn.loc.gov/2021032954
LC ebook record available at https://lccn.loc.gov/2021032955

British Library Cataloguing in Publication Data

A catalogue record for this book is available from the British Library

ISBN 978-1-80073-174-5 hardback
ISBN 978-1-80539-138-8 paperback
ISBN 978-1-80539-403-7 epub
ISBN 978-1-80073-175-2 web pdf

https://doi.org/10.3167/9781800731745

Contents

List of Illustrations ... vii

Preface ... viii

Introduction. The Greek Military Junta's Exceptionalism in Historical and Comparative Perspectives ... 1
Othon Anastasakis and Katerina Lagos

Part I. Historical and Ideological Background

1. The Greek Army in Politics, 1909–67 ... 15
André Gerolymatos

2. The Political and Ideological Origins of the *Ethnosotirios Epanastasis* ... 34
Katerina Lagos

Part II. Domestic Affairs

3. Economic Policy under the Greek Dictatorship ... 73
   Appendix: Data Sources ... 93
Andreas Kakridis

4. Foreign Investment under the Greek Military Regime: The American Experience ... 103
Nicholas James Kalogerakos

5. "Patient in a Cast": How the Greek Military Regime Traumatized Education ... 140
Othon Anastasakis

6. Can Dead Poets Speak Back? C. P. Cavafy, Cold War Propaganda, and the Greek Dictatorship ... 164
Foteini Dimirouli

7. Religion Enchained: The Church of Greece under
   the Military Junta 198
   Charalampos Andreopoulos and Athanasios Grammenos

Part III. External Affairs

8. Uneasy Alliances: Archbishop Iakovos and the Greek
   Colonels' Dictatorship 215
   Alexander Kitroeff

9. Uncle Sam Regrets: The United States and the Greek
   Coup of April 1967 240
   James Edward Miller

10. Britain, Europe, and the Greek Junta: "Business as Usual" . . 266
    Alexandros Nafpliotis

11. West Germany's Policy toward Greece during the Junta
    Period in the Context of "Burden-Sharing" 295
    Mogens Pelt

12. The Greek Military Regime and the Cyprus Question 320
    John Sakkas

Conclusions. The 1974 Moment of Rupture and the Legacies
of a Discredited Past 340
Othon Anastasakis and Katerina Lagos

Index 347

Illustrations

FIGURES

3.1. The Long-Term View: Real Gross Domestic Product
Growth and Employment Shares, 1955–75   76

3.2. Real Credit Growth: Private Sector Credits by Branch,
Deflated by Consumer Price Index, 1965–75   85

3.3. External Trade Balance: Exports, Imports, and Trade
Deficit, 1960–75, in Billions of US$ 88

3.4. Overheating? Inflation Rate (Year on Year) and Stock
Market Price Index, 1965–75   89

TABLES

3.1. Growth, Investment, and Fiscal Policy   82

3.2. Prices, Wages, and Monetary and Credit Policy   83

4.1. Greece: Balance of Payments Statistics, 1960–75   110

Preface

This idea for this book was conceived in April 2017 when a group of scholars were hosted at a three-day conference in Sacramento, California, to discuss the Greek military coup d'état on its fiftieth anniversary. This gathering, organized by the Hellenic Studies Program at Sacramento State University, was a great opportunity to revisit and analyze different aspects of a military regime that ushered in a dark chapter in contemporary Greek history.

The conference brought together historians, political scientists, literary experts, economists, sociologists, and anthropologists from all over the United States and Europe. During these three days, all these experts through their presentations explored a range of topics and revealed fascinating aspects of the seven-year military regime. It became evident to all of us that there was so much fresh and exciting information and analysis that emerged from this conference that we could simply not let this opportunity go wasted.

Up until that point, most of the scholarly studies on the subject had either focused on the political history of the Greek junta or were monographs on particular features of the dictatorship, but none had attempted to view this period in an all-inclusive, interdisciplinary manner.

Since that sunny weekend in Sacramento, we, the coeditors of this volume, never lost sight of a new exciting book project. We agreed to continue working with the majority of the paper presenters toward an edited volume that would include their original and groundbreaking scholarship. In the process, we added some more authors and new themes to build on the richness and interdisciplinarity of the project. The venture was fascinating for us, as editors as well as chapter contributors, and the longevity of the process, three-and-a-half years in the making, reflects the seriousness with which we all approached our subject matter.

We would therefore like to thank, first and foremost, all the individual authors of the chapters, who engaged so constructively with this book and put up with our often demanding editing process. They all held to our instructions and deadlines, producing memorable chapters in their own rights. This is a collective narrative of a dark period in Greek history, but it is also a collection of individual contributions which bring light to the different aspects of the regime.

In addition, we would like to thank our opening presenter at the conference, Dr. Alexandros Kokkinidis, who provided invaluable assistance and insight for the whole project.

Special thanks go to Nick Geller for his meticulous editing, his mastery of every conceivable form of citation style, and for his incredible collegiality, which resulted in a working relationship that we will never forget. We should also thank the language editor of the first draft, Nikos Filippakis, for his dedication during the initial phase of the book project.

All of these people have been an amazing group of colleagues to work with, and we are now fortunate to call them our friends.

We would also like to thank the anonymous reviewers for giving us constructive and highly complimentary feedback. They gave us a big boost to finalize our book, and we have tried to address all their comments.

Finally, we are also thankful to Berghahn Books because they embraced this book project from the start, and in particular Marion Berghahn, Mykelin Higham, and Chris Chappell for their support and guidance.

This volume would not be possible without the generosity of Angelo K. and Sofia Tsakopoulos, the Tsakopoulos Hellenic Foundation, and the Annunciation Endowment Fund. Both boards gave their unhesitating financial assistance to the conference and this publication. We are extremely grateful for their support.

Lastly, as enjoyable as the process has been from initial conference preparations to the final editing of the manuscript, we would like to express our sorrow for the loss of our beloved friend, colleague, and chapter contributor André Gerolymatos. His encyclopedic knowledge of all aspects of Greek military history coupled with his charismatic charm and leadership will be greatly missed. Despite the steady decline in his health, André made sure that his preliminary draft would be finished in time to join the other chapters. The edited version of his draft is now the first chapter of the volume, and we would like to dedicate *The Greek Military Dictatorship, 1967–74: Revisiting a Troubled Past* to André.

—Katerina Lagos and Othon Anastasakis
September 2021

Introduction
The Greek Military Junta's Exceptionalism in Historical and Comparative Perspectives

Othon Anastasakis and Katerina Lagos

Greece as the so-called birthplace of democracy appeared an international oddity in the eyes of many Westerners when in 1967 a group of Greek colonels overthrew the civilian government. The 1967 coup d'état brought about the longest dictatorship in the history of modern Greece. Looking back further, it was not the only military intervention in modern Greece's past; indeed, the country had experienced short military coups since the mid-nineteenth century and had lived through another long dictatorship by Ioannis Metaxas between 1936 and 1941 at the height of fascism in Europe. Yet what was unique about the Colonels' regime—unlike previous cases in Greece or contemporary cases in the Southern Europe or Latin America—is that the 1967 coup d'état took place at a time of strong economic growth in Greece, with the country firmly in the Western capitalist bloc, including a very promising association agreement with the democratic European Economic Community (EEC).

The present volume discusses this paradox and looks at the complexity of the military rule in Greece through a selection of contributions that examine the origins, nature, ideology, policies, and foreign politics of the regime. A collection of scholars who are experts in the field—most of them historians, but others from political science, international relations, political economy, religious studies, and literature—approach the military regime from internal and external relations perspectives. The book analyzes the military regime not simply as a unique period in modern Greek history, with a start date and an ending, but also through the prism of evolving domestic and international environments. The themes of continuity and rupture vis-à-vis the previous status quo are discussed throughout the book, whereby each contributor presents what was unique in the regime and what represented a continuity with past ideas, practices, and policies. While the book underscores the reactionary and often convoluted nature of the regime, it looks at what the Colonels did in order to remain in power, as well as their policies as governors responding to the exigencies of a country operating within the camp of modernizing Western liberal economies and societies.

The military regime in Greece has attracted the attention of many historians in the Anglophone literature. There are some noteworthy monographs on the political history of the regime from a top-down, elites perspective published during the 1970s and 1980s, with a fresh memory of the events (Clogg and Yannopoulos 1972; Andrews 1980; Woodhouse 1985, which is the most recent comprehensive analysis of the junta regime and provides a political history of the dictatorship). Other books include eyewitnesses and accounts with a more personal gaze at this period ("Athenian" 1972; Barkman 1989; Couloumbis 2004; Orestis 2009; Keeley 2010). In addition, there are analyses, which focus mostly on the origins and causes of authoritarianism in Greece, on the pre-1967 period, or the post-1974 transition to democracy (Papandreou 1970; Featherstone and Katsoudas 1987; Murtagh 1994). Finally, there are some more recent published books that touch on particular aspects of the regime, such as external bilateral relations, cultural issues, the junta's failed civilian experiment, or on the role of the youth at the time (Pelt 2006; Miller 2009; Doulis 2011; Kornetis 2013; Nafpliotis 2013; Karakatsanis 2018; Maragkou 2019; Tzortzis 2020). The present edited volume is broader in scope and includes a parallel discussion of politics, ideology, foreign policy, economics, education, religion, culture, diaspora, and external relations under Greece's military rule; as such, it can appeal to a more diverse audience. All these aspects are regarded comparatively, as part of an exceptional time in Greek history but also in connection with the country's historical continuum.

The origins of the military involvement in Greek politics goes far back into the nineteenth century, when links between civilian and military elites were established, with the latter often becoming politicized and tying their corporate interests to particular parties. What was unique about the 1967 military coup d'état was the almost complete alienation of the middle-rank officers from their political patrons. As André Gerolymatos and Katerina Lagos explain in the first section of this book, the Greek Civil War was a critical period that led to the "autonomization" of the Greek army from politics and the strengthening of the most reactionary anticommunist and antidemocratic fractions within the army, the precursors of the military junta—that is, the influential paramilitary organization known as IDEA (Ιερός Δεσμός Ελλήνων Αξιωματικών, Holy Bond of Greek Officers), whose members effectively imposed their coup in 1967.[1]

Post–World War II parliamentary rule in Greece during the 1950s and early 1960s was in essence an illiberal, half-baked democracy, marked by the exclusion of the Communist Party, discrimination against those associated with left-wing politics, manipulations of elections, and the use of repressive mechanisms (imprisonment or exile) toward dissidents. The political power of the anticommunist state rested on the triarchy of crown, parliament, and army. Within this triangle, the king of Greece at times seemed to perceive his powers to be limitless, and, frequently overstepping his constitutional rights, he intervened in party politics to pursue his personal agenda (Alivizatos 1986: 203–71). The political Right, through parliamentary and extra-parliamentary activities and with the help of the United States, managed to secure its dominant position in government for eleven uninterrupted years (1952–63).

The international environment, which is a theme discussed extensively in this book, was a very influential factor in Greece's turbulent post–World War II history, mostly as a result of the country's geopolitical significance. Postwar Greece was in many respects the microcosm of the international Cold War bipolarity, exemplified by the prolonged civil war in the 1940s and the victory of the Western over the communist forces. As a NATO member state from 1952, Greece acquired a special geopolitical position and was crucial to U.S. superpower interests in the Balkans and the Middle East; this contributed to the increasing role of the military and the strengthening of the institutional autonomy of the army in politics. Many members of the IDEA were educated in the United States, and they had espoused "new professional" doctrines of "counter-insurgency and internal security" (Stepan 1973: 50–53). As James Edwards Miller argues in his chapter, military assistance programs permitted the Greek government "both to strengthen its defensive capabilities through aid grants and to reallocate significant budgetary outlays to support important economic development programs." Eventually, U.S. economic assistance had to be reduced, which allowed for an increasing European influence in Greece's economy and society. Indeed, following the Association Agreement in 1961 with the EEC, the Greek economy was brought closer to the European fold—and with increasing bilateral economic links with the major Western European economies. As Alexandros Nafpliotis points out in his chapter, closer economic links with Germany, France, and Britain made it particularly difficult for these countries to sever relations with Greece when the military junta took over in 1967, and in some instances continued a "business as usual" practice.

Despite the hybridity of the democratic process and the ideological polarization, the Greek economy during the 1950s and 1960s recovered rapidly from the negative repercussions of the wars, with the help of American aid and direct foreign investment, and recorded impressive rates of growth. The main characteristics of this postwar "economic miracle" were the boosting of the manufacturing sector, the shift in investment from light consumer goods to durable and capital goods, the change in the structure of exports from agricultural to industrial goods, and a significant concentration of capital in industry (Mouzelis 1976). However, despite the impressive rates of economic growth, the main elements of Greece's prewar socioeconomic structure continued to dominate, marked by the powerful state sector, the inability to develop technologically the agricultural sector, and the ever-increasing power of shipping capital. The state sector continued to provide the bulk of employment for the majority of the middle and lower classes. As Andreas Kakridis argues in his chapter, "The quest for development was translated into the dual pursuit of *stability* and *investment*; both entailed a heavy dose of state intervention, albeit within the overarching framework of a market economy." While the economic changes of the 1960s did not affect in any radical way the peripheral status of the Greek economy in relation to the developed world, they brought about some qualitative changes in the standard of living of the population and strengthened the dynamism of the Greek society.

This rapid economic growth brought about the rise of a new middle class and with it the strengthening of a more demanding civil society seeking political change. The 1960s saw the ascendancy of the reformist Center Union government to power, and of its popular leader George Papandreou, challenging the domination of the postwar political triarchy. The Center Union professed a more progressive and inclusionary agenda, asking for the relaxation of the anticommunist state of repressive mechanisms, the submission of the armed forces under civilians, a more independent civil society, and a comprehensive educational reform. As Othon Anastasakis contends in his chapter on education, George Papandreou's educational reform stands out as one of the most significant reformist initiatives in Greece's educational history, entailing changes that challenged the decades old status quo to such a degree that the military junta made it one of its foremost priorities upon arrival in 1967 to overturn and break with this progress, as it clearly felt threatened by it.

Contrary to most Latin American counterparts, the breakdown of parliamentary democracy in Greece took place in the midst of an economic boom and not in the context of economic stagnation.[2] For this reason, the regime could not convincingly use a legitimizing developmentalist economic language as an excuse for intervention. In fact, as Kakridis argues, one can observe a high degree of continuity with the past in the economic policies adopted by the military rulers. The regime had therefore to resort to a sterile ideological discourse as is discussed in Lagos's chapter, where she argues that the ideological framework of the 21 April regime was confined within anti-communist, Greco-Christian generalities in their extreme Cold War usage, the only common ideological denominator within an otherwise diverse politically and ideologically military institution. This ideological framework looked totally antiquated, and was a solid rupture with the new Western societal discourses and movements of the late 1960s.

The fact that the 21 April regime did not face any credible internal political opposition allowed the small group of middle-rank officers, under the leadership of Georgios Papadopoulos, to sustain their power for as long as they did. To do this, they had to create their own alliances and networks of opportunistic supporters, as well as control institutions with some influence on Greek society, such as the Greek Orthodox Church. But even in this domain, as Charalambos Andreopoulos and Athanasios Grammenos argue in their chapter, they were not able to keep a consistent policy and exported their own divisions into the Church itself.

The military rulers were helped by the international power politics of the Cold War, which is what Nafpliotis and Mogens Pelt argue in their chapters, showing how Western countries continued to maintain relations with Greece's authoritarian rulers, primarily because it suited their own strategic as well as economic interests. Moreover, as Miller states in his chapter, in the case of the United States, support for democracy was clearly sacrificed on the altar of Cold War politics. Yet, despite the working relationship with the international community, in the end it was a foreign policy matter in Cyprus that acted as a catalyst for the collapse of the regime, a story which is aptly presented by John Sakkas in his chapter on the junta's policy vis-à-vis Turkey and Cyprus. Ironically, it was yet another humiliating external defeat, following the earlier 1897 Greco-Turkish War and the 1922 Asia Minor catastrophe, that sealed the fate of the military in Greek politics, this time in the right direction, leading to a successful transition to democracy and sending the military to the barracks where it belonged, as the ultimate rupture with the past.

The present volume is divided into three sections. The first section entails two chapters that look at the military and ideological origins of the 21 April regime. Gerolymatos provides an overview of the Greek military beginning in the early twentieth century. He argues that while the antecedents of military intervention can be traced back to the 1920s and 1930s, the Greek Civil War in the 1940s proved to be a seminal moment in the history of the military, as the emergent Greek National Army was fraught with factions and was weak in comparison to the Democratic Army. This prompted British—and later American—involvement to reorganize the Greek military and ensured that the officer corps would be beyond the reach of the political leadership. Lagos picks up the theme of the military's autonomy from political oversight and examines the growing involvement of the military in political affairs. The officers of the Greek army presented themselves as the praetorian guards of the Greek state and made sure to prevent any communist or left-leaning political party from acquiring power. However, once the Colonels acquired political power, they struggled to maintain unity and could not articulate a unified vision or political agenda for their regime.

The second part of the book looks at different policies of the regime in such fields as the economy, foreign direct investment, education, culture, and religion. In the area of economics, the dictatorship did not venture far from the policies adopted in the 1950s and early 1960s, and the Colonels sought to maintain economic growth, which, according to Kakridis, did not change key policy ideas or economic personnel. In fact, the shifts that occurred were those of policy emphasis, not major policy realignments. The Colonels tied the regime's survival to economic growth and consumerism; the additional resources generated were used to "co-opt and placate different social groups—not just the rich and powerful" (chapter 3, this volume). This proved to be a double-edged sword as it placed the economy under an increasing strain, which eventually caused macroeconomic derailment in 1973–74. A similar situation occurred when the dictators actively sought out foreign investment to generate desperately needed revenue. This pursuit resulted in a Byzantine dance between financial suitors and the established economic oligarchy to secure investment contracts in Greece. As Nicholas Kalogerakos explains, "Greece's doors were open for business," but foreign investors soon realized that their projects would face the same internal gatekeepers as before on their path to gaining approval from the Ministry of Coordination's Committee on Foreign Investment. Between preferential treatment for certain company proposals and outright suppression of potential competition for domestic companies, foreign corporations could not secure a deal with the Greek government without considerable internal cooperation and support. Ultimately, Kalogerakos demonstrates that the junta's declaration of support for foreign investment was more smoke and mirrors than a streamlined process for foreign investors, especially American investors. The Colonels may have been desperate for international recognition and foreign investment, but they were unwilling—or unable—to dismantle the prejunta power structure of vested interests within the economic establishment.

While the Colonels maintained the status quo for economic affairs, this was not the case with other government policies. Anastasakis explains that in the field of education, the Colonels pursued a reactionary agenda that fundamentally overturned all of the attempted reforms that George Papandreou and the Center Union Party had proposed with the 1964 Education Act. In addition, the dictatorship passed new laws to facilitate oversight and control of the youth, especially student organizations. In the end, the latter proved to be the regime's nemesis, and the reactionary university policies of the junta left a long-lasting legacy on Greece's post-1974 democracy. At some point, the regime tried, albeit unsuccessfully, to adopt a more technocratic agenda in education to respond to the objective needs of a changing liberal economy, a point that showed more clearly the conflicting nature of military officers as rulers in areas where they were utterly incompetent and fundamentally repressive. However, as Foteini Dimirouli explains, there were instances where the dictators used means other than repression and censorship to achieve their aims. The Colonels employed cultural appropriation and the redeployment of literary texts in the regime's discourse to further their political agenda. Using the national poet C. P. Cavafy as her case study, Dimirouli traces how Cavafy's poems were reinterpreted and recast to assert dictatorial legitimacy, ignite nationalistic sentiment, and vilify opponents. She asserts that poetry, like other art, "can operate as a cipher for causes that have little in common with prevailing readings of the work or with the discursive fields in which it was originally produced."

In the eyes of the Church, the Colonels took a cavalier and dismissive approach to the ecclesiastical hierarchy. Despite lauding the significance of Orthodox Christianity in the regime's social vision, the Colonels tried to control the ecclesiastical leadership for their own political purposes. Andreopoulos and Grammenos argue that the junta's interference in the Orthodox Church reached an unprecedented level. As they had done with their rupture in the field of education, within weeks after the coup, the Colonels replaced the Archbishop of Athens, Chrysostomos II, with a younger and more pliant Archimandrite Ieronymos and sought to control the Church in the name of its supposed salvation. However, Andreopoulos and Grammenos find that the Colonels' intervention was not one-sided; Ieronymos took advantage of his position to make changes within the Archdiocese hierarchy that violated Canonical law. As a result, tension and division developed within the hierarchy that ultimately led to Ieronymos's resignation in December 1973.

The third section of the book deals with external affairs and starts with a study of the linkages of the regime with a diasporic institution in the United States. Alexander Kitroeff examines the relations between the Colonels and one of the more prominent and often controversial leaders of the Church, Archbishop Iakovos of North and South America. Kitroeff highlights the mutual self-interest in fostering positive relations between the

Archdiocese and the junta regime. The Archdiocese Clergy-Laity Congress held in Athens in July 1968 was the high point of relations between Iakovos and the Colonels; the congress was a public relations success for the Colonels, as it projected a validation of the regime at a time when Greece had few allies. However, relations between the two declined in the face of the Colonels' dismissive and patronizing attitude toward the Greek diaspora and their blatant disregard of Iakovos's advice and offers of mediation with the U.S. government.

Staying with the United States, Miller explores the much discussed and most criticized role of the superpower. He challenges the notion that the Johnson administration helped bring the junta to power by examining both the years leading up to the coup as well as the initial relations between the two governments. Using recently declassified archival information, Miller argues that the United States, against what is often assumed, was not involved in the coup and expressed clear disapproval; yet the Johnson administration chose to keep steady communication with the dictatorship so that they could continue to influence the Colonels and persuade them to transition back to parliamentary rule.

Relationships with other Western actors, including Britain, West Germany, and EEC, are also examined in the book. More concretely, this volume delves into the major dilemmas of the Western European democratic states, confronted with the perennial question whether to engage with or break away from Greek military rule. While objecting to the dictatorial practices of the junta, the Western powers nevertheless had to consider security, economic, and political interests with an ally in a divided bipolar environment, and, with varying degrees of internal consent, they opted for continuity over rupture. Nafpliotis frames the discussion by examining Great Britain's relations with the military regime within the context of NATO, the Council of Europe, and the EEC, shedding light on how economic factors overrode political considerations in dealing with the Colonels. In the end, Western European countries tacitly legitimized the dictatorship by continuing to engage in diplomatic relations and trade agreements, overcoming their democratic sensitivities because it served their strategic and economic interests. As Nafpliotis demonstrates, Britain's behavior was not isolated; other European countries, such as France and West Germany, followed suit. Pelt picks up this theme in his chapter by analyzing West Germany's attempts to maintain a policy of nonintervention in Greek domestic affairs in the face of harsh criticism both at home and by some of Germany's allies in the Scandinavian region. As West Germany pursued a strategy "that on the one hand wanted to regain old markets and which on the other was designed to tie Greece to the West," Chancellor Kurt Kiesinger and Vice-Chancellor Willy Brandt could not disregard the concerns raised within their government as well as from neighboring allies. One of major considerations was West Germany's weapons trade with Greece; they were loath to terminate these lucrative deals and merely reduced the volume of sensitive arms deliveries instead of suspending them.

Finally, this section of the book addresses the regime's foreign policy in the utmost matter of national interest, Cyprus. Sakkas sheds light on the Colonels' duplicitous handling of the Cyprus problem. While the Colonels had voiced their support of enosis (union) for Cyprus from the outset of the dictatorship, behind closed doors, they pursued a solution based on partition. The Colonels deplored Archbishop Makarios's attempt to cultivate relations with the Soviet Union, and by June 1971 Papadopoulos sought to forge a deal with Turkey regarding Cyprus that he would impose on Makarios. Ultimately, the rift created between the junta and Archbishop Makarios continued to grow and came to a climax when Dimitrios Ioannides organized a coup d'état in the summer of 1974 to overthrow Makarios and forcibly unify Cyprus to Greece, leading to the collapse of the junta and the divided fate of Cyprus, which continues today.

In the conclusion, we discuss the meaning of the 1974 moment of the breakdown of the dictatorship and the subsequent legacies of the regime, arguing that July 1974 is mythologized in the minds of most Greeks as the moment of an irreversible transition to democracy and the victory of the latter over authoritarianism. Indeed, most of the actions by the first democratic governments were guided by the desire for the so-called dejuntifcation of Greek politics and society, as well as the rupture with the pre-1967 illiberal past, thus laying a solid foundation for democracy as the supposed only game in town. Yet, we also argue that the military regime left some legacies that continued to affect public perceptions toward democratic politics, civic resistance, and the role of external actors. To this day, the dictatorship remains a painful recollection for most Greeks with a living memory of it, many of whom are still alive to tell the story as they remember it, while others remain who prefer to forget.

This volume wishes not to forget but to build on the existing literature and revisit different aspects of the dictatorial period through research and investigation conducted by all of its contributors. It thus combines original archival information with in-depth scholarly analysis, in order to bring about innovative arguments on the nature of the regime. In the end, the book's added value lies in three important outputs: first, it is an updated account of a contested national story that comes more than half a century and two generations after the 1967 coup d'état; second, it provides for an interdisciplinary reading that covers different dimensions of the military regime, and in that sense the book stands as a unified interconnected narrative and at the same time provides for individual chapters with their own inherent value; and, last but not least, it is a reminder that there are many aspects of this turbulent period of Greek history that remain unexplored or underexplored and still require scholarly attention. In doing so, the Greek military regime stands out as a reminder of lessons learned from past political mistakes as well as irresponsible and dangerous leaderships.

Othon Anastasakis is the Director of South East European Studies at Oxford (SEESOX) and Senior Research Fellow at St Antony's College, University of Oxford. His most recent co-edited books include *Diaspora Engagement in Times of Severe Economic Crisis: Greece and Beyond* (Palgrave, 2022), *The Legacy of Yugoslavia: Politics, Economy and Society* (I.B. Tauris, 2020), and *Balkan Legacies of the Great War: The Past Is Never Dead* (Palgrave Macmillan, 2016).

Katerina Lagos is a Professor of History at California State University, Sacramento and the Director of the Angelo K. Tsakopoulos Hellenic Studies Center and Hellenic Studies Center. Her most recent publication is *The Fourth of August Regime and Greek Jewry, 1936-1941* (Palgrave, 2023).

NOTES

1. The history of the IDEA had its roots in the period of the Nazi occupation of Greece. It was originally formed by Greek officers in Palestine under the name of the ENA (Ενωσις Νέων Αξιωματικών, Union of Young Officers) and in October 1944 was transformed into the IDEA, an ideologically "pure" union of officers, who sought to promote their influence within the army. In their initial proclamation, the members of IDEA asked for the "forceful exclusion from the armed forces of officers with internationalist beliefs and nationally doubtful convictions" (Stavrou 1976: 116).

2. In Latin America, perennial structural problems of high inflation, balance of payment problems, and a high degree of dependence on the international economy exacerbated social tensions to such an extent that parliamentary institutions were not able to cope (Kaufman 1979: 190–96).

REFERENCES

Secondary Sources

Alivizatos, N. 1986. Oi politikoi thesmoi se krisi, 1922–1974. [Political institutions in crisis, 1922–74]. Athens.
Andrews, K. 1980. *Greece in the Dark: 1967–1974*. Amsterdam.
"Athenian." 1972. *Inside the Colonels' Greece*. Translated by R. Clogg. London.
Barkman, C. 1989. *Ambassador in Athens, 1969–1975: The Evolution from Military Dictatorship to Democracy in Greece*. London.
Clogg, R., and G. Yannopoulos, eds. 1972. *Greece under Military Rule*. London.
Couloumbis, T. A. 2004. *The Greek Junta Phenomenon: A Professor's Notes*. New York.
Doulis, T. 2011. *The Iron Storm: The Impact on Greek Culture of the Military Junta, 1967–1974*. Bloomington, IN.
Featherstone, K., and D. K. Katsoudas, eds. 1987. *Political Change in Greece: Before and After the Colonels*. London.
Karakatsanis, N. M., and J. Swarts. 2018. *American Foreign Policy towards the Colonels' Greece: Uncertain Allies and the 1967 Coup d'État*. New York.
Kaufman, R. 1979. "Industrial Change and Authoritarian Rule." In *The New Authoritarianism in Latin America*, edited by D. Collier, 165–253. Princeton.
Keeley, R. V. 2010. *The Colonels' Coup and the American Embassy: A Diplomat's View of the Breakdown of Democracy in Cold War Greece*. University Park, PA.
Kornetis, K. 2013. *Children of the Dictatorship: Student Resistance, Cultural Politics and the "Long 1960s" in Greece*. New York.
Maragkou, K. 2019. *Greece, Britain and the Colonels, 1967–74: Between Pragmatism and Human Rights*. London.
Miller, J. E. 2009. *The United States and the Making of Modern Greece*. Chapel Hill, NC.
Mouzelis, N. 1976. "Capitalism and Dictatorship in Post-War Greece." *New Left Review* 96 (March–April): 57–80.
Murtagh, P. 1994. *The Rape of Greece: The King, the Colonels and the Resistance*. London.
Nafpliotis, A. 2013. *Britain and the Greek Colonels: Accommodating the Junta in the Cold War*. London.
Orestis, V. 2009. *Confronting the Greek Dictatorship in the U.S.: Years of Exile, a Personal Diary (1968–1975)*. New York.
Papandreou, A. 1970. *Democracy at Gunpoint*. New York.
Pelt, M. 2006. *Tying Greece to the West: US–West German–Greek Relations 1949–74*. Copenhagen.

Stavrou, N. A. 1976. *Allied Politics and Military Interventions: The Political Role of the Greek Military*. Athens.

Stepan, A. "The New Professionalism of Internal Warfare and Military Role Expansion." In *Authoritarian Brazil*, 47–65. New Haven.

Tzortzis, I. 2020. *Greek Democracy and the Junta: Regime Crisis and the Failed Transition of 1973*. London.

Woodhouse, C. M. 1985. *The Rise and Fall of the Greek Colonels*. New York.

Part I

Historical and Ideological Background

Chapter 1

The Greek Army in Politics, 1909–67

André Gerolymatos

Military involvement in Greek politics was nothing new by the time the Colonels took power in 1967. The antecedents of the military intervention can even be traced to the first decade of the modern Greek state, during which the army intervened in Greece's political affairs (Gerolymatos 2009: 7). In 1843, the Athens garrison, led by General Dimitrios Kalergis, forced the first king of Greece, Othon I, to grant a constitution (Finlay 2014). Although the monarch had acquiesced to this demand at the beginning of his reign, he only acted on it when faced with a military revolt and possible revolution. By the end of the nineteenth century, Greece's defeat in the Greco-Turkish War of 1897 prompted military officers to press for reforms and modernization. Their requests fell on deaf ears, and, by October 1908, army officers organized themselves into the secret Military League. In a scene reminiscent of 1843, the Military League forced another king of Greece, George I, to grant a series of popular reforms and also secured the resignation of Prime Minister Dimitrios Rallis.[1] The Goudi Revolt of 1909 marks a new chapter in the military's involvement in Greek politics. From that point on, the Greek Army established itself an active participant in the political affairs of the country. This chapter will examine the significant role that the Greek Army would continue to play in the political arena—from the turbulent interwar years to the German occupation, and later to civil war of the 1940s and its aftermath.

THE ASIA MINOR CATASTROPHE AND THE INTERWAR YEARS

Prior to World War II, the Greek officer corps was riddled with factions and secret societies, not yet having coalesced into a single and ideologically cohesive body (Veremis and Gerolymatos 1991: 105–7). During the interwar period, however, groups within the officer corps had become integral participants in the unstable political climate that shaped the Greek state in the 1920s and 1930s. They became "arbiters in the struggle between the Liberal and Conservative (Populist) parties" and an integral part of the patron-client relationships dominated by the politicians (Veremis 1997: 7). Their composition had changed as a result of political and social changes that transpired between 1912 and 1923.[2] An increase in the military academy's admissions, for example, together with the introduction of free tuition in 1917, had opened up a military career to the less advantaged classes, while at the same time discouraging the sons of more prominent members of Greek society from joining its ranks (Veremis 1997: 6). Moreover, the Greek Army had expanded considerably between 1911 and 1919 in response to the Balkan Wars (1912–13), Greek participation in World War I, and the intervention in Asia Minor. This expansion necessitated a substantial increase in the officer corps, with most of the new officers coming from the reserves and from promotions in the field (Gerolymatos 2009: 8). Ironically, this expansion and diversity in recruits transformed the officer corps to be "more representative of Greek society and less willing to accept the supremacy of civilian rule" (Veremis and Gerolymatos 1991: 103; Veremis 1997: 38).

This same period saw a division of Greek society into two groups: the supporters of Venizelos (or Venizelists)—and his advocacy of Greece's entry into World War I on the side of the Entente—and, in contrast, the monarchists, who supported Constantine I and his policy of neutrality. The officer corps no less reflected this division of Venizelists and monarchists, a division that was only further compounded by the eventual victory of Venizelos in 1917 and the expulsion of King Constantine. The new additions owed their status and rank to Venizelos, and they represented a distinct entity within the academy-trained, prewar body of officers.[3] The officer corps, which had initially increased to meet the demands of war, contracted after the Asia Minor catastrophe, thus creating competition not only for promotion but also for professional survival in the postwar army (Veremis and Gerolymatos 1991: 103–5). The fear of early retirement made most officers vulnerable and ultimately susceptible to engaging in political intervention, and they opted to follow the fortunes of either the pro-Venizelos forces or those of the monarchy in the interwar period. As a result, the struggle between the Venizelist liberals and royalist conservatives also caused the Greek officers to fall into political rivalry and infighting (Mouzelis 1986: 98; Veremis and Gerolymatos 1991: 104–5).

During the interwar period, the officer corps and the Greek military in general mirrored the divisions within Greek society between the Venizelists and the royalists (Veremis and Gerolymatos 1991: 105). It is important to note, however, that these divisions within the officer corps, except for a small number of higher-ranking officers, did not represent distinct political entities or factions of officers devoted to a specific political cause. Instead, the armed forces were honeycombed with loose groupings of officers who gravitated to the Venizelists or royalists depending on their allegiance to senior military commanders who themselves were affiliated with a particular political party. Consequently, the fortunes of the officers were directly affected by the outcomes of the coups in the 1920s and 1930s, which were mounted by the supporters of Constantine I or those of Venizelos (Gerolymatos 2009: 9).

In the process, these loyalties quickly started to undermine the stability of the Greek state. A republican general, Leonidas Spais, later reflected in his memoirs that the minuet of party factions, combined with greed and acrimonious partisan politics, led the country to the great 1922 disaster in Asia Minor.[4] In the summer of 1922, the Greek Army was routed in Turkey; by September, it was streaming back to Greece in disgrace. As the soldiers returned home, a tide of refugees flooded the sun-drenched harbors of Athens and Thessaloniki. This sea of human misery was the price Greece had to pay for a military adventure that had begun in 1919, but whose origins were intertwined with the inception of the modern Greek state. Assigning blame had become the order of the day, and someone had to pay for the Asia Minor catastrophe as an atonement for the sin of defeat. It was left to the fractured military to choose the sacrificial victims.

By late fall of 1922, the army had selected six men to carry the burden and responsibility for the catastrophic defeat in Asia Minor: Prime Minister Dimitris Gounaris; Commander-in-Chief of the Greek Army Georgios Hatzianestis; Foreign Minister Georgios Baltazzis; Minister of the Interior Nikolaos Stratos; Minister of War Nikolaos Theotokis; and Finance Minister Petros Protopapadakis. Individually and collectively, these men directed the Greek state and also the military campaign. Although most Athenians nursed a secret desire for "the Six" (as they came to be known) to be spared, the army needed and demanded human sacrifices. In the last days of November, the army orchestrated a sham court in order to absolve the military from the disaster in Turkey and preserve its role as guardian of the state. The Six were quickly condemned to death for high treason.[5] Despite the cold rain that fell from early in the morning on 28 November 1922, approximately 150 men clustered together in a field adjacent to the Goudi military barracks, just a few kilometers north of Athens. They stood in silence, consumed by the restless energy of anticipation. They had come here to witness the execution of six men who were the most despised men in Greece. A light drizzle fell upon the spectators, some of whom were only partly aware that this particular execution now sealed the political schism that had dogged Greek society from the very beginning of the twentieth century.

The execution of the Six, however, was an aberration. Although coups and countercoups were part of the shuffleboard of Greek politics, they were relatively bloodless affairs (Gerolymatos 2009: 10). The application of mass killing, torture, and harsh imprisonment grew out of the cult of ideology and fear that plagued Greek society during the civil wars in the 1940s. Prior to 1922, the wrong end of a political conspiracy usually meant loss of office and influence, as well as the inability to compensate the followers of one party or another with rewards from the government's largesse. These shifts in fortune were temporary, however, and soon rectified by the next election or coup. While strong emotion and violence often accompanied major shifts in the power politics of the country, the execution of the Six introduced the prospect of death as an all too real punishment for political failure—a finality that few were prepared to countenance.

The army, or more specifically the officer corps, desperately needed to distance itself from the defeat in Asia Minor. As was the case with the military of the other Balkan states, the army officers considered themselves "the embodiment of the nation and the protectors of the state" (Gerolymatos 2009: 10). Any stigma of defeat or humiliation had to be deflected and consigned to unscrupulous politicians or to the Great Powers (Great Britain, France, and Russia). The Greek military invoked a "stab in the back" apologia as a means to explain their part in the cataclysm of 1922 and to preserve the role of the army as the guardian of Greece (Gerolymatos 2009: 10). However, this contempt for accountability only perpetuated a cycle of military interventions that frequently destabilized Greek society and guaranteed the army a disproportionate influence in the state. Consequently, the condemnation of the Six was simply another step in a self-serving process that enabled the military and the political opponents of the Six to avoid direct responsibility for the defeat. Although the disaster of Asia Minor was the immediate responsibility of the government in power, almost the entire Greek political and military establishment had played a part in bringing about this disaster. Tragically, the execution served to enshrine the political schism that had plagued Greek society almost from its inception and later, in a mutated form, would loom over the bloodletting of the civil wars in the 1940s.

One of the results of the Asia Minor catastrophe was that the army acquired a taste for power. In late September 1922, even before execution of the Six, a few army units that had been evacuated from Turkey reached Athens, and with little resistance took over Greece and proclaimed a new order.[6] The main leaders of the coup and members of the subsequent Revolutionary

Committee included Colonel Stylianos Gonatas, Colonel Nikolaos Plastiras, and Captain Nikolaos Phokas. For the sake of appearances, and under pressure from the British and French, these colonels set up a puppet government led by Sotirios Krokidas (Llewellyn-Smith 1973: 315). A short while later, that government was replaced by one, headed by Colonel Gonatas, dropping any pretense of civilian rule. On 26 September, the military issued an ultimatum to the government demanding, among other things, the removal of King Constantine I. The monarch agreed to leave Greece, which he did on 30 September, dying in Palermo, Italy, one year later. His eldest son, George, who had replaced Constantine for a short time, went into exile in 1924 when Greece became a republic (Gerolymatos 2009: 10).

The Greek army (more specifically the officer corps) desperately needed to distance itself from the defeat in Asia Minor, and getting rid of the monarchy was a small price to pay. The revolution of 1922 not only forced the abolition of the monarchy but also heralded a new era of direct intervention by the army in the making and unmaking of governments. In addition, each coup—whether successful or not—was followed by a purge of the armed forces (Gerolymatos 2016: 29). During the 1930s, the officer corps underwent several more purges that further deepened the ill will between conservative royalists and the liberal Venizelists—labels that still had less to do with any particular ideological stream than commitment to the leader of a political faction. The end result for most officers facing defeat in a coup was forcible retirement and a dramatic loss of income. Since most Greek officers relied on their salaries and did not have private means of support, the end of a military career meant certain poverty. For example, in the attempted coup of 1933, forty officers were removed, but after the 1935 coup attempt, another 1,500 more were cashiered. By 1940, as a result of the coups and attempted coups, approximately 4,500 officers had been forced into early retirement or had left the armed forces as a result of court-martials (Gerolymatos 2009: 11). As a group, these men represented a significant percentage of the officer corps, which in April of 1940 was comprised of a little more than 5,000 professional officers and another 10,000 in the reserves (Gerolymatos 1984: 70–71nn3–6).

In the earlier coups of the 1920s, those officers forced out of the army came from the ranks of the monarchists, but in the attempted coups of 1933 and 1935, the axe fell on mostly republican officers so that by 1940 almost all antimonarchists had been forced into retirement.[7] As a result, control of the armed forces reverted to royalist officers, who in conjunction with some members of the Populist Party (the traditional party of the royalists) began to clamor for the restitution of the monarchy. In 1932, the Populists had disavowed their allegiance to the crown, but, as Grigoris Dafnis observed, their rejection was superficial, and three years later (in 1935), they reasserted their support for George II (Dafnis [1955] 1974, vol. 2: 369).[8] Following the attempted coup of March 1935, the Populist Party emerged victorious at the polls, and tremendous pressure was placed on the new prime minister, Panagiotis Tsaldaris, to bring about an immediate restoration of the monarchy (Gerolymatos 2009: 11).

Tsaldaris had promised a referendum on the issue of the monarchy, but following his landslide victory in the 1935 general election, many in his party, and primarily those senior army officers, demanded that he abolish the republic and invite King George II to return to Greece.[9] When Tsaldaris refused, his government was promptly overthrown by the military. General George Kondylis, one of the conspirators, replaced him and upon assuming office declared the end of the republic and advanced the date for the referendum on the monarchy to 3 November 1935. The results of the plebiscite were outlandish even to the most credulous supporters of the monarchy: out of 1,492,992 votes cast, only a paltry 34,454 opposed the return of George II.[10]

The reinstatement of George II did not heal the fissures in Greek society. The elections of 1936 produced a parliament divided almost evenly between the Liberals and Populists, along with fifteen Communist deputies. Both major parties initiated talks with the Communists, and the Liberals actually managed to reach an agreement with them, but these efforts at political compromise were stillborn. When news of a possible Liberal-KKE (Κομμουνιστικό Κόμμα Ελλάδας, Communist Party of Greece) coalition was leaked, Alexander Papagos, the minister of army affairs, with the support of the chiefs of the air force, navy, and gendarmerie, informed the king that the armed forces would not countenance a government that included Communists (Koliopoulos 1977: 40).

In the absence of a majority government or coalition, George II appointed Constantine Demertzis to head a caretaker government to administer the country. Unfortunately, Demertzis died in April 1936, and a new interim leader was sought. However, selecting a new interim leader would be far more challenging as five other prominent political figures had died during the past year, including Kondylis, Venizelos, Tsaldaris, and Alexander Papanastasiou. At this critical juncture, the loss of some of Greece's most influential and experienced leaders prompted George II to select Ioannis Metaxas, the deputy premier and the leader of a small right-wing party, as the new head of government. Over the next few months, the growing labor unrest sweeping Greece provided the perfect opportunity for Metaxas, with the support of the king, to gain control of the state. On 4 August—the day before the twenty-four-hour general strike that had been declared by the Workers' Federation—Metaxas persuaded the king to suspend certain articles of the constitution and declare martial law in order to avert a Communist revolution.[11] In effect, on 4 August 1936, King George II gave Metaxas the authority to establish a dictatorship that lasted even beyond Metaxas's death in January 1941, until the exiled king reinstated the constitution in February 1942 (Gerolymatos 2009: 12).

Metaxas inherited an army commanded by predominantly royalist officers and an officer corps that was ideologically homogeneous for the first time in the history of Greece (Veremis 1997: 132). Metaxas rewarded the officers and strengthened their loyalty by increasing all types of military expenditure: "pay, arms, uniforms and barracks as well as roads and defense works" (Veremis 1997: 133). Consequently, by the beginning of the Italian invasion in October 1940, the Greek armed forces, purged of most men having Venizelist sympathies, provided the main prop for the monarchy and the Metaxas regime. This resulted in the politicization of most professional Greek officers, including those who retained their commissions and those in retirement or forced into the reserves. Those who kept their rank had a vested interest in the survival of the monarchy, but those who were drummed out of the service hoped for the day when the next coup would restore their commission and salary (Gerolymatos 2009: 13).

Despite the systematic purges within the army and the efficiency of the Metaxas security services, small groups of professional officers established antidictatorship cells within the army (Gerolymatos 2016). In March 1938, Epaminondas Tsellos formed the MEO (Μυστική Επαναστατική Οργάνωσιν, Secret Revolutionary Organization), whose goal was to remove the dictatorship by force. The military membership of the organization was comprised of mostly lower-ranking officers but also several colonels and two generals (General Achilleas Protosygkellos and General Andreas Platis, the deputy chief of the Hellenic Army General Staff) (Gerolymatos 1984: 70n2). Another cell, which had existed prior to the Metaxas dictatorship, was comprised of slightly lower-ranking officers; this cell had been formed in 1933 but remained dormant until 1940. Although neither posed a serious threat to the Metaxas regime, during the occupation some of their members played an active role in the resistance and assisted in the organization of ELAS (Ελληνικός Λαϊκός Απελευθερωτικός Στρατός, Greek People's Liberation Army) (Gerolymatos 1984: 70n2; see also Gerolymatos 2016).

WORLD WAR II AND THE OCCUPATION

After the 1935 coup, the royalist-dominated officer corps no longer followed the political leaders of any party but had themselves become the power brokers and potentially could impose their will upon the question of who was to govern.[12] The Venizelists, who had been compelled to leave the armed forces, filled the ranks of the main opposition groups to the monarchy and Metaxas. A number of them formed secret organizations, while others joined the British in covert groups that would eventually amalgamate into the Special Operations Executive (SOE), which had begun to organize embryonic clandestine networks in Greece. Until Metaxas refused to accept Mussolini's terms in October 1940, the British Foreign Office harbored deep suspicions against the Greek dictator.[13]

Despite the Foreign Office officials' disapproval of the SOE's activities, the British government was convinced that Greece would be overrun by the Axis, and therefore plans for an eventual resistance were essential. Since the Metaxas regime was determined to remain neutral, the SOE and the British intelligence services began to identify the Venizelist officers, Communists, and other revolutionary groups as potential recruits for a network of underground cells that would spring to life after Greece was occupied.[14] Another consideration was that if Metaxas brought Greece into the Axis alliance, then the same groups would be used to mount a resistance against the dictatorship (Gerolymatos 2009: 14).

The SOE's plans for resistance activity in an occupied Greece gathered additional momentum and more recruits after the outbreak of hostilities on 28 October 1940. When Metaxas decided to reject Mussolini's ultimatum, the British ceased to plan for organized opposition to him and concentrated instead upon the likely prospect that the Axis would overrun Greece. Effectively, the British still relied upon the Venizelist faction for recruits, as well as other organizations opposed to the Metaxas regime. One contributing factor was that the ideological division between the Venizelists and the royalists deepened during the war, when only 3,000 of the former were recalled to active duty. Another 1,500 troops, mostly those of higher rank, were kept from participating in the war, and many of them gravitated to the embryonic cells being organized by the British intelligence services (Gerolymatos 1984: 71).

As a leading Venizelist officer who had been implicated in several interwar coups, Colonel Euripides Bakirdzis[15] was an early link between British intelligence and the Venizelist groups opposed to Metaxas, later serving as an important contact between the emerging resistance organizations and the SOE.[16] For such officers, the Axis occupation represented simply another form of illegitimate authoritarian rule in Greece and provided an opportunity to establish a patriotic front against the new occupation forces. The royalist faction, on the other hand, faced the occupation of Greece as a cohesive and ideologically united group loyal to the monarchy and to the social status quo. However, as was the case with the Venizelist officers, this group also had to deal with the complicated prospect of resistance (Gerolymatos 2009: 14).

As the government of George II was preparing to go into exile, they had made no plans for the organization of a resistance movement to carry on the struggle in Greece. The royalist officers who wished to fight were encouraged by the government of George II to join the Greek armed forces in the Middle East and North Africa. About 2,500 troops did so, while others followed the lead of General Papagos and other senior royalist officers and abstained from joining the forces of the Greek government-in-exile or participating in any resistance activity. However, many royalist officers refused to remain idle and followed the example of the Venizelist officers, who had joined the resistance organizations that were formed in the fall of 1941 and winter of 1942. As a result, both EDES (Εθνικός Δημοκρατικός Ελληνικός Σύνδεσμος, National Republican Greek League) and ELAS acquired a considerable number of professional officers.[17]

In the case of ELAS, the number of royalist officers remained at approximately 600, along with 1,200 former permanent officers, essentially Venizelists, and 2,000 lower-ranking reserve officers (Gerolymatos 2009: 15). For EDES, it is more difficult to identify the percentage of royalist officers, at least in the early stages of the occupation. One constant factor, however, is that in the later years of the occupation, EDES units were dispersed and reformed (1943–44), and replacements came from the ranks of the royalist officers. This was further facilitated by the reconciliation between Napoleon Zervas, the head of EDES, and George II in March of 1943 (Gerolymatos 2009: 15; see also Gerolymatos 1985).

Indeed, the dynamics of the resistance movement and the political aspirations of those in and outside of occupied Greece had wreaked havoc on the Venizelist faction of Greek officers. Effectively, they fell into three categories. The first was composed of die-hard republicans who joined ELAS since EDES had ceased to represent their political sentiments. A second faction of Venizelists was represented by those individuals who suffered at the hands of ELAS during the dispersing of their guerrilla bands and found refuge or sought revenge by joining the Security Battalions organized by the Ioannis Rallis puppet government in 1943 under the control of the Nazis (Gerolymatos 2009: 15; see also Gerolymatos 1985: 19). By the end of the occupation, in fact, at least a thousand professional officers were serving in the Security Battalions, most of whom had been members of the Venizelist faction (Gerolymatos 1985: 20–21). The third group of republican officers were those who feared communism more than the king and followed the example of Zervas by making their peace with the monarchy.[18]

By contrast, the situation of the officers in the ELAS units continued to remain constant. The presence of well-respected Venizelist officers in ELAS, such as Stefanos Sarafis, as well as other well-known republican officers, such as Bakirdzis, Emmanuel Mandakas, and Alexandros Othonaios, attracted other Venizelists and professional officers from the regular army (Gerolymatos 2009: 16). Consequently, by the end of the occupation, the Greek officer corps had realigned politically as a result of their wartime experience. The royalist-Venizelist schism had been supplanted by a new polarization based on Cold War politics. The Left versus Right division that surfaced during the occupation took on new dimensions and came to dominate the political discourse in Greece during and after the occupation. A critical juncture occurred following the Dekemvriana (Δεκεμβριανά, December Events) of 1944; all officers affiliated with ELAS or any other left-wing organization were essentially barred from readmission into the new Greek National Army (Gerolymatos 2009: 16). The armed forces—those who had remained inactive during the occupation but supported the monarchy during the uprisings in the Middle East—were now the prerogative of the officers who fought with Zervas and the other officers who served in the Security Battalions. The latter were released from detention in order to support the British and Greek forces fighting against ELAS during the December Events (Veremis and Gerolymatos 1991: 114n41).

THE GREEK CIVIL WAR AND ITS AFTERMATH

After the occupation, the officer corps was once again honeycombed with secret leagues and associations (see Gerolymatos 2009 for a detailed discussion of the officer corps). The structure of these organizations was opaque, and some represented only a loose collection of officers with common professional interests (Veremis and Gerolymatos 1991: 115). To a great extent, these factions reflected the insecurity felt by the officers in the new Greek National Army, regardless of their prewar affiliations. Royalist officers who had sat out the occupation feared those who had joined the resistance or fought in the Middle East. The most vulnerable group were the former Venizelists who had accepted the monarchy and had been readmitted into the armed forces (Gerolymatos 2009: 16). During the 1946 government of Nikolaos Plastiras, many former republicans were reinstated. However, the short tenure of the Plastiras government brought back the old professional insecurities (Chouliaras and Georgakas 1985: 49). At the same time, the royalist faction saw many of its senior commanders lose their posts to former republicans, and they responded by forming secret organizations to protect themselves from retirement or dismissal (Gerolymatos 2009: 17).

Ultimately, the most influential group was IDEA (Ιερός Δεσμός Ελλήνων Αξιωματικών, Sacred Bond of Greek Officers), formed in late 1945 by the merger of ENA ('Ενωσης Νέων Αξιωματικών, Union of Young Officers) and other nationalist organizations (including Triana, an anticommunist secret organization of sabotage and intelligence) that arose during the war in the Middle East (Veremis 1997: 152; Gerolymatos 2009: 17). The goals of IDEA were to support the monarchy and defend the nation (Veremis 1997: 143). IDEA quickly expanded within the officer corps and eventually spread its influence throughout the army (Karigiannis 1950: 206–7). During the summer of 1946, IDEA intervened on behalf of the officers who had served in the Security Battalions and succeeded in having them reinstated into the army (Karagiannis 1950: 234; Grigoriadis 1975: 90–92). Nevertheless, little effort was made to address the issue of officers who had fought with ELAS during the occupation (Gerolymatos 2009: 17). Initially, 221 officers who joined ELAS were given appointments in the army, but shortly afterward they were placed on the inactive list (Gerolymatos 1985: 23–24n34).[19] Many of the officers excluded from the armed forces bore the brunt of the so-called white terror that inflicted Greece in the aftermath of the Varkiza Agreement. A year later, some of them took up arms and helped to create the Democratic Army, but hundreds of these former professional officers languished in detention and internal exile (Tsakalotos 1960: 47; Sarafis 1980: lxxvii; Alexander 1982: 161–62; Vaphiadis 1992: 128–29; Close and Veremis 1993: 99–100).

The Communist forces, unlike the Greek National Army, eventually established a cohesive officer corps that included some professional officers and experienced guerrilla commanders who had become adept at partisan warfare (Gerolymatos 2009: 17). Although some of these guerrilla commanders had served as reserve officers in the Greek Army, many had become officers during the occupation. Some were graduates of the ELAS military school in the mountains, while many others had earned their rank as a result of direct military experience in the field (Close and Veremis 1993: 103–4; Vaphiadis 1992: 146). The Greek National Army, on the other hand, entered the Greek Civil War (1946–49) riddled with factionalism and political intervention that extended to the operational level. Many units were relegated to defending static positions in order to protect a region represented by a powerful politician (Veremis and Gerolymatos 1991: 120).

Although well supplied and possessing considerable more firepower, the National Army was no match for the mobility and hit-and-run tactics of the Democratic Army (Gerolymatos 2009: 18). The rebels of the Democratic Army (DA) shifted their operations from the cities to the mountains and country towns, which kept the government troops off-balance and prevented them from using their resources to the maximum extent (Veremis 1997: 146). The officers who commanded the units of the new National Army also lacked experience in counterinsurgency warfare and had seen little action during the occupation; in contrast, those officers who had such experience from fighting in the guerrilla units of ELAS were excluded from the National Army and remained in detention camps for the duration of the war.[20] Both the lack of training in antiguerrilla warfare and the low morale in the National Army prompted a lackluster performance against the DA (Veremis 1997: 146–47). Their failure to destroy the Communist forces compelled the British, and later the Americans, to intervene and reorganize the Greek officer corps in a manner that would lead to military success. British and American intervention in the Greek Civil War had long-term consequences; the reorganization of the officer corps ensured that the armed forces would be beyond the reach of Greek political leadership in the postwar period (Gerolymatos 2009: 18). Admiral Petros Voulgaris, prime minister at the time, had initiated the process in June 1945 and gave the British Military Mission (BMM) executive authority over the organization of the Greek armed forces (Veremis and Gerolymatos 1991: 116–18).

The mechanism by which control could be asserted was the Supreme Military Council (established by the British and followed by the Americans) that included the head of the BMM as a nonvoting member. However, the other members of the council were given to understand that the chief of the BMM would prevail in military affairs. After the implementation of the Truman Doctrine in 1947, the Americans followed the British example and supported the independence of the Greek military from political intervention (Roubatis 1987: 74). Despite these changes, and despite considerable military aid from the United States, the Greek National Army continued to fail in its attempts to destroy the Communist forces. The Americans were ultimately forced to intervene directly in the overall strategic and tactical planning of operations so that Greece would not represent the first "domino" falling to communism in Southern Europe and Turkey (Karakatsanis and Swarts 2018: 8). For the next two years, U.S. officials were able to make considerable progress in creating a Greek National Army capable of countering a communist-dominated insurrection (Miller 2009: 21). Returning from imprisonment in a German concentration camp (Woodhouse 1972: 4), General Papagos was able to jolt the National Army into action and help lead it to victory in 1949. By the end of the civil war, the Americans opted to maintain greater control of the Greek military and made every effort to distance it from Greek politicians, while at the same time establishing direct links with the Greek officer corps. More significantly, the U.S. military advisors and the recently created CIA also developed close ties with IDEA, which by the end of the Greek Civil War had come to dominate the Greek Army(Veremis and Gerolymatos 1991: 122–23).

The end of the Greek Civil War and the onset of the Cold War had convinced the U.S. Joint Chiefs of Staff that Greece was not in a position to defend itself from aggression by any of the communist Balkan states or the Soviet Union without massive American support. Under these conditions, the primary function of the Greek army was to provide security against an internal threat.[21] Effectively, the role of the military was not only to prevent Communists or any left-wing organization from gaining control of the state; the army also had a political role to play in supporting anticommunist forces. In effect, U.S. policy toward Greece echoed the attitude of the officer corps and IDEA, which had already defined the role of the military as being the guardian of the state from internal as well as external forces.

In the period after the Greek Civil War, IDEA became a dominant force in the Greek Army and a rallying point for officers disaffected by the propensity of the monarchy to favor officers close to the palace (Veremis 1997: 152). The secret organization, consequently, shifted its loyalty to General Papagos, believing that he could counter the influence of the royal family in matters of promotion. Papagos was a hero of the Greek-Italian War (1940–41)[22] and responsible for the defeat of the Democratic Army. Although Papagos had been a devoted supporter of the monarchy, King Paul resented the growing influence of the general, and relations between the two became strained. This resentment was exacerbated by the fact that IDEA "had shifted its loyalty from the King to Papagos and had become the rallying point of officers whose professional ambitions were frustrated by the King's socially prominent military clients" (Veremis 1997: 152). In 1951, Papagos resigned as head of the army over a disagreement with Paul and decided to pursue a political position. His popularity as a strong leader, together with support from the military, led Papagos to a resounding victory in the 1952 elections. Members of IDEA were rewarded for their support of Papagos and assumed key positions in the army and in Greece's intelligence service, ΚΥΠ (Κεντρική Υπηρεσία Πληροφοριών, Central Intelligence Service)

Despite the fact that a significant number of IDEA members had been followers of Venizelos and opposed to the monarchy, they quickly pledged their loyalty to the king as a means of self-preservation.[23] They all rallied around the concepts of anticommunism and nationalism; in turn, many of these individuals' wartime actions were dismissed or deliberately overlooked. Even turncoat Venizelists who sought refuge in the Security Battalions were not held accountable for their actions. Quisling Prime Minister Ioannis Rallis had been tried as a collaborator after the occupation, but all charges with respect to the Security Battalions had been dismissed. The court ruled that Rallis did not break any Greek laws because the aim of the battalions had been to maintain law and order and internal security (Gerolymatos 1985: 25). The Cold War concepts of anticommunism and nationalism were convenient justifications for former members of the Liberal-Venizelist factions to mask their collaborationist past.

In addition, as IDEA expanded its influence in the army, former officers of the Security Battalions managed to gain greater control of the secret organization and use their influence to advance the careers of the former collaborationists. Colonel Christos Gerakinis, for example, became deputy director of the military academy, and some individuals, such as Colonels Charalambos Papathanasopoulos and Ioannis Plytzanopoulos, were relatively well known. However, many more remained anonymous and became the backbone of the 1967 junta (Gerozisis 1996, vol. 3: 824–25). The officers espoused the notion of national-mindedness (*ethnikophrones*), a self-proclaimed struggle against communism and opposition to all individuals and organizations of the Left more so than any ideological foundation.[24] This mantra of nationalist orthodoxy became "a guarantee of success and indeed of survival for the least prominent and able elements in the army" (Veremis 1997: 153).

Over the next fifteen years, IDEA and its offshoots, led by the future dictator, Georgios Papadopoulos, tightened their grip on the officer corps, and in 1967 took over the Greek state. Unsurprisingly, these officers soon rediscovered their antimonarchism, which they had conveniently abandoned in exchange for reinstatement into the army. The abortive countercoup staged by King Constantine II provided the Colonels an ideal opportunity to neutralize this potential political adversary and allow them free reign to pursue their own agenda and reward their loyal supporters. The armed forces, which were honeycombed with secret leagues and associations for much of the twentieth century, were now at the mercy of one of these secret associations and their so-called revolution.

André Gerolymatos was a professor of history and director of the Stavros Niarchos Foundation Centre for Hellenic Studies at Simon Fraser University. Professor Gerolymatos also held the Hellenic Canadian Congress of British Columbia Chair of Hellenic Studies at Simon Fraser University. He graduated from Loyola College and Concordia University with a BA with honors in classics. While at McGill University, he completed his MA in classics and subsequently was awarded his doctorate in history. His books include *The Balkan Wars* (Basic Books, 2002), *Red Acropolis Black Terror: The*

Greek Civil War and the Origins of Soviet-American Rivalry, 1943–1949 (Basic Books, 2004), *Castles Made of Sand: A Century of Anglo-American Espionage and Intervention in The Middle East* (St. Martin's Press, 2010). A specialist in military and diplomatic history, Dr. Gerolymatos served as a member of the Canadian Advisory Council on National Security. He was also a member of the board of the Alexander S. Onassis Foundation in the Unites States.

NOTES

1. According to Victor Papacosma (1977: 165), once Venizelos came to power in 1910, he sought to complete the general goals that the Military League had outlined but failed to attain immediately.
2. Veremis 2018 provides an excellent account of the history of the Greek officer corps up to the Metaxas dictatorship. For a theoretical examination of the subject, see Dertilis 1977. On the period after 1936 and the occupation, see Fleischer 1978: 5–36; Gerolymatos 1984: 69–79; 1992: 321–34; Hondros 1988: 33–48.
3. During the Balkan Wars, a new category of officers—namely, reserve officers—became part of the officer corps. According to Veremis (1998: 36–37), reserve officers had been granted regular commissions and, by 1920, formed the largest group of officers in the army lists. However, they were not accepted as equals by the academy-trained officers and hence out of professional necessity and because they acquired their commissions when Venizelos was prime minister, they tended to remain loyal to the liberal leader and opposed to the monarchy.
4. The disruption in the chain of command by the replacement of experienced officers in the armed forces in Asia Minor with less qualified Royalist commanders. This political intervention, according to Spais (1970: 144–45), was a contributing factor to the defeat of the Greek army in Turkey.
5. For a detailed and compelling account of the trial and execution, see Protaios (n.d.). Protaios, together with his own account, also includes the minutes of the Extraordinary Court Martial. In his study of the Greek expedition in Turkey, Llewellyn-Smith (1973) includes a discussion (in English) on the trial and execution of the Six.
6. On 28 September, part of the main army (12,000) marched into the capital in good order (Llewellyn-Smith 1973: 314).
7. The purge of Royalist officers in 1922 was followed by the dismissal of 1,800 republican officers because of the unsuccessful coups of 1933 and 1935 (Gerolymatos 1984: 71n7).
8. Dafnis ([1955] 1974) attributes the Populist victory to the strong backing of the middle class. He points out, however, that this support did not translate into endorsement of the monarchy, but instead the rejection of the Liberal Party.
9. A critical factor in the victory of the Populists was the boycott of the elections by the Venizelists.

10. According to the American ambassador Lincoln MacVeagh (Chouliaras and Iatrides 1985: 60), the number given for the monarchist vote was higher by a margin of 400,000 votes than the total vote cast by all parties in any previous election. Fleischer (1988: 54) adds that the Danish ambassador in Athens commented that the entire process was a farce and "the greatest comedy performed on the European scene for a long time."
11. Metaxas (1964: 222–23 [4 August 1936]) confided in his diary that the country was on the eve of a communist revolution. Communist propaganda, he wrote, had already infiltrated the civil service and threatened to paralyze the state, and it had started eroding the discipline of the armed forces.
12. Metaxas, in particular, was aware that the officer corps could challenge his position as the dictator of Greece and placed considerable emphasis on establishing reliable security services (Gerolymatos 1992: 31). However, during the short period of the 4 August regime, King George II exercised considerable influence over the armed forces, whose mostly Royalist officers looked to him as both the legitimate head of state and the primary guarantee of maintaining their professional careers (Veremis and Gerolymatos 1991: 105).
13. Sir Sydney Waterlow, the British Ambassador to Athens, attempted to convince King George II to remove Metaxas but met with little success (British National Archives [BNA], Athens Telegram No. 185, 6 October 1938, FO 371/22362). Metaxas (1964: 359 [19 March 1939]) for his part confided in his diary that the British did not like the dictatorship, and he feared British intrigues against his regime.
14. This policy of using political revolutionaries and groups opposed to their own governments was not only characteristic of SOE's activities in Greece but was also based on a broader concept that such groups were by their very nature ideally suited to participate in clandestine networks (Gerolymatos 1992: 132–35).
15. Colonel Euripides Bakirdzis was the leader of one of the underground cells organized by the British MIR (Military Intelligence Research) and Section D (a department of the British Secret Intelligence Service) to resist the Germans. Later, both the MIR and Section D would be taken over by the SOE (Special Operations Executive) (Gerolymatos 1991: 38).
16. Another important consideration for the continued (and almost exclusive) use of opponents of the Metaxas regime by the SOE after the occupation was that the organization in Athens had little or no contact with the intelligence services, ministries, or individuals close to the Greek government. Consequently, after the fall of Greece and the rapid withdrawal of the British military and intelligence forces from the mainland, there was no opportunity or time either to establish contacts with the agencies and individuals that represented the monarchy and the Metaxas regime or cooperate with them in the organization of clandestine networks that would operate after the Axis occupation (Gerolymatos 1992: 54–55).
17. According to Veremis and Gerolymatos (1991: 105–6), one important factor that led many Greek officers to follow different resistance organizations and

clandestine groups was that the breakdown of political authority in Greece after the beginning of the occupation led to the absence of political control and direction over the officer corps. In the ensuing vacuum of legitimate authority, many Greek officers were left free to follow a course of action motivated by patriotism, a spirit of defiance against the Axis forces in Greece, or their own political beliefs. Some joined the Greek forces in the Middle East, others followed the guerrilla bands in the mountains, and even others opted to enlist in the Security Battalions of the Rallis puppet government out of fear of communism, revenge, or simple self-interest. See Gerolymatos 2009, 15.

18. The same conditions applied to the Greek armed forces in the Middle East, particularly after the mutinies in 1943 and 1944. Republican officers either accepted the monarchy or were purged, while others ended up in prison camps as a result of their part in the uprisings of the Greek forces in the Middle East.
19. See also the United States National Archive (USNA), Records of the Office of Strategic Services, NARS RG 226 L 57536.
20. Harry Truman Library, President's Secretary File, SR-10, BOX 259 (cited in Close and Veremis 1993: 104–5).
21. According to Roubatis (1987: 72–79, 125–27, 131), it was only in the mid-1960s that the United States partially amended this strategy.
22. According to C. M. Woodhouse, Papagos was initially reticent about organizing resistance against the Axis occupiers. In fact, Woodhouse states that Papagos took a "wait and see" stance. Papagos's arrest and deportation to Germany in the summer of 1943 caused a vacuum in effective military leadership of the military hierarchy (see Clogg and Yannopoulos 1972: 4). Papagos was released in May 1945 and returned to Greece to participate and provide leadership in the Greek Civil War.
23. See Gerolymatos (1996: 42) for a detailed overview of the complexities of political identification that resulted for thousands of resistance fighters after the liberation of Greece in the fall of 1944.
24. Grigoriadis (1984: 189) writes that the fear of the Left and anticommunism surpassed the prewar political schism and that the opposition to EAM-ELAS-KKE was extended to include all individuals and organizations who did not identify with right-wing political ideology and the monarchy. Those who did defined themselves as *ethnikophrones*, a term which during the occupation defined not only those who supported the monarchy but also conservative republicans. The political ideology of the ethnikophrones, states Grigoriadis, manifested itself as a fear of the Left and developed greater impetus after the December Events and the Varkiza Agreement. According to Tsakalotos (1960: 399), a prewar republican but a postwar monarchist, opposition to communism transcended any other political sentiments among the officer corps. Veremis and Gerolymatos (1991: 116) add that in the postoccupation period the emergence of the Left was one factor, but the direct intervention of the British provided a new element in also redefining the dynamics of the political and military relationship.

REFERENCES

Archives

London, United Kingdom
    British National Archives (BNA)
Independence, MO, United States
    Harry Truman Library
Washington, DC
    United States National Archive (USNA)

Secondary Sources

Alexander, G. M. 1982. *The Prelude to the Truman Doctrine: British Policy in Greece, 1944–1947*. Oxford.
Chouliaras, Y., and D. Georgakas, eds. 1985. "Documents: Dispatches of Lincoln MacVeagh." With an introduction. *Journal of the Hellenic Diaspora* 12(1): 29–52.
Close, D. H., and T. Veremis. 1993. "The Military Struggle, 1945–9." In *The Greek Civil War, 1943–1950: Studies of Polarization*, edited by D. H. Close, 97–128. London.
Dafnis, G. (1955) 1974. *I Hellas metaxy dyo polemon, 1923–1940* [Greece between two wars, 1923–40]. Reprint. Athens.
Dertilis, G. 1977. *Koinonikos metaschminatismos kai stratiotiki epemvasi, 1880–1909* [Social transformation and military intervention, 1880–1909]. Athens.
Finlay, G. 2014. *History of the Greek Revolution*. Vol. 2. Cambridge.
Fleischer, H. 1978. "The 'Anomalies' in the Greek Middle East Forces, 1941–1944." *Journal of the Hellenic Diaspora* 5(3): 5–36.
———. 1988. *Stemma kai svastika* [Crown and Swastika]. Vol. 1. Athens.
Gerolymatos, A. 1984. "The Role of the Greek Officer Corps in the Resistance." *Journal of the Hellenic Diaspora* 11(3): 69–79.
———. 1985. "The Security Battalions and the Greek Civil War." *Journal of the Hellenic Diaspora* 12(1): 17–27.
———. 1991. "British Espionage in Greece, 1941–1942." *Journal of Modern Hellenism* 8: 37–48.
———. 1992. *Guerrilla Warfare and Espionage in Greece, 1940–1944*. New York.
———. 1996. "The Battle for Athens: Strategy and Tactics." *Journal of the Hellenic Diaspora* 22: 39–56.
———. 2009. "The Road to Authoritarianism: The Greek Army in Politics, 1935–1949." *Journal of the Hellenic Diaspora* 35: 7–26.
———. 2016. *An International Civil War: Greece, 1943–1949*. New Haven, CT.
Gerozisis, T. 1996. *To soma ton axiomatikon kai i thesi tou sti synchroni elliniki koinonia 1821–1975* [The officer corps and its place in contemporary Greek society 1821–75]. 3 vols. Athens.

Grigoriadis, F. N. 1975. *Istoria tis neoteris Elladas* [History of modern Greece]. Vol. 10, *Emfylios polemos, 1944–1949: To deftero antartiko (1946–1949)* [Civil war, 1944–49: The second guerilla war (1946–49)]. Athens.

Grigoriadis, S. 1984. *Dekemvris-Emfylios, 1944–1949: Synoptiki istoria* [December–Civil War, 1944–49: Concise history]. Athens.

Hondros, J. L. 1988. "Too Weighty a Weapon: Britain and the Greek Security Battalions, 1943–1944." *Journal of the Hellenic Diaspora* 15(1–2): 33–48.

Iatrides, J. O., ed. 1980. *Ambassador MacVeagh Reports: Greece, 1933–1947*. Princeton.

Karagiannis, G. 1950. *To drama tis Ellados, 1940–1952: Epi kai athliotites* [The tragedy of Greece, 1940–52: Heroics and atrocities]. Athens.

Karakatsanis, N., and J. Swarts. 2018. *American Foreign Policy towards the Colonels' Greece*. New York.

Koliopoulos, J. S. 1977. *Greece and the British Connection, 1935–1941*. Oxford.

Metaxas, I. 1964. *To prosopiko tou imerologio* [His personal diary]. Vol. 4, *1933–1941*, edited by P. Vranas. Athens.

Miller, J. 2009. *The United States and the Making of Modern Greece: History and Power, 1950–1974*. Chapel Hill, NC.

Mouzelis, N. P. 1986. *Politics in the Semi-Periphery: Early Parliamentarism and Late Industrialization in the Balkans and Latin America*. London.

Protaios, S. n.d. *I diki ton Exi* [The trial of the Six]. Athens.

Llewellyn-Smith, Michael. 1998. *Ionian Vision: Greece in Asia Minor, 1919–1922*. 2nd ed. Ann Arbor, MI.

Roubatis, Y. P. 1987. *Tangled Webs: The U.S. in Greece, 1947–1967*. New York.

Sarafis, S. 1980. *ELAS: Greek Resistance Army*. London.

Spais, L. 1970. *Peninta chronia stratiotis* [Fifty years a soldier]. Athens.

Tsakalotos, T. 1960. *40 chronia stratiotis tis Ellados: Pos ekerdisame tous agones, 1940–1949* [40 years as a private of Greece: How we won the struggles, 1940–49]. 2 vols. Athens.

Vaphiadis, M. 1992. *Apomnimonevmata* [Memoirs]. Vol. 5, *Εμφύλιος* [Civil war]. Athens.

Veremis, T. 1997. *Military in Greek Politics: From Independence to Democracy*. Montreal.

———. 2018. *Oi epemvaseis tou stratou stin elliniki politiki, 1916–1936* [The interventions of the army in Greek politics, 1916–36]. Athens.

Veremis, T., and A. Gerolymatos. 1991. "The Military as a Sociopolitical Force in Greece, 1940–1949." *Journal of the Hellenic Diaspora* 17(1): 103–28.

Woodhouse, C. M. 1972. "The 'Revolution' in Its Historical Context." In *Greece under Military Rule*, edited by R. Clogg and G. N. Yannopoulos, 1–16. London.

Chapter 2

The Political and Ideological Origins of the *Ethnosotirios Epanastasis*

Katerina Lagos

In Georgios Papadopoulos's first speech to the press following the coup d'état on 21 April 1967, he publicly explained the factors that prompted him and fellow military colleagues to overthrow the state, and described the type of government that they wished to establish. At this inaugural press conference, Papadopoulos considered the military intervention to be comparable to surgery by referring to Greece as a "sick patient" on the operating table that needed restraints in order for the "operation" to succeed (Papadopoulos 1968, vol. 1: 11). This medical analogy has been cited repeatedly to characterize the motives and agenda of the Junta dictatorship.

Their repressive actions garnered them rebuke and international condemnation to the point where anyone who was associated with the junta was either in prison or considered persona non grata for any Greek political party in the Metapolitefsi (regime change). Recent publications on the junta have attempted to contextualize the dictatorship in Greek history by either making comparisons to previous twentieth-century dictatorships in Greece or drawing wider, transnational comparisons to Latin America (Bermeo 1995; Aguilar and Kovras 2019). Domestically, the most common comparison is made with the Metaxas dictatorship, 1936–41, and scholars have identified apparent similarities in language, ideology, and repression (see, e.g., Angelis 2016; Kouki and Antoniou 2017). Yet the similarities to the Metaxas dictatorship can only go so far; there are fundamental differences between the two regimes that make the comparison inconsequential. The military dictatorship of 1967–74 sought to follow the historical tradition of the Goudi Coup of 1909.[1] As seen with the previous Greek military dictatorships in the twentieth century, their ideology was vague and undefined; at best, it was a reflection of Cold War military ideology blended with pre-existing nationalist ideals. For the seven years that the junta was in power, their behavior, policies, and ideological statements were widely ridiculed and disparaged by contemporary scholars and journalists.

This chapter will explore the historical and military background in which the Colonels rose to power. It will be argued that, while the post–World War II military had been reformed in a manner that made it politically homogenous, there were various factions within the military who had differing notions of "protecting the social order"—notions that also incorporated their own professional advancement. With the growing political instability of the mid-1960s, various groups within the army started to conspire to plan a military overthrow of government. The Colonels' coup is the outcome of one of these conspiracies; it also reflected the self-promotion of these officers. Once in power, they employed a combination of ideas from the past that served as the ideological vision of the regime: anticommunism and the establishment of a so-called Greco-Christian civilization. The ethos of the army, in which the Colonels were situated, was carried through to the junta dictatorship as part of its expressed ideology regarding anticommunism. In addition, the Colonels articulated aspects of nineteenth-century nationalist ideology as the second part of its ideology that was based on the linear progress of the Greeks and their role in Western civilization. Thus, the Colonels did not develop an ideology for their regime, but instead relied on ideas found in the past.

While many scholars consider the dictatorship as a rupture in Greek politics, there are underlying aspects of continuity to both the pre- and post-war periods—as seen especially in the ideological statements of the regime—that warrant a closer inspection of the junta and its stated agenda. The regime's leadership highlighted the coup as a "revolutionary" event, marking a break from the past. Georgios Georgalas, one of the two ideologues of the regime,[2] explicitly stated that the Colonels' coup represented a complete revolution since, he argued, it did not have a class or political party affiliation. Georgalas (1967: 6) also referenced French revolutionary language by making parallels to a "new chapter" in Greece; the junta had established their own "Year 0" by "destroying the political 'establishment.'" From this perspective, there was no past—"no yesterday"—in the political realm (Georgalas 1967: 6). This rebirth was captured in the emblem of the regime that included the darkened profile of an army soldier against the background of a phoenix rising from flames. This imagery symbolizes both the country's and army's resurrection (the latter of which is at the heart of the dictatorship). Georgalas underscored this symbolism in his assertions that the regime was establishing a new political foundation and anticipated that they would achieve a national regeneration for all Greeks. For Georgalas, the mission of the dictatorship was a new version of the Megali Idea (Μεγάλη Ιδέα, Great Idea),[3] called the "Great Synthesis" (Μεγάλη Σύνθεσις) (Georgalas 1967: 9). These French Revolutionary aspirations, together with language drawn from Greek nationalist discourse, highlight the self-perception of the dictatorship as a vehicle for change and an appeal for unity.

Yet while the leaders sought a break from the political past, their actions belied a more traditional approach to military interventions in Greek affairs during the postwar years. The Colonels' coup reflected a perceived duty to maintain conservative political rule, while also promoting the officers' own corporate interests and political agenda. With King Constantine's countercoup, however, the historic link between the military and the king was broken. The junta leadership lost their titular leader, marking a distinct rupture between the regime's leadership and the Greek monarchy. Compounding the situation were the simmering tensions that existed between the various factions in the leadership—the "hard-liners" and "soft-liners"[4] being the most prominent groupings—which began to weaken the tenuous unity of the regime. Ultimately, the combination of the friction between the various factions of the regime, together with Papadopoulos's personal ambitions, undermined the regime's tenuous unity and would later lead to its implosion.

THE GREEK MILITARY IN THE PRE-WORLD WAR II PERIOD

The Greek military has been an active participant and catalyst in political affairs from the establishment of the modern Greek state. As agents of change, the military took the initiative to break the Gordian knots of political conflict. Beginning in 1843 and up through World War II, the Greek military—especially the army—intervened in Greek political affairs in conjunction with politicians to help end stalemates and usher in political change. In the years following the Greek Civil War, the military considered its perceived mission to protecting the Greek nation and remaining vigilant in defending the country from communism (Hatzivassiliou 2006: 8). Yet there is a fundamental difference from the past (pre-Metaxas), as André Gerolymatos argues in his chapter, in that the composition of the military was far more politically homogenous, was more autonomous in its political agency, and was fully committed to upholding anticommunist values. It is within this context that the leaders of the junta dictatorship—George Papadopoulos, Stylianos Pattakos, and Nikolaos Makarezos—came to see their role in supposedly saving Greece from communism in 1967.

During the nineteenth century, the revolts of 1843 and 1862 represent instances where the military intervened swiftly to push a political agenda; in 1843, the military revolted against King Othon and forced him to accept a constitution. In 1862, the military, together with members of the political world, once again revolted against Othon, but this time Othon was forced to abdicate the throne. In both instances, the military ended the deadlock that had existed in the political realm. Neither of these revolts resulted in a military dictatorship, nor was there any intention by the military officers to retain political power. However, these two revolts established a precedence in Greek political affairs that continued into the twentieth century. From 1909 and on, Greek military intervention would be a constant factor in political affairs and condition the army officers' raison d'être vis-à-vis the state.

The Goudi Coup of 1909 represents a watershed year in Greek politics and can be seen as the beginning of twentieth-century politics for Greece.[5] The aborted attempt to unify Crete to Greece, and the political tensions that ensued, prompted the Military League (organized by noncommissioned and junior army officers who emulated the Young Turks of the Ottoman Empire) to take action. The revolt brought about significant political reforms, forced the resignation of two prime ministers (Dimitrios Rallis and Kyriakoulis Mavromichalis), and ushered Eleftherios Venizelos to power. None of the Military League's leaders acquired political power; instead, the leaders sought to secure political reforms and then return power back to political leaders. With Venizelos's assumption of power, he inaugurated a series of reforms and modernization programs; included in this program of reforms was the reorganization and training of the Greek military forces. The army, navy, and incipient air force all underwent improvements that would enable Greece to mobilize over 130,000 men by the beginning of 1912 (Papacosma 1977: 164). Venizelos's military restructuring would bear fruit; during the Balkan Wars of 1912–13, Greece secured a substantial territorial and population increase, as well as rehabilitating the military's morale and prestige (damaged as a result of the humiliation suffered during the Greco-Turkish War of 1897).

The rehabilitation of the Greek military did not last long, however. The constitutional crisis resulting from the disagreement over Greece's entry into World War I spilled over to the military. The National Schism divided the Greek military into Venizelist and anti-Venizelist factions; with every change in political administration came a corresponding purging of the military to ensure politically loyal officers and soldiers.[6] With King Constantine I's abdication in 1917, Venizelos arrived in Athens, assumed political power, and immediately declared war on the Central Powers.[7] Royalist officers and those sympathetic to King Constantine were purged from the military; more than 1,500 royalist officers were cashiered, while a small number were imprisoned or exiled (Veremis 1997: 178). Despite the factionalism and loss of experienced officers, the Greek military provided noteworthy participation in the final months of the war. The national elections of November 1920 resulted in Venizelos's defeat and the return of the royalist political faction under Dimitris Gounaris. The following month, Gounaris organized a plebiscite that brought back King Constantine from exile. In addition, Gounaris renewed Venizelos's Asia Minor campaign and brought the dismissed and exiled royalist officers back into their posts. Venizelist officers were either dismissed or voluntarily resigned.

The Greek military was soundly defeated in 1922 by the Turkish forces, under the leadership of Mustafa Kemal (later Kemal Ataturk), and this defeat—termed the Asia Minor Catastrophe—also proved destructive to the unity and integrity of the Greek military. The Catastrophe also underscored the deleterious consequences of repeatedly purging the military for political purposes. The Greek army "disintegrated and rebelled against the royalist politicians, blaming them for bringing about a national disaster" (Kapetanyannis 1986: 90). A self-termed Revolutionary Committee formed by Colonel Nikolaos Plastiras and other military leaders overthrew the Gounaris government and forced King Constantine to abdicate the throne. Plastiras purged the fractured military yet again by cashiering over 1,000 anti-Venizelist officers. In order to shift the responsibility for the Catastrophe away from the military and place the blame squarely at the feet of the royalist government, Plastiras orchestrated a military trial convicting former Prime Minister Gounaris along with members of his cabinet, including Georgios Hatzianestis, commander-in-chief of the Greek Army, and sentencing them to death. The execution, as Andre Gerolymatos explains in his chapter, was an aberration in the history of the military; however, it is "from this period that a latent antipolitical undercurrent [appeared] in the nationalist attitudes of the military" (Kapetanyannis 1986: 90). With Plastiras's mission complete, he resigned in January 1924 and transferred political power back to Venizelos.

The next two major coups that occurred prior to the outbreak of World War II were organized by Theodoros Pangalos (1925–26) and Ioannis Metaxas (1936–41).[8] These dictatorships had a common foundation; they both sought to bring stability and order. They also inaugurated a new ideological justification for their actions in helping curb a new enemy: international communism. Pangalos and Metaxas equally persecuted communists within Greece and actively sought educational reforms to weed out communist instructors and/or ideas. Both dictators received votes of confidence from their respective parliaments prior to suspending parliament and assuming dictatorial rule. In addition, neither envisioned his dictatorship as a temporary interlude in Greek politics and made no mention of transitioning back to parliamentary rule. It is this overarching objective that differentiates the Pangalos and Metaxas dictatorships from all other twentieth-century coups.

In addition, Ioannis Metaxas had significant political experience and had formed his own erstwhile political party, the Free-Thinkers Party (Κόμμα των Ελευθεροφρόνων), fifteen years before he assumed dictatorial power. He was a long-standing royalist politician who gained the confidence of King George II and his acquiescence for the establishment of a dictatorship. Metaxas's cabinet was comprised primarily of politicians and not military officers. Yet it is the Metaxas dictatorship of 1936–41[9] that has drawn the most numerous comparisons with the junta dictatorship of 1967–74. These comparisons have been based on the similar rhetoric of the two regimes and the fact that members of the junta had received their military training during the years of the Metaxas dictatorship. Beyond the military background of the leaders and rhetorical similarities of the two regimes, there are significant differences that set them apart. The Metaxas dictatorship was a police state and not a part of the framework of the army. In contrast, the junta dictatorship was a military regime comprised of midlevel army officers who had no political experience, had usurped power to promote their own interests, and had no support from King Constantine II.

The political context in which the two dictatorships existed were also very different: Metaxas reflected the interwar period and the political trends of authoritarianism and fascism, while the junta reflected the Cold War period and its geopolitical conflicts. Finally, those who find close affinity between the two dictatorships—both during and after the fall of the junta—rely on fascism as the linking factor. While there continue to be debates on the political nature of the Metaxas dictatorship, little credence can be given to the fascist orientation of the junta dictatorship. The comparison "of the junta to Metaxas on the basis of fascist ideology appeared and gained prominence at the time of the dictatorship because it allowed its opponents to understand their predicament, classify the junta and present it to the world, and ultimately appeal for international support" (Kouki and Antoniou 2017: 471). Even Papadopoulos distanced himself from a comparison to Metaxas and instead envisioned himself not as a fascist leader but rather as a modern-day Venizelos who sought to modernize the country (Kouki and Antoniou 2017: 472). Repeated references to the Colonels' coup beginning in the Goudi barracks were published in newspapers such as *Nea Politeia* and *Makedonia* as a way to highlight this historic link (Kouki and Antoniou 2017:

467). Ultimately, the junta dictatorship cannot be seen a postwar sibling of the Metaxas dictatorship, despite its superficial similarities.

POSTWAR POLITICS AND THE RISE OF THE COLONELS

The Greek Civil War was a major turning point in contemporary Greek history that also had drastic implications on the Greek military, especially the army (for the theoretical debates of the Greek military's "professionalization," see Huntington 1968; Kourvetaris 1969; Kapetanyannis 1986; Tsarouhas 2005). American involvement to help defeat the communist insurgents (Democratic Army) reflected a new role for the United States in Greek affairs. American involvement in Greek political, economic, and military affairs was premised on the new Cold War reality and Marshall Plan ideas of modernization. To fulfill these two aims, significant funding poured into Greece. Between 1947 and 1966, Greece received 3.75 billion USD (Tsarouhas 2005: 8). In addition, the "Americans assumed direct control of virtually all key ministries, under terms carefully stipulated in a number of bilateral agreements" (Iatrides 2003: 79) that ensured American interests prevailed over domestic political squabbling. The Greek military was fundamentally reorganized and reoriented based on American military standards. It was restructured in a manner that precluded it from organizing a successful military offensive, being relegated to serving as a secondary-status military capable only of defensive action (Dokos 2004: 45). To mitigate this downgrade in status, the armed forces exclusively received and were equipped with "American arms," and "the hundreds of officers who received graduate military training in the United States welcomed the continuity of their host country's influence" (Dokos 2004: 45). By the early 1960s, the military was comprised of roughly 120,000 men and officers in the army, 19,000 officers and men in the navy, and 23,000 officers and men in the air force (Kourvetaris 1969: 45). These numbers also belie the preponderance of the army and, subsequently, its ability to intervene in Greek political affairs.

During the period of 1950–66, approximately 11,805 officers were trained in the United States. American "training [was] never limited to acquisition of technical skills; it [was] always placed in the wider context of a process by means of which 'professional capabilities' [were] fully shaped. From this point of view the shaping of attitudes towards 'national security,' broad political issues, the conceptualization and perception of the 'enemy' and the type of war to be fought [were] considered as being of paramount importance" (Kapetanyannis 1986: 22). As a result, the doctrine of "national security" taught in American military schools and academies contributed decisively to shaping the ideas of whole generations of new military leaders. It not only contained "an explicit ideology for military intervention in domestic politics but also a claim to political power by the national military forces" (Kapetanyannis 1986: 71). To reinforce this doctrine, the American CIA helped establish the Greek KYP (Κεντρική Υπηρεσία Πληροφοριών, Central Intelligence Service) in 1953, which served as a bastion of right-wing politics and kept uncomfortably close ties to its American counterpart (Iatrides 2003: 87).

For Greece, the experience and trauma of the Greek Civil War galvanized the armed forces to adopt and maintain a hardline adherence to anti-communism and conservatism, which dovetailed nicely with American and NATO interests (Dokos 2004: 56). The self-perception of the military as "an indispensable instrument of progress and modernization stemmed in part from the variety of social programs and economic development projects in which the armed forces had been employed since 1945" (Kassander 1986: 292–93; cited in Dokos 2004: 56). Most of the officer corps tended to come from rural areas in Greece and were typically from the poorer southern regions, "a traditional recruiting pool for the Civil Service—and to a considerable degree from the lower classes" (Kapetanyannis 1986: 72–73). For those who enrolled in the Greek Army service school, the training[10] for the noncommissioned officers (NCO) employed "the methods and curriculum patterned after those of their U.S. counterparts."[11]

The overall improvements introduced by the United Sates were greatly enhanced by Greece's membership in NATO (Iatrides 2003: 81), and soon the Greek military "unequivocably [sic] assumed that [Greece's] national interests would always have to be identical with those of the US and NATO" (Kapetanyannis 1986: 29). The officer corps

> became the most prominent centre for the production, formulation and dissemination of the new regime's official ideology: militant and uncompromising anti-communism.... The military could not stomach any dealings with yesterday's enemies.... Their contemptuous view of politics as a corrupt and socially divisive activity detrimental to national objectives, contributed to a basically anti-political and anti-democratic stance which reduced Parliament and representative institutions to a mere talking club incapable of solving the country's problem[s]. (Kapetanyannis 1986: 94–95)

The officer corps viewed itself as "embodying the national ideals of Greece and equated the goals of the armed forces with those of the nation" (Kassander 1986: 292–93; cited in Dokos 2004: 56). This view was codified in the 1952 Greek constitution, whereby the military answered to the king (their commander-in-chief) and made no mention of the role that the government had in the supervision of the military (Greek Constitution of 1952, Article 32; see also Christidi 1965: 23; Kourvetaris 1969: 96).[12] The role of the postwar Greek military was structured in a manner that it became a semi-autonomous arm of the government that reported directly to the King, while successive prime ministers, including Konstantinos Karamanlis and George Papandreou, would be unable to interfere in the military's administration or leadership (Terlexis 1971: 451).[13] The link between the Greek military and the king was so intertwined that by 1962 King Paul could openly state to officers of the Thessaloniki garrison, "I belong to you and you belong to me" (Siotis 1971: 31).

Beginning in 1952 with the election of Alexandros Papagos, conservative rule dominated the Greek political landscape. Similarly, the late 1940s and early 1950s in the United States were dominated by Cold War ideology and anticommunist persecution (most notably led by Senator Joseph McCarthy); in both countries, political and military interests converged on these issues. During the height of the Civil War, three factors were put in place to help bolster the military battle against communism in Greece and shape the postwar political landscape. First, during the height of the war in 1947, the Communist Party was banned. Second, Law 509 was passed at the same time that "enabled the police to take action against anyone suspected of left-wing activities, while public sector employment presupposed the production of a 'certificate of social beliefs' that denounced communism and left-wing ideological convictions" (Tsarouhas 2005: 8). The third factor came in 1948 with the establishment of the TEA (Τάγματα Εθνοφυλακής Αμύνης, National Defense Battalions), which were to assist in the pursuit and apprehension of leftist political sympathizers. The battalions comprised a militia-type organization that facilitated the army and city police in maintaining internal security.[14] Up until 1967, approximately "21,997 people were deprived of their citizenship and 1,722 people were deported to internal exile" (Close 2002: 95). A new form of nationalist fundamentalism dominated Greek identity that "presented an image of Greece as a besieged nation warding off communist adversaries and upholding Western values" (Veremis and Koliopoulos 2004: 18).

The surprise selection of Konstantinos Karamanlis as the new head of the Greek Rally Party in 1955,[15] following the death of Prime Minister Papagos, brought into power an individual who espoused strident anticommunist political sentiments, as well as steadfast support for the United States. Karamanlis and foreign policy advisors Evangelos Averoff and Konstantinos Tsatsos considered themselves "staunch supporters of America's leadership role in the free world and of its containment policy" (Iatrides 2003: 87). Karamanlis was suspicious of Nikita Krushchev's attempts to improve relations between Greece and the Soviet bloc and spurned overtures for diplomatic relations. During this period, Krushchev developed a growing interest in the Eastern Mediterranean and pursued a multifaceted "offensive on diplomatic, trade and cultural fronts aimed at further weakening Greek ties with the West, increasing popular support for front parties in Greece and fostering growth of a climate in which legalization of the outlawed Communist Party could be achieved."[16] Karamanlis was derisive of the Soviets' overall political policy of détente, which he considered disingenuous and reflecting the "gangster face of communism."[17] In addition, Karamanlis had a jaundiced perception of the Balkan communist states, which he felt were actively pursuing a "push to the Aegean."[18]

Karamanlis's militant anticommunist stance was not supported by the majority of the Greek population. A growing anti-American sentiment in Greece (shaped in part by the Cyprus crisis and anti-Greek pogrom in Istanbul), coupled with an "international climate that was increasingly opposed to Cold War divisions and the dangerous nuclear arms race," helped create fertile ground for opposition parties to exploit (Iatrides 2003: 86). As a result, Greek opposition parties sympathetic to the Soviet Union and its overtures began gaining popular support. The EDA (Ενιαία Δημοκρατική Αριστερά, United Democratic Left) party capitalized on the growing tensions in Cyprus as well as the stagnant employment situation for the working class. The EDA courted Greek workers by blaming Karamanlis and the ERE (Εθνική Ριζοσπαστική Ένωσις, National Radical Union) for the general "conditions of chronic unemployment, low living standards and lack of economic opportunities."[19] For government officials in Athens and Washington, the EDA's rising popular appeal, together with their "total identification with Soviet foreign policy objectives under the guise of a thinly veiled pacifism and neutralism" (Kapetanyannis 1986: 94), made them a potential threat to conservative political rule. In 1958, the EDA received more votes than the moderate Liberal Party, and this translated into seventy-eight seats in parliament (out of three hundred).[20] The sudden spike in the EDA's electoral outcome prompted concern within Karamanlis's ERE party, as well as in U.S. political circles, for the future.

According to U.S. intelligence officials, the 1958 elections reflected a weakening of ERE and moderate political parties. In contrast, EDA was projected to become the principal opposition party with an estimated increase of 30 percent in their electoral percentage in future elections. U.S. intelligence officials noted that drastic measures were being considered by King Paul to prevent the "communist-front" EDA from participating in any form of coalition government. Should the "elements composing ERE" begin to disintegrate, or if Karamanlis's frustration with the negotiations over Cyprus should prompt him to resign, American officials were confident that "any EDA bid for power would almost certainly be blocked through [the] establishment of a Palace-backed anti-Communist coalition, or possibly by creation of an authoritarian regime based on military support."[21]

Political tensions regarding the Cyprus issue and the domestic economic situation dominated Karamanlis's second term in office. Negotiations regarding the fate of Cyprus proved increasingly challenging for the prime minister. A perception grew within Karamanlis's cabinet that any negotiations within NATO would result in a solution that was disadvantageous to the interests of Greece and the Greek Cypriots.[22] The growing violence on Cyprus prompted the British to relinquish their control of the island; in 1959, the Zurich conference brought Great Britain, Greece, and Turkey to the negotiating table and resulted in Cypriot independence with a constitution that provided generous representation to the Turkish minority on the island. The failure to achieve enosis (union) with Greece proved to be a devastating blow to Karamanlis. In addition to his foreign policy blunder, growing attacks against Karamanlis for his economic policies undermined the ERE's ability to govern. Karamanlis acknowledged that Greece was "being confronted by an economic and political crisis arising from its inability to expand agricultural exports, especially tobacco, and its shortage of investment capital."[23] With the rising attacks against him by his political opponents and accusations of scandals in the Greek press,[24] Karamanlis found himself in an untenable situation.[25] On 20 September 1961, he resigned, and national elections were scheduled for 29 October.

The 1961 elections proved the American intelligence officials correct in their predictions regarding military intervention. To help stave off the rising popularity of EDA and the newly formed Center Union Party (led by George Papandreou), an organized campaign, codenamed "Plan Pericles," was put into operation to ensure a victory for ERE. The organizers of the plan were "a group of army officers, appointed by the general staff [who cooperated] with the police" in a systematic way throughout the country. Massive electoral irregularities and acts of intimidation and brutality occurred; army officers and police threatened villagers in the countryside to switch their votes to ERE (Koliopoulos and Veremis 2010: 137), while in the metropolitan areas, illegally registered individuals packed certain districts to change the electoral outcome. One residence alone listed 218 police living there (Close 2002: 104). Although ERE emerged victorious with 176 and 50.8 percent of the vote, George Papandreou challenged the outcome of the election. The Supreme Court upheld the validity of the election, and this decision sparked Papandreou's "relentless struggle" (Roubatis 1987: 157) to defeat ERE in the next elections.[26]

Many of the officers involved in Plan Pericles were members of clandestine military organizations, including future dictator Colonel Georgios Papadopoulos. Most of these military organizations originated during and after World War II and sought to promote their members professionally. The most prominent organization was the EENA (Εθνική Ένωσις Νέων Αξιωματικών, Union of Young Greek Officers) formed in 1958. EENA supported the king and conservative rule, but the organization was comprised of lower-level junior officers. The leadership of the EENA included Colonel Georgios Papadopoulos, Nikolaos Makarezos, and Stylianos Pattakos. EENA was an offshoot of the IDEA (Ιερός Δεσμός Ελλήνων Αξιωματικών, Sacred Bond of Greek Officers), which originated in the Middle East during the Greek Civil War (Kourvetaris 1969: 26),[27] where "new military units were formed out of the remnants of the Greek army defeated by the Germans and the local Greek community under the aegis of the British command" (Kapetanyannis 1986: 137).[28] Members of the EENA maintained the ethos of the Greek military to protect the country from communist infiltration, and the 1961 elections ensured that the individuals involved could carry out their actions without recrimination.

Within two years of his reelection, Karamanlis would tender his resignation again and leave Greece for Paris, France, where he would remain until 1974. In the midst of several crises plaguing Karamanlis, a group of officers prepared to take action in April 1963 in order to stabilize the political situation. The U.S. military attaché in Athens "learned that a group of army officers led by Brigadier General Odesseus [sic] Angelis, Colonel Alexandros Hatzipetros and Lieutenant Colonel George Papadopoulos . . . was preparing to seize power. Acting on his own, Ambassador Henry R. Labouisse communicated to the conspirators his strong disapproval of the proposed coup" (Iatrides 2003: 88). With this stern warning, the officers did not execute their plans. Papandreou emerged victorious in the elections, and, in 1964, he was able to govern Greece with a majority in parliament. During his short term in office, Papandreou attempted to carry out his political agenda of income redistribution and social justice (Papandreou 1970: 126–27). He began to dismantle aspects of the anticommunist state by relaxing police measures, releasing most of the political prisoners, and dissolving many anticommunist vigilante groups (Close 2002: 107). Papandreou also began a diplomatic campaign to reestablish political relations with the communist Balkan states, including Bulgaria, Yugoslavia, and Romania.[29] Papandreou sought to establish relations with the Soviet Union but failed due to Soviet demands for Greece to leave NATO and recognize the KKE (Greek Communist Party) (Koliopoulos and Veremis 2010: 139). To the young King Constantine, the extreme political right, and the military

(Roubatis 1987: 213–14),[30] Papandreou was treading dangerous ground with these discussions with the Soviets and needed to be removed from power.

An opportunity arose for King Constantine in July 1965. Tensions between the king and Papandreou reached a boiling point when Papandreou asked Constantine to assume the portfolio of the Ministry of Defense, replacing Petros Garoufalias. Constantine refused Papandreou's request on the grounds that this appointment would create a conflict of interest. Papandreou's son, Andreas, was under investigation for his involvement in a left-wing clandestine organization named the Officers Save Fatherland Ideals Democracy Meritocracy (whose acronym, ASPIDA, spelled "SHIELD" in Greek). Andreas was accused of being "the leader and inspiration behind the ASPIDA group whose primary aim was to take Greece out of NATO and to set-up a Nasser-type populist-socialist state" (Kourvetaris 1969: 135–36). In response to King Constantine's rejection, Papandreou submitted his resignation. For several weeks following Papandreou's resignation in July, riots and demonstrations plagued the country (Schwab and Frangos 1973: 9–10). These protests, together with an uptick in worker and farmer strikes, gave conservatives the impression of a general breakdown of order.[31]

The July events (termed Ιουλιανά) prompted a heightened sense of fear in the palace, the military, and members of the extreme right. King Constantine actively sought to lure Center Union deputies away from their party (Αποστάτες) and help form a government with the ERE. A government was formed under the leadership of Stefanos Stefanopoulos and would last until December 1966, when the head of the ERE, Panayiotis Kanellopoulos, withdrew his support for the government (Miller 2009: 124). A caretaker government was put in place under the leadership of banker Ioannis Paraskevopoulos, and new elections were scheduled for May 1967. This would be the fourth caretaker government since July 1965 and reflected a regression to the political instability of the interwar years.

With the politicians unable to sort out their differences, various military groups began discussing action to bring the chaos to an end. Rumors of coups began to circulate widely; Andreas Papandreou stated in an article on 9 March that "forces within Greece were plotting either to rig elections schedules for 28 May or to prevent them from being held by imposing a dictatorship . . . planned by a 'junta whose tentacles spread from the palace to foreign intelligence services, the extreme right and the economic oligarchy'" (Schwab and Frangos 1973: 11). George Papandreou expressed similar concerns to American ambassador Phillips Talbot on 17 March,[32] perhaps with the unspoken hope that American officials might intervene.[33] While both Andreas and George Papandreou referenced the "junta" as a group of army generals and politicians who were supported by King Constantine, another midlevel group of army officers were also secretly planning their next steps[34]:

> Thirty to forty middle-grade military officers worked quietly over a period of time to perfect a plan which paralleled roughly that of the General Staff's longstanding plan to prevent a Communist take-over. It was the plan of the General Staff, with which some members of the coup group were plugged in at key posts, which provided the middle-grade officers with natural cover. This circumstance, together with the impeccable military records of the junior officers and their quiet, determined efficiency, afforded them that element of surprise necessary for the coup's implementation.[35]

These officers were members of the EENA and titled themselves the Revolutionary Council (following in the tradition of Plastiras's Revolutionary Committee). This Revolutionary Council was founded in 1963, and its members had "become progressively more disillusioned with the deteriorating political situation and the inability of the politicians to solve Greece's problems." In addition, they harbored resentment against Papandreou because the military was "left out of the big pay increases given to the Police, the Judiciary, and the huge constituency of teachers." To add insult to injury, many of the EENA members were transferred from Athens to the provinces in 1964 and would remain there for the duration of Papandreou's tenure in office.[36] Ironically enough, several of the EENA members were assigned to the same provincial post and continued to plot their next steps without interference.

The lead member of the Revolutionary Council was Colonel Georgios Papadopoulos, who had figured prominently in the 1961 Plan Pericles, had direct connection with the United States military, and was a part of KYP. Papadopoulos, along with Nikolaos Makarezos and Stylianos Pattakos, were brought back into Athens in late 1965 by General Gregory Spandidakis, who was the head of the General Staff under the short-lived Stefanopoulos government. Papadopoulos took advantage of his reassignment and gained access to the confidential negotiations regarding military intervention by his superiors. In addition, all of Papadopoulos's coconspirators were transferred to key positions in the General Staff, which allowed them to control the centers of military administration (Kapetanyannis 1986, 298). Spandidakis tasked Papadopoulos to revise the NATO-approved Plan Prometheus, designed to prevent a communist overthrow of government. In addition, by December 1966, Papadopoulos and other members of the Revolutionary Council met at the home of Lieutenant Colonel Ioannis Ladas. Here they discussed the political situation and toyed with the idea of establishing a dictatorship.[37] When parliament was dissolved on 15 April 1967, the Colonels decided to take action. The inner executive circle of the National

Council, known as the Revolutionary Group, met at Pattakos's house in the Athenian suburb of Ano Patissia on Tuesday, 18 April, to finalize their plans. It is at this point that Papadopoulos became the formal leader of the Colonels, and the date for the coup was scheduled for the night of 20–21 April (Woodhouse 1985: 20–21).

As the praetorian guards of the Greek nation, stepping into the political arena was part of the army's history and modus vivendi. From the end of the Civil War, four different military interventions and coups were planned: 1951, 1955, 1961, and 1963. Although none of the coups were carried out, the fact remains that the military was considered a vital tool to help maintain conservative and anticommunist rule in Greece. While the fear of a communist overthrow was not generally accepted by the majority of the Greek populace as a credible or impending threat, nonetheless, the perception that George and Andreas Papandreou would again come to power and lead the country down a new politically precarious path proved terrifying to the king, the military, and the extreme right.[38] In their collective mind, the Papandreous represented conduits to the communist bloc and under no circumstance could this be tolerated. This was also reflected in the timing and initial justification for the coup. George Papandreou was scheduled to speak in Thessaloniki on 23 April, and the Colonels cited this event as a precursor for a communist revolution occurring in Thessaloniki that day (Schwab and Frangos 1973: 19). A government spokesperson reported that "a Communist insurrection had been planned and that George Papandreou ... had conspired with the Communists to provoke a riot as he addressed his followers."[39] With the immediate threat of a communist takeover on the horizon, the Colonels launched their coup d'état using a NATO-devised plan to confront a communist overthrow of Greece. Once the Colonels took power, what remained to be seen for the self-styled *Ethnosotirios Epanastasis* (Εθνοσωτήριος Επανάστασης, Revolution to Save the Nation), was whether they would adhere to the ideological mission and historical precedents of previous military interventions or take Greece down a different political path.

THE *ETHNOSOTIRIOS EPANASTASIS* IN POWER

The coup d'état began at 2:00 AM on 21 April 1967. Military forces departed from the ΚΕΤ (Κέντρο Εκπαιδεύσεως Τεθωρακισμένων, Armored Training Center) and had spread throughout the streets of Athens by 2:45 AM. Light tanks went to the king's residence at Tatoi; another group of tanks went to take over control of the central telephone exchange and radio station, while a third group rounded up political prisoners and senior officers. By 3:00 AM, Athens had been completely overtaken by the coup.

General Spandidakis had given the order to launch Plan Prometheus and to secure all military divisions in their places and close off the borders of Greece. All attempts to recover legitimate rule by the king, the navy, or other loyal political authorities were intercepted by supporters of the coup and suppressed. Even the police had quickly capitulated and began patrolling the streets to ensure that no one dare come outside. By 6:00 AM, Greece was fully under the control of a military dictatorship. A radio broadcast came on shortly thereafter and announced the change in government. A so-called royal decree was read over the radio and detailed the suspension of various articles of the Greek Constitution,[40] in addition to outlining the new restrictions that were put in place. Later that evening, the identity of the dictators was made public. The regime's leadership would be in the hands of Colonel Papadopoulos, Brigadier General Pattakos, Lieutenant General Spandidakis, and Colonel Makarezos. Former Supreme Court Prosecutor Konstantinos Kollias was selected to serve as the premier of the dictatorship, and the remainder of the administration was comprised of civilian individuals.

A few days later, on 27 April, Papadopoulos would give his first press conference, in which the colonel outlined the context and justification for the coup and made the infamous analogy to Greece as a diseased patient. He also referenced the communist threat to the country and said that "70 trucks' worth of evidence" would be made available to the press at a later date (Papadopoulos 1968, vol. 1: 13). Quickly, it became apparent that the junta dictatorship did not have an articulated ideology that preceded their assumption of power. While the Colonels may have shared vague ideological notions for the regime, they relied on Georgalas and Papakonstantinou to articulate their so-called ideology over the course of the months and years following their seizure of power. This ideology was premised on two aspects: (1) anticommunism and (2) the creation of a Greco-Christian civilization. By the end of 1967, Georgalas published a short pamphlet, titled *The Ideology of the Revolution: Not Dogma, but Ideals*, which stated the two goals of the dictatorship: "The first, the immediate goal, was to save the country, during this critical moment, from the slide to chaos, a schism, and red communism. The second, more general motive, is for National Regeneration; meaning our liberation from the economic, intellectual, social, administrative, and political underdevelopment and our ascent to the heights of a new summit" (Georgalas 1967: 7–8). Disregarding the supposed fears of a communist revolution, the second goal of the regime left many unanswered questions. What

"National Regeneration" meant and exactly how the Greeks were to ascend new heights were never delineated in any concrete terms.

The clearest connection between the junta dictatorship and the prejunta period can be seen in the Colonels' advocacy of anticommunism as a pillar of their ideology. Anticommunism was part of the political discourse from the 1920s and figured prominently in the Pangalos and Metaxas dictatorships. In the postwar period, a strong anticommunist ideology was developed among the army officer corps. This ideology was incorporated in the oath of allegiance that the officers swore to King Constantine (Kourvetaris 1969: 96). As discussed earlier, anticommunism was also part of the Rally Party and ERE's political agenda. This overlapped with the military's postwar mission and dovetailed nicely with NATO's political outlook. The fear of communism was emphasized as the justification for the Colonels' coup d'état. On 27 April, when Papadopoulos gave his first press conference, he outlined the context and justification for the coup and made the infamous analogy to Greece as a diseased patient. While Papadopoulos never produced any of the "70 trucks' worth of evidence," the mantra of anticommunism was consistently reiterated throughout the duration of the dictatorship. By 1970, the anticommunist justification continued to be reiterated. Georgalas gave a speech at a foreign correspondents dinner where he identified 1965 as the point at which the revolution began. He stated that in

> 1965, in particular, we experienced a crisis which was not just political but national, a crisis which called for an immediate revolutionary solution. . . . [Our] Revolution took place to save Greece from chaos, civil war, and submission to Red totalitarianism. It took place to prevent the country from slipping into communism and to maintain it within the bosom of free western nations, of which Greece constitutes a vital and inalienable element. (Georgalas 1971: 46)

The crisis that Georgalas identifies were the July events that involved George Papandreou and King Constantine. Papandreou is indirectly considered the source of the communist fear and the vehicle by which Greece would be led to "Red totalitarianism."[41]

In addition to maintaining anticommunism as an ideological foundation for the regime, the Colonels sought to appropriate the term "revolution" and delegitimize its use in communist discourse. Georgalas, a former communist himself, denounced communism as a partisan counterrevolution whose "change" would have been fatal to the country (Georgalas 1967: 5). He argued that the communist "effort to create a society in which everything would develop according to a 'plan' [had] led to the Berlin Wall, which stands in the heart of Europe, and is a symbol of its failure" (Georgalas 1971: 45). In addition, since communist revolution was premised on the working classes, this was only partially reflective of society and therefore partisan. In contrast, the Colonels' "revolution" was one that incorporated all of Greek society and therefore was a "true" revolution. This pansocial perspective was echoed by Papadopoulos in a speech given to wartime veterans of northern Greece. During this speech, Papadopoulos made the analogy between the Colonels and Greek society. He identified the regime as a group of individuals who did not represent one economic class or political faction; rather, they represented the entire Greek nation. This notion of collectivity was not new to Papadopoulos—it was a sentiment engrained in the Colonels from their military training. Cadets were taught that their military calling was "sacred" and that "in times of extraordinary danger and threat, [the cadets would] be the only hope for the nation's territorial integrity and internal tranquility" (Kourvetaris 1969: 51). Since the Colonels represented the entire Greek nation, they perceived their actions as a national revolution designed to protect the nation from external threats.

Like all Greek army officers, Papadopoulos also considered the military profession as the repository of Greco-Christian ideals (Anastasakis 1992: 160). As Andreopoulos and Grammenos discuss in their chapter on the Greek Orthodox Church, the Colonels idolized the past and glorified the present and future of the nation through the work of the army and the Church (Mikedakis 2007). The Colonels relied on the Church "as a mechanism against Communism and in the reproduction of the already established ideology of Helleno-[Christianity]" (Gazi 2004: 62–78). This ideology "combined ancient Greece, the Byzantine Empire, and modern Greece, arguing that the Greek nation was unique, blessed by God, characterized by historical, cultural, and biological continuity, and that a true Greek must be Orthodox—implying that religion and the nation were inseparable and that the true Greek identity necessarily consisted of both of these elements" (Sakellariou 2013: 157–59; cited in Sakellariou 2019: n3). Papadopoulos's repeated assertion of a Greco-Christian civilization thus tapped into longstanding concepts of Greek nationalism as an unbroken link from antiquity to the present and grounded in the religious principles of Greek Orthodoxy.[42] However, the Colonels also saw their regime as a break from the immediate past, conceptualizing themselves as the saviors of a diseased and misled nation and the only ones who could bring back the nation to health and instruct its people on the "proper" civic morals. By presenting the regime as the only means for salvation, Papadopoulos belied a Manichean worldview: "If then the revolution fails, the result will be chaos."

Language also played a formative role in the Colonels' vision of a Greco-Christian Civilization, and they were quick to engage in this debate. Adamantios Korais's creation of the "Katharevousa" language rules (making

Modern Greek conform to classic Greek) provided a linguistic component for the continuity argument by linking antiquity to the present, which would guide "the production of Greek national culture which sees itself as exclusively linked to Greek 'nature'" and to its historic past (Koundoura 2007: 32). The Colonels circled back to the language controversy and quickly issued government decree #129 on 5 September 1967 that "Katharevousa" would be used for all oral and written schoolwork beginning in the fourth year of elementary school. Reasserting Katharevousa's prominence would reinforce the link between ancient and contemporary Greece, while also serving as the catalyst for a new, lofty Greek civilization. In addition, restoring Katharevousa to linguistic dominance also served as the regime's contribution to the language debates of the late nineteenth and early twentieth centuries. The linguistic debates took on political dimensions in the early 1920s whereby conservatives, including military dictator Theodoros Pangalos, considered supporters of the demotic language to be "advocates of communism" (μαλλιαροκομμουνισμός) (Maria Repousi 2012). Regime officials cast similar opprobrium on demotic developments by adding an ethnic component to their condemnation, calling the demotic a "semi-barbarian Turko-Hellenic language" (Polychronopoulos 1980, vol. 2: 546; cited in Anastasakis 1992: 220). As explored in Othon Anastasakis's (1992) thesis on education, the dictators had a fixation on Katharevousa. Anastasakis (1992: 221) speculates that due "to their own poor educational achievements, [regime leaders] perceived the use of the katharevousa idiom as a sign of education, as a status symbol, reminiscent of the 19th-century perception of the language issue." The revival of Katharevousa thus served a binary purpose: first, it reinforced the regime's campaign against communism and foreign enemies; and, second, it underpinned the regime's ideological placement within a purified, chronologically unbroken, and reified nationalist paradigm.

The combination of linguistic continuity to territorial/racial components of Greek identity came together, as Constantine Tsoukalas argued: "'Race, blood, land, and climate,' in other words, the cornerstones of nineteenth century definitions of the nation, were added to the 'metaphysical and hypostatic totality' that modern Greek ideologists see as making up Greekness. For them, 'Greek culture is untranslatable to the effect that non-Greeks can only catch a glimpse of the divine essence'" (Tsoukalas 1993, cited in Koundoura 2007: 33). This nationalist conceptualization would figure prominently in Papadopoulos's speeches. To wounded veterans in Thessaloniki, Papadopoulos stated:

> Today, we are taking on the responsibility for ourselves, in order to embark on the correct road which will result in the continuation of Greek history. We,

ourselves, have returned upholding the order and the inheritance we have received for the victims and wounded, those who sacrificed themselves and their regiment members on the hills of Greece, drenching them with blood, so this land would remain Greek.... It is enough that the Greeks remember that they are Greeks, that they are the descendants of a people, who were always loyal to their destiny, for this people operated within an auspicious state, governed by Greco-Christian ideals, which have no relation with the jungle. (Papadopoulos 1968, vol. 1: 37 [21 May 1967])

To Papadopoulos, the wartime veterans provided the link between the land, blood, and race that Tsoukalas referenced. As the veterans serve as the link between the Greeks and the land, the veterans also become historic links between successive generations of Greeks, by virtue of the fact that there have been continuous wars and revolutions in which Greek warriors have participated. References to ancient battles and the Colonels' ascent to power as a revolution thus placed the Colonels' regime within the historical and teleological progression of Hellenism. It is no accident that Colonel Pattakos used well-known phrases, such as "come and take [them]" (μολὼν λαβέ, attributed to King Leonidas of Sparta), to highlight Greek bravery, especially in the postwar context of foreign enemies surrounding Greece.[43]

Additionally, Georgalas (1967: 5) emphasized that the regime's actions were part of a revolution that would fulfill the aspirations of the Greek race, making Greece the contemporary beacon for Western civilization.[44] Papadopoulos echoed these statements in his early speeches and consistently emphasized the superiority of the so-called Greco-Christian civilization, and how this civilization would "make Greece a pole of ideological spiritual attraction" (Woodhouse 1985: 32). Other members of the regime followed suit, including Minister of the Interior Ioannis Ladas, who stressed that the regime was tasked with the lofty mission of guiding Greek civilization to a new "Golden Age" (Woodhouse 1985: 32). In fact, Ladas maintained that "human civilization was wholly fashioned by [the Greek] race. Even the enemies of Greece," he said, "recognize that civilization is an exclusively Greek creation . . . [and the Greeks] could continue to radiate civilization in all directions" (*Apoyevmatini*, 6 August 1968; cited in Clogg 1972: 41). A historical parallel to this notion of creating a new Hellenic civilization could be seen in the Metaxas dictatorship. Metaxas himself eschewed military expansion and instead sought a cultural regeneration whose product would be the "Third Greek Civilization," alongside ancient Greece and Byzantium. This Third Greek Civilization would serve as a contemporary intellectual beacon for Western civilization and raise the esteem of the Greek people worldwide. While the junta leaders repeatedly referenced a Greco-Christian society, it could be argued that this reflected less of an ideological link with the Metaxas dictatorship and more of a reconnection of both regimes to a preexisting nationalist discourse (Sakellariou 2008). Like Metaxas, Papadopoulos and other regime leaders never articulated exactly how this was to be accomplished in practical terms. By 1968, these statements dissipated (Papadopoulos 1968, vols. 2–4), and only the theme of anticommunism (together with nationalist slogans incorporating the country, religion, and family) continued to be emphasized (Papadopoulos 1968, vols. 2–4).

Since the period of the dictatorship, the Colonels' ideological pronouncements have prompted scholars to dismiss them as meaningless verbiage (Woodhouse 1985: 32) and hackneyed slogans (Close 2002: 116), or lacking ideological components altogether (Clogg 1972: 36). Most scholars agree that many of the junta's ideological statements can be traced back to the rhetoric of the Metaxas period, since nearly half of the lead members of the dictatorship graduated from the Military Academy in 1939 and 1940 (Zaharopoulos 1972: 31–32) and therefore would have been imbued with Metaxist propaganda. Two of the most prominent slogans for the regime were "Greece of the Christian Greeks" (Ελλάς Ελλήνων Χριστιανών) and "Fatherland, Religion, Family" (Πατρίς, Θρησκεία, Οικογένεια), which were reminiscent of the interwar period. As stated earlier, much of Metaxas's ideological vision was not novel but stemmed from pre-existing nationalist ideas (for an overview of the use of "Fatherland, Religion, Family" as a slogan that emerged in 1880, see Gazi 2011). For the junta leaders, their so-called ideological vision for Greece also relied on these same preexisting ideas, coupled with the Greek army's ideology of protecting the nation from external and internal threats.[45] This was useful rhetoric for the regime leaders, but they were not in a position to carry out this ideological vision. As soldiers, their expertise was in carrying out military plans and not developing ideological frameworks; this would help explain why the junta leaders outsourced their intellectual labor—ironically, to former communists, who were presumably adept at theoretical and ideological discourse.[46] The fundamental problem for both dictatorships was the nebulous nature of their visions and the inability of either regime to explain how their respective vision would be realized. For Metaxas, the growing hostilities on the European continent would overshadow any theoretical concerns about the direction of the regime. In contrast, the junta leaders did not have an external crisis that could be used to divert attention, and they were faced with growing criticism for their lack of progress in domestic reforms. Within the regime, the two prominent factions, with stark differences in their approach to carrying out the regime's political agenda, grew further apart and competed for political dominance.

The vagueness of the junta's ideological vision and its lack of connection to the regime's political agenda was immediately evident in the early days of the dictatorship. In May 1967, U.S. ambassador Talbot sought information concerning the new regime leaders and their political objectives (for a nuanced analysis of the U.S. foreign policy toward the dictatorship, see Karakatsanis and Swarts 2018). According to Talbot's sources, the regime "considered itself as [a] reformist element whose objectives were to seize power and revitalize Greek institutions generally in line with principles which governed IDEA."[47] During the same month, U.S. secretary of defense Robert McNamara was able to meet with Greek minister of defense Lieutenant General Spandidakis to get clarification on the regime's objectives. Spandidakis stated that the regime had developed a four-point program that it wished to implement. These four objectives were: (1) to reorganize the government mechanism; (2) to establish economic control; (3) to revise the Greek Constitution to "bring it up to date"; and (4) to "return the country to a constitutional order."[48] Spandidakis did not offer concrete ways in which this agenda was to be carried out, nor say how long it would take to fulfill their objectives. In order to allay McNamara's possible concerns regarding the ideological orientation of the regime, Spandidakis concluded the meeting with the assertion that "all of us are of a democratic point of view; we are not going to establish a Fascist regime in Greece."[49] Throughout all of these meetings, U.S. officials were left with the impression that the "junta's vision of a purified political and social atmosphere may be unrealistic and its capability to realize it may be doubtful, but its resolve to see it through is firm and so far unquestioned."[50]

The immediate actions of the junta regime swept across all aspects of Greek society. Policy statements were issued identifying the impending changes: "social reforms, assistance and reformation of the Church, help for workers, more assistance to mothers, aid for youth, social justice generally and love for the villages. Taxes would be reformed, economic developed supported and education advanced" (Schwab and Frangos 1973: 20). In addition, the Cyprus conflict would be settled "quickly and finally" (Woodhouse 1985: 23). In reality, many "reforms" were made to some of the sectors listed: the educational system, the Church hierarchy, the local administration, social policies, the press, and finally the political system. However, these reforms were often ill-conceived and reflected the hypocrisy of the regime's statements of eliminating corruption and facilitating efficient local government. In the case of the Greek economy, Spandidakis's claims of "establishing economic control" were never explained; in fact, the same investment patterns and personnel continued to exist from the prejunta period.

THE KING'S COUNTERCOUP AND THE
COMPETING FACTIONS IN THE REGIME'S LEADERSHIP

The one unpredictable factor in the initial months following the coup was King Constantine. The link between the military and the king has been a constant factor since the establishment of the Greek state. The king has been the head of the military, and this role was reinforced and expanded during the postwar period. As explained earlier, the king's oversight of the military superseded the government's oversight; from 1947, the Greek military became a semiautonomous sector of the state and no longer answered to a sitting prime minister. The king was responsible for awarding promotions to a given officer,[51] and thus an officer's career and advancement was in the hands of the king. However, the Colonels' coup came as a surprise to King Constantine, and he frantically sought a way to extricate himself from an increasingly compromising situation.

During the period prior to the coup, the king cooperated with the organization of the Generals' coup. The coup[52] was led by Spandidakis and internally named "Ierax (Hawk) Number Two."[53] King Constantine had supported the organization of the General's coup as a means to prevent George and Andreas Papandreou from returning to power in May. Nevertheless, Constantine was caught unawares by the Colonel's coup on 21 April (Woodhouse 1985: 23). Once the coup began, tanks came and surrounded the King's residence at Tatoi; his personal secretary, Major Michael Arnaoutis, was arrested, and his phone lines were cut. Constantine had two secret telephone lines: one of the lines provided direct contact to the naval base at Skaramanga, while the second line connected him to the Police Emergency Center in Maroussi (Woodhouse 1985: 24–25). As Constantine was preparing orders for both military divisions, members of the coup discovered the secret line to the naval base and quickly cut it. Using the second line, Constantine was able to make contact with Rallis (former minister of public order) and instructed him to communicate with the Army III Corps stationed in northern Greece and order them to make their way down to Athens to resist the coup. Although Rallis dispatched the directive, "two staff officers who were members of the conspiracy had intercepted and suppressed it" (Rodakis 1975, cited in Woodhouse 1985: 25). All attempts to forestall the coup were frustrated, and, by 6:30 AM, the coup leaders arrived at the king's residence. In the meantime, a forged decree on behalf of Constantine was made public on the radio, justifying the events that had just taken place.

The personal safety of King Constantine and his family hung in the balance during the initial hours of the coup.[54] Constantine initially requested U.S. Marines to land in Greece to help reassert his control over the armed forces, but his request was denied.[55] Instead, Assistant Secretary of State Talbot offered to assist the king and his family to evacuate Greece via U.S. helicopters.[56] Later that day, Constantine met with the leaders of the so-called National Revolution to discuss their next steps. Constantine tried to persuade them to "end their mutinous action and return to duty" (Woodhouse 1985: 26), but he was unsuccessful. Throughout the negotiations, King Constantine was able to secure Kollias (chief prosecutor of the Άρειος Πάγος [Areios Pagos, Supreme Civil and Criminal Court of Greece]) as prime minister of the new regime. Both U.S. officials and King Constantine determined that remaining in Greece would be in the country's best interest. Talbot considered Constantine the best hope for influencing the new leaders and, hopefully, returning Greece back to constitutional rule.[57]

From this point, Constantine's main objective with the junta leaders was for them to draft a new constitution that would pave the way for a return to democratic government.[58] This request was not an unusual one; historically, Greek military coups had typically came to power with the objective of stabilizing a turbulent political situation, securing political reforms, and then returning power into the hands of politicians. The Goudi Coup of 1909 was a reference point for the junta leaders; one of the significant outcomes of Goudi was the revision of the 1864 Greek constitution.[59] Similarly, the junta leaders considered that their main political objective was to reform the country and then guide it (in improved fashion) back to parliamentary rule. Based on this historical precedence, the king appealed to the leaders' sense of military duty and obligation vis-à-vis the Greek state. Over the course of the summer and fall, it became evident that there was a fundamental difference between prior coups and the junta dictatorship. Within the Revolutionary Council, there was discord regarding if and when a new constitution should be written, which divided the council into two mutually antagonistic camps—hard-liners and soft-liners. Papadopoulos and Pattakos wished to proceed immediately with the drafting of the new constitution, but other members (including Lieutenant Colonel Ioannides) wanted to maintain dictatorial rule and focus on what they felt were the goals of the revolution. A tug-of-war ensued that placed King Constantine, U.S. officials, and Papadopoulos on one the side of constitutional reform, and extremist factions and junior officers opposing the reform on the other.

By late fall, Constantine's frustration with and disgust for the regime leaders prompted him to plan his own countercoup. Throughout the country, pockets of popular resistance against the regime were developing, but the regime was able to quickly arrest any individual or group considered to be conspiring against the regime (Woodhouse 1985: 38). King Constantine organized his countercoup for 13 December because several indispensable officers were to retire soon after (Woodhouse 1985: 38). Constantine had relied on the unanimous loyalty of the military; he was mistaken. By evening, it was apparent that the countercoup was a failure. From Kavalla, King Constantine left Greece with his family to Rome. This departure symbolized Constantine's withdrawal from the political situation in Greece, as well as from his role as leader of the Greek military forces. A new political paradigm would be established in the country, and Papadopoulos's ambitions would take the regime in new, unchartered territory, creating more friction between the two major factions within the regime administration, especially the younger officers.[60]

CONCLUSION

The junta dictatorship of 1967–74 came to power on the pretense that there was an impending communist overthrow. Since the end of the Greek Civil War, the Greek military became a politically homogenous body whose raison d'être was to defend national independence, the territorial integrity of the state, and the existing political and social system against any perceived threats. Conservative Greek politicians subscribed to the Cold War mentality and became staunch defenders of the political order. Postwar Greek governments considered themselves surrounded by hostile countries—the communist Eastern Bloc and Turkey—and invested disproportionately in the military as a means of deterrence.

The Colonel's coup on 21 April 1967 followed a historic pattern of military behavior and coups. Since the turn of the century, military coups have taken action to solve what they perceived as political impasses. They also served as a means for factions within the military to promote their own interests and political agenda. The Colonels' coup reflected both of these aspects. The Colonels voiced similar concerns of external threats and the need to reestablish order and stability. They also sought to promote their own corporate interests and had no qualms about marginalizing senior members of the military or the king himself. However, the unity of the coup and its vague mission of purification and moral order soon collapsed after a series of events, beginning with King Constantine's countercoup. The political relation between the king and the military was broken; no longer could Constantine evoke his father's message of belonging to the officers of the military.

Continued pressure by the United States to move forward with a constitution and return to parliamentary government exacerbated preexisting divisions between the hard-liners and soft-liners among the junta's leadership. This internal schism between the two factions also underscored the inherent problems with the ideological vision of the regime: the hard-liners had no wish to move forward with constitutional reforms and a transition back to parliamentary government; rather, they wanted to maintain political control indefinitely. By contrast, the soft-liners (in varying degrees) sought to pursue constitutional reform in tandem with carrying out the political agenda. However, Papadopoulos's attempted reforms did little to improve the country and only generated increasing protest both from within and outside of Greece. Many of the same problems that had existed before in Greece—corruption, nepotism, and abuses of power—continued unabated during the dictatorship. As Papadopoulos and the soft-liners forced the creation of the 1968 constitution, the hard-liners and other smaller factions within the leadership[61] complained that he had moved "too swiftly towards return to civilian rule, thereby jeopardizing the future careers of all who took part in [the] coup and the officer corps in general."[62]

Ultimately, Papadopoulos was no longer satisfied with being the titular head of a national revolution; rather, he sought complete power for himself. By 1973, Papadopoulos had orchestrated a plebiscite on the fate of the Greek monarchy and secured 78.6 percent of the popular vote in favor of abolishing the monarchy. More importantly, Papadopoulos also became president of the government and intended to stay in power until 1981. He had institutionalized himself in power and marginalized both his soft-liner colleagues and hard-liner opponents (Grigoriadis 1975). This action sealed Papadopoulos's fate, however. The Athens Polytechnic uprising of November 1973 was not the *cause* of Papadopoulos's fall; it was the needed excuse to justify his overthrow and bring Ioannidis and the hard-liners to power.

Katerina Lagos is a Professor of History at California State University, Sacramento and the Director of the Angelo K. Tsakopoulos Hellenic Studies Center and Hellenic Studies Center. Her most recent publication is *The Fourth of August Regime and Greek Jewry, 1936-1941* (Palgrave, 2023).

NOTES

1. A group of junior army officers banded together in a secret society called the Military League and rebelled against political corruption and foreign policy failures. Their motivation ranging from the defeat of the Greek forces in 1897 to the weakness of the Athenian government to achieve Cretan enosis to Greece, the junior officers rebelled in order to bring about reforms and new leadership in power. Once they had achieved their mission, the Military League disbanded.
2. Theophylakos Papakonstantinou was the second ideologue of the dictatorship.
3. The Megali Idea was the dominant foreign policy from the inception of the Greek state up through the Asia Minor Catastrophe in 1922. This foreign policy sought to enlarge the Greek state at the expense of the Ottoman Empire.
4. The division between hard-liners and soft-liners is a broad division; within the hard-liners were other smaller factions of varying political viewpoints. Two factions within the hard-liners include those who were neofascists and those who did not have a political doctrine. The latter faction included Dimitrios Ioannides, who overthrew Papadopoulos. Within the soft-liners, other divisions existed. Finally, there were other factions within the junior officers, who had their own outlook on the regime (Anastasakis 1992: 195–96).
5. The advent of Venizelos to power brought sweeping changes in the political, economic, and social world of Greece (Papacosma 1977).
6. Thanos Veremis outlines the characteristics of the military from 1897 through 1936 and organizes them into five groups based on military patron-client relationships. Veremis (1997: 81, 87) argues that after the Balkan Wars, "the social structure of the officer corps changed, increasing the dependence of officers on politicians. . . . Their susceptibility to political manipulation temporarily increased the subjective control of civilian attitudes and civilian patrons."
7. The Central Powers consisted of Germany, Austria-Hungary, Bulgaria, and the Ottoman Empire.
8. There were a number of short-lived or unsuccessful coups from 1926 to 1935: Georgios Kondylis, 1926; Nikolaos Plastiras, 1933; Eleftherios Venizelos, March 1935; and Georgios Kondylis again, October 1935. In August 1926, Kondylis overthrew the Pangalos dictatorship and remained in power until national elections could be completed in November 1926. Plastiras attempted to organize a coup in March 1933 in response to the anti-Venizelist electoral victory, but it failed due to lack of support, and Plastiras himself was forced to leave Greece. The March 1935 attempted coup was organized by Venizelos and Plastiras (not in Greece at the time of the attempted coup) but failed to get support. This coup marks the end of Venizelos's participation in governmental affairs, and both he and Plastiras were condemned to death in absentia. The final coup before the Metaxas dictatorship (1936–41) occurred in October of the same year; it overthrew the Panagis Tsaldaris government and led to Kondylis assuming the position of prime minister until his death in February 1936. All of these short-

lived coups and attempted coups can be seen as expressions of the antagonism of the National Schism.
9. The author considers the end of the Metaxas dictatorship to be the date of the dictator's death, 29 January 1941. While members of the dictatorship continued to govern Greece during the occupation, they were free to act on their own and actively exhibit Nazi sympathizing and antisemitic beliefs. This behavior should not be conflated with the political outlook and agenda of Metaxas while he was still alive and in power.
10. Typically, during the postwar period, the length of an army cadet's professional training lasted for four years (see Kourvetaris 1969: 50).
11. Central Intelligence Agency (CIA) Library, no. CIA-RDP01-00707R0002001 10030-0; National Intelligence Services (NIS), "Greece: Armed Forces," March 1974.
12. With the junta's 1968 revised constitution, the military owed their "allegiance to the country, the national ideals and traditions and service to the nation." There were two other duties assigned to the Greek military: "The mission of the military is to defend national independence, the territorial integrity of the state and the existing political and social system against any insidious attempt.... The mission of the military man is opposed absolutely to those ideologies that aim to overthrow and undermine the existing political or social order, or to subvert the national convictions of the Greeks. Furthermore, the mission of the military is opposed to those political parties connected with principles and programs which have been dissolved and outlawed" (Greek Constitution of 1968, Articles 129–30: 53–54).
13. Article 32 of the 1952 constitution stipulated that the king was the commander-in-chief of the armed forces. However, Terlexis agrees with Roy C. Makrides's observation (1968: 151) that Article 32 was interpreted by the military to mean that it took its orders directly from the king and not an elected government.
14. CIA Library, no. CIA-RDP01-00707R000200110030-0; NIS, "Greece: Armed Forces," March 1974, 23.
15. When King Paul passed over Stephanopoulos and Kanellopoulos for the leadership of the Greek Rally Party, there was significant surprise and concern by politicians on both sides of the Atlantic. According to Solon Gikas (former army and defense chief, former minister, former head of IDEA), the army was planning a coup right after the death of Papagos, most likely out of concern for the political future of the country. Gikas was the chief of staff during this period and used his leadership to prevent the coup from being carried out, most likely once it was clear that Karamanlis would be a strong supporter of the conservative agenda and the United States (Couloumbis 2004: 93).
16. *Foreign Relations of the United States (FRUS), 1958–1960*, vol. 10. *Eastern Europe; Finland; Greece; Turkey*, pt. 2, no. 240, Operations Cooperating Board Report on Greece (Nsc 5718/1), "Operations Coordinating Board Report," Washington, DC, 14 May 1958.

17. *FRUS, 1958–1960*, vol. 10, *Eastern Europe; Finland; Greece; Turkey*, pt. 2, no. 293, "Telegram from the Embassy in Greece to Secretary of State Herter, at Paris," Athens, 17 May 1960. In 1958, 47 percent of the Greek population considered economic growth, improvement in the standard of living, and price stability to be the biggest political issues (Close 2002: 104).
18. *FRUS, 1961–1963*, vol. 19, *Eastern Europe; Cyprus; Greece; Turkey*, no. 312, "Memorandum of Conversation," Washington, 19 April 1961.
19. *FRUS, 1958–1960*, vol. 10, *Eastern Europe; Finland; Greece; Turkey*, pt. 2, no. 243, "National Intelligence Estimate; The Outlook for Greece's Stability and Foreign Position," Washington, DC, 23 September 1958.
20. *FRUS, 1958–1960*, vol. 10, *Eastern Europe; Finland; Greece; Turkey*, pt. 2, no. 239. "Memorandum for the Files," Washington, DC, 14 May 1958.
21. *FRUS, 1958–1960*, vol. 10, *Eastern Europe; Finland; Greece; Turkey*, pt. 2, no. 243. "National Intelligence Estimate; The Outlook for Greece's Stability and Foreign Position," Washington, DC, 23 September 1958. King Paul is considered the originator of the extraparliamentary solution and to have imitated his brother, King George II, who granted permission to Metaxas to become dictator; see CIA Library, no. CIA-RDP79-00927A004000030003-4, "The Monarchy and Stability in Greece," 5 April 1963, 4.
22. *FRUS, 1958–1960*, vol. 10, *Eastern Europe; Finland; Greece; Turkey*, pt. 2, no. 287, "Telegram from the Embassy in Greece to the Department of State," Athens, 10 November 1958.
23. *FRUS, 1958–1960*, vol. 10, *Eastern Europe; Finland; Greece; Turkey*, pt. 2, no. 292, "Secretary's Meeting with Greek Prime Minister," Athens, 4 May 1960.
24. *FRUS, 1958–1960*, vol. 10, *Eastern Europe; Finland; Greece; Turkey*, pt. 2, no. 301, "Memorandum of Conversation," Athens, 14 December 1960. Karamanlis was also embroiled in a personal scandal that involved Nazi official Max Merten. In an article in *Der Spiegel* published in September 1960, Karamanlis was directly accused of being a Nazi collaborator and of having been "rewarded with the contents of a warehouse confiscated from a Jewish merchant" (Archer 2016: 5).
25. According to John O. Iatrides (2010: xx), "American policy makers in the State Department, the National Security Council, and the White House had failed to appreciate the extent to which domestic developments and frustrations, including growing anti-American sentiment across the political spectrum, had undermined Karamanlis's standing."
26. Andreas Papandreou (1970: 6) refers to this term as the "unyielding fight."
27. IDEA initially began as a military league "with the initials SAN whose aim was anti-communist and which was renamed IDEA ... when the expeditionary Army arrived in Greece in 1944." Thanos Veremis (1997: 143) identifies the winter of 1945 as the founding period of IDEA.
28. There were several other wartime secret military organizations, including the left-wing ASO (Αντιφασιστική Στρατιωτική Οργάνωση, Antifascist Military Organization), pro-fascist "National Nemesis," right-wing ENA (Ενωσις Νέων Αξιωματικών, Union of Junior Officers), and SAN (Association of Young Of-

ficers), which reflected the degree to which the officer corps and troops were factionalized and politicized. With the exception of ASPIDA (Shield), whose year of origin is unclear, the other left-leaning organizations ceased to exist following the purging of the military of all leftists.

29. With regard to Bulgaria, George Papandreou held a similar position as Karamanlis. Both were concerned with a possible military conflict with Bulgaria. However, Papandreou sought to open up dialogue with Bulgaria and other Balkan states as part of his strategy to be "an ally of the west and a friend of the east" (Papandreou's speech to parliament on 20 December 1964; cited in Hatzivassiliou 2006: 126).

30. Roubatis (1987: 213–14) discusses the creation of the Greek "establishment" that controlled Greece in the post–World War II period.

31. Between 1963 and 1965, 1,001 strikes occurred in comparison to 432 strikes between 1959 and 1962. In addition, 698 strikes had occurred between 1966 and April 1967. This highlights the dramatic upswing in domestic tension during the politically turbulent years prior to the dictatorship (Kapetanyannis 1986: 191).

32. *FRUS, 1964–1968*, vol. 16, *Cyprus; Greece; Turkey*, no. 162, "Memorandum of Conversation," Athens, 17 March 1967.

33. While there has been significant debate regarding the involvement of the United States (and Great Britain) in the execution of the coup d'état, recent scholarship based on newly released archival documents has moved away from this position (Maragkou 2006: 427–43).

34. There was a third "junta" comprised of lower-division army captains, who were accused of organizing a coup. However, this group—according to C. M. Woodhouse (1985: 15)—could be considered insignificant since "it simply consisted of a group of junior officers who were worried about their prospects of promotion."

35. Linden Baines Johnson (LBJ) Library, State Dept. Administrative History, box 2, *Administrative History of the Department of State*, vol. 1, chapter 4, sect. J, "Greece in Political Crisis"; cited in Maragou 2006.

36. CIA Library, OCI no. 0721/67, no. 0000227056, "Intelligence Memorandum: Military Takeover in Greece," 21 April 1967.

37. *FRUS, 1964–1968*, vol. 16, *Cyprus; Greece; Turkey*, no. 245, "Field Information Report," Athens, 20 December 1966.

38. According to James Edward Miller (2020: 13–14), "Both [the] American political forces and Greek political elites focused so intensely on the disruptive role of one of the central protagonist in events leading to the coup, Andreas George Papandreou, that they misjudged the proximity of a military takeover. Fixation on the Andreas 'threat' led many conservatives to conclude that a coup was preferable to a Papandreou government." Robert Keeley (2010: 71), a United States Foreign Service officer stationed in Greece, also wrote that "the Palace, the ERE hard core, the military, the conservative establishment—are determined that they will not permit the Papandreous to come to power."

39. Gikas claimed that there was a strong possibility that riots would have occurred during Papandreou's speech. According to Gikas, farmers were descending to Thessaloniki from neighboring areas, and when the government gave orders to shoot at the farmers, these orders were deliberately disobeyed (see Couloumbis 2014: 92–93).
40. Article 91 of the 1952 Greek Constitution stated that "Ο Βασιλεύς δύναται, μετά πρότασιν του Υπουργικού Συμβουλίου, εν περιπτώσει εμπολέμου καταστάσεως η επιστρατεύσεως ένεκεν εξωτερικών κινδύνων η σοβαράς διαταραχής η εκδήλου απειλής της δημοσίας τάξεως και ασφαλείας της χώρας εξ εσωτερικών κινδύνων, σ'αναστείλη διά Βασιλικού διατάγματος εις όλην την επικράτειαν η εις μέρος αυτής την ισχύν των άρθρων 5, 6, 8, 10, 11, 12, 14, 20, 95 και 97 του Συντάγματος η τινών τούτων και θέτων εις εφαρμογήν τον εκάστοτε ισωύοντα νόμον 'περί καταστάσεως πολιορκίας' να συστήση εξαιρετικά δικαστήρια" [The King may, following a proposal by the Council of Ministers, in the event of a state of war or mobilization due to external dangers or serious disturbance or the manifestation of a threat to public order and security of the country from internal threats, suspend by Royal Decree throughout all its territory or areas therein the validity of articles 5, 6, 8, 10, 11, 12, 14, 20, 95 and 97 of the Constitution or any of these and implement the respective law "on the state of siege" to establish extraordinary courts].
41. While George Papandreou was not viewed as a politician who would lead Greece to communism, there was general fear that Andreas would do so. George's brief role in politics during the Greek Civil War period reflected his anticommunist outlook. However, his advanced age (George Papandreou would die in 1968) and the fear that George could be influenced or manipulated by his son Andreas (who did inspire concern by Greek officials, military leaders, and U.S. policymakers) prompted fear of his reelection.
42. The theory of the German philologist Jacob Phillip Fallmerayer (1790–1861) regarding the ethnic lineage of the modern Greeks prompted a multivolume response by a young academic, Constantine Paparrigopoulos (1815–91). Fallmerayer's theory "not only deprived modern Greeks of their foremost source of pride and equated them with lesser breeds like the Slavs [Fallmerayer's language], but removed their European credentials as well. For if they are not the linear descendants of 'the Glory that was Greece,' then they had no real place in European civilisation" (Livanios 2008: 262). In response, Paparrigopoulos helped to reinforce the linear descent of the Greeks and also the lofty position of the Greeks in Western civilization (for an expansive discussion of nineteenth-century Greek nationalism, see Livanios 2006).
43. As discussed in Foteini Dimirouli's chapter, the dictators took great care to incorporate classic texts and well-known contemporary writers (such as C. P. Cavafy) as a strategy of cultural legitimation for the regime.
44. Ironically, the Colonels were critical of the Western world and renounced Western sociocultural values.

45. The Greek officers felt that the ideological position of the Army Officer Corps was intertwined with the ideal mission of the military man in general. The raison d'être of the military was included in the 1968 Greek Constitution, which calls for the military's "faith and allegiance to the country, the national ideals and traditions and service to the nation. Furthermore, the mission of the military is to defend national independence, the territorial integrity of the state and the existing political and social system against any insidious attempt." In another paragraph, it was stated that "the mission of the military man is opposed absolutely to those ideologies that aim to overthrow and undermine the existing political or social order, or to subvert the national convictions of the Greeks. Furthermore, the mission of the military is opposed to those political parties connected with principles and programs which have been dissolved and outlawed" (1968 Greek Constitution, Articles 129–30; cited in Kourvetaris 1969)
46. Whether the dictators tried to highlight the fact that these individuals were communists who had supposedly converted or ones who simply had experience in developing ideological material (in contrast to the Colonels) is open to debate.
47. *FRUS, 1964–1968*, vol. 16, *Cyprus; Greece; Turkey*, no. 284, "Telegram from the Embassy in Greece to the Department of State," Athens, 5 May 1967.
48. *FRUS, 1964–1968*, vol. 16, *Cyprus; Greece; Turkey*, no. 286 (2018Z), "Telegram from the Mission to the North Atlantic Treaty Organization and European Regional Organizations to the Department of State, Paris, 9 May 1967.
49. Ibid.
50. CIA Library, no. 1255/67, "Intelligence Memorandum: The Situation in Greece," 6 July 1967.
51. The king based his decisions on the recommendation of the minister of national defense, which was in turn based on the decision of the military service councils (Kourvetaris 1969: 62).
52. To communists, this coup was labeled the "palace coup"; see *Foreign Broadcast Service Information Service (FBSI)* 1966, "Daily Report: Foreign Radio Broadcasts," nos. 246–52, 1966.
53. *FRUS, 1964–1968*, vol. 16, *Cyprus; Greece; Turkey*, no. 275, "Intelligence Information Cable," Athens, 9 March 1967: 260.
54. U.S. intelligence reports reference King Constantine's fear for his life. Although highly debated, Ioannides was claimed to have considered executing Constantine.
55. *FRUS, 1964–1968*, vol. 16, *Cyprus; Greece; Turkey*, no. 275 (2030Z), "Telegram from the Embassy in Greece to the Department of State," Athens, 21 April 1967.
56. Ibid.
57. *FRUS, 1964–1968*, vol. 16, *Cyprus; Greece; Turkey*, no. 278, "Telegram from the Department of State to the Embassy in Greece," Washington, DC, 22 April 1967.

58. *FRUS, 1964–1968*, vol. 16, *Cyprus; Greece; Turkey*, no. 281 (2300Z), "Telegram from the Embassy in Greece to the Department of State," Athens, 25 April 1967.
59. The new constitution was promulgated in June 1911.
60. *FRUS, 1969–1976*, vol. 30, *Eastern Europe; Eastern Mediterranean, 1969–1972*, no. 244, "Memorandum of Conversation," Washington, DC, 2 April 1969.
61. CIA Library, no. CIA-RDP79T00975A025000040001-9, "Central Intelligence Bulletin," 4 August 1973.
62. *FRUS, 1969–1976*, vol. 30, *Eastern Europe; Eastern Mediterranean, 1969–1972*, no. 302 (1555Z), "Telegram from the Embassy in Greece to the Department of State," Athens, 8 February 1971.

REFERENCES

Periodicals

Apoyevmatini
Der Spiegel
Makedonia
Nea Politeia

Archives

Washington, DC
  Central Intelligence Agency (CIA) Library

Published Primary Sources

Foreign Relations of the United States (FRUS)
Foreign Broadcast Service Information (FBSI)

Secondary Sources

Aguilar, P., and I. Kovras. 2019. "Explaining Disappearances as a Tool of Political Terror." *International Political Science Review* 40(3): 437–52.
Anastasakis, O. 1992. "Authoritarianism in 20th Century Greece: Ideology and Education under the Dictatorships of 1936 and 1967." DPhil thesis, London School of Economics and Political Science, University of London, U.K.
Angelis, V. 2016. "Change and Continuity: Comparing the Metaxas Dictatorship and the Colonels' Junta in Greece." *Mediterranean Quarterly* 27(3): 38–52.

Archer, W. "The Merten Affair." MA thesis, California State University, Sacramento.
Bermeo, N. 1995. "Classification and Consolidation: Some Lessons from the Greek Dictatorship." *Political Science Quarterly* 110(3): 435–52.
Clogg, R. 1972. "The Ideology of the 'Revolution of 21 April 1967.'" In *Greece under Military Rule*, edited by R. Clogg and G. Yannopoulos, 36–58. New York.
Close, D. 2002. *Greece since 1945: Politics, Economy and Society*. London.
Couloumbis, T. A. 2004. *The Greek Junta Phenomenon: A Professor's Notes*. New York.
Dokos, T. 2003. "Greece in a Changing Strategic Setting." In *Greece in the Twentieth Century*, edited by T. A. Couloumbis, T. Kariotis, and F. Bellou, 42–68. London.
Gazi, E. 2004. *O defteros vios ton Trion Ierarchon: Mia genealogia tou "Ellinochristianikou Politismou"* [The second life of the Three Hierarchs: A genealogy of "Greek Christian Civilization"]. Athens.
———. 2011. "'Fatherland, Religion, Family': Exploring the History of a Slogan in Greece (1880–1930)." Paper presented at the Modern Greek Studies Association Annual Symposium, NYU, New York, October. Retrieved 18 November 2020 from https://www.academia.edu/1057905/Fatherland_Religion_Family_Exploring_the_History_of_a_Slogan_in_Greece_1880_1930_.
Georgalas, G. 1967. *I Ideologia tis epanastaseos: Ochi dogmata, alla ideodi* [The ideology of the revolution: Not dogma, but ideals]. Athens.
———. 1971. "Against the Establishment." Επιθεώρηση Κοινωνικών Ερευνών 7(7–8): 45–47.
Grigoriadis, S. 1975. *I istoria tis diktatorias* [The history of the dictatorship]. Athens.
Hatzivassiliou, E. 2006. *Greece and the Cold War: Front Line State, 1952–1967*. New York.
Huntington, S. 1968. *The Soldier and the State: The Theory and Politics of Civil-Military Relations*. New Haven, CT.
Iatrides, J. O. 2003. "The United States and Greece in the Twentieth Century." In *Greece in the Twentieth Century*, edited by T. A. Couloumbis, T. Kariotis, and F. Bellou, 69–110. London.
———. 2010. "Prologue." In Keeley 2010, xiii–xxviii.
Kapetanyannis, V. 1986. "Socio-political Conflicts and Military Intervention: The Case of Greece, 1950–1967." DPhil thesis, University of London.
Karakatsanis, N. M., and J. Swarts. 2018. *American Foreign Policy towards the Colonels' Greece: Uncertain Allies and the 1967 Coup d'Etat*. New York.
Kassander, P. 1986. "National Security." In *Greece: A Country Study*, edited by R. S. Shinn, 292–93. Washington, DC.
Keeley, R. V. 2010. *The Colonels' Coup and the American Embassy: A Diplomat's View of the Breakdown of Democracy in Cold War Greece*. University Park, PA.
Kouki, E., and D. Antoniou. "Making the Junta Fascist: Antidictatorial Struggle, the Colonels, and the Statues of Ioannis Metaxas." *Journal of Modern Greek Studies* 35(2): 451–80.
Koliopoulos, J., and T. Veremis. 2010. *Modern Greece: A History since 1821*. London.
Koundoura, M. 2007. *The Greek Idea: The Formation of National and Transnational Identities*. London.

Kourvetaris, G. "The Contemporary Army Officer Corps in Greece: An Inquiry into its Professionalism and Interventionism." PhD dissertation, Northwestern University, Chicago.

Livanios, D. 2006. "The Quest for Hellenism: Religion, Nationalism and Collective Identities in Greece (1453–1913)." *The Historical Review/La Revue Historique* 3: 33–70.

———. 2008. "The Quest for Hellenism: Religion, Nationalism and Collective Identities in Greece, 1453–1913." In *Hellenisms: Culture, Identity, and Ethnicity from Antiquity to Modernity*, edited by K. Zacharia, 237–69. Aldershot and Burlington, VT.

Makrides, R. C. 1968. "Greek Political Freedom and United States Foreign Policy." *Massachusetts Review* 9(1): 147–54.

Maragkou, K. 2006. "The Foreign Factor and the Greek Colonels' Coming to Power on 21 April 1967." *Southeast European and Black Sea Studies* 6(4): 427–43.

Mikedakis, E. 2007. "Renouncing the Recent Past, 'Revolutionising' the Present and 'Resurrecting' the Distant Past: Lexical and Figurative Representations in the Political Speeches of Georgios Papadopoulos (1967–1973)." PhD dissertation, University of South Wales, Sydney, Australia.

Miller, J. E. 2009. *The United States and the Making of Modern Greece*. Chapel Hill, NC.

———. 2020. "'Papandreou Derangement Syndrome'? The United States and the April 1967 Coup." In *The Greek Junta and the International System: A Case Study of Southern European Dictatorships, 1967–74*, edited by A. Klapsis, C. Arvanitopoulos, E. Hatzivassiliou, and E. G. H. Pedaliu, 13–27. New York.

Papadopoulos, G. 1968 *To Pistevo Mas* [Our creed]. Vol. 1. Athens.

Papandreou, A. 1970. *Democracy at Gunpoint*. New York.

Polychronopoulos, P. 1980. *Paideia kai politiki stin Ellada: Kritiki analysi kai axiologisi ton ideologikon kai gnostikon leitourgion tou scholikou systimatos, 1950–1975* [Education and politics in Greece: Critical analysis and evaluation of the ideological and cognitive functions of the school system, 1950–75]. 2 vols. Athens.

Repousi, M. 2012. *Ta Marasleiaka, 1925–1927* [The Marasleiaka, 1925–27]. Athens.

Rodakis, P. 1975. *Oi dikes tis chountas* [The junta trials]. Vol. 1, *I diki ton protaition* [The trial of the instigators]. Athens.

Roubatis, Y. 1987. *Tangled Webs: The U.S. in Greece, 1947–1967*. New York.

Sakellariou, A. 2008. "Diktatories kai orthodoxi ekklisia stin Ellada ston 20o aiona: Politikes, oikonomikes kai ideologiko-noimatikes scheseis ypo kathestota ektaktou anangkis" [Dictatorships and the Orthodox Church in Greece during the twentieth century: Political, economic, and ideological relations under regimes of emergency]. PhD dissertation, Panteion University of Social and Political Sciences, Athens, Greece.

———. 2013. "Religion in Greek Society: State, Public or Private?" In *Religion beyond Its Private Role in Modern Society*, edited by W. Hofstee and A. van der Kooij, 153–66. Leiden.

———. 2019. "Authoritarianism and the Greek Orthodox Church: Historical and Contemporary Aspects." Society Analysis and Political Education, Rosa Luxemburg Foundation. Retrieved 18 November 2020 from https://www.rosalux.de/en/publication/id/40942/.

Schwab, P., and G. D. Frangos, eds. 1973. *Greece under the Junta*. New York.

Siotis, J. 1971. "Some Notes on the Military in Greek Politics." *Epitheorisis koinonikon erevnon* 7(7–8): 29–38.

Terlexis, P. 1971. "The Military and the Greek Constitution: A Comparison between the New and the Old Document." *Western Political Quarterly* 24(3): 449–55.

Tsarouhas, D. 2005. "Explaining an Activist Military: Greece until 1975." *Southeast European Politics* 6(1): 1–13.

Tsoucalas, C. 1993. "Greek National Identity in an Integrated Europe and a Changing World Order." In *Greece, the New Europe, and the Changing International Order*, edited by H. Psomaides and S. Thomadakis, 57–78. New York.

Veremis, T. 1997. *The Military in Greek Politics: From Independence to Democracy*. London.

Veremis, T., and J. Koliopoulos. 2003. "The Evolving Content of the Greek Nation." In *Greece in the Twentieth Century*, edited by T. A. Couloumbis, T. Kariotis, and F. Bellou, 13–31. London.

Victor Papacosma, S. *The Military in Greek Politics: The 1909 Coup d'État*. Kent, OH.

Woodhouse, C. M. 1985. *The Rise and Fall of the Greek Colonels*. New York.

Zaharopoulos, G. 1972. "Politics and the Army in Post-War Greece." In *Greece under Military Rule*, edited by R. Clogg and G. Yannopoulos, 17–35. New York.

Part II

Domestic Affairs

Chapter 3

Economic Policy under the Greek Dictatorship

Andreas Kakridis

Compared to other aspects of the Greek dictatorship, its economic policies have not received much attention. Furthermore, the relevant assessments remain largely polemical. The Colonels continually talked about boosting growth and putting an end to party politics.[1] Their opponents charged them with profligacy, venality, and ineptitude; criticism was often peppered with tales of scandal and corruption—invariably anecdotal.[2] Nevertheless, both sides converged on one point: for better or worse, the junta's economic policy represented a break with the past.

This notion of discontinuity permeated much of the literature that emerged in the immediate aftermath of the junta's collapse. Critics went to great lengths to confirm the regime's poor record and the policy blunders that led to the country's eventual macroeconomic derailment in 1973–74 (Nepheloudis 1973; Pesmazoglou 1974: 75–108; Kafiris 1975; Karagiorgas 1978 [originally published in *Anti*, 1 and 7 September 1974]).[3] Even those authors on the Left who interpreted the regime as being a natural product of capitalist development in the periphery ascribed its emergence to a radical break *within* the capitalist alliance (the classical reference here being Poulantzas 1975; see also Nikolinakos 1974). Echoes of these arguments persisted for several decades, as the history of the junta languished in relative obscurity. It is only in recent years, not least thanks to the increased use of archival material, that the regime's economic policies have been revisited, often in ways that challenge our earlier preconceptions (see, e.g., Meletopoulos 2008; Tsakas 2015, 2018; Kazakos 2016; Melistas 2016).

This chapter surveys the existing literature and evidence in order to present a more nuanced assessment, focusing on a handful of key policy areas, such as public finance, investment, money and banking, trade, and incomes policies. In doing so, it seeks to challenge the notion of policy discontinuity, arguing that key policy ideas, objectives, and instruments did not change in 1967; nor did much of the economic personnel or institutions. The shifts that occurred were shifts in emphasis, not major policy realignments.[4] Some of them were conjunctural, while others reflected the junta's reluctance to jeopardize growth, which was seen as essential to the regime's survival. The reliance on economic performance as a legitimizing device proved to be a double-edged sword, inasmuch as it put the economy under increasing strain, eventually causing macroeconomic derailment. As for the political economy underpinning the regime, the commonplace notion that the Colonels favored only a narrow circle of big business and army cadres is found to be as tenuous as the regime's own claims of impartiality. Lending and growth provided the junta with the additional resources with which to co-opt—or at least try and placate—large segments of the population. The very tenacity with which expansionary policies were pursued is telling of the regime's desire to use the economy to offer something to everyone.

THE ECONOMY: A LONG-TERM VIEW

Before turning to policy as such, the next paragraphs consider economic performance.[5] Greece was a poor but rapidly growing economy. The immediate postwar years had been plagued by meager output, widespread food shortages, huge budget deficits, and rampant inflation; a protracted civil war had sown further destruction and delayed economic recovery relative to other countries. By 1955, however, not least thanks to substantial injections of American aid, financial stability had been restored, and most sectors had regained, if not surpassed, their prewar production levels.

Over the subsequent two decades, the Greek economy grew by an average of 6.6 percent annually, registering one of the highest growth rates among countries in the Organization for Economic Co-operation and Development (OECD). Total output more than tripled; by 1975, per capita GDP stood at 42.6 percent of U.S. levels—up from a modest 20.6 percent two decades earlier.[6] Industry, particularly heavy industry, became the main engine of growth and was bolstered by high rates of capital accumulation: energy, metal processing, and chemicals registered double-digit growth rates, as overall industrial output expanded by an average of 9.2 percent annually. Of course, manufacturing was growing from a low starting point, and most sectors were still dominated by small-scale firms of questionable efficiency. Nevertheless, by 1975, industry accounted for almost a third of output and employment—up from about a fifth in 1955. Most of its gains were made at the expense of agriculture, which shrank in *relative* output and shed almost half its workforce. The remaining income—approximately half the economy's total GDP—was generated by the service sector, which created most new jobs and grew in line with total output.

There was nothing particularly unique about this process of extensive growth and structural transformation, which was typical of many poorer countries at the time, including many European countries during the so-called golden age of the postwar period (for a general discussion, see, e.g., Chenery 1960; Kuznets 1966; for applications to postwar Europe, see Temin 2002; Eichengreen 2007: 86–130). The shift from agriculture to industry and services, underpinned by labor mobility and high rates of investment, was common to all of them. In Greece, more than a million people migrated from the countryside to the cities, and from low- to high- (or, at least, higher-) productivity employment. Athens doubled in size, and the country's demographic and social landscape underwent a radical transformation. Several hundred thousand Greeks emigrated, most of them to West Germany, Australia, and North America. Their exodus, usually temporary, helped raise rural productivity, while their remittances became a precious source of capital to finance Greek imports, which were chronically above exports.

In this context, it is hardly surprising that most economists tend to subsume the junta years under a broader historical period, spanning the mid-1950s to the mid-1970s (see, e.g., Alogoskoufis 2006). Plotting real GDP against time, and distinguishing between agriculture and industry, figure 3.1 highlights the continuity in the underlying trend lines. From this perspective, the only remarkable thing about the economy under the dictatorship is just how *unremarkable* it is. Granted, 1966–67 witnessed a minor slowdown, but this was soon overcome as the economy picked up speed, at least until 1974, when Greece had its first major postwar recession. Arguably, however, the crash was a singular event, the product of an international oil shock and the Cyprus crisis; and while the latter can certainly be traced back to the Colonels' abortive foreign policy, neither was directly related to their economics. The 1974 slump notwithstanding, most key economic indicators do not reveal a radical break after the 1967 coup. Of course, continuity in performance does not necessarily imply continuity in policy; the next section thus turns to economic policymaking.

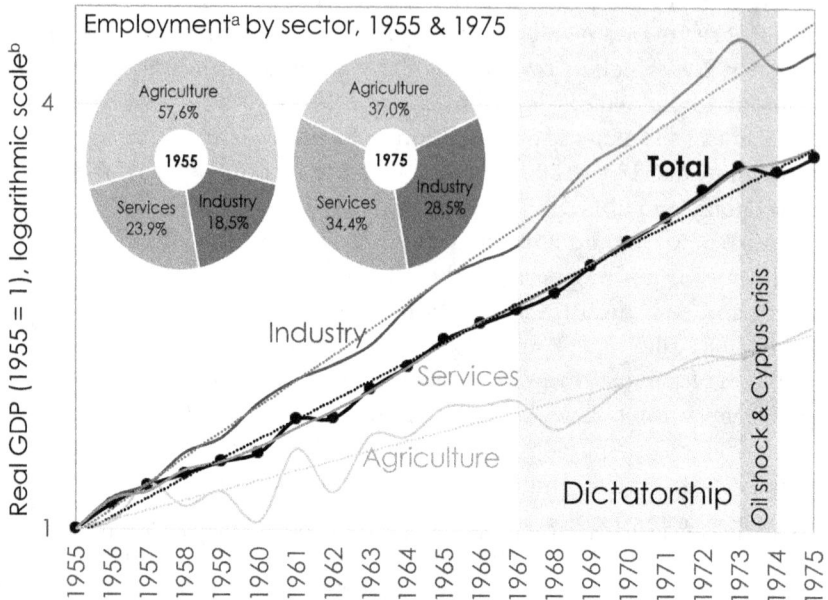

Figure 3.1. The Long-Term View: Real Gross Domestic Product Growth and Employment Shares, 1955–75. Source: See Appendix.

a. Employment shares calculated through linear interpolation from decennial census data.
b. GDP data in constant 1970 prices, converted into an index (1955=1) and plotted on a logarithmic scale, along with their trend lines; agricultural and industrial output plotted separately in order to highlight relative performance.

THE POSTWAR POLICY CONSENSUS: DEVELOPMENT THROUGH STABILITY AND INVESTMENT

In the early 1950s, after several years of intellectual fermentation and ideological conflict, ideas about the economy in Greece crystallized into a policy consensus. Economic development became the overarching objective. This was usually measured in terms of growth, but everyone knew it to be a more complex structural process of modernization, with a clear bias toward industry. In policy terms, the quest for development was translated into the dual pursuit of *stability* and *investment*; both entailed a heavy dose of state intervention, albeit within the overarching framework of a market economy.[7]

Stability subsumed several policies aimed at creating an economic environment favorable to investment and growth: safeguards for private property rights, wage growth moderation, a reliable currency, balanced budgets, and steady access to international trade (for a contemporary, almost canonical account, see Zolotas 1965). Some of these prescriptions stemmed from the trauma of recent hyperinflation: following the successful devaluation of 1953, Greek monetary authorities sought to keep inflation low and treated the drachma's peg to the U.S. dollar with an almost religious reverence. Fiscal policy remained conservative: public spending was modest, and budgets were kept balanced. Labor unions were tightly controlled, keeping nominal wage increases close to the rate of productivity growth; unit labor costs were thus kept in check, safeguarding price stability and fueling the profits necessary to finance additional rounds of investment. Low inflation was also integral to the country's balance of payments, whose persistent deficit on current account—mitigated by invisible earnings from migrant remittances, tourism, and shipping—was a long-standing policy concern. Political considerations aside, the 1961 Association Agreement with the European Economic Community (EEC) sought to ensure preferential access to key export markets and signaled the country's commitment to the Western, multilateral trading system.[8]

For its part, investment was needed to overcome capital shortages, which were considered to be the main obstacle to accelerated development and industrialization.[9] Investment could be public, particularly in key infrastructure, such as energy, water, transport, or telecommunications, where state ownership was commonplace. Since this was the only type of public expenditure that could be debt-financed, the public investment budget—published separately since 1952—was always in deficit. Whatever part was not covered by ordinary budget surpluses was chiefly financed through treasury bills, state-issued bonds, and foreign credits. Most investment, however, was private. Here, the state was expected to intervene in markets in order to attract, stimulate, and channel resources into those activities that were deemed most conducive to development: industry rather than commerce; exports rather than imports; new rather than traditional crops; long-term rather than short-term projects. To this end, successive postwar governments used a battery of surcharges, tax breaks, licensing requirements, regulations, and incentives to attract foreign capital, tilt relative prices, and shape factor costs across industries and (to a lesser extent) geographical areas.

The most integral component of this mechanism was the banking system and *financial repression*: the systematic use of credit and monetary policy instruments to capture and divert savings into desired uses. Minimum reserve requirements forced banks to hold public debt—thus guaranteeing the favorable placement of state-issued treasury bills. Administratively determined maximum interest rates distinguished between different types of loans: cheaper loans for agriculture and industry, more expensive ones for commerce—unless they were meant to finance exports. With the cost of capital set administratively, credit had to be rationed: mandatory credit ceilings by type of loan were combined with financial penalties for those who failed to meet the targets. At the center of this intricate web sat the Monetary Committee, a powerful organ housed at the Bank of Greece and headed by the minister of coordination. The Committee met on a weekly basis to adjust the regulatory threads and fine-tune the flow of liquidity into the public and private sectors; for all intents and purposes, it was Greece's "silent planner."[10]

Needless to say, this was not a liberal policy regime. Property rights were upheld and most economic activity "fell within the sphere of private enterprise," but state intervention was widespread.[11] Markets were born free, but everywhere they were in chains.

ECONOMIC POLICY AFTER 1967: A TALE OF CONTINUITY

Policy Objectives, Policy Blueprints, and Policymakers

Rapid development, through stability and investment, under the watchful eye of the state: this had been the pillar of economic policy in the 1950s and 1960s. The events of 1967 did not change them. For all its messianic fervor and revolutionary rhetoric, the junta lacked a coherent, let alone a radical, ideological framework—especially in economics, where it mainly promised to deliver the fruits of development by eliminating the alleged waste and corruption of its political predecessors.[12] It is worth pointing out how this emphasis on corruption—which later re-emerged as a major line of criticism *against* the regime—rested on an implicit convergence of policy means and ends. In other words, the lack of fundamental ideological cleavages shifted the discussion from the choice of policy objectives to the honesty or efficiency with which a common set of objectives had been pursued.

The government of Konstantinos Kollias, sworn in immediately after the coup, promised "to accelerate growth" and promote "prosperity for all, within the framework of monetary stability" and "in line with the country's commitments towards the EEC," not least by "concentrating investment" where it mattered most (see "Οι οικονομικοί στόχοι της νέας κυβερνήσεως" [The new government's economic objectives], *Oikonomikos Tachydromos*, 4 May 1967, 1–2; "Συγκεντρωτική η επενδυτική πολιτική της εθνικής επαναστατικής κυβερνήσεως" [The new revolutionary government's policy shall concentrate investment], *To Vima*, 18 January 1968, 1). Similar ideas were echoed in the speeches of the regime's leader, Georgios Papadopoulos, and elaborated on by Nikolaos Makarezos, the member of the junta's triumvirate who also served as its minister of coordination until 1973. Subsequent governments under Spyridon Markezinis and Adamantios Androutsopoulos reiterated their commitment to this overarching policy consensus.[13]

The same principles underpinned the regime's five-year *Economic Development Plan for Greece (1968–72)* and its lesser known successors. Published in December 1967, the plan was indicative[14] and thus of limited practical significance for the private sector; nevertheless, it mapped out the regime's public investment priorities and served as a bellwether of overall economic policy. Aiming for an annual growth rate between 7.5 percent and 8.5 percent, the plan reiterated the core tenets of the policy consensus, including the emphasis on balanced budgets and monetary stability, the priority regarding infrastructure and industry, and the need to improve competitiveness, not least with a view to adapting "to the economic conditions in the countries of the EEC" (Ministry of Coordination 1967: 21). In fact, the plan was almost identical to a similar document covering the 1966–70 period, which had been commissioned by the centrist government of George Papandreou (Centre of Planning and Economic Research 1965; for a detailed comparison of the two documents, see Melistas 2016: chapters 1–3). Both relied heavily on the work of the Centre for Planning and Economic Research (CPER), an agency set up by George Papandreou's son, Andreas, back in 1959; a quick glance at the names of those involved in the 1968–72 plan reveals several long-standing advisors to the Ministry of Coordination and the Bank of Greece, as well as many of Andreas Papandreou's early recruits.

Reference to economists behind the 1968–72 plan raises a broader point about people and institutions: economists in postwar Greece, particularly those who participated in policymaking, were a tight-knit and hierarchical community, clustered around banks, universities, and the civil service (Kakridis 2009b). The junta did not change that: lacking an independent body of experts, the regime relied heavily on existing institutions and their personnel. Ministers may have come from the army and the judiciary, but the underlying apparatus was largely left intact. Some senior figures resigned or were removed, but they were quickly replaced by their subordinates, with the explicit intention of maintaining institutional stability and policy continuity.[15] Thus, most of the regime's supposedly new economists were hardly new at all: sharing a common professional trajectory, many of them had been members of the EES (Εταιρεία Ελληνικών Σπουδών, Society for Greek Studies), a mainstream economic think tank dating back to the 1950s, and had served in various posts, forging ties with professional associations and the business community (on the Society's role in binding together many of the junta's [new] economic advisors, see Meletopoulos 2008: 283–304; for a discussion of the ties of various economists to the Federation of Greek Industry [SEB], see Tsakas 2018). In this context, it is hard to imagine where major policy innovations—those little earthquakes Papadopoulos liked to talk about—would originate.

Policy Record: Stability

As a matter of fact, there were no earthquakes. The principal tenets of the policy consensus were upheld. Tables 3.1 and 3.2 summarize key economic and policy indicators between 1967 and 1974. Given the singularity of 1974, when the oil shock and the Cyprus crisis sent the economy into a tailspin, the tables distinguish between two junta period averages: one restricted to the precrisis years, 1967–73, and one incorporating 1974. Comparisons with previous years tell a story of continuity: deviations are few and modest, especially if 1974 is treated as an outlier.

Much like its predecessors, the junta strove to preserve economic stability. Private property rights were upheld, while foreign investors continued to enjoy generous protections and incentives. The dollar peg was maintained, even as the gradual collapse of the Bretton Woods Agreement signaled the realignment of key European exchange rates.[16] Foreign trade continued on a multilateral basis and the tariff cuts agreed on with the EEC in 1961 were implemented fully, as the regime went at lengths to normalize international relations and restart the accession process, which the EEC had frozen after the coup. Despite the loss of some 100–200 million USD in EEC credits, the halt in negotiations was a source of political, rather than economic, consternation and did not cause any substantial changes in trade orientation (for the regime's own views on EEC policy, see Dimopoulos 1979).[17]

Monetary policy kept prices stable, at least until 1973, when penned up inflationary pressures were compounded by the hike in energy costs. Wage policy remained constricted, with nominal wage increases set in line with productivity growth. The regime upheld the minimum wage hikes that had been agreed on for 1967 but soon clamped down on union activity and made subsequent collective wage agreements subject to ministerial decree (Katsanevas 1983: 75). Real wage growth was kept below productivity, thus permitting wider profit margins and continued gains in unit labor costs. Minimum wage increases were kept *below* average wage growth, signaling the regime's determination to boost competitiveness. The outbreak of inflation in 1973 reversed some of these patterns, but not the overall tenor of the junta's wage policy.

Fiscal policy also held few surprises. Despite subsequent charges of profligacy, ordinary budgets remained in surplus and financed part of public investment, the balance being covered through bonds. Public indebtedness expanded, but not much faster than output, keeping debt close to a fifth of the GDP—a figure dwarfed by developments in subsequent decades.[18] The cut in income, profit, and inheritance tax rates was offset by rapid growth and the abolition of various tax breaks and exemptions. Tax revenues grew faster than output, but their structure hardly changed. There is no evidence of massive hiring and—prior to the Cyprus crisis—no rapid buildup of spending on security and defense. Expenditures remained low, including social spending on education, health care, and social insurance. However, this was hardly new: the emphasis on rapid growth meant that redistribution would have to wait. In the words of Ilias Balopoulos, a senior economist at the time, the junta's emphasis on "production first and redistribution later" signaled a return to the economic orthodoxy of Konstantinos Karamanlis, albeit without the "populism" and "petty interests" that came with parliamentary politics (interview quoted in Meletopoulos 2008: 306).[19]

Policy Record: Investment

Investment also remained at the heart of economic policy. In fact, the share of gross fixed capital formation in GDP increased to 28.4 percent, up from an average of 22.9 percent in the 1960–66 period. This is in line with international comparisons suggesting that autocratic regimes tend to attain higher rates of capital accumulation, presumably because of their willingness to suppress current consumption to accelerate growth.[20]

Needless to say, the above refers to the *quantity* of investment. In terms of *quality*, the junta claimed to have rationalized things; critics spoke of mismanagement and low-yielding projects. Recent work by Nikos Melistas lends support to the critics: focusing on the regime's public investment record, he documents the persistence of inefficiencies, overspending, and political interference to favor specific projects and regions (Melistas 2016). Corruption or inefficiency aside, there are other reasons to expect the junta's investments to have yielded less: with the exception of a few refineries and shipyards, the post-1967 period lacked the large-scale, emblematic investments that had set the tone in the late 1950s and 1960s. Furthermore, public investment focused extensively on construction and (secondary) road building. Scattered across the map, such projects were consistent with the junta's promise to transform Greece into "an endless construction site" but faced lower returns than large-scale infrastructure projects (Bank of Greece 1978: 675).

Table 3.1. Growth, Investment, and Fiscal Policy. Source: see Appendix.

	Period averages:									
	1960–66	1967–73	1967–74	1967	1968	1969	1970	1971	1972	1973	1974
GDP growth, real (%)	7.3	7.6	6.4	4.7	5.7	9.3	8.3	8.0	9.1	8.3	-1.8
Productivity[a] growth (%)	9.5	8.6	6.6	6.9	8.5	11.9	9.0	7.5	9.6	7.0	-6.5
Investment[b] (% of GDP)	22.9	28.4	27.9	23.3	26.8	28.6	27.4	29.0	31.8	31.7	24.7
Public investment (% of total)	30.1	28.9	29.1	29.8	26.9	28.1	28.2	31.3	30.3	27.8	30.1
Construction (% of total)	69.1	65.5	64.7	64.9	68.7	66.8	64.4	64.1	65.2	64.3	59.6
Housing (% of total)	39.2	30.1	29.8	28.9	28.7	29.8	30.3	30.5	31.2	31.2	27.9
Ordinary budget balance (% of GDP)	0.7	0.5[c]	0.3[c]	0.3	0.6	0.8[c]	0.9	0.2	-0.1	0.6	-0.9
Revenue (% of GDP)	17.6	21.2	21.1	20.5	21.9	21.8	21.4	21.3	21.4	20.3	20.6
Direct taxes (% of revenue)	17.3	20.0	20.9	17.4	18.6	19.1	19.6	21.6	22.2	21.6	27.3
Expenditure (% of GDP)	16.8	20.7	20.8	20.2	21.3	21.0[c]	20.5	21.1	21.4	19.7	21.5
Public security (% of exp.)	6.9	5.9	5.9	5.6	5.9	6.3	6.2	6.0	5.5	5.4	5.9
Defense (% of exp.)	20.4	19.3	19.7	20.3	19.1	20.4	20.2	18.0	18.0	18.8	22.5
Defense [NATO defin.[d]] (% of exp.)	26.6	25.7	25.4	24.4	25.7	26.8	27.2	26.3	25.1	24.6	22.8
Investment budget balance (% of GDP)	-3.5	-4.1	-4.0	-2.8	-3.9	-4.1	-4.3	-4.3	-4.9	-4.5	-3.5
Overall budget[e] balance (% of GDP)	-2.7	-3.6	-3.7	-2.5	-3.3	-3.3	-3.4	-4.1	-4.9	-3.9	-4.5

a. Real GDP per person employed; derived from ESA-95 adjusted data.
b. Gross fixed capital formation (i.e., excludes changes in inventories).
c. Excludes 7,049 mil. Greek drachmas for the cancellation of farmer debt in 1969, which corresponded to another 3.1% of GDP that year.
d. The NATO definition of defense expenditure diverges from the national definition (as derived from budget data), not least by including pensions paid to retirees.
e. All budget data refers to the *central* (not general) government–i.e., excludes the surpluses generated by local authorities, social security funds, and public enterprises.

Table 3.2. Prices, Wages, and Monetary and Credit Policy. Source: see Appendix.

	Period averages:										
	1960–66	1967–73	1967–74	1967	1968	1969	1970	1971	1972	1973	1974
Exchange rate (Greek drachmas/$)	30.0	30.0	30.0	30.0	30.0	30.0	30.0	30.0	30.0	29.6	30.0
Inflation rate (%)	2.2	3.3[a]	6.6	1.7	0.3	2.5	3.0	3.0	4.3	15.5	26.9
Wage[b] growth, nominal (%)	9.4	10.7	10.5	9.5	9.8	9.6	8.8	8.0	12.6	17.2	19.3
Wage[b] growth, real[c] (%)	7.1	6.2	3.7	7.7	9.4	7.0	5.7	4.8	7.9	1.5	-6.0
Real unit labor costs[d] growth (%)	-3.1	-3.3	-2.5	0.2	-0.3	-5.1	-3.9	-2.4	-2.2	-9.4	3.9
Money supply[e] growth (%)	15.0	14.6	15.2	21.1	4.2	8.2	10.9	13.8	23.1	22.5	19.7
Money supply[e] (% of GDP)	18.9	22.0	22.0	23.0	22.3	21.4	21.1	21.5	23.0	21.8	22.0
Loans[f] (as % of GDP)	35.5	51.5	52.1	42.2	45.3	48.5	52.1	56.6	60.4	55.5	56.4
Agriculture (% of loans)	27.0	17.9	17.9	23.5	19.9	18.1	16.8	16.1	15.2	15.9	17.8
Industry (incl. energy) (% of loans)	40.7	40.9	41.0	41.0	41.2	41.1	41.1	41.6	40.6	40.0	41.3
Commerce (% of loans)	15.2	11.0	10.7	12.9	12.2	12.0	11.1	10.2	9.4	9.4	8.6
Housing (% of loans)	5.0	12.1	12.0	7.6	10.6	12.6	13.1	13.3	13.8	13.4	11.6
Tourism (% of loans)	2.6	4.9	5.1	3.2	3.8	4.2	5.0	5.3	6.0	6.5	6.8
Loan growth, nominal (%)	15.3	19.4	19.5	15.6	15.6	20.9	21.1	21.2	22.3	19.4	20.4
Loan growth, real[g] (%)	11.4	13.1	11.3	12.2	13.6	16.9	16.4	17.4	16.3	-0.4	-0.2

a. Restricted to the six years from April 1967 to April 1973, to net out the effect of the 1973 oil shock (see annual data for details).
b. Compensation per employee, on a national accounting basis; derived from ESA-95 adjusted data.
c. Compensation per employee, deflated by consumer price index; derived from ESA-95 adjusted data.
d. Ratio of compensation per employee to nominal GDP per person employed; derived from ESA-95 adjusted data.
e. Narrow money—i.e., notes and coins in circulation and short-term (current) bank accounts.
f. Loans outstanding at the end of the calendar year, excluding loans to the central government.
g. Deflated by GDP deflator.

As total investment increased, its composition did not change significantly. Public investment accelerated, including so-called parallel investment projects by major public corporations in energy and telecommunications. Private investment, which accounted for more than two-thirds of total capital formation, grew even faster. As before, a host of administrative and financial sticks and carrots were used to attract and channel resources into preferred uses. Several laws provided the appropriate tax incentives and legal guarantees for investment, including foreign investment, which continued to enjoy preferential treatment. Credit remained the main policy lever: total lending grew by almost 20 percent annually, providing a sizeable stimulus. Interest rates were still set administratively and loans were systematically rationed by the Monetary Committee.

In this context, Makarezos may have professed his "insistence on the principles of economic liberalism," but his liberalism was as genuine as Papadopoulos's democratization (Makarezos 2006: 84). In reality, financial repression and silent planning continued unabated—as did a host of price and wage controls. Subsequent claims that the junta's economics were "liberal"—let alone "neoliberal"—are entirely misplaced.[21] The state was still very much present in the economy—not as an instrument of redistribution or welfare provision, nor as source of Keynesian demand management, but as the guarantor of stability and promoter of capital accumulation.

SHIFTS IN EMPHASIS AND AN EXPLANATION: GROWTH-LEGITIMATION

We have seen how the junta shared the same objectives, used the same policy instruments, and even relied on the same institutions and personnel as its predecessors. Whatever policy differences existed were differences in emphasis or implementation, sometimes prompted by changes in the domestic business cycle and international circumstances.

Trademark Policies: Construction, Tourism, Shipping, and Foreign Capital

It is worth taking a moment to test this theory against some of the most common claims made to highlight the junta's alleged break with the past. These claims include placing too much emphasis on tourism, fueling a real estate boom through unregulated construction, offering shipowners large tax breaks to get them to repatriate their fleets and business, or, more generally, that the regime courted big business and offered large concessions to

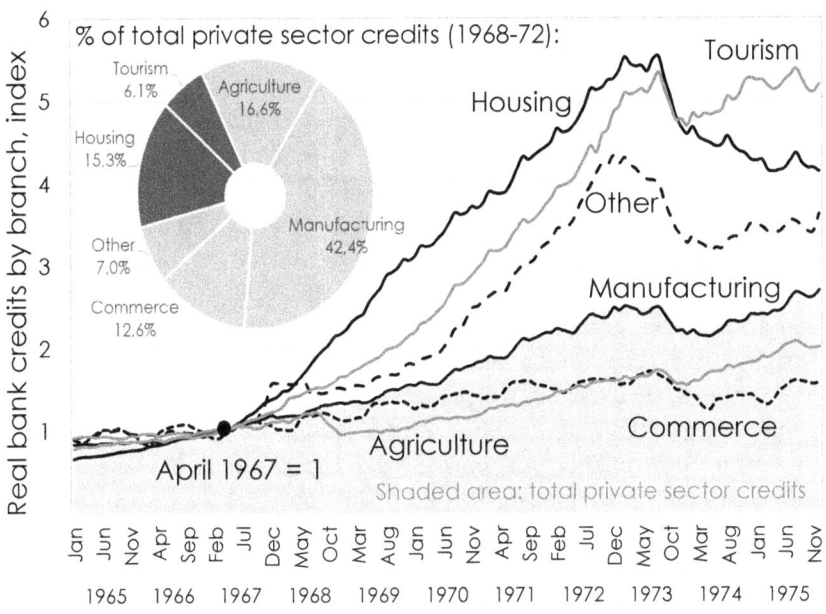

Figure 3.2. Real Credit Growth: Private Sector Credits by Branch, Deflated by Consumer Price Index, 1965–75. Source: see Appendix.

attract foreign capital. Needless to say, these claims are all true. However, none of them represented a major break with the past.

Concessions to foreign investors had been present at least since the landmark law 2687/53 and had invariably attracted the ire of opposition parties, not to mention competing business interests.[22] Eager to strengthen its foreign ties and project an image of stability, the junta redoubled efforts to secure foreign capital. This often led to boisterous announcements of half-baked deals—as in the notorious cases of Litton Industries, the proposed Onassis industrial complex in Megara, or the road-building contract with the MacDonald Corporation—all of which were eventually abandoned. Furthermore, faced with resistance from local business circles and the uncertainty created by the regime's own fickleness, foreign enterprises often saw their investment plans pitted against each other or frustrated completely.[23] This is highlighted in Nicholas Kalogerakos's chapter in this volume, which details the fate of several American investment projects during the dictatorship. Generally, the actual amount of inward foreign direct investment (FDI) declined after 1967, as did the size of the average investment project (Giannitsis 2011). Capital imports under law 2687/53 never surpassed 0.5 percent of GDP—a figure hardly consistent with either triumphant press releases or cries of colonial exploitation!

Much of the foreign capital mentioned above came from Greek shipowners, many of whom repatriated their fleets and offices after 1967. Special legislation provided incentives for foreign shipping companies to establish branches in Greece; taxes were cut, and telecoms and maritime insurance improved, while generous credits were made available for local shipbuilding. Nevertheless, the junta may have been more forward than its predecessors, but it was hardly breaking new ground: sizeable tax cuts had already been introduced during the Karamanlis and Papandreou premierships. Moreover, the success of the repatriation policy owed much to international developments, such as high freight prices and discrimination against "flags of convenience" (Harlaftis 1993: 142–56).

As for construction and tourism, the regime made credit conditions more elastic, subsidized mortgage rates, and offered a host of regulatory and tax incentives.[24] Many of these measures were first introduced in 1967 as part of the junta's efforts to boost a sagging economy, but they were not rolled back until 1973, when signs of overheating had become too strong to ignore (more on this later). Tracking credits by sector, figure 3.2 highlights the relative rise in loans for housing and tourism, *relative* being the key word: at their peak, these loans still represented little more than 20 percent of total lending; manufacturing alone received more than twice as much. Thus, despite the Colonels' increased willingness to finance construction, the share of housing in total investment actually *declined* after 1967 (see figure 3.2 above).

In short, even the junta's trademark policies are consistent with those of its predecessors. Despite the occasional shift in emphasis, all of them ultimately involved the use of tax and credit incentives to promote investment and maintain high rates of economic growth. In fact, most shifts can be interpreted in light of the junta's emphasis on growth as a legitimation device.

Growth-Legitimation and Its Perils

Growth was essential to the dictatorship because it helped legitimize its existence. The underlying rationale was that as long as material conditions kept improving, people were expected to protest less about the erosion of civil liberties and democratic institutions (on the use of growth to legitimize autocratic regimes, see Schmidt 2012). To quote Papadopoulos (1968: 22) in a moment of disarming honesty, during a press conference held on 4 May 1967: "The Government's basic intention is to provide the people with the best possible living conditions. . . . The folk saying is correct: 'a hungry bear won't dance' [νηστικό αρκούδι δε χορεύει]. People struggling to make ends meet are restless. We don't need restlessness right now. We are in no mood to tolerate any reaction."

By extension, compared to its democratic predecessors, the dictatorship was more willing to boost aggregate demand and downplay the macroeconomic risks associated with higher growth rates. Private sector lending was the main policy lever at its disposal; public spending—investment in particular—also helped, but the small size of the Greek budget curtailed its potency.[25] There is ample evidence that the junta pushed lending further than its predecessors. In 1967, total loans outstanding (net of public borrowing) stood at around 40 percent of GDP; by 1972, that figure had climbed to 60 percent, implying a sizeable boost to aggregate demand. The process was self-reinforcing, inasmuch as lending fueled deposits, which commercial banks translated into further lending.[26]

It was not just the volume of stimulus that mattered—timing was also important. Early measures to boost construction were fine-tuned to pull the economy out of a slowdown: construction is known to react quickly, requires few imports, and creates more jobs than other types of investment. However, once growth had rebounded, the government should have reversed course to combat what foreign observers were describing as an "over-rapid credit expansion in certain sectors."[27] Instead, Greek policymakers remained complacent. In the words of one senior official, "As early as 1970, economic developments ceased to be closely monitored, and a spirit of perilous euphoria prevailed" (Constantinos Thanos, quoted in Markezinis 1979: 342).

Antagonism between different factions of the regime may have played their part in this. The spring of 1970 witnessed a major reorganization within the Ministry of Coordination: orchestrated by Makarezos, this caused consternation among senior officials aligned with Papadopoulos. Those same officials returned to power in the summer of 1971, when Papadopoulos scuttled the Ministry of Coordination and transferred many of its powers to a new agency under his control. The Monetary Committee was also downgraded, a decision that would be reversed again in 1973 (Bank of Greece 1978: 645–46; Melistas 2016: 142–56). Needless to say, these frequent overhauls undermined policy consistency, not least since new officials sought to surpass their predecessor's growth record. In September 1971, at a time when the economy was already booming, the newly appointed deputy minister for government policy, Ilias Balopoulos, proposed a new round of expansionary measures so that "international statistics [could] show Greece growing by more than 7 percent annually."[28]

Balopoulos went on to boast that Greece's record growth had been accomplished under conditions of monetary stability. However, as he was writ-

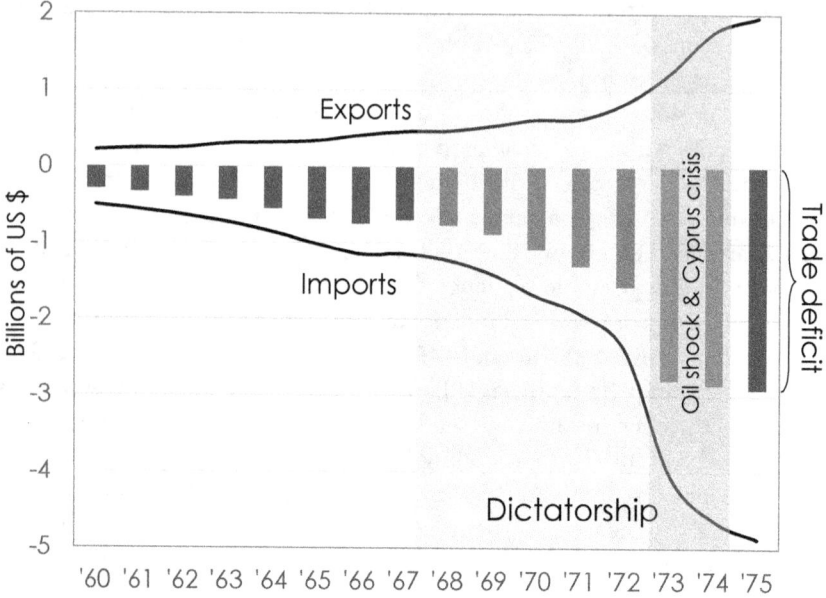

Figure 3.3. External Trade Balance: Exports, Imports, and Trade Deficit, 1960–75, in Billions of USD. Source: see Appendix.

ing his proposals (1972), pressures were already building up in the economy. On the internal front, inflation was about to breach the 5 percent limit; Makarezos had introduced price controls, but these were beginning to undermine agricultural production and cause shortages.[29] The other pressure point was external: growing rapidly, Greece was absorbing an ever-increasing volume of imports (figure 3.3). For all its efforts, including "Buy Greek" campaigns and export subsidies, the junta was faced with a ballooning trade deficit, which needed financing. Foreign loans were hard to come by, at least on favorable terms: U.S. civilian aid had decreased markedly, and the EEC had frozen long-term credits to Greece. Short-term supplier credits and the Eurodollar market picked up the slack, albeit at a higher cost. More viable alternatives included emigrant remittances, tourist receipts, shipping monies, and foreign direct investment.

Herein lies a key aspect of the junta's trademark policies that is generally overlooked. The emphasis on tourism was linked to its value as a source of foreign exchange. The wooing of shipowners had far less to do with tax revenues than with foreign exchange, including the incomes of Greek seamen. The same can be said of the almost desperate quest for foreign capital:

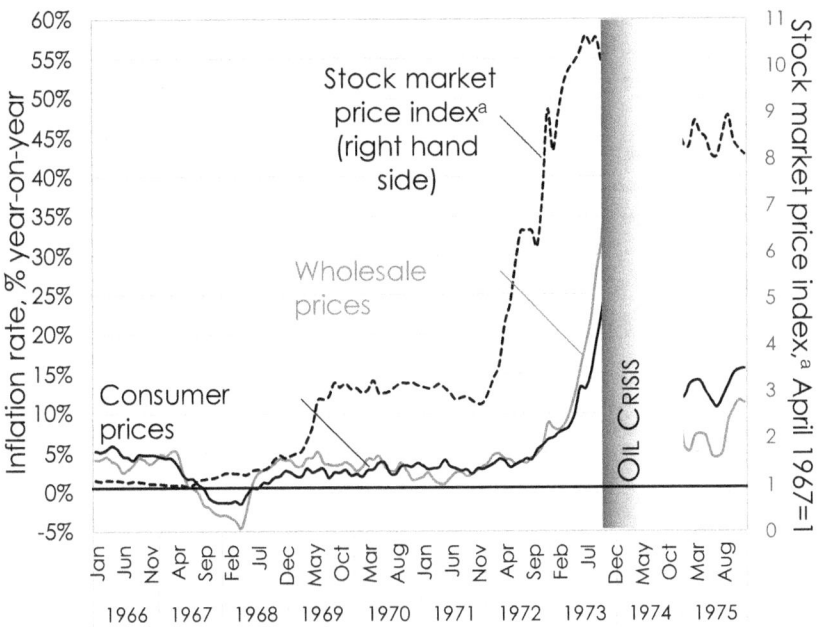

Figure 3.4. Overheating? Inflation Rate (Year on Year) and Stock Market Price Index, 1965–75. Source: see Appendix.

a. Index of manufacturing stock prices.

no matter their viability, FDI projects could finance part of the trade deficit. Even the peculiar decision to follow the dollar and *devalue* the drachma in 1973—at a time when the Greek economy was dangerously close to overheating—can be explained in terms of the regime's constant fear of a balance of payments crisis.[30] In a similar vein, foreign banks were invited to establish local branches—provided they offered foreign exchange loans to the Greek state. Local construction firms secured lucrative public contracts as long as they promised to raise capital abroad and cede the corresponding foreign exchange to the government.

This was not the only link between construction and the regime's hunger for foreign exchange. In postwar Greece, real estate had become the preferred means of saving. Alternative investments were scarce, and financial repression kept deposit rates low, so most people put their savings into bricks and mortar. These were not just *any* people. By the late 1960s, thousands of Greeks were working abroad, earning money in coveted foreign currencies. Their savings were a potential foreign exchange windfall: helping them build a house back home was the best way to get those savings into the country. In 1968, Greek foreign workers and seamen were granted preferential interest rates on deposits with Greek banks. By 1972, more than half the country's foreign currency deposits originated from such accounts, which often ended up financing domestic construction. Part of the junta's favorable policy toward homebuilding can be traced back to the need to capture emigrant savings at a time when the balance of payments was in trouble and the number of *Gastarbeiters* (guest workers) was at its peak.

In short, some of the dictatorship's allegedly bizarre or concessionary policies were less irrational or scandalous than critics suggest. At the very least, they fit into a broader model of economic management with an almost singular emphasis on growth. Whether this was a *viable* model is debatable. The oil shock and Cyprus crisis brought growth to an abrupt end; however, there are good reasons to believe the economy had already been heading for trouble. Inflation had been picking up well before the outbreak of the Yom Kippur War, which caused the spike in oil prices (figure 3.4). Excess liquidity had already been fueling bubbles in real estate and the stock market. By 1973, policymakers were no longer willing to ignore the warning signs and hit the brakes: various types of loans were suspended, credits contracted, and the budget was revised, cutting investment and current spending (Bank of Greece 1978: 656). Before long, this sudden policy reversal would have caused a recession. Furthermore, the Colonels' high-handedness, arbitrary legal interventions, and general disregard for precedent undermined the rule of law to an extent that also undermined long-term growth (Kazakos 2016: 153). The oil shock and the Cyprus crisis merely precipitated the inevitable.

More generally, the early 1970s marked a turning point in the global economy. As the United States struggled with stagflation and Europe's golden age was drawing to an end, new industrial economies were emerging in Asia. The collapse of fixed exchange rates eliminated a key anchor from an international financial system that was becoming increasingly turbulent. This new landscape called for a new policy consensus, one that the regime—boycotted by the majority of Greek politicians and beset by its own internal power struggles—was neither willing nor able to provide. One can only speculate as to whether a democratic government would have reacted differently. The junta's control of the press and its extensive use of propaganda certainly precluded open debate on economic policy, while the rise of hard-liners after the Ioannidis coup alienated several business stakeholders. Ultimately, however, none of this mattered: the regime's undesirability did not hinge on the dexterity of its macroeconomic management; for all its efforts, the dictatorship never succeeded in legitimizing political repression through economic growth.

CONCLUSION

Upon seizing power, the Colonels claimed that they would accelerate growth because they (alone) could rise above the fray of party politics and pursue the necessary reforms. That was the reasoning behind Papadopoulos's pointed remark—addressed to those who called for a more rapid return to democracy—that "parliaments cannot make the leap to economic development."[31] This chapter has argued that junta policymakers walked in the footsteps of their predecessors and relied on familiar policy instruments, pushing some of them to their limits. Let us now turn to the regime's alleged autonomy from political interference and special interests.

Political scientists remind us that all regimes—including nondemocratic ones—require the support of some "winning coalition" to keep them in power (De Mesquita et al. 2003: 7). This was no less true of the Colonels, who originally capitalized on those conservative elements who had been preparing for a coup sanctioned by the king, but soon found themselves in need of broader support. As economic policy was used to garner this support, policy decisions became subject to pressures from special interests. Concessions were made; favors were exchanged; demands were appeased. Loukas Patras's ambitious plan to reform social insurance, for instance, was blocked by the reactions of bank clerks and the army's rank-and-file (Karter 2011: 94; for the regime's social policy, see Sotiropoulos 1999). Far from being allocated "scientifically," public investments were used as political bargaining chips. Makarezos's personal archive contains dozens of appeals by local authorities, senior members of the clergy, and friends, who sought to bypass official channels in order to fund their pet projects; scribbled on the letters' margins are notes of the steps taken each time (Melistas 2016: 199–207).[32] The junta's fragmentation added a further layer of complexity to the process, as each member of the triumvirate acted independently and sought to forge alliances with different interest groups.

In this context, analysis has usually focused on the regime's relationship with big business. O'Donnell's (1979: 292) model of bureaucratic-authoritarianism—tailored to the Latin American experience—was invoked to suggest a close alliance between the Colonels and "the upper fractions of a highly oligopolized and transnationalized bourgeoisie," forged to overcome an economic crisis coupled with popular unrest (the classic reference being O'Donnell 1973). In a similar vein, Nicos Poulantzas (1975: 21, 46) ascribed the junta's rise and fall to shifts in the "internal balance" between a domestic and *comprador* bourgeoisie—with divergent attitudes toward foreign capital. More recently, Christos Tsakas (2018 and the references cited therein) has sought to revise and refine these arguments, claiming that the challenge posed by the prospect of EEC membership led Greek business to support the dictatorship at first, only to change course once the regime appeared to be threatening the prospect of Greece's full membership.

Drawing upon a rich tapestry of sources, Tsakas is careful to avoid many of the pitfalls of earlier applications of bureaucratic-authoritarianism to Greece, as discussed in Nancy Bermeo's (1995) classic critique. Nevertheless, the suggestions that the 1965 political crisis "had a heavy impact on the economy" (Tsakas 2018: 694), or that Greece's problems of industrialization were similar to those implied by Guillermo O'Donnell's paradigm for Latin America, are exaggerated. Subsequent policy continuity is also inconsistent with the predictions of the bureaucratic-authoritarian model. Moreover, Tsakas may be correct to suggest that historians should revisit the connection between the junta and the EEC, but the role of business considerations in this interaction is tenuous. Greek business did not acquiesce to the Colonels because "business-friendly politics were crucial to economic convergence with the EEC" (Tsakas 2018: 701); it did so because business-friendly politics were good for business—regardless of the EEC. At no point during the dictatorship did business seek to dismantle financial repression or give up its protection to accelerate convergence with the EEC. Moreover, it is not clear what *economic* motives would lead Greek industrialists—whose unhindered access to European markets had been ensured since 1969—to agonize over the timing of the country's accession. Unlike farmers, who had every right to complain about their exclusion from the Common Agricultural Policy (CAP), industrialists were in no rush to face unfettered competition from the rest of Europe. After all, most of them did not survive the subsequent transition.

Attention to the regime's business ties is linked to the notion that the junta's "winning coalition" consisted of a narrow circle of army cadres and business moguls—to the exclusion and detriment of broader segments of society, notably workers and farmers. This is hard to reconcile with available data. Throughout the dictatorship, Greek workers saw their real wages grow steadily and enjoyed several goods at subsidized prices; consumer loans, public housing, and cheap mortgages helped boost living standards further. Army personnel received generous pay raises, while the discharge of many "undesirable" officers increased upward mobility by unclogging the middle ranks of the officer corps (see Veremis 1997: 154, 161; more data is available in Gerozisis 1996: 1243–61). Civil servants and the army were offered access to cheap loans as well as various other housing opportunities. Relative agricultural prices may have languished until 1971, but they benefited considerably from the subsequent inflation. Additionally, farmers enjoyed expanded welfare coverage and subsidized credits, while some of their pre-1967 debts were written off.[33]

In general, lending and growth provided the junta with the additional resources with which to co-opt and placate different social groups—not just the rich and powerful. The oft-repeated claim that income inequalities widened under the Colonels is impossible to either confirm or dismiss on the basis of available evidence.[34] The same applies to claims of decreased or increased corruption, although there is no doubt corruption existed. Furthermore, there are good reasons to suspect that the junta had an impact on institutions that matter for economic prosperity in the long run, such as the civil service, education, and the judiciary. However, research in these areas remains scant. The time is thus ripe to revisit both the economics and the political economy of the Greek dictatorship. As additional archival material becomes available, economists and historians have much to learn from the study of the junta and from each other.

APPENDIX: DATA SOURCES

National accounting data covering (real and nominal) GDP and gross fixed capital formation (CFCF or investment) and their sectoral breakdowns were taken from Ministry of Coordination 1976 (for 1959–73) and Ministry of Coordination 1979 (for 1974–75).

An alternative, less detailed series that is ESA-95 compliant is also available from Ministry of National Economy 2001 and from the European Commission's AMECO database (Spring 2019 version). AMECO was used to derive productivity, (real) wage growth, and competitiveness, using (real) GDP per person employed, nominal compensation per employee (HWCDW; national accounting basis) and real unit labor cost (QLCD).

Successive issues of the *Statistical Yearbook* of Greece, published annually by the National Statistical Service of Greece, were used to extract data on population and census-based sectoral employment. Data from "Table II:3—Cash Transactions of the State" were used to construct public finance statistics. Data from "Table IX:4—Current Expenditures of Civil Ministries, Public Security Forces and Ministry of National Defence" were used to distinguish between civilian and security/military spending (NATO-defined defense expenditures were derived from IMF reports). Data from "Table XXIII:1—Balance of Payments, Global Data" were used to construct balance of payments statistics.

Successive issues of the Bank of Greece's *Monthly Statistical Bulletin* were used to extract data on the consumer and wholesale price indices, stock market prices, the exchange rate, money supply, and bank deposits and credits (aggregate and by sector).

Andreas Kakridis is an economist turned economic historian, who specializes in Greece. He studied at Oxford and Athens and defended his thesis—devoted to development theorizing in postwar Greece—in 2009. Since then, he has taught at the University of Athens and the Ionian University, where he is currently assistant professor of economic history. His latest book, Κυριάκος Βαρβαρέσος: Η βιογραφία ως οικονομική ιστορία [Kyriakos Varvasessos: A biography as economic history] (Bank of Greece, 2017) is a biography of a prominent central banker whose life spans Greece's economic history from the mid-1920s to the mid-1950s. Since 2017 he is also the scientific advisor to the Bank of Greece Historical Archive, arguably one of Greece's most important archives for economic research.

NOTES

1. The regime's side is summarized by Makarezos 2006; cf. the policy review offered by Papadopoulos in his speech during the opening ceremonies of the 33rd Thessaloniki International Expo on 31 August 1968, as published in Papadopoulos 1969: 42–46, as well as the propaganda brochure titled *Five Years of Economic Progress, 1967–1972* (Ministry of Government Policy Public Relations Service 1972).
2. Early critics of the regime's economic policy include Pesmazoglou 1972 and Kanellopoulos 1978 (written in 1973 and originally published in *Oikonomikos Tachydromos*, 5 and 10 September 1974). Tales of scandal circulated widely in the press after the regime's collapse; many of them were recently reproduced by Eleftheratos 2015.
3. The economic chapters of Grigoriadis 1975 deserve special mention for their many insights and level-headedness.
4. The term is taken from Iordanoglou (2003: 81), who makes a similar argument about continuity.
5. Subsequent paragraphs are inevitably condensed; interested readers can turn to Kostis 2019; Iordanoglou 2020. For those who do not read Greek, Freris 1986: chapters 4–5; and Augustinos 1991 both offer concise, if somewhat dated, introductions.
6. Comparative GDP per capita figures drawn from the Maddison Project Database, version 2018 (see Inklaar et al. 2018).
7. Once again, the summary offered abstracts from many of the relevant details; for an intellectual history of the postwar "development consensus," see Kakridis 2009a; for details on the corresponding policy regime, see Pagoulatos 2003: 20–79; Iordanoglou 2020.
8. The prospect of subsidized credits also played its part: the Association Agreement foresaw the provision of 125 million USD in credits through the European Investment Bank over the period of 1962–67; additional funds were expected later, not least as part of Greece's convergence toward the Common Agricultural Policy (CAP) (Yannopoulos 1975).

9. To quote the economist who would later serve as deputy governor of the Bank of Greece during the dictatorship, "The lack of sufficient capital is the common denominator of all problems of economic development" (Panas 1955: 191).
10. The term was coined by Thomadakis 1994: 40; for a more detailed account of monetary policy instruments, see Zolotas 1965, chapter 2; and *Greece: Recent Economic Developments*, 19 January 1972: 69–71 (EBD/SM/72/7, Ref. 205024, IMF Archives); the system was revamped in 1966, the key innovation being the link forged between so-called primary reserve requirements and different loans, which sought to equalize the net return of different types of loans to commercial banks (by counterbalancing more lucrative, high-interest loans with higher reserves).
11. The formulation is taken from a lecture by Xenofon Zolotas (1958: 24) titled "Monetary Stability and Economic Development." In the same lecture, Zolotas went on to explain how "the government's role in this respect is to establish on the one hand, a favourable framework within which private enterprise may operate successfully, and on the other, create incentives which would make the main productive investments attractive and discourage non-productive ones"; should private enterprise prove "unwilling or unable" to make the necessary investments, then the state was justified in stepping in to undertake them. In practice, of course, the Greek state often fell short of these goals, either failing to favor private enterprise or favoring some enterprises more than others.
12. On the junta's ideology (or lack thereof), see Clogg 1972; Meletopoulos 2008: 147–339. For an early taste of the regime's views on economic policy, see the propaganda pamphlet *Why Did the Revolution of April 21st Take Place?* (Panhellenic Confederation of the Reserve Officers 1968).
13. Shifts in emphasis reflected shifting circumstances: for example, faced with rising inflation, Markezinis (1979: 340–47) placed more emphasis upon stability.
14. Indicative planning is a specific type of economic planning (not to be confused with Soviet-style central) that essentially plans for the whole economy, but the state only controls the public investment part and (perhaps) some regulatory dimensions. Thus, the numbers for the private sector are only indicative—and meant to help private investors plan their actions—rather than implementable.
15. Thus, Demetrios Galanis became governor of the Bank of Greece at the behest of Zolotas, who resigned from the post in August 1967; see Bank of Greece 1978: 696. Similarly, many of the Ministry of Coordination's directors-general, including long-serving advisor to Konstantinos Karamanlis, Ioannis Labroukos, were also encouraged to maintain their posts.
16. In the course of the 1960s, the postwar Bretton Woods system of fixed exchange rates came under increasing strain. In August 1971, the U.S. dollar—which lay at the center of the system—was devalued; subsequent efforts to salvage it proved insufficient, and the dollar was devalued again in February 1973 (Garber 1993: 461–85).
17. The negotiation freeze is discussed at length in Van Coufoudakis 1977; Pesmazoglou 1999 offers an excellent summary of the economic and political issues at play.

18. According to Ministry of National Economy 1998, public debt as a percentage of GDP rose from 16.2 percent in 1967 to 17.6 percent in 1974; *Eurostat* currently puts the latter figure at 21.2 percent of GDP. Neither figure is consistent with claims that the regime overborrowed, though there was certainly evidence of the regime being forced to borrow on less favorable terms.
19. In practice, of course, the regime's ability to resist "populism" and "petty interests" proved just as limited, if not more so (see conclusion).
20. Note that this does *not* imply that autocracies actually succeed in delivering higher growth rates; evidence suggests that these regimes are associated with greater *variation* in growth rates (see Przeworski et al. 2000; Tavares and Wacziarg 2001; Knutsen 2011, 2018).
21. Present in many of the early (polemical) analyses of the regime's policy (e.g., Pesmazoglou 1972: 77), such claims crop up frequently in the literature (see, e.g., Meletopoulos 2008: 451; Kazakos 2001: 275; Close 2002: 120; Nikolopoulos 2011: 654).
22. The most prominent prejunta example being Pechiney's aluminum project, which was dismissed as scandalous and exploitative by the Centre Union and the Left (Kostis 1999).
23. Note how this means that, when made, requests for additional concessions could reflect the additional risk premium that came from making a deal with a military regime whose stability and internal cohesion were in question.
24. The policy is best summarized in successive OECD *Country Reports*; for a list of measures targeting tourism, see Appendix III in *Greece: Recent Economic Developments*, 31 July 1973 (EBD/SM/73/184, Ref. 197520, IMF Archives).
25. IMF estimates fiscal policy to have added an average of around 1 percent to growth rates in the 1967–72 period; see "Table IV" in *Greece: Recent Economic Developments*, 31 July 1973: 128 (EBD/SM/73/184, Ref. 197520, IMF Archives).
26. Thus, liquid assets (cash, deposits, bond holdings, etc.) rose from 58.7 percent of disposable income in 1967 to 75.9 percent in 1972—a rate of expansion more than double that of the 1962–67 years; See Bank of Greece 1973: 28.
27. *Greece: Staff Report and Proposed Decision for the 1970 Article XIV Consultation*, 15 July 1970: 12 (EBD/SM/70/151, Ref. 239234, IMF Archives).
28. Deputy Minister for Government Policy to H.E. the Prime Minister, "Εισήγησις επί της βραχυχρονίου κυβερνητικής πολιτικής, εν τω πλαισίω του Προγράμματος Κυβερνητικής Δράσεως 1972" [Proposal on the government's short-term policy, within the framework of the 1972 Program of Government Action], 20 September 1971, File 7/B, document 38, Archive of Nikolaos Makarezos.
29. Price controls had been introduced by law 918/1971. Their removal by Markezinis in 1973 prompted Makarezos's resignation; as is often the case, the underlying reasons were political rather than economic (see Markezinis 1979: 340–43; Makarezos 2006: 265–68).
30. Following the collapse of the Smithsonian Agreement, the U.S. dollar devalued by 10 percent relative to gold and most European currencies on 12 February 1973; focused primarily on the balance of payments, the Greek government de-

cided to maintain the drachma's peg to the dollar (as it had also done in 1971), effectively devaluing the drachma by approximately 6–7 percent relative to its trading partners. For the policy rationale, see Makarezos 2006: 251–52, and the official communiqué of the Bank of Greece governor, Demetrios Galanis, to the IMF, as reproduced in *Greece: Exchange System*, 15 February 1973 (IMF Archives, EBD/73/42, Ref. 199886); for a critique, see "Πού οφείλονται αι δυσμενείς εξελίξεις και τι πρέπει να γίνη" [What is causing unfavorable developments and what needs to be done], *To Vima*, 28 September 1973, 1–2. The decision was reversed in October of the same year, but it was too late.
31. See the front page of the newspaper *To Vima*, 7 September 1969.
32. Melistas 2016 finds that Makarezos's home region of Fokida received between four and five times more public investments per capita than the rest of the country.
33. On 30 March 1968, Papadopoulos announced the cancellation of farmers' debts. The cancellation benefited more than 750 thousand farmers and 1,200 cooperatives and involved some 7 billion drachmas in loans granted by the Agricultural Bank prior to 21 April 1967, which would henceforth be taken over by the Treasury; see *Greece: Recent Economic Developments*, 16 July 1970: 12 (EBD/SM/70/152, Ref. 239220, IMF Archives). At the time of the announcement, most loans were not being serviced, so the cancellation helped farmers contract new loans. Needless to say, the decision was popular with farmers, who were otherwise faced with a phasing out of more generous price supports, due to a drastic overhaul of the farm support system in 1967.
34. Estimates based on income taxes, such as those in Leivada and Tsakloglou 1993: 422–40, inasmuch as they exclude more than two-thirds of the population, cannot be considered reliable. Reliable estimates start from 1974, as discussed in Tsakloglou 1993.

REFERENCES

Periodicals

Anti
Oikonomikos Tachydromos
To Vima

Archives

Rethymno, Crete
    Archive of Nikolaos Makarezos
Washington, DC
    International Monetary Fund (IMF) Archives

Secondary Sources

Alogoskoufis, G. 2006. "The Two Faces of Janus: Institutions, Policy Regimes and Macroeconomic Performance in Greece." *Economic Policy* 10(20): 147-92.
Augustinos, G. 1991. "Development through the Market in Greece: The State, Entrepreneurs, and Society." In *Diverse Paths to Modernity in Southeast Europe: Essays in National Development*, edited by G. Augustinos, 89-133. Westport, CT.
Bank of Greece. 1973. *Ekthesis tou dioikitou tis Trapezis epi tou isologismou tou etous 1972* [Governor's report for the year 1972]. Athens.
———. 1978. *Ta prota peninta chronia tis Trapezis tis Ellados (1928-1978)* [The first fifty years of the Bank of Greece (1928-78)]. Athens.
Bermeo, N. 1995. "Classification and Consolidation: Some Lessons from the Greek Dictatorship." *Political Science Quarterly* 110(3): 435-52.
Centre of Planning and Economic Research. 1965. *Draft of the Five-Year Economic Development Plan for Greece (1966-1970)*. Athens.
Chenery, H. B. 1960. "Patterns of Industrial Growth." *American Economic Review* 50(4): 624-54.
Clogg, R. 1972. "The Ideology of the 'Revolution of 21 April 1967.'" In *Greece under Military Rule*, edited by R. Clogg and G. Yannopoulos, 36-58. New York.
Close, D. H. 2002. *Greece since 1945: Politics, Economy and Society*. London.
Coufoudakis, V. 1977. "The EEC and the 'Freezing' of the Greek Association, 1967-1974." *Journal of Common Market Studies* 16(2): 114-31.
Dimopoulos, A. G. 1979. *I koini agora kai i syndesis (1969-1972)* [The common market and the association (1969-72)]. Athens.
Eichengreen, B. 2007. *The European Economy since 1945: Coordinated Capitalism and Beyond*. Princeton.
Eleftheratos, D. 2015. *Lamogia sto chaki: Oikonomika "thavmata" kai thymata tis chountas* [Swindlers in khakis: Economic "miracles" and victims of the junta]. Athens.
Freris, A. F. 1986. *The Greek Economy in the Twentieth Century*. London.
Garber, P. M. 1993. "The Collapse of the Bretton Woods Fixed Exchange Rate System." In *A Retrospective on the Bretton Woods System: Lessons for International Monetary Reform*, edited by M. D. Bordo and B. Eichengreen, 461-94. Chicago.
Gerozisis, T. A. 1996. *To soma ton axiomatikon kai i thesi tou sti synchroni elliniki koinonia* [The officer corps and its position in modern Greek society]. Vol. 3. Athens
Giannitsis, A. 2011. "Exoterikos daneismos kai exoteriko dimosio chreos" [External borrowing and external public debt]. In *Oikonomiki istoria tou ellinikou kratous: Oikonomikes leitourgies kai epidoseis* [Economic history of the Greek state: Economic functions and performance], vol. 2, edited by T. Kalafatis and E. Prontzas, 525-97. Athens.
Grigoriadis, S. 1975. *Istoria tis diktatorias* [History of the dictatorship]. 3 vols. Athens.
Harlaftis, G. 1993. *Greek Shipowners and Greece, 1945-1975: From Separate Development to Mutual Interdependence*. London.
Inklaar, R., H. de Jong, J. Bolt, and J. van Zanden. 2018. "Rebasing 'Maddison': New Income Comparisons and the Shape of Long-Run Economic Development." *GGDC Research Memorandum* GD-174. Groningen.

Iordanoglou, C. I. 2003. "I oikonomia, 1949–1974: Anaptyxi kai nomismatiki statherotita" [The economy, 1949–74: Development and monetary stability]. In *Istoria tou neou Ellinismou, 1770–2000* [History of modern Hellenism, 1770–2000], vol. 9, *Nikites kai ittimenoi, 1949–1974: Neoi ellinikoi prosanatolismoi–Anasynkrotisi kai anaptyxi* [Winners and losers, 1949–74: New Greek orientations—Reconstruction and development], edited by V. Panagiotopoulos, 59–86. Athens.

———. 2020. *I elliniki oikonomia meta to 1950* [The Greek economy after 1950]. Vol. 1, *Periodos 1950–1973: Anaptyxi, nomismatiki statherotita kai kratikos paremvatismos* [Period 1950–73: Development, monetary stability, and state interventionism]. Athens.

Kafiris, V. 1975. "The Greek Economy under the Dictatorship (1967–1974): An Overview." *Journal of the Hellenic Diaspora* 2(3): 37–41.

Kakridis, A. 2009a. "The Quest for Development: Theorising Economic Development in Post-war Greece (1944–1967)." PhD diss., Panteion University of Political and Social Sciences, Athens, Greece.

———. 2009b. "Continuity and Change: Mapping the Community of Economists in Greece (1944–1967)." *European Journal of the History of Economic Thought* 16(4): 625–64.

Kanellopoulos, A. 1978. "Thrylos kai alitheia ston oikonomiko tomea" [Legend and reality in the economic field]. In *Meletes pano sti synchroni elliniki oikonomia* [Studies on the modern Greek economy], edited by S. Papaspiliopoulos, 35–50. Athens.

Karagiorgas, D. 1978. "Oi oikonomikes synepeies tis stratiotikis diktatorias" [The economic consequences of the military dictatorship]. In *Meletes pano sti synchroni elliniki oikonomia* [Studies on the modern Greek economy], edited by S. Papaspiliopoulos, 17–34. Athens.

Karter, G. P. 2011. *"Ta kafsima eteleiosan . . .": Apo tin politikopoiisi Papadopoulou stin "metapolitefsi" Karamanli* ["We ran out of fuel . . .": From Papadopoulos's politicization to Karamanlis's "Metapolitefsi"]. Athens.

Katsanevas, T. K. 1983. *Ergasiakes scheseis stin Ellada: To thesmiko plaisio kai oi syllogikes diapragmatefsis* [Labor relations in Greece: The institutional framework and collective bargaining]. Athens.

Kazakos, P. 2001. *Anamesa se kratos kai agora: Oikonomia kai oikonomiki politiki sti metapolemiki Ellada* [Between state and market: Economy and economic policy in postwar Greece]. Athens.

———. 2016. "Politikoi thesmoi kai oikonomiki anaptyxi: I empeiria tis diktatorias, 1967–1974" [Political institutions and economic development: The dictatorship experience, 1967–74]. In *I diktatoria ton syntagmatarchon kai I apokatastasi tis dimokratias* [The Colonels' dictatorship and the restoration of democracy], edited by P. Sourlas, 137–67. Athens.

Knutsen, C. H. 2011. "The Economic Effects of Democracy and Dictatorship." PhD diss., University of Oslo, Norway.

———. 2018. *Autocracy and Variation in Economic Development Outcomes*. V-Dem Working Paper 80. Gothenburg.

Kuznets, S. 1966. *Modern Economic Growth*. New Haven.

Kostis, K. P. 1999. *O mythos tou xenou i i Pechiney stin Ellada* [The myth of the foreigner or Pechiney in Greece]. Athens.

———. 2019. *O ploutos tis Elladas: I elliniki oikonomia apo tous Valkanikous polemous mechri simera* [The wealth of Greece: The Greek economy from the Balkan Wars until today]. Athens.

Leivada, A., and P. Tsakloglou. 1993. "Oikonomiki anisotita stin Ellada: Diachroniki metavoli kai diastromatiki analysi" [Economic inequality in Greece: Intertemporal change and cross-sectional analysis]. In *Diastaseis tis Koinonikis Politikis Simera* [Aspects of social policy today], edited by N. Petralias, 422–40. Athens.

Makarezos, N. I. 2006. *I oikonomia tis Ellados (21ῃ Ἀπριλίου 1967–8ῃ Ὀκτωβρίου 1973)* [The Greek economy (21 April 1967 – 8 October 1973)]. Athens.

Markezinis, S. V. 1979. *Anamniseis, 1972–74* [Memories, 1972–74]. Vol. 6. Athens.

Meletopoulos, M. I. 2008. *I diktatoria ton syntagmatarchon: Koinonia, ideologia, oikonomia* [The Colonels' dictatorship: Society, ideology, economy]. 3rd ed. Athens.

Melistas, N. 2016. "'I chounta ekane erga': Anaptyxiakos programmatismos kai programmata dimosion ependyseon sto deftero miso tis dekaetias tou '60" ["The junta built things": Development planning and public investment programs in the second half of the '60s]. MA thesis, University of Crete, Rethymno, Greece.

de Mesquita, B. B., A. Smith, R. M. Siverson, and J. D. Morrow. 2003. *The Logic of Political Survival*. Cambridge, MA.

Ministry of Coordination. 1967. *Economic Development Plan for Greece (1968–1972)*. Athens.

———. 1976. *National Accounts of Greece, 1958–1975*. Athens.

———. 1979. *National Accounts of Greece, 1970, 1973–1977*. Athens.

Ministry of National Economy. 1998. *I elliniki oikonomia, 1960–1997* [The Greek economy, 1960–97]. Athens.

———. 2001. *Main National Accounts Aggregates of the Greek Economy, 1960–1999 (ESA-95)*. Athens.

Ministry of Government Policy Public Relations Service. 1972. *Five Years of Economic Progress, 1967–1972*. Athens.

Nepheloudis, V. A. 1973. *Apomythopoiisi me ti glossa ton arithmon: Kritiki analysi ton oinomikon kai koinonikon exelixeon stin eikosaetia, 1950–1970* [Using the language of numbers to dispel myths: Critical analysis of economic and social developments in the two decades, 1950–70]. Athens.

Nikolinakos, M. 1974. *Widerstand und Opposition in Griechenland: Vom Militärputsch 1967 zur Neuen Demokratie*. Darmstadt.

Nikolopoulos, I. 2011. "Oikonomia kai politiki tin periodo tis stratiotikis diktatorias (1967–1974)" [Economy and politics during the period of military dictatorship, 1967–74]. In *Oikonomia kai politiki sti synchroni Ellada* [Economy and politics in modern Greece], edited by T. Sakellaropoulos, 643–54. Athens.

O'Donnell, G. A. 1973. *Modernization and Bureaucratic-Authoritarianism: Studies in South American Politics*. Berkeley.

———. 1979. "Tensions in the Bureaucratic-Authoritarian State and the Question of Democracy." In *The New Authoritarianism in Latin America*, edited by D. Collier, 285–318. Princeton.

Pagoulatos, G. 2003. *Greece's New Political Economy: State, Finance, and Growth from Postwar to EMU*. St. Antony's Series. Basingstoke, U.K.

Panas, E. G. 1955. "Ta mesa pros anaptyxin ton oikonomikos ypaneptygmenon choron" [The means to develop economically underdeveloped countries]. *Epitheorisis oikonomikon kai politikon epistimon* [Review of economic and political sciences] 10(3–4): 184–204.

Panhellenic Confederation of the Reserve Officers. 1968. *Why Did the Revolution of April 21st Take Place?* Athens.

Papadopoulos, G. 1968. *To pistevo mas* [Our creed]. Vol. 1. Athens.

———. 1969. *To pistevo mas* [Our creed]. Vol. 3. Athens.

Pesmazoglou, V. 1999. "Elliniki diktatoria (1967–1974) kai EOK: Oikonomia, politiki, ideologia" [The Greek dictatorship (1967–74) and the EEC: Economy, politics, and ideology]. In *I diktatoria, 1967–1974: Politikes praktikes–Ideologikos logos–Antistasi* [The dictatorship, 1967–74: Political practices–Ideological rhetoric–Resistance], edited by G. Athanasatou, A. Rigos, and S. Sepheriadis, 92–114. Athens.

Pesmazoglou, J. 1972. "The Greek Economy since 1967." In *Greece under Military Rule*, edited by R. Clogg and G. Yannopoulos, 75–108. New York.

———. 1974. *Agonistika* [Militant (texts)]. Athens.

Poulantzas, N. 1975. *La crise des dictatures: Portugal, Grèce, Espagne*. Paris.

Przeworski, A., M. E. Alvarez, J. A. Cheibub, and F. Limongi. 2000. *Democracy and Development: Political Institutions and Well-Being in the World, 1950–1990*. Cambridge.

Schmidt, M. G. 2012. "Legitimation durch Performanz? Zur Output-Legitimität in Autokratien." *Totalitarismus und Demokratie* 9(1): 83–100.

Sotiropoulos, D. A. 1999. "'O Bourlotieris kommounistis kai o peinas kai nistis ergatis': I koinoniki politiki tis diktatorias" ["The insurgent communist, and the poor, hungry worker": The dictatorship's social policy]. In *I diktatoria, 1967–1974: Politikes praktikes-Ideologikos logos-Antistasi* [The dictatorship, 1967–74: Political practices–Ideological rhetoric–Resistance], edited by G. Athanasatou, A. Rigos, and S. Sepheriadis, 115–31. Athens.

Tavares, J., and R. Wacziarg. 2001. "How Democracy Affects Growth." *European Economic Review* 45(8): 1341–78.

Temin, P. 2002. "The Golden Age of European Growth Reconsidered." *European Review of Economic History* 6(1): 3–22.

Thomadakis, S. 1994. "Adiexoda tis anasynkrotisis kai oikonomikoi thesmoi tou metapolemikou kratous" [Reconstruction impasses and economic institutions in the postwar state]. In *I elliniki koinonia kata tin proti metapolemiki periodo (1945–67)* [Greek society in the first postwar period (1945–67)], edited by N. Petralias, 34–40. Athens.

Tsakas, C. 2015. "Oi Ellines viomichanoi brosta stin evropaiki proklisi: Kratiki stratigiki kai idiotika symferonta apo ti syndesi me tin EOK stin apokatastasi tis dimokratias" [Greek industrialists and the European challenge: State strategy and private interests from the association with the EEC to the restoration of democracy]. PhD diss., University of Crete, Rethymno, Greece.

———. 2018. "Europeanisation under Authoritarian Rule: Greek Business and the Hoped-for Transition to Electoral Politics, 1967–1974." *Business History* 62(4): 686–709.

Tsakloglou, P. 1993. "Aspects of Inequality in Greece: Measurement, Decomposition and Intertemporal Change: 1974, 1982." *Journal of Development Economics* 40(1): 53–74.

Veremis, T. 1997. *The Military in Greek Politics: From Independence to Democracy*. Montreal.

Yannopoulos, G. N. 1975. *Greece and the European Communities: The First Decade of a Troubled Association*. Beverly Hills.

Zolotas, X. 1958. "Monetary Stability and Economic Development." Athens.

———. 1965. *Monetary Equilibrium and Economic Development*. Princeton.

Chapter 4

Foreign Investment under the Greek Military Regime
The American Experience

Nicholas James Kalogerakos

When the Greek military regime seized power, the dictators declared they would cleanse the corrupt civil bureaucracy, eliminate red tape that stalled decision-making in government, and, most importantly, aggressively attract foreign direct investment. The regime, craving international acceptance, specifically U.S. approval, proclaimed Greece's doors were open for business. The Colonels claimed to be less selective and more disposed to consider and extend concessions for foreign investment. Attractive terms were added to the arguments of efficiency in the administration and social calm, to counteract uncertainties of a relationship with a government that did not have the confidence of the Greek people. This attitude was predicated on the calculation that the establishment of operations and interests in Greece by major foreign firms could secure much-needed public relations and political support on an international scale (Pesmazoglu 1972: 97). At the same time, however, the regime's opponents feared the dictators would expose Greece to uncontrolled U.S. economic imperialism.

Since the end of the Greek Civil War, some U.S. corporations had coveted expansion plans in Greece.[1] Greece had, for the period, favorable foreign investment laws, specifically Greece's basic investment law 2687/53, which stipulated that foreign companies established in Greece were entitled to the same treatment as that extended to domestic companies (nondiscriminatory treatment). American business investment in Greece during the immediate post–Marshall Plan assistance years was propped up by U.S. economic assistance. When the United States ended its economic assistance program to Greece in 1963, which coincided with Greece's Association Agreement with the European Economic Community (EEC) in 1962, the Greek government took steps to protect domestic business interests. They established domestic development banks that solidified collusive bank-industry relationships, but also resulted in hindering competition and preserving oligopolistic structures.

There are indeed continuities with the democratic governments that established clientelistic networks with the Greek business establishment—networks that continued to operate during the military regime's rule, but with one major difference. The dictators bestowed on the Greek economic establishment such undue influence and power that major foreign investment projects had to be filtered through them to ensure their interests were not being compromised. Most American investors quickly realized that the Greek economic establishment and their patrons in government organizations were not willing to allow foreign companies to compete in the Greek marketplace. Unfortunately, American businessmen seeking opportunities in Greece more often than not turned their backs on investing in Greece. They departed disappointed, disillusioned, and frustrated.

AMERICAN ECONOMIC ASSISTANCE

Following the termination of Marshall Plan assistance in 1952, the U.S. government urged the Greek government, through the continuation of sound economic policies and the passage of appropriate legislation, to obtain private financing for economic development projects in Greece. In return, the United States would assist the Greek government's efforts to attract American capital for investment opportunities in Greece.[2] Despite this push by the Americans for Greece to finance its economic development through private U.S. capital markets, the availability of American economic aid would remain the cornerstone to U.S. foreign investment in Greece over the next decade. The Greek Government made a substantial request for American economic aid in 1956 and 1957. In addition to a 60 million USD aid level for ordinary foreign exchange and budgetary deficits, Greece was in need of 68 million USD of special assistance, totaling 128.2 million USD (compared to the 33 million USD extended in FY 1956) for the support of additional agriculture and economic development programs.[3] The Greek government's long-range agricultural improvement program had two main parts: improved farm production (agricultural machinery) and improved food processing (canning).⁴ Overall, the Greek government's ambitious economic development program called for the rapid expansion of the industrial sector, the extraction and processing of Greece's extensive mineral wealth, and the establishment of a vibrant tourist industry by building more hotels and roads. However, by the late 1950s, the United States was in the process of winding down its economic assistance to Greece. This was made clear in a letter from President Dwight Eisenhower replying to Prime Minister Konstantinos Karamanlis's request for additional economic assistance: "I must point out, however, that the total of our aid programs for the coming fiscal year may very well be reduced from last year. This will raise problems with respect to individual programs in many countries. I am sure that you understand that our aid to Greece will therefore have to be determined in the context of other priority needs for our aid throughout the world."⁵ Nonetheless, the Greek government pressed the Americans for financial assistance under the U.S. Development Loan Fund (DLF). Most notably, 75 million USD over a three-year period was required for four key projects: (1) a fertilizer plant at Ptolemais; (2) the national highway from Athens north to Thessaloniki and on to the Yugoslav border; (3) the thermo-electric plant at Ptolemais; and (4) the electric power and irrigation dam on the Akheloos River.⁶ Ultimately, in 1959, the United States provided 12 million USD DLF assistance to Greece for the nitrogenous fertilizer plant, which had also been supplemented by West German capital and some domestic capital.⁷

American policy direction on economic assistance to Greece did not change when President John F. Kennedy entered the White House. In fact, Kennedy, having to confront recessionary pressures at home, wanted America's European allies to share more of the burden on foreign economic assistance. He outlined as "a high priority" in National Security Action Memorandum No. 22 "the development of formulas for fair sharing in both foreign aid and military partnership, with our European allies, as well as with arrangements that will ease the balance of payments problem of the United States."⁸ Kennedy would completely reorganize U.S. foreign aid with the passage of the Foreign Assistance Act of 1961. This "New Look" to U.S. foreign aid, as described by Deputy Special Assistant for National Security Affairs Walt Rostow to Kennedy, clearly indicated that "the goal is to help other countries learn how to grow. Aid ends when self-sustained growth is achieved and borrowing can proceed in normal commercial ways."⁹

As the United States was ending its economic assistance, Western Europe significantly increased their investment in Greece, most notably by France and West Germany. In 1960, Greece had undertaken the construction of a hydroelectric project on the Akheloos River for the supply of electric power to an aluminum smelter operated by France's Pechiney conglomerate (which used domestically mined bauxites). The cost of the project was undertaken by Greece's Public Power Corporation, estimated at 49 million USD and equivalent to 65.3 percent of Pechiney's investment in the smelter of 75 million USD. Pechiney had achieved favorable concessions that included obtaining a fifty-year contract with the Greek government for cheap electricity rates. In return, Greece would provide Pechiney's subsidiary, Aluminium de Grèce, with loans at an interest rate of 4.5 percent for infrastructure projects with expenditures in excess of 1 million USD (Dokopoulou 1986: 224–25). At the same time, the American Ambassador expressed the U.S. government's concern at the reported proposal to require a 51 percent Greek interest in certain development industries. Karamanlis did not seem disturbed at the possible chilling effects for private foreign investment. He emphasized that any such measure would only be applied to what he described as a limited category of industries producing for the domestic market.[10]

Moreover, in 1962, the West German government backed the Megalopolis Power Station Project, and, in November 1963, West Germany and Greece signed a credit agreement of DM 200 million. Together with the previous investment of DM 200 million credits granted to Greece in November 1958, the total of West German state loans to Greece by 1964 came to DM 403.35 million. By financing the Megalopolis Power Station, West Germany became directly involved in a project of great national prestige (Pelt 2006: 231). In a last attempt to maintain U.S. economic aid to Greece, the American ambassador explained that Greece had made great strides in the past decade and that "aid to Greece should not by any means be considered a 'reward for good behavior,' but rather an investment toward sound and attainable mutual goals. We are getting good return on our investment."[11] However, any thought of U.S. economic assistance being extended beyond 1963 was quashed when Vice President Lyndon Johnson, while visiting Greece, bluntly told the Greeks, "The United States cannot return to a bilateral economic aid relationship with Greece."[12] Washington was clear concerning its belief in Greece's growing ability to sustain a satisfactory rate of economic growth without American economic assistance: "At this stage we regard Greece's own efforts as the essential ingredient, with inflows of foreign capital being attracted by Greece's successes in the economic field rather than, as in the past, Greece's economy being impelled toward growth by foreign assistance. We therefore reiterate our view that the GOG [government of Greece] should continue to press ahead wherever possible at this time in its economic programs."[13]

PROTECTING THE GREEK ECONOMIC ESTABLISHMENT

Many view 1961 as a fundamental turning point in Greece's economic program, as it gradually shifted toward an export-oriented industrialization policy and export-led growth. Greece began attaching major importance to the export potential of investments as a criterion for granting foreign investment approvals. This competitive turn, necessitated by the 1961 Association Agreement of Greece with the EEC (effective from 1962), also meant that the objective of protecting domestic industries from the entry of foreign competitors would ostensibly cease to be a priority (Pagoulatos 2003: 74). Greece was seen to play a role in the southern EEC periphery as an export platform for multinationals, attracted by the country's comparative advantages. A key argument for southern enlargement of the EEC was the prospective increase in the export-processing investment by multinationals, especially U.S.-based ones, which would take advantage of the cheap labor of peripheral economies and low cost inputs from EEC affiliates to export to EEC or underdeveloped countries (Dokopoulou 1986: 205–6).

Yet, as Evangelia Dokopoulou (1986) argues, the economic development policies of Greece regarding trade never identified the United States as an important export market. The United States was viewed more as a potential source of foreign direct investment, to which most favorable concessions from the 1950s to mid-1970s were offered. Great emphasis was placed on trade with Arab countries, partly related to lower transportation costs on exported manufactures (Dokopoulou 1986: 214–15). During the 1960s and until the mid-1970s, manufactured exports of Greece grew annually on average 10.7 percent between 1960 and 1970, and 12.3 percent between 1970 and 1976; the share of manufactured exports as a percentage of all Greece's merchandise exports rose from 9 percent in 1960 to 48 percent in 1975 (Dokopoulou 1986: 209).

Greece's Association Agreement with the EEC included ceasing protection of domestic industries from the entry of foreign competitors; nevertheless, the Greeks took measures to ensure that their domestic business interests remained protected. Three development banks (all established in 1962–64) specialized in industrial investment. The state-owned Hellenic Industrial Development Bank (ETVA) was the largest, while the National Investment Bank of Industrial Development (NIBID) was established by the state-controlled National Bank, and the Investment Bank by the privately owned Commercial Bank group. The ETVA was established through the merger of two public development organizations, the Industrial Development Corporation and the Economic Development Financing Corporation.

The ETVA organized industrial zones in the Greek periphery but operated more as a lending rather than as an investment institution. While ETVA was to undertake higher risks than commercial banks by investing in new industrial ventures or dynamic smaller-scale firms, ETVA extended lower-interest, long-term financing to enterprises already financed by commercial banks. These development banks were underequipped in transferring technical know-how or developing internal mechanisms for evaluating the technical and financial feasibility of potential industrial projects (Pagoulatos 2003: 71).

George Pagoulatos (2003) has argued that the banks' inability to monitor industrial clients was effectively exacerbated by the closed family structure of most domestic firms. Frequently, bank participation in the governing boards of industrial clients took a more informal and personal nature—boards occasionally being staffed with retired bank officials. This reflected clientelistic networks of mutual accommodation between Greek industrial customers and bank personnel. Lines of preferential credit to client firms protected the firms' oligopoly or monopoly position in their sector. Instead of promoting industrial development, close and collusive bank-industry relationships hindered competition and perpetuated the market's oligopolistic structure. They blocked the entry of new competitive business rivals and protected established firms from the need to modernize (Pagoulatos 2003: 71-72). Instruments of industrial protectionism and government intervention, apart from special tax treatment, included the certificate of expediency, often used to block competition to the benefit of established local monopolies, and import licensing, also aimed at protecting domestic firms from competing imports. Other forms of industrial protection included tariffs, quotas, import payment controls, and preferential treatment of domestic producers in state purchases (Pagoulatos 2003: 73).

Andreas Kakridis in this volume challenges the notion of policy discontinuity by the military regime from previous democratic governments. He argues that key policy ideas, objectives, and instruments did not change in 1967; nor did much of the economic personnel or institutions. Lacking an independent body of experts, the regime relied on existing institutions and their personnel. While ministers may have come from the military regime's leadership group, the bureaucracy was largely left intact. Some senior figures resigned or were removed, but were soon replaced by their juniors, with the explicit intention of maintaining institutional stability and policy continuity. The institutions, instruments, civil servants, and policies that attended to domestic business interests during the previous democratic governments continued to remain integral to the dictatorship's economic development program.

In fact, the military regime's five-year economic development program (1968–72) was largely based on a draft program for 1966–70 and expanded on the instructions of previous democratic governments. However, a significant deviation by the regime from the economic conceptions of previous democratic governments can be seen in its exceptionally high reliance on business operators for initiating and executing organizational activities and investments of major importance (Pesmazoglu 1972: 77–78). The former deputy governor of the Bank of Greece, John Pesmazoglu, correctly claimed at the time that "the regime has shown far more of its true nature in its dealings with the business community, whose co-operation it has regarded as essential. . . . But the more effective wooing has been done by accepting proposals or requests by business groups or particular concerns in a spirit of loose laissez-faire" (Pesmazoglu 1972: 77). The military regime's heavy dependence on the Greek economic establishment for economic growth not only exposes the corruptibility of interventionism by the regime's clientelistic considerations but consequently resulted in deterring foreign direct investment (FDI).

FDI is difficult to capture from statistics of the 1960s and 1970s, not least since it entails assumptions about investor *intentions*, such as duration, and the desire to control the target business. The author is unaware of any Greek national or international source that would track what is now described as FDI for Greece in the 1960–75 period—let alone isolate FDI originating from the United States. Researchers would be cautious not to place too much trust in any FDI data compiled prior to 1980. Available data comes from Greece's Balance of Payments statistics, as compiled by the Bank of Greece and reported in its *Monthly Statistical Bulletin*. Aside from the usual imports, exports, and invisible items, such as tourism and shipping receipts, the Balance of Payments also tracks the "movement of capital," which is relatively close to what is now reported as the financial account. Given the substantial deficit on goods trade, which was not covered entirely by invisible earnings, the country's overall current account was always in deficit and had to be matched by corresponding capital inflows (financial account surplus). Those inflows increased substantially during the dictatorship, largely because they had to match the corresponding widening trade deficit (table 4.1).

Clearly, this does not signal success in attracting FDI. Most of these inflows were loans: supplier credits, bond sales, and loans to Greek public corporations syndicated abroad. Some of these inflows were the result of Greek emigrants purchasing real estate in Greece (surreptitiously labeled "Private sector capital imports for other purposes" in table 4.1). If one nets out most of the above, what remains is an inflow category called "Private

Table 4.1. Greece: Balance of Payments Statistics, 1960–75. Source: Bank of Greece, Monthly Statistical Bulletin, 1960–75.

	1960	1961	1962	1963	1964	1965	1966	1967	1968	1969	1970	1971	1972	1973	1974	1975
Trade deficit as % of GDP	-9.5%	-9.5%	-10.8%	-10.6%	-12.0%	-13.0%	-12.8%	-11.1%	-11.4%	-11.6%	-12.6%	-13.6%	-14.3%	-19.6%	-16.9%	-14.7%
Current account deficit as % of GDP	-2.9%	-2.6%	-2.9%	-2.0%	-4.4%	-5.2%	-4.5%	-3.5%	-3.6%	-4.4%	-4.7%	-3.4%	-3.3%	-8.2%	-7.2%	-5.1%
Financial account surplus (million USD)	89.8	127.8	168.0	148.1	211.1	234.3	265.4	180.4	265.1	316.2	375.1	479.3	841.2	1,035.0	1,046.6	1,266.7
as a % of GDP	2.9%	3.7%	4.5%	3.6%	4.6%	4.4%	4.6%	2.9%	3.9%	4.1%	4.4%	5.0%	7.6%	7.3%	6.2%	6.4%
Private sector capital imports for business purposes (million USD)	15.3	18.6	27.5	44.3	48.2	84.4	69.1	53.7	53.9	82.5	156.4	99.1	90.2	145.1	187.2	194.7
as a % of total capital imports (i.e., the financial account surplus)	17.0%	14.6%	16.4%	29.9%	22.8%	36.0%	26.0%	29.8%	20.3%	26.1%	41.7%	20.7%	10.7%	14.0%	17.9%	15.4%
Capital imports under L.D. 2687/53	5.9	7.3	14.7	28.9	44.7	72.2	48.5	32.6	33	25.8	50	42.4	55.8	61.6	66.9	23.6
as a % of total capital imports (i.e., the financial account surplus)	6.6%	5.7%	8.8%	19.5%	21.2%	30.8%	18.3%	18.1%	12.4%	8.2%	13.3%	8.8%	6.6%	6.0%	6.4%	1.9%
as a % of GDP	0.2%	0.2%	0.4%	0.7%	1.0%	1.4%	0.8%	0.5%	0.5%	0.3%	0.6%	0.4%	0.5%	0.4%	0.4%	0.1%
Private sector capital imports for other purposes (million USD)	31.8	36.3	40.8	43.5	53.1	58.0	65.3	54.4	71.9	80.1	95.6	138.2	190.2	270.6	245.3	312.4
as a % of total capital imports (i.e., the financial account surplus)	35.4%	28.4%	24.3%	29.4%	25.2%	24.8%	24.6%	30.2%	27.1%	25.3%	25.5%	28.8%	22.6%	26.1%	23.4%	24.7%
as a % of GDP	1.0%	1.0%	1.1%	1.1%	1.1%	1.1%	1.1%	0.9%	1.1%	1.0%	1.1%	1.4%	1.7%	1.9%	1.5%	1.6%

sector capital imports for business purposes," which represents approximately a quarter of the net surplus. Since those numbers include *any* loan contracted by nonbank private corporations outside Greece, one would not classify them as FDI—but they could be considered an upper bound to any reasonable estimate. A reliable lower bound could be capital injected through Law 2687/53, the legislation under which most foreign direct investments would be categorized (see table 4.1). This indicates that despite the many announcements of new investment projects, the military regime failed to produce an acceleration of FDI (not only American FDI, but overall)—at least the FDI that would flow through Law 2687/53. In fact, average FDI inflows relative to GDP never surpassed the peak they reached in the mid-1960s, when most of the Karamanlis government's major investment projects (e.g., Pechiney) were in full swing.

During the junta years, capital imports under law 2687/53 never surpassed 0.5 percent of GDP. Moreover, the actual volume of FDI declined after 1967, and so did the size of the average investment project (Giannitsis 2011). One must also be cognizant of the fact that some of the funds injected through Law 2687/53 during the dictatorship were shipping funds, and therefore it is debatable whether one would consider their origin truly "foreign."

"GREEK MANUFACTURERS ARE NO ANGELS"

There are indeed continuities between the military regime's heavy dependence on the Greek economic establishment for economic growth, while catering to their interests, and the practices pursued previously by Greek governments during the 1950s and 1960s. Prodromos Bodosakis-Athanasiadis was arguably the most dominant Greek businessman and industrialist during the 1930s. As the head of the largest armaments firm in the Balkans and Near East and the most important link between Greek and German industry, he had cultivated close personal relations with political insiders of the Ioannis Metaxas regime (1936–41) and with the dictator himself. Bodosakis fled Greece shortly before the Nazi invasion during World War II and eventually made his way to the United States. Since his armaments firm was established using German technology and know-how, and because he was considered one of the world's most prominent arms dealers, American authorities closely tracked Bodosakis's activities. A report from the director of Naval Intelligence in 1942 titled "Greek American Fascism" referred to Bodosakis as "a thoroughly disreputable character, by some considered the most dangerous of all Greeks" (Pelt 2006: 71). Bodosakis kept in touch with leading members of the Greek government in exile, as well as with Greek liberal political and military circles based in Egypt. He had a number of leading Greek military men and politicians on his payroll, including future Greek prime ministers. However, it would be Bodosakis's close connections with the minister of economic coordination, Spyridon Markezinis, who was responsible for the Greek economic development plan and its execution, that would ensure Bodosakis's influence on the postwar Greek economic landscape (Pelt 2006: 72–73).

Through his extensive prewar relations to German business interests, including a partnership with the German industrialist Bertold von Bohlen Krupp, Bodosakis contributed to paving the way for an official West German– Greek understanding regarding the participation of West German industry in the Greek development plan through the Erhard-Markezinis agreement in 1953. Unsurprisingly, Bodosakis had strong personal business interests in several major projects in the Greek development plan listed to receive assistance from West German industry, notably the Ptolemais Project, the Larymna nickel mines, and the installations planned for the manufacture of nitrogenous fertilizers through his Hellenic Company of Chemical Products and Fertilizers Ltd. (Pelt 2006: 92). Consequently, Markezinis was accused of pursuing a policy that heavily favored Greek business interests and was too centered on cooperation with West Germany. As Mogens Pelt clearly indicates, no projects benefited more by the Erhard-Markezinis agreement than those under Bodosakis's control (Pelt 2006: 84).

In addition to Bodosakis, there were other significant players in the Greek financial landscape during this period. The Eliopoulos brothers— Elias, George, and Athanassius—rose to international notoriety as "the Drug Barons of Europe" after they launched their narcotics smuggling operation, which would span the globe in 1927. Elias had visited China and arranged to ship raw opium to two complicit manufacturers in France, and by May 1928 was selling diverted pharmaceutical grade narcotics to America's major illegal drug distributors, most notably to mafia crime boss Charles "Lucky" Luciano. In 1930, the Eliopoulos brothers financed a clandestine laboratory in Turkey, and thereafter narcotics from Turkey and China were routed to France and then shipped to the United States (Valentine 2006: 10). Following the seizure of 17,500 cans marked "Furs," each containing one ounce of morphine, shipped from Istanbul to Brooklyn aboard the *SS Alesia* in 1930, Elias in Athens felt so secure that he was beyond the reach of U.S. law enforcement that he confided to a U.S. federal narcotics agent about his trip to China and how he set up business with an associate in Tientsin (Tianjin). Elias predicted an annual turnover of tons of illicit narcotics to the United States (United States Drug Enforcement Administration 2018: 17). As Gerard Piel described in *Life* magazine in 1943, "The House of Eliopoulos functioned as the central bank and clearing house for the biggest share of the world's illicit trade in opium, morphine and heroin ever organized in one system."

In 1932, the Eliopoulos brothers were exposed for manipulating the illicit drug trade. The United States Drug Enforcement Administration credits the Eliopoulos brothers as the originators of the "double deal": in order to ensure that their customers would not grow to become a competitive threat, the brothers would "snitch" on them to U.S. customs authorities (United States Drug Enforcement Administration 2018: 17). The Eliopoulos brothers soon retired from the drug smuggling trade and heavily invested their fortune in Greece's bourgeoning mining industry, notably in bauxite, barite, bentonite, pearlite, and gold mines. Their crown jewel was Bauxites Parnasse S.A., which they founded in 1934, possessing bauxite-rich deposits in the Parnassus region.

In 1941, prior to the Nazi invasion and occupation of Greece, the Eliopoulos brothers fled to New York and assumed that the statute of limitations would protect them from prosecution. In 1943, Elias and George were brought to trial in a Brooklyn federal court for smuggling 1 million USD worth of morphine into the port of Hoboken in 1931. Both brothers were convicted of all charges but were later acquitted as the statute of limitations had indeed been exceeded. Eventually, the indictments were rendered null and void (Gingeras 2014: 53). By 1947, the Eliopoulos brothers returned to a liberated Greece to resume their mining operations. But when the Greek mining industry received American assistance through industrial loans and programs of "stockpiling strategic materials," these aid loans took the privileged direction of the mines of the Greek Chemical Products and Fertilizers Company of the Bodosakis Group and the bauxite mines of the Skalistris Group (Papastefanaki 2013: 171–72). Late into 1955, the Eliopoulos brothers' Bauxites Parnasse mines sat idle (Papastefanaki 2013: 173).

The establishment in Greece of the Pechiney alumina and aluminum plant in 1960 had given great impetus to the Greek bauxite mining industry. Yet, prior to the opening of the refinery, there were serious concerns that mineral-rich deposits were being mined and exported. In February 1962, Pechiney's Aluminium de Grèce reached an agreement with the Barlos Brothers Company for the delivery of 4.725 million tons of bauxite for the period of 1965–83. After the Greek government intervened, Aluminium de Grèce also reached an agreement with the Eliopoulos brothers' Bauxites Parnasse to purchase 175,000 tons of bauxite per year for thirty years at competitive prices (Papastefanaki 2013: 177). By 1971, Bauxites Parnasse mined approximately 1.3 million tons of bauxite and controlled 60 percent of the domestic production per year (United States Department of the Interior, Bureau of Mines 1971: 3).

As a result of the Greek government's commitment in the original 1960 agreement to assure Pechiney ownership of 30 million tons of bauxite over thirty years, Greek bauxite miners were compelled to perform extensive exploration work in order to increase the amount of available ore while maintaining their traditional exports of bauxite. George Eliopoulos indicated that the Eliopoulos brothers alone spent several million dollars in scientific mining exploration in the Mount Parnassus area with the result that since 1962 they had established "sure and very probable" bauxite deposits of approximately 60 million tons. "Probable and geographically probable" deposits in the Eliopoulos mining properties on generous long-term, fifty-year leases from the government were estimated at over 100 million tons. In 1968, Bauxites Parnasse delivered to the Pechiney alumina plant between 225,000 and 250,000 tons of bauxite per year. In addition, in 1967, the Eliopoulos brothers exported a total of approximately 550,000 tons (including 200,000 tons to Soviet Russia) as their share of total Greek exports of bauxite from approximately 1.2 million tons during that year.[14]

Pechiney made a proposal to expand its Distomo plant to produce an additional 250,000 tons of alumina for export. This would earmark for Pechiney an additional 500,000 tons of Greek bauxite ore. The 64 million USD expansion program would raise Pechiney's production capacity to 475,000–500,000 tons of alumina and 150,000 tons of aluminum per year by the end of 1971. Bauxite consumption at the company's alumina plant was expected to be 1 million tons per year. The total investment in production facilities since the start of operations in 1960 would reach 200 million USD by the end of 1971. Meanwhile, Bauxites Parnasse had a 6 million USD investment program underway by 1971, including a beneficiation plant, which expected to raise bauxite production capacity to 2 million tons by 1975 (United States Department of the Interior, Bureau of Mines 1971: 3).

For a while, the Eliopoulos brothers carried on negotiations with Pechiney for a joint venture in establishing a separate 250,000-ton alumina plant for which bauxite would be supplied exclusively from the Eliopoulos mining operations. However, these negotiations fell through, whereupon the Eliopoulos brothers made an independent application to the Foreign Investment Committee to invest approximately 40 million USD in an alumina/aluminum plant at Itea in a joint venture with a U.S. firm (speculated to have been the Reynolds Metal Company).[15] In response, Aluminium de Grèce bought 50 percent of the shares in Delphi Bauxites in 1968, and in 1972 it acquired 75 percent of the Barlos Brothers Company mines in Distomo. However, a clause included in a contract signed between Pechiney and the junta in 1969—which stipulated that the Greek government had to maintain Aluminium de Grèce's priority in the supply of bauxite (Papastefanaki 2013: 178–79)—acted as a deterrent to other interests from entering the Greek alumina/aluminum industry.

Prominent Greek industrialists were vocal early on of critical missteps the junta was making, most notably Demetrios Angelopoulos, the head of Halyvourgiki Steel. Angelopoulos feared that "through incompetence or lack of expertise on the part of the persons responsible for economic and fiscal policy, serious mistakes [were] being made which could damage the economy." Regarding the investment climate, Angelopoulos could detect plenty of evidence that the attitude of the business community was, as a whole, one of hesitancy and skepticism. There were certainly some firms, such as Halyvourgiki, which had long planned improvements or expansion and had decided to proceed with their plans. But overall, Angelopoulos claimed the "climate has not been propitious enough to be conducive to large scale investments." He stressed that lack of confidence in the economic and financial policies of the regime, as well as the existence of considerable uncertainty about the future, were factors that tended to exert a braking effect on productive investment. Ominously, he seemed reasonably confident that the interests of Greek industrialists would soon improve.[16]

George Anastassopoulos, the president of the Athens Merchants' Association, complained that the military regime lacked experience and expertise, and that they made mistakes that could have been avoided. He specifically referred to the regime's tendency to promulgate decree-laws without adequate study and preparation, with the result that some of the regime's most important emergency laws had to be suspended and revised within days after they were issued. From a business perspective, this was not conducive to faith and confidence in the efficiency and understanding of the government. Nevertheless, Anastassopoulos clearly indicated that "the business community is anxious to see the Papadopoulos Government improve its performance and succeed in its efforts to promote the economic development of the country. To achieve this the Government needs the assistance and advice of the business community." Anastassopoulos explained that "it is the duty of business to help the Government in a positive and active way. The Revolution is a reality, which it would be futile and unrealistic to ignore."[17]

In fact, Greek industrialists would attain an extraordinary amount of influence through the Five-Year Economic Development Program Committee. The Committee was established to review and essentially influence draft legislation and regulations for sections of the program. The "Working Parties" would provide a thorough analysis of the problems falling into their respective areas of responsibility, draft the necessary enabling legislation or implementing regulations, and have their recommendations referred by the Committee to the appropriate ministries for further review and elaboration before they were enacted by the Cabinet into decree ("emergency") laws. The Committee was also a sounding board for any comments or ideas that private business wished to present. The Committee would often hold informal hearings with representatives of Greek business who were believed to be in a position to make constructive suggestions. The views of the business community would be largely reflected through Committee member Demetrios Marinopoulos of Famar (pharmaceuticals) and Printemps-Prisunic (self-service stores) and president of the Federation of Greek Industries (FGI).[18] While Greek industrialists in the past had tremendous influence over government direction, such as Bodosakis, they largely operated in the background. The junta took the unprecedented step of formalizing FGI influence in government decision-making structures.

Greek industrialists were indeed appreciative for a seat at the center of government. Christopher Katsambas, a leading Greek cotton textile manufacturer and head of the Piraiki-Patraiki Cotton Manufacturing Company, had a twenty-minute private meeting with Prime Minister Georgios Papadopoulos at the prime minister's request. Papadopoulos explained he urgently wanted to meet with Katsambas because he had heard many positive things about him as the "dean of Greek manufacturers." Papadopoulos also told Katsambas that he considered him not only a leading Greek businessman, but also a public figure since Katsambas was President Emeritus of the Federation of Greek Industries and active president of the Greek Cotton Textile Manufacturers Association. Katsambas expressed to Papadopoulos that the Greek manufacturers had every reason to be thankful to the Revolutionary Government for what it had done for Greek industry as a whole. Katsambas stated, "No other Greek Government has ever tried to help Greek industry as much as the present Government." He added that there were still many problems to be solved, but the Greek manufacturers had at least the satisfaction that they were being listened to sympathetically, and that an honest effort was being made to find solutions to their problems. Katsambas extolled particularly the restoration of order and discipline in the factories and the elimination of disruptive wildcat strikes.[19]

Katsambas then told Papadopoulos that the Greek manufacturers had one major complaint: no prime minister of Greece in the postwar period had visited the headquarters of the Federation of Greek Industries. He attributed this to the fact that, "for political reasons, the Greek industrialists have never been a desirable element for politicians to be openly friendly with." He added that since the present government had no such inhibitions, the Greek manufacturers considered themselves greatly honored for the opportunity to host the prime minister. Katsambas complained that Greek industry and the Greek manufacturers had been "badly abused and demeaned" in the past as "exploiters and suckers of the blood of the working people," and that there was little they could do to defend themselves against such unjust accusations. He conceded that "the Greek manufacturers are no angels but that until Greece can breed more progressive and more altruistic and publicly minded industrialists, Greece's economic development must remain a responsibility of the present generation."[20]

The military regime's first attempt to attract FDI proved to be its most futile. In a desperate need to shore up its international credibility, notably to maintain working relations with the United States, and show to the world that Greece was open for business, it almost immediately signed a contract with the American multinational Litton Industries to promote economic development in specific regions of Greece and attract foreign direct investment. The Litton case is also particularly notable in that the Greek economic establishment flexed its authority to not only crush a foreign competitor that threatened its interests, but also proved to the dictators—who had proclaimed, "We do not belong to the economic oligarchy"—that the economic establishment could not be bypassed.

LITTON IN GREECE

Litton Industries' spectacular success in industry by the early 1960s convinced its leaders that their highly publicized methods in technical organization and project planning could organize and program solutions for diverse economic and social problems. Litton believed they could create economic models that would pinpoint key investment opportunities in developing countries (McGrew 1972: 66). Litton's interest in making Greece the test case for its claim to possess a special competence for tackling economic development predates the actual contract signing on 16 May 1967 by several years. Discussions first began under the George Papandreou government (1963–65), and, when it fell, negotiations continued with the successor governments. A government-financed Litton feasibility study in 1965 recommended that a development center be established on the island of Crete and the Western half of the Peloponnesus, both areas suffering economic stagnation.[21]

The Litton contract was both ambiguous and overreaching. Litton's responsibilities were vaguely outlined to encompass the "development of resources, social and economic in nature, which are directly related to economic growth." Litton was to establish procedures, methods, and measures for the development of the two regions, evaluate and revise existing plans and programs, act as supervising and surveying agent of development works, train government officials in modern management techniques, and solicit foreign capital ("Greece-Litton Industries" 1969: 19; see McGrew 1972: 67). While the twelve-year contract was subject to periodic review, either party reserved the right to terminate the relationship. The government could cancel the agreement if capital investments did not total at least 120 million USD by the end of the first two years and 240 million USD by the end of the first four years. As stipulated in the contract, the government was obliged to reimburse Litton for all costs incurred in performing its contractual obligations ("Greece-Litton Industries" 1969: 21; see McGrew 1972: 67–68).

The initiative for negotiations with the Greek regime came from the military regime itself. Pierre Guillaume, executive officer at Litton Industries Benelux, received a telephone call while in Washington in late April from an official of the Ministry of Coordination inviting him to Athens. Litton was anxious to implement a development program in Greece because it offered a unique combination of two key factors: real potential for agricultural, industrial, touristic, and general infrastructural development; and secondly, pleasant living conditions, which could easily attract qualified personnel to work in the country. In the initial stages of the program, covering the balance of 1967, Litton's work was largely administrative. During this period, Litton did not expect to initiate specific development projects or procure any funds for projects. The main task was to conduct preliminary feasibility studies and prioritize ventures. Litton had not resolved to undertake any particular project, and formal construction on any project was unlikely to begin before mid-1968. Litton's approach to the contract in 1967 contradicted their aim of completing as many projects as possible. Litton was clearly aware of the political implications of its contract with the regime. Future Greek governments or political parties could oppose the program and seek to terminate it. Litton believed its best protection against such an eventuality was "to complete several key projects as rapidly as possible so that, by the time any political attacks begin against the program, there will be works accomplished that speak for themselves, and broad support from the Greek public that benefits from these works."[22] But by concentrating its efforts on tourism, Litton faced harsh criticism in the United States. Many in the U.S. Congress opposed the Greek regime by discouraging Americans from traveling to Greece. Congress heavily criticized the American Society of Travel Agents (ASTA) for proceeding with their annual conference in Athens. In response to Congress's continuing discouragement of American tourism to Greece, the U.S. Embassy delivered a sharp warning:

Attempting to discourage tourism to Greece would be considered as reflecting a major change in our policy—from correct reserve to overt hostility. As a result, our ability to exert constructive influence in Athens would be lessened. We have invested a lot of money in building up the economy of Greece, which has heavy dependence on tourism. We would be working against our own interests by discouraging [tourism to Greece]. [Such action] . . . would work against the interests of the Greek people, while it is doubtful that it would produce a helpful effect on the policy of the regime.[23]

In fact, the prospects for Greek tourism had rebounded by mid-1968 and appeared strong for 1969. A sharp upturn in tourist arrivals began in August 1968 and carried through to September. Although difficult to explain the reasons for this revival, it seemed to indicate that the tourism picture was beginning to return to normal.[24]

Despite the gloomy outlook for Litton in Greece by 1968, there were several investments under negotiation that had considerable economic prospects. The most intriguing was a proposal by Fiat for a car assembly plant in Greece with a capacity of five thousand units a year. Negotiations with Fiat had reached a fairly advanced stage. The key issue was whether local importers of automobiles would be able to exert enough influence on the Greek regime to keep Fiat out. In this regard, the major obstacle was Sarakakis Bros., the largest importer of vehicles and related machinery.[25] National Can was also seriously interested in establishing a can manufacturing plant near Patras. Finally, a major tourist development proposal was being devised by Litton staff in late 1968 involving a complex of hotels, bungalows, and private villas on Crete, in which Litton itself would invest its own capital. Inexplicably, the details of this project were shrouded in secrecy by Litton's senior staff until it was ready for presentation to the government.[26] But Litton never attained the necessary data from the government to conduct a proper feasibility study. Poor planning led Litton to renege on its commitment to invest 3 million USD in the complex.[27]

One serious error Litton committed was its supposition that its contract with the government assured the company cooperation with government services, banks, and other public entities. An experienced businessperson in the Greek marketplace could have predicted that these agencies, being fiercely competitive with one another, would inevitably treat Litton as an unwelcome rival. The company found to its dismay that it was cut off from important sources of information, and that organizations such as the Greek Industrial Development Bank actually discouraged foreign parties from collaborating with it. More importantly, whereas Litton had assumed that its responsibility for a given investment was essentially fulfilled once it delivered a capital commitment to the government, it discovered that the real struggle only began at that point. William McGrew, a regional office director for Litton in Patras, explained:

> Before it could be approved and Litton receive credit for it, each project had to be nursed through the labyrinthine Greek bureaucracy where vested business interests lurked to stifle new competition . . . . Litton never got "plugged in" politically. It failed to perceive the character of the Greek power game, in which close personal relationships are essential. When its projects were undermined by working level bureaucrats in league with business rivals, its managers lacked the support of men at the ministerial level who could squelch those pressures. (McGrew 1972: 73)

According to McGrew, Litton's best effort—the bid by Fiat to establish Greece's first automobile plant—was quashed as a result. Jaques Warschauer, the general manager of Litton Greece, often complained that "the Establishment" seemed certain to oppose any project that might in the least prove competitive. Frank P. Butler of the U.S. Embassy recalled that shortly following the coup, the United States started to watch with great interest the government's ability to cope with two problems: tax reform and foreign investment. He wrote, "We thought that it might be difficult for the Government substantially to change the course of the economy much if the 'establishment' could successfully oppose tax reforms and keep competitive foreign investment out. It certainly has been successful with regard to taxes and apparently it is doing alright with regard to competition."[28] McGrew had become sharply critical of the Litton operation in Greece. He informed the U.S. Embassy that he would remain for the final few months of his contract, but he had no wish to "go down with a sinking ship." McGrew had been led to believe that Litton would ostensibly seek out development opportunities, produce feasibility studies, and with this background material in hand, use the vast industrial connections of the Litton "empire" to solicit the necessary private investment capital. Instead, he found that the Litton people in Athens were indecisive about their role, commenting, "One week they are interested in finding investment opportunities; when this effort bogs down, they say 'well, it doesn't matter, we are really here to act as a catalyst in getting the Greek Government to development [sic] the country.'"[29] McGrew discovered that no mechanisms had been established for organizing investment funds. He explained that Litton's conception of its role as "catalyst" was causing friction with the Ministry of Coordination. Litton's staff was "unbelievably arrogant" in supposing it had the authority to instruct the government in development matters.[30] Except for himself, there was no one on Litton's staff who spoke Greek or had any conception of the Greek culture. Moreover, the Greek office lacked a development economist. McGrew complained that the director, Warschauer, "cannot organize his own office, let alone the Western Peloponnesus." According to McGrew, Greek officials had recognized Litton's ineffectiveness and were beginning to avoid contact.[31]

The lack of direction for Litton in Greece could partially be blamed on the incompetence of its executives. Warschauer complained to the U.S. Embassy that more than half of the visit to Greece by Roy Ash (president of Litton Industries U.S.) was spent vacationing outside Athens with his wife and children. He made no calls to government officials. While Ash probed into project proposals, he made no outside effort to move them forward. Ash probably recognized the magnitude of the problem at hand: first, there was no infrastructure on Crete or in the Western Peloponnesus to support a development program of the size contemplated; second, capital could not be obtained at the interest rates specified in the contract; and finally, the power of vested interests, the economic "establishment," to stop competitive projects was overwhelming.[32]

By mid-1968 Litton had failed to produce the breakthrough it needed to protect its relations with the government and its international reputation. Locating projects presented no particular problem, but a key obstacle to progress was financing. Greece was not considered by many foreign firms an outstandingly good risk. Litton was now hoping its contract with the Greek regime would evolve, at least tacitly, into a new and broader arrangement, under which Litton could become the government's general economic advisor. If Litton did assume such a role, there would have been much opposition from the Greek business community. No one had come forward from the Greek business community to champion Litton's cause in the interest of Greece's overall development. The business community remained disinterested and slightly antagonistic toward Litton.[33]

Neither was there wide support in the bureaucracy, especially in the Ministry of Economic Coordination. Coordination with the government was never good. One of the most serious problems was that various government agencies were undertaking projects in the Western Peloponnesus and Crete, which Litton only learned from newspapers. Additional problems continued to surface. The government began to exercise its right to review all Litton expenditures, including the right of veto on hiring. New financial controls were imposed by the Greek regime, which went so far as to require Litton employees to obtain a signed receipt for taxi fares.[34]

Criticism of Litton also came from outside of Greece. Hans O. Schmitt of the International Bank for Reconstruction and Development, after observing Litton operations, expressed that the Litton staff, with few exceptions, were woefully short on development experience, and that development programs had to be socially and politically as well as economically acceptable.

The Litton staff gave Schmitt a glowing account of the projects they had in waiting, but when Schmitt asked them to "squeeze the air out," the list of works in progress or projected was "pathetic." The Greek officials whom Schmitt talked to were ready to give up on Litton. According to Schmitt, the only way Litton could save its reputation in Greece was to cut its staff to the core voluntarily, concentrate on a few projects, and pursue these projects with more vigor and astuteness than previously.[35]

The first decisive evaluation of Litton's performance was fixed by the contract for May 1969. The company was to be engaged in the implementation of programs totaling at least 120 million USD. At this two-year juncture, projects with committed capital backing and government approval numbered four: a brewery, a small electronics plant, a hotel which Litton did not originate but assisted in arranging partial financing, and a can factory. Total value was an estimated 11.5 million USD; less than half represented foreign financing. Litton argued, with considerable justification, that several other investment proposals were being delayed by the government's slowness in approving them. According to Litton, capital secured within Greece and from abroad totaled approximately 50 million USD (McGrew 1972: 68). Nonetheless, by any calculation, Litton had fallen far short of its contractual goal.

Despite Litton's management not having the requisite experience and connections in Greece to facilitate their negotiations, other major American multinationals continued to be stymied when they attempted to enter the Greek marketplace, especially when their proposals directly competed with the interests of major players of the Greek economic establishment. Despite these multinationals' sophisticated business models and track record of sound organization and expertise, their efforts were thwarted if they tried to enter any project without a partnership, consortium, or joint venture agreement with central figures of the economic establishment. Such was the experience of beverage giant Pepsi-Cola, which challenged Coca-Cola and Tom Pappas for a slice of the Greek soft beverage market.

COCA-COLA VS. PEPSI-COLA

During the late 1940s, the Coca-Cola Company rapidly expanded its overseas operations so that by 1950 a third of its profits came from outside the United States. In the postwar period, many Europeans regarded the expansion of Coca-Cola into their countries as American economic imperialism. Most Europeans feared that Coca-Cola would harm their domestic wine, mineral water, and fruit juice industries (Standage 2005: 257). Coca-Cola's close association with American values also worked against it in another part of the world: the Middle East. In 1966, an Israeli businessman accused the Coca-Cola Company of avoiding the Israeli soft drink market in order to protect its business in the much larger Arab market. The Arab world, with its ban on alcoholic drinks and hot climate, was a promising market for Coca-Cola; its annual profits in the region totaled approximately 20 million USD. Accusations of antisemitism mounted, and prominent Jewish organizations in the United States began to boycott Coca-Cola. The company responded by announcing it would license an Israeli bottling franchise in Tel Aviv. This in turn provoked the Arab League to call on its members to boycott Coca-Cola. The company refused to back down, and the Arab boycott came into force by August 1968 (the boycott would last into the late 1980s) (Standage 2005: 261). Realizing that Coca-Cola would have to exit the Middle East market quickly, company executives looked next door to an untapped market in Greece and contacted one of its key industrialists, Tom A. Pappas, to partner with him in establishing a bottling plant in Greece.

Pappas, a Greek American, had learned early on how to cut through Athens' labyrinth bureaucracy to attract U.S. capital to Greece. His greatest business achievement came in 1962, when Standard Oil (New Jersey) went into partnership with him. When the Greek government sought bids for a new oil refinery, Pappas and Esso outbid Aristotle Onassis and fourteen other competitors by proposing a package deal that called for the construction of a massive industrial complex, which included a steel mill in Thessaloniki. The Esso-Pappas refinery also had an exclusive contract with Pappas's Atlantic Maritime Enterprises Company and its fleet of ten oil tankers to transport the oil for the refinery ("Entrepreneurs: The Greek for Go-Between," *Time*, 14 February 1969).[36] After learning of the Pappas–Coca-Cola venture brewing in Greece, the Pepsi-Cola Company gained a greater interest in entering the Greek marketplace.

Nick Podlesski, Pepsi-Cola's vice president, had contacted the alternate (deputy) minister of coordination, John Rodinos-Orlandos, to inquire whether the Ministry of Coordination would be prepared to consider "in principle" the issuance of a bottling and distribution license for Pepsi-Cola if the total required investment of approximately 2 million USD was made entirely in hard currency rather than on the basis of a vague government requirement demanding at minimum an investment in foreign exchange of 1.2 million USD, plus a local investment in drachmas, and a "special contribution" in the form of a tourist or other unrelated project. The alternate minister was intrigued by the proposal since it provided a basis for direct negotiations with the Pepsi-Cola Company rather than with third-party applicants, which mainly tried to obtain a license for cola drinks with the intention of reselling them at a premium. He expressed that the Ministry had become exasperated with these types of middlemen. Additionally, the Pepsi-Cola proposal was appealing since it represented a sizable direct investment in foreign exchange.[37]

Nonetheless, the alternate minister noted he was not at liberty to make a commitment to even consider the Pepsi-Cola proposal without placing in jeopardy other proposals that were pending before the Committee on Foreign Investment and were in the framework of package deals, relating the issuance of a bottling and distribution license for a cola beverage to a variety of ancillary investment projects. Coca-Cola and Royal Crown Cola were at the top of the list. The alternate minister indicated that such proposals were under consideration and anticipated a decision by the end of June 1968. He added that he was mindful of the fact that these proposals had greatly impeded the licensing of cola beverages in Greece, but he was confident the Ministry of Coordination would adopt a more clearly defined policy on the matter. The alternate minister concluded that a plan was being considered for levying a special consumption tax on cola drinks, without making the retail price of such drinks prohibitive, in order to provide an adequate margin of protection for the local soft drinks and fruit juice industries.[38]

Podlesski, following his failed negotiations with the Panagopoulos family of IVI (IVI had obtained the contract for bottling Schweppes products in Greece), felt tremendously affronted by information reaching him from various sources that the government was seriously considering granting Pappas exclusivity rights for several years for the preparation, bottling, and marketing in Greece of all cola-type beverages. As part of his package proposal, Pappas would invest 30 million USD in fresh fruit and vegetable canning and fruit juice production primarily for export, as well as in soft drink production for domestic distribution. Pappas was being given license to produce and distribute Coca-Cola and "cola-type beverages" in Greece, for which he would establish four plants—in Athens, Thessaloniki, Chania (in Crete), and Patras.[39]

During a meeting with John Nassoufis, secretary general of the Ministry of Coordination, Nassoufis informed Podlesski that no final decision had yet been determined on the Pappas package proposal, but that a decision would be forthcoming. Nassoufis also stated bluntly that the government was free to decide whether it was in Greece's interest to grant exclusive rights for soft drinks to anybody willing to make a 30 million USD investment in manufacturing, intimating that Podlesski had no right to complain. He added that if Pepsi-Cola would make a proposal involving an aluminum plant, a steel mill, or a food-processing complex or offer the government a 200 million USD loan at zero interest, the government would be prepared to forget Pappas and offer Pepsi-Cola an exclusive franchise. Podlesski commented that Nassoufis's attitude throughout the meeting was "smart-alecky, unabashedly arrogant, and extremely unpleasant." Nassoufis concluded the meeting by urging Podlesski to "hurry up and make an application" but went on to state that he would not promise that a decision on the Pappas proposals would be held up waiting for the Pepsi-Cola proposal.[40]

Moreover, Podlesski's repeated telephone calls over a period of three weeks to Rodinos-Orlandos for an appointment with the alternate minister to discuss the possibilities of obtaining permission to bottle and distribute Pepsi-Cola in Greece remained unsuccessful. Disillusioned and frustrated, Podlesski complained that he did not know whether to give up and leave Greece or persist in his efforts to see the alternate minister. When U.S. Embassy officials finally contacted the alternate minister's office on Podlesski's behalf, his secretary claimed the alternate minister had been "too busy" to see Podlesski. In fact, Rodinos-Orlandos later conceded that an understanding "en principe" had been reached with Pappas for the Coca-Cola franchise, but there were still some details to be negotiated. In response to a question whether there was room for licensing another cola-type beverage in Greece, the alternate minister replied that it would be unthinkable, having "squeezed the juice" out of Pappas for a comprehensive package proposal involving an investment of approximately 30 million USD, to turn around and allow other foreign soft drink manufacturers to come in on the basis of a relatively small investment of 2 or 3 million USD.[41]

Ultimately, Pappas was given exclusivity protection for his Coca-Cola venture for a period of eighteen months (rather than thirty-six months as Pappas had originally requested), which in effect meant that no licenses for other types of soft beverages would be issued until the first Coca-Cola bottling plants were built and operating.[42] Yet Vernon Hoppers and John Theologitis of Coca-Cola Middle East were apprehensive regarding the implications of Article 15 of the Tom Pappas Decree (#593 of 7 September 1968), establishing a rather vague and inconclusive wholesale price determination formula for Coca-Cola. The Coca-Cola representatives agreed that using the "highest-priced" local lemon and orange juice–based soft beverage as a basis for determining the wholesale price of Coca-Cola was problematic in the sense that local competitors would take advantage of this clause and place a juice-based product on the market with a price tag that would raise the price of any cola-based beverage to prohibitive heights. They also agreed that the determination of the actual cost of production of Coca-Cola as a basis for the assessment of the contemplated consumption tax on Coca-Cola products and the establishment of a required 80 percent price differential in relation to local soft drinks was bound to generate problems of implementation. They feared it might prove difficult to reach agreement with bureaucratically minded Greek civil servants on costing, and that this provision would become a source of constant friction and argument with the price control authorities.[43]

The Coca-Cola representatives further pointed out that since Article X of Greece's basic investment law 2687/53 stipulated that foreign companies established in Greece were entitled to the same treatment as that extended to domestic companies (nondiscriminatory treatment), the validity of the provision in paragraph 1 of Article 15 of the Tom Pappas Decree that a unilaterally applied consumption tax (a tax that does not have equal incidence on domestic soft drinks) could be contested in court on the grounds that a law of constitutional effect, such as PL 2687/53, could not be abrogated by a ministerial decree. Nevertheless, they all agreed it would have been unwise for Coca-Cola to start this venture in Greece with an attempt to rescind through litigation a basic provision of the Tom Pappas Decree, and it would be better if mitigation of the unjust requirement could be achieved through negotiation. When asked how much the Coca-Cola Company had to do with the promulgation of the Tom Pappas Decree, Hoppers stated that at no stage was his company intimately involved in Pappas's negotiations with the Ministry of Coordination, although he was personally informed from time to time of the general trend and progress of the talks.[44]

Kadry Mahmoud and Podlesski of PepsiCo International also complained that the wording of Article 15 was so inexact that it would eventually prove to be problematic for Pappas, as well as for any other producer of cola-based drinks in Greece. First, the language of Paragraph 1, Article 15 made the imposition of a consumption tax on cola-based beverages potential ("may be levied") rather than mandatory. The ambiguity of the tax provision had significantly added to the imponderables of making a meaningful economic feasibility study for a cola-based beverage bottling operation in Greece. Additionally, the provision in Paragraph 2 determining the amount of consumption tax to be levied on cola-based drinks, based on production costs, opened up vast vistas of bureaucratic interference in the determination of actual production costs. According to the PepsiCo officials, the situation suggested a careless approach on the part of the negotiators of the Coca-Cola agreement, in utter disregard of the facts and figures involved in the bottling of a cola-based drink in Greece.[45]

Socrates Vekris, Pappas's attorney, would later admit that Pappas's representatives in the negotiations were handcuffed by the strongly biased attitude of the government's representatives against Coca-Cola as a potential competitor to the Greek citrus fruit juice and soft drink industries. As a result, Pappas's representatives were compelled to hedge and, as a matter of strategy, decided to accept the best obtainable terms by deliberately ignoring or condoning certain ambiguities in the hope that these might be clarified to better advantage at a later stage, once the project commenced. Vekris explained that originally the Ministries of Finance and Agriculture preferred a 100 percent price differential between Coca-Cola and local soft beverages without accounting for production costs. This would have been catastrophic, and he therefore agreed to a flexible tax consumption provision predicated on cost and a resulting minimum price differential of 80 percent. Other price-control measures were also considered, such as raising the duty on the cola concentrate or establishing a specific tax per bottle of Coca-Cola, all of which were deemed excessively prejudicial and potentially more dangerous than the 80 percent price differential formula based on cost of production. It was considered the lesser of many evils.[46]

In fact, with such puzzling conditions on paper, cola companies such as Pepsi-Cola would remain highly skeptical of investing in Greece. Once Coca-Cola began production in Greece, they rewrote the rules under which they operated. By May 1972, four years after the original agreement, the Pappas investment pledge was diminished by 87 percent to a 2.5 million USD investment. According to the government, the reduction was necessary due to a shortage of raw materials needed to build the canning plants. Coca-Cola, however, had no such problems in acquiring the necessary materials for their own construction requirements (Hougan 1972).[47]

GERBER VS. NUTRICIA

The Greek economic establishment also moved to suppress, if not entirely eliminate well-established American competition in Greece. Such was the case when Demetrios Marinopoulos and Nutricia made a play to challenge Gerber's near monopoly of the Greek baby food market. The Greek regime, fearful of a major American corporation being run out of Greece, impotently urged that all three parties cooperate. Gerber's International Division Vice President Frank A. Meyer had been in Athens several days to confer with the company's distributors, Hellacana Trading Co.–Spyropoulos Bros., and officials of the ETVA concerning Gerber's plans to establish a baby food manufacturing unit in Greece within the framework of the company's overall world expansion plans.

At the time, Gerber had been importing its products to Greece and controlled 90 percent of the Greek baby food market. Meyer learned after he arrived in Athens (from ETVA) that Famar S.A. (Marinopoulos Bros.–manufacturers of pharmaceutical products and operators of a chain of supermarkets) and Nutricia N.V. (Dutch manufacturer of baby foods) had concluded a licensing arrangement for the production of baby foods in Greece and had filed an investment proposal with the Ministry of Coordination. Meyer was informed that a provision included in the Famar-Nutricia-Greek government negotiations would grant Nutricia exclusive investment rights for a period of four years from the date of approval of the investment. Meyer understood that this provision, if included in the investment agreement, would torpedo his plans to begin operations in Greece. Meyer did not object to Nutricia's legitimate right to negotiate and conclude a licensing arrangement; his firm did not fear competition in any part of the world. However, he wanted to secure the government's assurances that Gerber would not be prohibited from operating in Greece, and that it be given an option to submit an investment proposal.[48]

Nassoufis noted at first glance that the odds seemed to favor a Gerber investment—a total outlay of 2 million USD, a 25 percent export commitment,[49] and a product of high quality and worldwide reputation. Nonetheless, he expressed some doubt regarding the seriousness of Gerber's interest since no formal application had been filed with the Foreign Investment Service. He wondered why Gerber wanted to invest 2 million USD in Greece since it already controlled 90 percent of the market through imports. Long before the preliminary Gerber investment inquiry, Demetrios Marinopoulos, the president of the FGI, explored possibilities of establishing a baby food manufacturing industry in Greece. He made overtures to Gerber, but found it was not interested. He then approached Nutricia, which showed keen interest. After preparing a feasibility study, Marinopoulos filed an application with the Foreign Investment Committee of the Ministry of Coordination for permission to establish a plant in Greece in association with Nutricia and the NIBID, with each partner taking approximately a 33.3 percent equity interest in the proposed venture, which, however, would have been much smaller in size than the one contemplated by Gerber. At the same time, Marinopoulos applied for a four-year exclusivity protection during which period no other license for a similar industry would be issued.[50]

Nassoufis stated that, quite frankly, both Economic Coordination Minister Nikolaos Makarezos (one of the ruling triumvirate dictators) and he were anxious to assist Marinopoulos in his venture because "he was a progressive young industrialist and also because he had been of great help to the Government in the early days of the Revolution when the economy was going through a difficult period."[51] But Nassoufis kept the approval of the Marinopoulos project in abeyance for a week as a means to explore the possibility of an association between Gerber and Marinopoulos-Nutricia, one in which Gerber would replace the NIBID with a 33.3 percent interest. His aim was that Gerber would to enter into direct negotiations with Marinopoulos; he would lend his full support to such negotiations, and, if necessary, he would pressure Marinopoulos to be more flexible in his demands. However, Marinopoulos was already complaining that his project was being held up by an administration that professed to be against bureaucracy and bureaucratic delay.[52]

This arrangement was completely unacceptable to Gerber. Meyer explained that Gerber already controlled 90 percent of the Greek market, not factoring in its vast technical know-how. Gerber received substantial royalties elsewhere simply for their know-how; "producing baby food is not easy," Meyer argued. Nonetheless, the government did not want to offend Marinopoulos, a leading progressive industrialist, president of FGI, and ardent supporter of the military regime; nor did it want to drive out Gerber and its sizable foreign investment. Therefore, Nassoufis strongly urged that Marinopoulos and Gerber cooperate.[53]

Frustrated by these developments, D. Zepos, Gerber's legal representative in Greece, spoke disparagingly about how Marinopoulos, through a series of calculated steps, was attempting to push Gerber out of the Greek marketplace. He nevertheless remained confident that the preliminary investment application filed by Meyer was so attractive that the Ministry of Coordination would have to think twice before turning it down in favor of the Marinopoulos proposal. Gerber also offered to back up its 25 percent export commitment with any kind of guarantee (legal or financial) that the government might consider appropriate, and, furthermore, it offered to put up a substantial bond in the form of a cash deposit or bank letter of guarantee to the effect that the proposed investment would be completed within the stipulated deadline. Zepos remained hopeful that the Marinopoulos application would not be approved with a four-year exclusivity clause.[54]

But in actuality, cooperation with Marinopoulos was Gerber's only option. During a lunch meeting, Meyer and Marinopoulos discussed the possibilities of a joint venture in baby food production. Gerber became extremely reluctant to enter a joint proposition, especially a three-way one with Famar and Nutricia, which would require Gerber to contribute (and thereby reveal) essentially all their technology and relinquish control of the market. Meyer indicated that he could not think of any terms on which this would have been acceptable. In contrast, Marinopoulos did not believe it was fair for the government to permit a foreign company to compete on the basis of an application submitted after his. He attempted without success to reassure Meyer that Gerber's secrets would be safe, citing the fact that Famar already produced drugs for several different U.S. firms under contract with no leakage. Meyer pointed out that while drugs required simple formulations, baby foods involved an entire industrial ambiance, including temperature and humidity control in the factory, which could not be divided or compartmentalized between different participants in the process.[55]

Meyer attempted to determine whether Marinopoulos's proposition was in fact well thought out or whether it was just a preemptive strike to obstruct Gerber's expansion plans. It appeared that Marinopoulos had given some thought to production but virtually none to distribution. The total Greek market was 3.5 million jars. The economic capacity of what Marinopoulos proposed would be 10 million jars annually. He gave assurances that Gerber could keep and even increase its present market through imports. Marinopoulos simply stated he would export the difference, but neither he nor Nutricia had an established export network comparable to Gerber's, and Nutricia's competitive position in likely export markets were not nearly robust enough to ensure substantial exports. Marinopoulos also claimed he would not seek to exclude imported Gerber products through higher tariffs—he even offered to put it in writing, which Meyer asked him to do on the spot. But it appeared inevitable that the government would not have looked kindly on a domestic plant running far under capacity and possibly losing money, while large quantities of foreign exchange were being spent to import closely competing products.[56] Meyer concluded that Gerber had more to lose than to gain in a three-way deal between Gerber, Marinopoulos, and Nutricia and decided to walk away from negotiations. Unfortunately, Meyer's worst fears for Gerber became a reality: Nutricia flooded the Greek market, and consumers were hard pressed to find Gerber products in Greece.

CONCLUSION

The Greek military regime did not enhance Greece's attractiveness to American foreign investors. The measures that the regime implemented were often counterproductive, notably the incentives for the establishment of manufacturing industries in provincial areas (e.g., outside the greater Athens area). The disadvantages of being located away from the capital area far outweighed the tax and other advantages provided by existing legislation. A provincial industry could import its machinery and plant equipment duty- and tax-free; enjoyed a 10 percent reduction in social security (IKA) payments and a 30 percent cut in turnover tax; was exempt from the 6 percent tax on payrolls and accorded more favorable treatment in depreciation allowances and tax-free reserves; but, on the other hand, the company was forced to pay much higher wages and salaries for skilled workers and office employees who could not be recruited locally and who had to be transported from Athens at a considerable extra expense and loss of company paid time. More importantly, companies incurred heavy expenses in obtaining a supply of electric power and a telephone connection in the provincial areas.[57]

William P. Wassman, project manager for Union Carbide, which was constructing a new 1.6 million-USD factory in the Thebes area, approximately 70 kilometers outside Athens, complained that for one telephone line the company was charged by the OTE 175,000 drachmas, or about 6,000 USD. In addition, Union Carbide had to spend a disproportionately large amount to drill artesian wells (including one dry hole) for the plant's water supply. The extra costs involved in shipping out raw materials and transporting finished products to Athens were also considerable. Wassman claimed, "When the chips are down, whatever tax and other advantages the company derives from its out-of-town location are, in the long run, practically wiped out by direct and indirect increases in product cost." He viewed the incentives to provincial enterprises with considerable skepticism and felt that a concerted effort was needed to "bring into sharper focus the inexpediency and counter-productiveness of the present policy of forcing foreign investors, without discrimination, to build their plants in provincial areas, against the recommendations of experts and their own better business judgment."[58]

A long track record of U.S. economic assistance to Greece did not materialize into a preference for conducting business with American corporations, particularly following the Association Agreement of Greece with the EEC. Subsequently, the economic development banking systems that were established in the early 1960s, which aimed to protect and further the interests of the Greek economic establishment, continued to function effectively during the years of the junta. Lines of preferential credit to client firms protected the firms' oligopoly or monopoly positions in their sectors. Instead of promoting economic development, close and collusive bank-industry relationships hindered competition, blocked the entry of new competitive business rivals, and perpetuated Greece's oligopolistic structure (Pagoulatos 2003: 71–72). It is worth reiterating that despite the military regime's grandiose announcements trumpeting elaborate foreign investments, average FDI inflows relative to GDP never surpassed the peak they reached in the mid-1960s, when most of the Karamanlis government's major investment projects became operational.

The junta was desperate for international recognition and foreign investment, but was unwilling to dismantle the already-established power structure of vested interests and the economic establishment, which mobilized to quash potential foreign investment projects. In fact, this economic and political power structure was reinforced by the military regime's leaders and the economic establishment exerting their increased influence to protect their interests. Major figures in the economic establishment continued to curb foreign investment by attaining exclusivity rights on entire sectors in the Greek marketplace, while the regime's leaders treaded lightly around these figures in order to not offend the economic establishment. As a result, potential American investors did not find Greece "open for business," but rather faced an emboldened economic establishment that successfully continued to stifle American competition.

Nicholas James Kalogerakos received his graduate degree in the history of international relations from the London School of Economics and earned his doctorate in modern history from the University of Oxford, St. Antony's College. His doctoral thesis is titled "Dealing with the Dictators: The United States and the Greek Military Regime, 1967–1974." He was also the last doctoral student of the modern Greek historian, Richard Clogg. Nicholas has taught modern European history at the University of Ottawa, specializing in European integration. He has served as a senior policy advisor for the federal Canadian Ministers of International Development and Citizenship and Immigration and as a director in the office of the Minister of National Revenue. Nicholas is currently associate director of policy and research to the federal Canadian Leader of the Official Opposition.

NOTES

1. Large American financial institutions such as First National City Bank and Chase Manhattan would finance major industrial projects in Greece. Petrochemical companies, including Standard Oil's ESSO and chemical conglomerates Dow Chemical and Allied Chemical, and industrial behemoths, such as Union Carbide, established operations in Greece under their banners. Other American companies chose to be more covert by establishing subsidiaries, such as Parsons and Whittemore's Thessalian Pulp and Paper.
2. *Foreign Relations of the United States (FRUS), 1952–1954*, vol. 8, *Eastern Europe; Soviet Union; Eastern Mediterranean*, no. 442, 9 May 1953.
3. *FRUS, 1955–1957*, vol. 24, *Soviet Union; Eastern Mediterranean*, no. 295, 26 May 1956.
4. Ibid., no. 302, 15 November 1956.
5. Ibid., no. 309, 16 August 1957.
6. *FRUS, 1958–1960*, vol. 10, *Eastern Europe; Finland; Greece; Turkey*, pt. 2, no. 230, 6 January 1958.
7. Ibid., no. 255, 29 January 1959.
8. *FRUS, 1961–1963*, vol. 9, *Foreign Economic Policy*, no. 91, 20 February 1961.

9. Ibid., no. 94, 28 February 1961.
10. *FRUS, 1958–1960*, vol. 10, *Eastern Europe; Finland; Greece; Turkey*, pt. 2, no. 301, 14 December 1960.
11. *FRUS, 1961–1963*, vol. 16, *Eastern Europe; Cyprus; Greece; Turkey*, no. 325, 1 January 1962.
12. Ibid., no. 346, 6 June 1963.
13. Ibid.; no. 352, 7 August 1963.
14. National Archives (NA), John Enepekides to Frank P. Butler, Memorandum–EMB/ECON, "Visitors and Telephone Calls of More than Routine Interest" (hereafter "Visitors and Telephone Calls of MTRI"), 14 June 1968, Lot Files, Lot 71D6, Folder: E-7 Visitors of More than Casual Interest (hereafter Visitors of MTCI) (January–June) Greece 1968, 1 of 5, Box 14.
15. Ibid.
16. NA, John Enepekides to Frank P. Butler, Memorandum–EMB/ECON, "Visitors and Telephone Calls of MTRI (Week of June 24–29, 1968)," 24 June 1968, Lot Files, Lot 71D6, Folder: E-7 Visitors of MTCI (July–December) Greece 1968, 4 of 4, Box 16.
17. NA, John Enepekides to Frank P. Butler, Memorandum–EMB/ECON, "Visitors and Telephone Calls of MTRI," 2 May 1968, Lot Files, Lot 71D6, Folder: E-7 Visitors of MTCI (January–June) Greece 1968, 2 of 5, Box 15.
18. NA, John Enepekides to Frank P. Butler, Memorandum–EMB/ECON, "Visitors and Telephone Calls of MTRI (Week of June 10–15, 1968)," 12 June 1968, Lot Files, Lot 71D6, Folder: E-7 Visitors of MTCI (January-June) Greece 1968, 1 of 5, Box 14.
19. NA, John Enepekides to Frank P. Butler, Memorandum–EMB/ECON, "Visitors and Telephone Calls of MTRI (Week of December 9–14, 1968)," 10 December 1968, Lot Files, Lot 71D6, Folder: E-7 Visitors of MTCI (January-June) Greece 1968, 5 of 5, Box 15.
20. NA, John Enepekides to Frank P. Butler, Memorandum–EMB/ECON, "Visitors and Telephone Calls of MTRI (Week of December 9–14, 1968)," 10 December 1968, Lot Files, Lot 71D6, Folder: E-7 Visitors of MTCI (January-June) Greece 1968, 5 of 5, Box 15.
21. NA, John Rubel, Litton, to David E. Bell, Administrator for Agency for International Development, 17 September 1965, File: Bureau of Near Eastern and South Asian Affairs, Office of the Country Director for Greece, Records Relating to Greece, 1964–66, Folder: Defense Affairs–DEF 19 Military Assistance (MAP) Greece 1966, Box 11. See also McGrew 1972: 67.
22. NA, Memorandum of Conversation, Ambassador Phillips Talbot, Mr. Roy Ash, President, Litton Industries US, Mr. Pierre Guillaume, Executive Officer, Litton Industries Benelux, Mr. Edward Cohen, Economic Officer, Embassy Athens, "Litton Industries Agreement with GOG," 25 May 1967, Lot Files, Lot 69D553, Folder: FN 9 Foreign Investment Greece 1967, Box 5.
23. NA, L. Milner Dunn, NEA/GRK to L. Battle, NEA, "Suggestion of Senator Pell concerning October 1967 Meeting of ASTA (American Society of Travel

Agents) in Athens," 1 September 1967, Lot Files, Lot 69D553, Folder: YP Tourism Greece 1967, Box 5. The Greek government viewed with concern the proposed introduction of restrictive measures aimed at curbing American tourism abroad. According to the State Department, 152,000 Americans entered Greece during the period of April–December 1967, representing 17.5 percent of the entire tourist inflow, but more than 30 percent of the total earnings in foreign exchange. This favorable balance had previously helped to remedy part of the traditionally unfavorable gap in the balance of trade between the two countries (1967: exports from Greece 60 million USD, imports from the United States 149 million USD, Greek deficit 89 million USD). Considerable funds had been channeled into the tourist industry both in the form of infrastructure financing as well as private investments. This latter sector comprised large interests of American capital invested in hotels, airlines, and shipping services. The intended restrictions were bound to create adverse effects on the Greek balance of payments. President Johnson, in his State of the Union message, stated that restrictions could be imposed "without unduly penalizing the travel of... people who have relatives abroad whom they need to see." Among Americans visiting Greece, a large number represented citizens of Greek origin. The proposed measures would nonetheless hamper these people from visiting their relatives abroad. The Greek government understood the serious reasons that prompted the United States to take restrictive measures on American tourism abroad. However, it consistently requested that a more flexible approach in the case of Greece would be fully justified, considering the impact of tourism on the Greek economy, which was undergoing a delicate process of development and readjustment. NA, Royal Greek Embassy, Washington DC, "Aide-Memoire," 8 February 1968, Lot Files, Lot 71D6, FN-12 US Balance of Payments Greece 1968, Box 16.
24. NA, Memorandum of Conversation, Evangelos Elliades, Director, Foreign Operations, Bank of Greece and Barrington King, "Prospects for Greek Balance of Payments in 1969," 21 October 1968, Lot Files, Lot 71D6, Folder: FN-12 U.S. Balance of Payments Greece 1968, Box 16.
25. William Mancha of the Ford Motor Company contacted the American Embassy to inquire about Fiat's reported interest in establishing an auto plant in Patras. He indicated that Ford would be "perturbed" if the arrangement involved import restrictions on other makes or automobiles and possibly an exclusivity period for Fiat, which would prohibit other companies for a number of years that might conceivably be interested in a similar agreement. NA, John Enepekides to Frank P. Butler, Memorandum–EMB/ECON, "Visitors and Telephone Calls of MTRI (Week of December 16–21, 1968)," 23 December 1968, Lot Files, Lot 71D6, Folder: E-7 Visitors of MTCI (January–June) Greece 1968, 4 of 5, Box 15. Fiat would eventually establish operations in Greece after the fall of the dictatorship in 1975, via a licensing agreement with Autokinitoviomihania Ellados (Greek Automobile Industry), assembling a model based on the Fiat 127 and using imported parts from Italy. Members of the ownership group included the owners of the company that imported Fiats to Greece.

26. NA, Memorandum of Conversation, William W. McGrew, Regional Office Director, Litton Industries, Patras, and Barrington King, Embassy Economic Officer, 15 October 1968, Lot Files, Lot 71D6, Folder: FN-9 Foreign Investment Litton Greece 1968, Box 16.
27. NA, Memorandum of Conversation, Hans O. Schmitt, Chief of Mission, IBRD Economic Mission to Greece, Miss Nurit Wahl, Economist, IBRD Mission, Mr. Butler, Economic Counselor, Mr. Churchill, Economic Officer, Mr. King, Economic Officer, "Conclusions of the IBRD Mission to Greece," 5 November 1968, Lot Files, Lot 71D6, Folder: 11-1 Credit Loans (International Ex-Im Banks) Greece, Box 16.
28. NA, Frank P. Butler, to L. Milner Dunn, NEA/GRK, "Litton–Greece," 31 July 1968, Lot Files, Lot 71D6, Folder: FN-9 Foreign Investment Litton Greece 1968, Box 16.
29. NA, George T. Churchill to Daniel Brewster NEA/GRK, "William McGrew's Comments on Litton Industries," 30 September 1968, Lot Files, Lot 71D6, Folder: FN-9 Foreign Investment Litton Greece 1968, Box 16.
30. Ibid.
31. Ibid.
32. NA, Frank P. Butler, to L. Milner Dunn, NEA/GRK, "Litton–Greece," 31 July 1968, Lot Files, Lot 71D6, Folder: FN-9 Foreign Investment Litton Greece 1968, Box 16.
33. NA, Memorandum of Conversation, Richard Kulp, Litton Industries, Frank P. Butler, and Barrington King, 29 May 1968, Lot Files, Lot 71D6, Folder: FN-9 Foreign Investment Litton Greece 1968, Box 16.
34. Ibid.
35. NA, George T. Churchill, Economic Counselor, to Mr. Butler, NEA/GRK, "Views of Hans Schmitt, IBRD Team," 6 November 1968, Lot Files, Lot 71D6, Folder: 11-1 Credit Loans (International Ex-Im Banks) Greece, Box 16, NA.
36. Esso-Pappas formed the major part of a 190 million USD complex that also included a petrochemical plant operated by Ethyl Corp., a fertilizer plant, and the steel mill in which Republic Steel had a 15-percent share. Altogether there were seven companies which in 1968 had 111 million USD in sales. Pappas was chairman of three of the seven companies.
37. The conversation occurred on 9 April 1968. See NA, John Enepekides to Frank P. Butler, Memorandum–EMB/ECON, "Visitors and Telephone Calls of MTRI," Lot Files, Lot 71D6, Folder: E-7 Visitors of MTCI (January–June) Greece 1968, 2 of 5, Box 15.
38. NA, John Enepekides to Frank P. Butler, Memorandum–EMB/ECON, "Visitors and Telephone Calls of MTRI," Lot Files, Lot 71D6, Folder: E-7 Visitors of MTCI (January–June) Greece 1968, 2 of 5, Box 15.
39. The conversation occurred on 13 June 1968. See NA, John Enepekides to Frank P. Butler, Memorandum–EMB/ECON, "Visitors and Telephone Calls of MTRI (Week of June 10–15, 1968)," 17 June 1968, Lot Files, Lot 71D6, Folder: E-7 Visitors of MTCI (January–June) Greece 1968, 1 of 5, Box 14.

40. The conversation occurred on 17 June 1968. NA, John Enepekides to Frank P. Butler, "Visitors and Telephone Calls of MTRI (Week of June 17–22, 1968)," 24 June 1968, Lot Files, Lot 71D6, Folder: E-7 Visitors of MTCI (January–June) Greece 1968, 1 of 5, Box 14.
41. The conversation occurred on 11 July 1968. NA, John Enepekides to Frank P. Butler, Memorandum–EMB/ECON, "Visitors and Telephone Calls of MTRI (Week of July 8–13, 1968)," 15 July 1968, Lot Files, Lot 71D6, Folder: E-7 Visitors of MTCI (July–December) Greece 1968, 4 of 4, Box 16.
42. Along with fruit juice and fresh fruit and vegetable canneries in various parts of Greece, the Coca-Cola bottling and distribution project would provide jobs for approximately 650 office employees and 4,000 factory and other workers. Approved in Royal Decree 593. The conversation occurred on 12 September 1968. NA, John Enepekides to Frank P. Butler, Memorandum–EMB/ECON, "Visitors and Telephone Calls of MTRI (September 9–14, 1968)," 16 September 1968, Lot Files, Lot 71D6, Folder: E-7 Visitors of MTCI (July–December) Greece 1968, 3 of 4, Box 16.
43. The conversation occurred on 13 November 1968. NA, John Enepekides to Frank P. Butler, Memorandum–EMB/ECON, "Visitors and Telephone Calls of MTRI (Week of November 11–16, 1968)," 18 November 1968, Lot Files, Lot 71D6, Folder: E-7 Visitors of MTCI (July–December) Greece 1968, 1 of 4, Box 15.
44. NA, John Enepekides to Frank P. Butler, Memorandum–EMB/ECON, "Visitors and Telephone Calls of MTRI (Week of November 11–16, 1968)," 18 November 1968, Lot Files, Lot 71D6, Folder: E-7 Visitors of MTCI (July–December) Greece 1968, 1 of 4, Box 15. Hoppers added that it was his idea that no reference should be made in the decree to production costs and that if the Greek government insisted on the inclusion in the agreement of a price differential clause for the protection of the domestic soft drink industry, such clause should have been couched in much more explicit language and should have set a narrower margin of protection for domestic soft drinks—not in excess of 50 percent on a wholesale price basis. However, Pappas claimed throughout the negotiations the government was adamant on this point.
45. The conversation occurred on 31 October 1968. NA, John Enepekides to Frank P. Butler, Memorandum–EMB/ECON, "Visitors and Telephone Calls of MTRI (Week of October 28–November 2, 1968)," 4 November 1986, Lot Files, Lot 71D6, Folder: E-7 Visitors of MTCI (July-December) Greece 1968, 1 of 4, Box 15.
46. The conversation occurred on 15 November 1968. NA, John Enepekides to Frank P. Butler, Memorandum–EMB/ECON, "Visitors and Telephone Calls of MTRI (Week of November 11–16, 1968)," 18 November 1968, Lot Files, Lot 71D6, Folder: E-7 Visitors of MTCI (July–December) Greece 1968, 1 of 4, Box 15.
47. This case corresponded with the former Deputy Governor of the Bank of Greece John Pesmazoglu's statement in 1971 that there existed a tendency by

foreign enterprises to obtain the special advantages of foreign investment (such as exclusivity clauses), but they had no intention of implementing the corresponding investments, a practice that was bound to increase uncertainty and hesitation by other would-be domestic or foreign investors (Pesmazoglu 1972: 97–98).

48. The conversation occurred on 18 October 1968. NA, Office of the Commercial Attaché to Frank P. Butler, Memorandum–EMB/ECON, "Visitors of MTCI," Lot Files, Lot 71D6, Folder: E-7 Visitors of MTCI (July–December) Greece 1968, 2 of 4, Box 15.
49. This document indicates 5 million USD and a 50 percent export guarantee but was corrected in other documents to 2 million USD and a 25 percent export guarantee.
50. NA, John Enepekides to Frank P. Butler, Memorandum–EMB/ECON, "Visitors and Telephone Calls of MTRI," 8 November 1968, Lot Files, Lot 71D6, Folder: E-7 Visitors of MTCI (July–December) Greece 1968, 1 of 4, Box 15.
51. Ibid.
52. Ibid.
53. The conversation occurred on 20 November 1968. NA, Office of the Commercial Attaché to Frank P. Butler, Memorandum–ad EMB/ECON, "Visitors of MTCI November 18–22, 1968," 25 November 1968, Lot Files, Lot 71D6, Folder: E-7 Visitors of MTCI (July–December) Greece 1968, 1 of 4, Box 15.
54. The conversation occurred on 2 December 1968. NA, John Enepekides to Frank P. Butler, Memorandum–EMB/ECON, "Visitors and Telephone Calls of MTRI (Week of December 2–7, 1968)," 9 September 1968, Lot Files, Lot 71D6, Folder: E-7 Visitors of MTCI (Jan-June) Greece 1968, 5 of 5, Box 15.
55. The conversation occurred on 25 November 1968. NA, Office of the Commercial Attaché to Frank P. Butler, Memorandum–EMB/ECON, "Visitors of MTCI November 18–22, 1968," 25 November 1968, Lot Files, Lot 71D6, Folder: E-7 Visitors of MTCI (July–December) Greece 1968, 1 of 4, Box 15.
56. The conversation occurred on 25 November 1968. Ibid.
57. The conversation occurred on 29 August 1968. NA, John Enepekides to Frank P. Butler, Memorandum–EMB/ECON, "Visitors and Telephone Calls of MTRI (August 19–31, 1968)," 09/03/1968, Lot Files, Lot 71D6, Folder: E-7 Visitors of MTCI (July–December) Greece 1968, 3 of 4, Box 16.
58. Ibid. Emmanuel Kambouris, of Ideal-Standard (a subsidiary of American Standard), complained of similar typical frustrating difficulties facing foreign companies investing in Greece. In order to have a direct telephone line connecting its factory at Thebes with Athens, Ideal-Standard reluctantly agreed to pay a bill for 200,000 drachmas from OTE. However, a single line proved inadequate, and the company applied for another two lines. In fact, the company went as far as to purchase at its own expense the necessary multiplex equipment for use on the proposed two new lines. Ideal-Standard was informed by OTE that it would not only pay for the equipment, but also defray all import duties and taxes to clear it through customs. Furthermore, Ideal-Standard would have to pay all

installation expenses, plus a stiff monthly rental for use and maintenance. The proposed arrangement involved an additional initial outlay for the two lines (including the delivered cost of the imported equipment) of between 250,000 and 300,000 drachmas (8,500–10,000 USD). Ideal-Standard believed such treatment of a foreign company contemplating a total investment of more than 4 million USD and making a substantial contribution to the industrial development of a Greek provincial area was completely unfair and unwarranted. The conversation occurred on 28 August 1968. NA, John Enepekides to Frank P. Butler, Memorandum—EMB/ECON, "Visitors and Telephone Calls of MTRI (August 19–31, 1968)," 3 September 1968, Lot Files, Lot 71D6, Folder: E-7 Visitors of MTCI (July–December) Greece 1968, 3 of 4, Box 16.

REFERENCES

Periodicals

Life
Time

Archives

Washington, DC
   National Archives (NA)

Published Primary Sources

Foreign Relations of the United States (FRUS)

Secondary Sources

Dokopoulou, E. 1986. "Multinationals and Manufactured Exports from the Enlarged EEC Periphery: The Case of Greece." In *Industrialization in Developing and Peripheral Regions*, edited by F. E. I. Hamilton, 205–31. London.

Giannitsis, A. 2011. "Exoterikos daneismos kai exoteriko dimosio chreos" [Foreign loans and foreign public debt]. In *Oikonomiki istoria tou ellinikou kratous: Oinomikies leitourgies kai epidoseis* [Economic history of the Greek state: Economic functions and performances], edited by T. Kalafatis and E. Prontzas, vol. 2, 525–97. Athens.

Gingeras, R. 2014. *Heroin, Organized Crime, and the Making of Modern Turkey*. Oxford.

"Greece-Litton Industries: Agreement for the Development of Crete and the Western Peloponnesus." 1969. *International Legal Materials* 8(1): 18–30.

Hougan, J. 1972. *Helen Vlachos Doesn't Love You Anymore: Conversations with a Greek in Exile*. London.

McGrew, W. W. 1972. "Litton's 'Noble Experiment.'" *Columbia Journal of World Business* 7(1): 65.

Pagoulatos, G. 2003. *Greece's New Political Economy: State, Finance, and Growth from Postwar to EMU*. London.

Papastefanaki, L. 2013. "'Greece Has Been Endowed by Nature with This Precious Material . . .': The Economic History of Bauxite in the European Periphery in the 20th Century." In *Aluminum Ore: The Political Economy of the Global Bauxite Industry*, edited by R. Gendron, M. Ingulstad, and E. Storli, 158–84. Vancouver.

Pelt, M. 2006. *Tying Greece to the West: US–West German–Greek Relations 1949–1974*. Copenhagen.

Pesmazoglu, J. 1972. "The Greek Economy since 1967." In *Greece under Military Rule*, edited by R. Clogg and G. Yannopoulos, 75–108. London.

Piel, G. 1943. "Narcotics: War Has Brought Illicit Traffic to All-Time Low but U.S. Treasury Fears Rising Postwar Addiction." *Life*, 19 July.

Standage, T. 2005. *A History of the World in Six Glasses*. New York.

Time. 1969. "Entrepreneurs: The Greek for Go-Between." 14 February.

United States Department of the Interior, Bureau of Mines. 1971. "I. Commodity Review: Aluminum and Bauxite. Greece." *Mineral Trade Notes* 68(8): 3–4.

United States Drug Enforcement Administration. 2018. "The Early Years." In *History*, 12–29. Washington, DC. Retrieved 1 September 2020 from https://www.dea.gov/sites/default/files/2018-05/Early%20Years%20p%2012-29.pdf.

Valentine, D. 2006. *The Strength of the Wolf: The Secret History of America's War on Drugs*. New York.

Chapter 5

"Patient in a Cast"

How the Greek Military Regime Traumatized Education

Othon Anastasakis

The relationship between authoritarian regimes and education is by definition competitive, combative, and conflictual, and, for autocratic rulers, education is always one of their core concerns, a source of potential opposition. As a conduit of liberal thinking, the youth, the students, and the academics have the potential to cause damage and become a basis of resistance and challenge to the autocratic authority of a dictatorial regime.

An authoritarian regime has a number of options and instruments when dealing with the sensitive sector of education. At first, it can use ideological instruments of propaganda, indoctrination, and censorship aimed at justifying the exceptional and repressive character of its rule; the instruments of indoctrination and controlled information can be more visible and explicit in the formative years of primary and secondary education through the redrafting of or ad hoc interventions in textbooks, the nationalistic teaching of history, and the manipulation of the content of the school curricula. Purges of professors, teachers, or other dissenters are common practices, and new officials loyal to the regime are put in place. In addition, dictatorships make ample use of coercive mechanisms to repress universities and any rebellious student movements. Finally, authoritarian regimes control the educational apparatuses by centralizing power and modifying previous structures and institutions with new ones, adjusting them to the purposes of the regime (for a comparative study, see Connelly and Grüttner 2005).

My focus in this chapter is on the relationship between the Greek military junta and the field of education during the seven-year rule, 1967–74. I will be looking at four important dimensions: first, the educational beliefs of the Greek military mind and their approach toward the youth; second, the reactionary and counter-reformist nature of the regime; third, the policy-making of the military government through the adoption and implementation of relevant laws; and, finally, the postjunta legacies of the regime's authoritarian educational practices, bearing in mind that the discrediting of the military regime came in large part from the student movement and the Polytechnic uprising in 1973.

The following study is based on a combination of selected primary and secondary research material to show some of the ideological underpinnings in the military junta's world of education. Regarding the educational policy, in particular, there are a number of useful sources, including ministerial councils concerning the drafting of laws, the actual legislature, the publications of some of the regime's ideologues, and analysis based on newspapers and political reviews of the 1970s.[1]

The chapter argues that the Greek military rulers, during their stay in power, reversed the educational reforms that had been adopted in the recent parliamentary years, echoing the rigidity and reactionary nature of the military mind. Nevertheless, caught in the middle of a rapidly growing Greek economy, the military rulers were torn between their illiberal and repressive practices and an objective need to modernize the field of education. While modernization in advanced capitalist societies is the product of democratic education, in authoritarian regimes of limited or repressed pluralism, the need for modernization and economic liberalization comes into conflict with their propensity to control the scientific and intellectual debate. At a time of an increasing internationalization of education and information in the Western world of the 1960s and 1970s, marked by the rapid spread of liberal ideas, the controversies and contradictions of the regime became much more evident in the field of education (for a comparative study with contemporary regimes in Latin America, see Sanders 1981: 11).

The appointment of eight ministers and eight junior ministers of education in the seven years of military rule, each of a different professional background, was typical of the Greek military regime's undecided and vacillating "experimentation" with education. The ministers of education and religious affairs included, in chronological order, Konstantinos Kalampokias (April–December 1967), a member of the Supreme Court of Justice; Theofylaktos Papakonstantinou (December 1967–June 1969), a journalist and political analyst; Georgios Papadopoulos (June 1969–July 1970), the leader of the military regime; Nikitas Sioris (July 1970–August 1971), a businessman and economist; Gerasimos Frangatos (August 1971–July 1972), a professor of organic chemistry; Nikolaos Gantonas (July 1972–October 1973), a military officer; Panagiotis Sifnaios (October–November 1973), a politician and journalist; and Panagiotis Christou (November 1973–July 1974), the ex-rector of the University of Thessaloniki and a professor of theology who assumed the ministry during the last phase of the military regime when Dimitris Ioannides was in power.[2] This haphazard group of individuals shows the wavering of the regime between the reactionary, the repressive, the ideological, the pseudoliberal, and the pseudotechnocratic policies.

Throughout his tenure as the junta strongman, Papadopoulos often employed medical metaphors, whereby the junta assumed the role of the "medical doctor," with the "patient" being Greece (*Makedonia*, 28 April 1967). Typically, the rulers portrayed themselves as the "doctors" who operated on the "patient" by putting the patient into an orthopedic walking cast and applying restraints on the patient, or tying him/her onto a surgical bed and anaesthetizing him/her in order to perform the "operation," so that the life of the patient" would then not be "endangered" during the operation (McDonald 1983: 110). Such metaphors reflected the rhetorical extremities to which these middle-rank officers as political rulers would often resort. Ironically, during the course of the regime, it became apparent how such metaphors became relevant to the country's condition, and how many wounds the military junta itself inflicted on Greek politics and society. Needless to say, it was in the field of education that such backward and authoritarian blows were felt the most.

THE MILITARY MIND

For autocrats, education is always a threat to the system because it provides a platform for challenge to their authority. However, in some cases, it can also be an opportunity to spread their message and influence on the youth. Here, Juan Linz's division between totalitarian and authoritarian systems is helpful for understanding the dictatorial regimes' approach toward education and youth. According to Linz, totalitarian regimes are characterized by "a monistic centre of power," "a more or less intellectually elaborate ideology," and an "active mobilisation through a single party," and exist where ideology holds a holistic conception of man and society (Linz 2000). Fascist regimes during the interwar period sought a totalitarian control over education, and because they saw themselves as radical alternatives to the status quo, they sought to create youth movements with a long-term ideological appeal and a complete control of the content of information. Similarly, the communist regimes imposed their own educational culture under the totalitarian domination of the state and the one-party system, from the Soviet and Eastern European variations to Mao's Little Red Book. Authoritarian systems under military rule are, on the other hand, systems with limited and controlled political pluralism, more often than not without an elaborate and guiding ideology and lacking the ability to create influential parties or youth movements. A second relevant distinction when studying the ideational environment of autocracies is that between ideologies and mentalities: ideologies are systems of thought, more or less intellectually elaborated and organized by intellectuals or pseudointellectuals themselves or with their assistance; mentalities are disparate ways of thinking and feeling, more emotional than rational, that provide noncodified ways of reacting to different situations (Vovelle 1990).

The ideological justifications for the imposition of military rule and the exercise of dictatorial power in Greece can be compared to its contemporaneous Latin American military regimes—although there are some differences with respect to the more technocratic outlook of the Latin American type (Linz and Stepan 1978; O'Donnell 1988); they also share some similarities with the much longer personality-driven dictatorships of Franco in Spain and Salazar in Portugal (Payne 1986). Like them, the 21 April regime lacked an organized system of belief or a comprehensive authoritarian ideology in order to interpret its surrounding reality, and in order to mobilize society around a convincing narrative. The military junta resorted to unconvincing justifications of its repressive tactics, torn by ideological contradictions and conflicting points of view among its own elites (Clogg 1972: 51). The ideological justifications of the military junta, far from presenting a coherent ideological alternative, reflected some controversial, and often personal, military mentalities, with some minimum common denominators around the notions of ultranationalism, Greco-Christianity, and anticommunism.

The 21 April regime's "ideology" was formed through the officers' own militaristic education, their powerful position in the post–World War II Greek state, their clientelist connections with civilian elites, and the power attributed to them by U.S. interference during the anticommunist Cold War environment. Greek officers believed that the army was the embodiment of national ideals, identity, and consciousness (Kouvertaris 1971). They felt that they represented and lived by a set of superior moral values. To them, the military profession was a repository of Greco-Christian ideals. The officers' inability to form a coherent nationalist philosophy resulted in the production of a series of nonsensical rhetorical statements, typical of their ill-based intellectual skills and of their ideological confusion, for example: "The Greeks have always been Greeks of Greece, Greeks of the

Greek nation" (Papadopoulos 1969 [29 March] in his speech to the students of Thessaloniki). The ideological motto of the junta government was expressed in the "Greece of Christian Hellenes." The Greek officers' self-image contained an underlying element of puritanism and a religious moral certainty. Their own ideological indoctrination as young officers involved an extensive censorship of their reading material and their own radio station, which was not submitted to any governmental control, transmitting programs of a clearly political and partisan character (Meynaud [1966] 2002). Broadcasting centers in every major military unit, special time allotted in training schedules for National Ethical Instruction of the troops, lectures on politics and the ideology of international communism, newspapers, and journals—all of these constituted the systematic methods of indoctrination of the postwar military mind (Kapetanyannis 1986: 116).

The military rulers rejected the descriptions of fascism, totalitarianism, and even dictatorship as a definition of the nature of their intervention, while they used the term "revolution" to such an extent that it became a very common word in the official vocabulary of the regime, in their effort to persuade the populace of their intention to radically alter the political life of Greece; revolution defined more "as an attitude of mind and a moral stance, an expression of the soul rather than as a material expression" (*Eleftheros Kosmos*, 21 November 1972). The leaders of the 21 April military intervention and their theorists also rejected the notion of the "coup d'état," presenting their intervention as being a necessary "revolutionary change," brought about by a group of nationally minded, middle-ranking officers (Georgalas 1970). Despite an apparent initial ideological unity among the leaders of the military regime with respect to some very general ideas and objectives, the junta was a military bloc composed by a number of middle-class officers, whose mentalities and ideational fixations are better understood in the context of their ideological variants. As in most other similar cases of dictatorships, the Greek junta and its civilian supporters were divided between hard-liners versus soft-liners, religious versus secular, economically liberal versus state centralizers, militaristic versus technocratic, status quo versus the modernizers. All these tendencies permeated the mentalities of the junta rulers, as well as those who collaborated with them, and appeared most prominently and erratically in the field of education.

REACTION AND COUNTER-REFORM IN GREEK EDUCATION

Since the late nineteenth century, Greek education provided the platform for competing discourses, ideological battles, and a series of reforms and counter-reforms. The system was always highly centralized and controlled by a powerful Ministry of Education, and successive governments used education as a means to legitimize their political and ideological hegemony. Having imported some Western structural and administrative models, the majority of the internal struggles within education focused mostly on ideological and cultural issues and involved the content of school curricula, pedagogical methods, and especially the language question (purified/Katharevousa vs. demotic/popular), which for much of the twentieth century dominated many ideological debates among politicians and intellectuals, among liberals and conservatives (Frangoudaki 1977). Despite the increasingly public and free character of Greek education, the system overall retained, since its inception, a classicist orientation, insufficient vocational training, and a religious homogeneity around the Orthodox Christian faith, all of which often contradicted the liberal pressures coming from the more advanced Western capitalist societies, of which Greece was claiming to be part during the interwar and the post–World War II contexts (Dimaras 1974–1988, vol. 1).

Toward the end of the 1950s came the first timid attempts at transforming school programs and reorganizing education toward more technical alternatives following the report by a 1957 Commission on Education, which deliberated on the needs of the Greek educational system in the context of a growing Western economy. But it was the reform proposed in 1964, following the rise of the Center Union party and its charismatic leader George Papandreou to power,[3] which would become among the most significant moments in Greece's educational history. Papandreou consistently demanded the democratization and modernization of Greek society. The accession of George Papandreou to power in 1963, following eleven years of uninterrupted, harsh, and highly exclusionary right-wing rule, resulted in the enactment of a comprehensive and all-encompassing educational reform, which was a response to the needs of a growing Greek economy, on the one hand, and the demands for a more democratic education, on the other.

The Center Union's educational reform had been at the time one of the most comprehensive reforms in the history of Greek education and had involved the reorganization of education at all three levels, primary, secondary, and tertiary. Indeed, Law 4379/1964, prepared by Evangelos Papanoutsos, one of the most prominent liberal pedagogists at the time, covered a wide range of issues, which included, among others: free public education provided at all levels; the extension of compulsory education to nine years; the division of secondary education into two stages (the gymnasium and the lyceum, three years each); the official recognition of demotic (spoken) language, elevated to the status of the then dominant Katharevousa (purified); reformation of the curricula in primary and secondary education; increased emphasis given to mathematics and the natural sciences to balance the traditionally classicist education; teaching of ancient texts from translations, with original texts to be studied only at the lyceum; introduction of new courses in secondary education, such as economics, sociology, philosophy, and law; a marked reduction in the emphasis placed on classics and an increase in the hours devoted to Modern Greek and foreign languages; the introduction of voluntary courses at the lyceum; Latin on a voluntary basis at the lyceum to be studied only by those who intended to specialize in theology, literature, and law; abolition of the half-term semester examinations in secondary education; introduction of a free meal service for primary school children; reorganization of the entrance examinations for higher education; and the school leaving certificate (*Akadimaiko Apolytirio*) to be taken in some fifty provincial examination centers instead of, as previously, only in Athens and Thessaloniki (for information on the Center Union's educational reform, see Dimaras 1974–1988, vol. 2; 1978; Vrychea and Gavroglou 1982; Noutsos 1988; Bouzakis 2011; Foukas 2018).

In higher education, the Center Union government introduced the University of Patras and the philosophical faculty at the University of Ioannina. The Teachers' Training College was reorganized and its period of study extended from two to three years in order to improve the quality of the teaching personnel. Finally, the Athens Pedagogical Institute was set up to undertake fundamental research into Greek educational and pedagogical issues. In 1966, a draft law on higher education proposed the connection of economic development with the role of the university, giving further emphasis to the creation of new universities and challenging the strong and monolithic institution of the professor's chair. The overall character of these educational provisions reflected the social, political, and economic needs of Greece at the time. The 1964 Education Act became essentially redundant after the government of George Papandreou fell in July 1965. It was not enacted by the subsequent government and was officially overturned by the 21 April regime. However, it remained the pivotal moment in the history of Greek education for the depth and breadth of its scope and transformative ambition (Dimaras 2000).

. One of the first and immediate policies of the military regime was to reverse the changes that had been initiated by the 1964 reform and bring education back to its pre-1964 status. Thus, they believed that the goals of "order and stability" would be served better because they saw such changes as directly threatening the sustainability of their dictatorial rule ("Leading Greek Educationalist" 1972: 133). Emergency Law 129/1967, "On the Organization and Administration of Education," completely and systematically demolished the 1964 reform and brought about the outright abrogation of most of the recent changes that had been proposed, including the return to six-year compulsory education; a school-leaving age of twelve instead of fifteen years; abolition of the lyceum and the reimposition of the pre-1964 unified gymnasium, the latter divided into the lower and higher gymnasia, one of a classical orientation, and the other of a vocational orientation; the return to the system of exams that the previous system had abolished; the period of teacher training reduced from three years to two; and abolition of the baccalaureate and a return to the previous system of entrance to higher education examinations.

In addition, a new scheme was introduced that once again changed the orientation of secondary education and abolished the concept of "general education" that had guided the spirit of the 1964 reform. The curriculum of the gymnasia, based on Law 129/1967, did away with the schoolbooks proposed by the 1964 reform (published under the auspices of the Pedagogical Institute) and replaced them with textbooks published before 1963; the regime reintroduced the half-year semester examinations; they reimposed Latin as a compulsory language, increased the hours of studies of Ancient Greek and reduced the hours of mathematics and Modem Greek; they abolished courses such as the "Elements on the Democratic System," "Education of the Citizen," "Introduction to Sociology," and "Elements of Economic Science," replacing them with courses such as "The Principles of the 21 April "Regime." Ancient Greek was given renewed emphasis at the expense of modem languages, and all the voluntary courses were abolished. The demotic language was only to be taught during the three first years of primary education (see "Decision by the Minister Kalambokias," published in *To Vima*, 13 June 1967). In 1969, a new program for secondary education was introduced in order to replace the previous 1967 one. Subsequent changes in the curricula enhanced the character of classicist and religious education (Royal Decree 702/69, *Government Gazette*, 31 October 1969).

The Pedagogical Institute was abolished, and all of its members were dismissed or demoted; the Institute, which had attracted the participation of famous Greek scientists, was abolished because, according to the military rulers, its spirit was "contrary to the national traditions and the long history of the Greek people" ("Declaration of the Minister," *Eleftheros Kosmos*, 20 June 1967). In its place, the pre-1964 Higher Council of Education was reestablished (going back to 1914 regulations) and given overall supervision of educational matters. A further decree ruled that all candidates were required to have a "certificate of good conduct" in order to be admitted to the university (Royal Decree 454/67, article 5). A free meal service for primary schoolchildren was abolished, and measures concerning the appearance of pupils in schools were strictly applied.

The military rulers had a fixation with the Katharevousa language and only allowed the use of demotic in the first three years of primary education, under the general provision that it should be "void of extremities and idioms, and corresponding to the perceptive capacity of the pupils in these forms." In the other years, the use of Katharevousa was imposed strictly. Military rulers used to call the demotic a "semi-barbarian, Turko-Hellenic language" (Polychronopoulos 1978, vol. 2: 546). In 1968, the junta's constitution declared Katharevousa the official language of the state. Schools had to also teach students in this language, and all textbooks (except those in primary school) would be written in the purified Greek. Teachers who were opposed to the change (from demotic to Katharevousa) were immediately dismissed from their teaching posts. Most of the military rulers themselves employed the use of Katharevousa in their speeches, legal documents, and regime books, as a status of Greekness and in the spirit of Greco-Christianity.

YOUTH DEMOBILIZATION

The military junta's attitude to the youth was largely shaped as a reaction to the previous reformist climate in education, as well as the student and wider youth mobilization, in the context of a broader international movement of student unrest and reactions during the 1960s (Rico and Huerta 2019; on Greece, see Kornetis 2013). In his book, *The Crisis of the Consumerist Society*, Giorgos Georgalas (1971), one the main propagandists of the 21 April regime, went on an outright offensive against the values of the Western world and against the practices and ideas of Western youth, whose decadence was expressed in the events of 1968 in France, the hippy movement in the United States, and the various anarchists and nihilists of Western societies. He developed the notion that there was a conspiracy against the cultural self-sufficiency of the Greek nation and against the regime of 21 April, a conspiracy guided by the decadent values of the West, such as the hippy movement, anarchism, nihilism, and "eudemonism." He regarded the youth as being vulnerable to the ideas of communism and anarchism, as a result of frustration that had led young people into disobedience and a desire to overturn the status quo. In his book, he stated, "The youth is turning toward more leftist orientations, with a tendency to anticonformism.... Although the new generations are being educated and exposed to more knowledge, they remain immature and are being seduced by the idea that they are entitled to impose their opinion" (Georgalas 1971: 80). The younger generation, and especially the students who were "unbearably bored," were considered persistent bearers of a revolting tendency influenced by "well-fed intellectuals" (Georgalas 1971: 80). The conversion of the international student movements from orthodox Marxism to more radical forms of revolutionary action, inspired by the examples of Mao, Castro, or Che Guevara, had persuaded Georgalas by the early 1970s that communism had ceased to be a major threat, and he perceived that anarchism had come to hold a greater attraction for young people, given that "communism seeks to take advantage of a situation in which decadence has taken root, but when communism had itself been discredited there is a revival of anarchism" (Georgalas 1971: 80).

The regime's policy toward the youth, informed by ideas such as the above, involved the immediate dissolution of all youth organizations of different ideological persuasion, including the Lambrakis Youth Movement,[4] which was associated ideologically and politically with the Center-Left; the EREN, which was the youth organization of the conservative party ERE (Ἐθνικὴ Ῥιζοσπαστικὴ Ἕνωσις, National Radical Union); and the EDHN (Ἐθνικὴ Δημοκρατία Νεολαία, Greek Democratic Youth), the youth organization of the Liberal Party (*Eleftheros Kosmos*, 30 April 1967). Shortly afterward, Odysseas Angelis, the leader of the General Army Staff, ordered the dissolution of 279 organizations and associations (see remarks of A. Lentakis in *Anti* 18 [3 May 1975]: 32). In addition, pupils at primary and secondary school levels were not allowed to attend any youth organizations, with the exception of the Greek Boy Scouts, the youth section of the Greek Red Cross, and Orthodox Sunday schools. Moreover, school communities involved in various types of extracurricular activities were not allowed at all by the junta (message from the Minister Kalampokias in *Eleftheros Kosmos*, 13 May 1967).

In 1968, the military regime created a special department within the General Secretariat of the Prime Minister's Office under the title Direction of the Youth (Law 551/20-9-68), aiming at controlling the Greek youth, the student movement, and other youth organizations. It involved the financing of supervisory councils and the publishing of propagandist magazines (See remarks of A. Lentakis in *Anti* 18 [3 May 1975]: 22). The only attempt by a few members of the military elite to create a youth organization was the revival of Alkimoi (a 1930s organization which had existed intermittently since then; see Daloukas 2013). Its leadership was given to Konstantinos Plevris, the leader of the 4 August Party,[5] but the movement had very limited appeal and membership.

The regime issued Law 93/1969, "On the Rights and Duties of the Students," involving sanctions for disobedient students. This was a clearly and explicitly disciplinary and intimidating document, on the model of the 1929 Idionymon, with similar vocabulary and ideas concerning students.[6] The disciplinary punishments in cases of offenses such as the dissemination of subversive ideas, incitement to strike, and disrespect for the principles of the state varied from a reprimand to permanent expulsion from all institutions of higher education, or interruption of the deferment from military service. Articles 120 and 123 of the law stated that

> students will be punished if they aim at the implementation of ideas having as an obvious goal the overthrow, by whatever means, of the existing social regime or try to convert others to those ideas, or propagate such ideas in whatever way and by whatever means, or propagate ideas of organisations aiming at detaching a part from the whole of the State. Students intending to call fellow students of one or more schools, or a group of students, to a meeting should, twenty-four hours in advance, in writing, ask for permission from the Rector, stating the place, the day and the time, as well as the purpose of the assembly ... otherwise they will be punished. (Translation from "Education: A Farewell to Freedom," *Greek Report*, February 1969, 5–6)

Occasionally, the regime would also use some incentives, such as the abolition of the "certificates of good conduct," the offers of free books, scholarships, exam accommodations, interest-free loans, free medical care, and new halls of residence, in its efforts to appease students.

CENSORSHIP, INDOCTRINATION, AND PROPAGANDA

One of the initial acts of the military governors was their decision to censor a long list of printed publications—books, newspapers, and periodicals. The first official act came from the Ministry of Education (Act 12/5/67), which forbade the circulation of 647 books by both Greek and foreign authors (mostly Marxist, historical, and literary works), 83 newspapers, and 44 periodicals. Any booksellers who continued to sell the forbidden books made themselves liable to imprisonment under the 1912 law "On the Establishment of a State of Siege." The list even included some unexpected entries, such as George Finlay's *History of the Greek Revolution* and Konstantinos Paparrigopoulos's *History of the Greek Nation*, the latter author considered to be the founder of modern Greek historiography and of the principle of Greek continuity from antiquity to the present. The Ministry of Presidency monitored publications, the press, and public events. Independent censorship committees were set up, consisting of lawyers, philologists, authors, employees of the Ministry of Press, policemen, and military men (Grigoriadis 1975, vol. 1: 114). The audiovisual, printed, and performed material, which the censors of the regime banned, involved references to popular uprisings, sex, "subversive theories," and ideas that exercised "a bad influence upon the youth" or were offensive to the nation, the Christian religion, and the government ("Athenian" 1972: 96–97; cited in Asimakoulas 2009: 29).

In a spirit of widespread control of information, even preschool kindergarten books were stamped before military censors would allow their circulation. It should be noted, however, that in general, the school textbooks approved by the junta were not radically different from their predecessors' books—the pre-1964 textbooks. In the history textbooks, there were a few additions and changes concerning modern Greek history in order to provide the necessary justification of the military intervention. Greater emphasis was placed on periods of warfare in the study of Greek history, thus presenting the national history as a series of military victories and giving the army the leading role as the heir to the ancient spirit and guardian of the national heritage. In the history textbooks, the depiction of the glory of war was pursued systematically, while the underrepresentation of other important political and intellectual accomplishments revealed the one-sided military perception of history (Polychronopoulos 1978, vol. 2: 546). Papakonstantinou, the regime's press director and one of the ministers of education (1 November 1967 to 20 June 1969), wrote the book *Political Education*, which was distributed at all stages of primary, secondary, and higher education and was considered the epitome of the regime's political philosophy based on the projection of the religious spirit and the reinforcement of anticommunist propaganda.

Royal Decree 702/69 was a typical example of an attempt to impose a militaristic mentality in pupils at a very sensitive and susceptible age in primary education. This law touched on aspects of everyday school life (saluting the flag, compulsory carrying of satchels), promoted a formalistic primary learning, left no room for any teachers' initiative, and was full of allusions to religion. Several members of the military junta advocated close connections with the Orthodox Church, the most vociferous proponent being Brigadier Stylianos Pattakos, one of the members of the regime's leading Triumvirate,[7] a member of the religious brotherhood Zoi (Ζωή, Life), an organization which had close links with the regime and influenced the regime's policy in church and educational matters. This overtly puritanical church organization contributed to the imposition of some of the most prudish educational measures enforced by the regime, such as the bans on beards for schoolboys and miniskirts for schoolgirls, draconian film censorship, compulsory church attendance, etc. ("Ζωή, σωτήρ, οι έλληνες επίσκοποι και η χούντα" [Zoi, Sotir, the Greek bishops and the junta], *Hellenic Review* 1 [September 1968]: 27).

CONTROL AND INFILTRATION OF THE EDUCATIONAL APPARATUS

Estranged from the previous civilian political establishment and isolated from all mainstream intellectuals and pedagogues, the military rulers interfered in educational matters through the control of institutions and the use of clientelistic methods, overthrowing the previous educational status quo and establishing new educational networks, relying on opportunistic supporters and loyal officers in crucial educational posts.

The Constitution of 1968 stated that the general directives of national educational policy should be formed, as prescribed by law, after consultation with the National Council of Education. The competence of the National Council of Education was to give its opinion on the general guidelines on educational matters, as well as its aims, mission, and ideological orientation. This was composed of the archbishop of Athens, the president of the Constitutional Court, the leader of the Armed Forces, the president of the Academy of Athens, the rectors of the Universities of Athens, Thessaloniki, and of the Polytechnic of Athens, and the senior general inspector of secondary education.

The regime appointed some of its supporters to the Professors' and the Teachers' Unions so as to be able to control the actions and decisions of these unions. The vacant seats created by the series of dismissals in the universities were filled by people "in agreement with the social status quo and national ideals" (Gregoriadis 1975: 115). Governmental control over the institutions of higher education became stifling, reaching its peak with the infamous institution of the government commissioner and the appointments of retired army officers in higher educational institutions. The government commissioner exercised state surveillance over higher education by seeing that laws and governmental policies were being applied. He was present at the meetings of the various administrative bodies, and he offered his opinion and made propositions (Law Decree 180/69, 30 April 1969). Furthermore, Royal Decree 322/69 defined the details regarding the seat of the commissioner and the people working around him in the Universities of Athens and Thessaloniki, the Polytechnic of Athens, the Higher Agricultural School of Athens, the Higher Industrial School of Athens and Thessaloniki, and the Higher School of Fine Arts. While the post of the governmental commissioner had been first introduced in 1931, the aims, content, and the type of appointee changed completely under the dictatorship. The person appointed became a type of police inspector in the universities. The institution of the government commissioner was included in the military regime's constitutions, both in 1968 and 1973.

The military government intervened in the elections of professors either by refusing to appoint the choice of the competent electoral bodies or by making appointments without respecting the electoral procedures (see remarks of G. Papadimitriou in *Politis* 2 [June 1976]: 21). Moreover, the minister of education had a free hand to announce the occupant of a vacant seat if he so wished (Law Decree 429/70, "On the Proclamation of a University Seat"). Law Decree 672/70 stated that deans and rectors were no longer to be elected by their respective senates but were to be appointed by the ministry from a list of three candidates chosen by the senates. The same principles were applied for the assistant teaching staff based on Law 553/68. All the candidates had to submit their applications for appointment to the Ministry of Education, accompanied by the curriculum vitae on their and their families' political convictions and affiliations. The purge of some unwanted university professors was also achieved by the lowering of the retirement age from 70 to 65. The junta obliged professors to sign "declarations of loyalty" to the regime. A series of Constituent Acts defined the conditions according to which the teaching staff might be considered disloyal to the regime and therefore subsequently be dismissed or forced to resign. The purge of schoolteachers, while on a relatively small scale, was carefully selected, concentrating on some indicative leading figures in the profession, in order to preempt the wider community of teachers and deprive them of their leaders.

Following these purges and the subsequent appointments of people loyal to the regime, there was a long list of professors, readers, and assistant staff who collaborated with the military junta, aiming at their personal professional ascendancy. Some of them offered their support to the regime's ideology and propaganda, with the publication of pro-government books and articles, laudatory speeches, and membership in pro-dictatorship associations. Others collaborated with the security police in passing on information on students and professors. Others accepted political and administrative appointments offered by the regime. By appointing professors as experts to the ministries, the military junta tried to give a technocratic and specialist facade to the government. Nineteen professors became ministers or deputy ministers, while other professors became general secretaries of ministries, general directors, prefects, bank governors, presidents of administrative councils, etc. (see remarks of D. Daveas in *Politis* 2 [June 1976]: 23–28).

The regime used police surveillance and police informers among students to control and monitor university life and to suppress the student movement, and there were often threats not to grant passports, scholarships, and tuition fees to students in foreign countries. Reflecting their conspiratorial and paramilitary mentality, they created the equivalent mechanism in the educational establishment, the "parallel student" organization, which played an active role in the destabilization and the demobilization of the student movement. During the 1960s, before the advent of the dictatorship, the EKOF (Εθνική Κοινωνική Οργάνωσις Φοιτητών, National Social Organization of Students) had actively participated in the university environment as a counterbalance to the growing center-left and left-wing student movements. It had been created by the right-wing government of ERE, and had been supported financially by it.[8] During the period of the junta, EKOF was the only student organization that was not dissolved, while the military rulers made extensive use of previous EKOF members in crucial ministerial, prefectural, diplomatic, and other posts.[9]

THE PSEUDOMODERNIZING AND PSEUDOLIBERAL FACADE

During the 1950s and 1960s, the Greek economy grew rapidly and recorded very high rates of growth, which were among the highest in Europe at an average of 7 percent. Indeed, following the food shortages, budget deficits, and rampant inflation caused by the Nazi occupation (1941–44) and the subsequent Greek Civil War (1944–49), from the mid-1950s onward, the country started witnessing major economic changes, marked by price stability and growth, supported by U.S. aid and foreign direct investment from Western Europe. A noticeable shift from agriculture to industry and services resulted in demographic change and labor mobility through emigration from the countryside to the cities, with the capital Athens, in particular, doubling in size during the 1950s and 1960s. The main characteristics of postwar economic development were the boosting of the manufacturing sector, the shift in investment from light consumer goods to durable and capital goods, the change in the structure of exports from agricultural to industrial goods, and a significant concentration of capital in industry. While the economic changes of the 1950s and 1960s did not affect in any radical way the peripheral status of the Greek economy in relation to the developed world, they brought about some qualitative transformations in the standard of living of many Greeks, including a rise in education. As a result, state education expanded, and the number of pupils who graduated from secondary school to go on to higher education rose steadily; the number of registered students in higher education nearly tripled from 25,658 in the 1960–61 academic year to 72,269 in 1970–71 (Karamanolakis 2015: 44).

The military regime governed in the midst of a growing economy that continued to increase until 1973 before being affected severely by the oil crisis. Similarly, the gross product of the industrial sector reached the peak of a rapidly increasing development that had started in 1958. In addition, employment in the secondary sector increased dramatically, and a change in the composition of industrial production took place as well (Pesmazoglou 1999: 205-12). Following a reactionary, antireformist start in education, the military regime was required to respond to the changing environment, marked by continuous growth and industrialization, by introducing economically driven changes to the country's education system.

Toward the end of the 1960s, the World Bank issued a compelling report on the need for better technical education in Greece. Its primary findings concerned the inability of technical schools in Greece to respond to the needs of the diversification of the economy. It was stated that Greece spent the lowest amount of money in Europe on industrial and technological research and placed its emphasis on the traditional sectors of nutrition and textiles. It also argued that the lack of technical and specialized education contributed to the production and reproduction of the already existing traditional structures of the Greek economy, without creating the circumstances for the development of technically advanced and dynamic sectors (Pesmazogou 1999: 331).

As a response to this, a new educational institution came into existence in 1970, following the adoption of Law 652/1970, "On Technical and Professional Education," in the form of KATE (Κέντρα Ανωτέρας Τεχνικής Εκπαιδεύσεως, Centers of Higher Technical Education), which were based on the World Bank's recommendations and with the financial assistance of the bank in order to respond to the need for specialized studies in agriculture, industry, health, and the processing of food. On the other hand, the creation of KATE was also a way to absorb the surplus of demand for higher education, avoiding potential social pressures.

In 1971, the regime established a Committee for the Study of Education, comprised of six university professors, two general educational administrators, three teachers, and one technical education specialist. It was appointed in order to provide recommendations on how to improve Greece's school system, which included among others, extending compulsory schooling to nine years and expanding vocational programs. The committee also stressed the importance of science and mathematics in the curricula, as well as placing more emphasis on specialized technical education (Georgiadis 2007), some of which was reminiscent to the guidelines of the 1964 reform. Parallel to that, another Committee on Higher Educational Matters proposed the diversification and expansion of the institutions of higher education (Vrychea and Gavroglou 1982: 68-71). Such proposals were followed up by legislation on the independence of the University of Ioannina in 1970, composed of the Schools of Philosophy, Physics, and Mathematics, which had previously been a charter of the Aristotle University of Thessaloniki

(Law Decree 746/70, *Government Gazette*, 12 December 1970), and the creation of the University of Crete (established in 1973 and started functioning in the 1977–78 academic year) and the University of Thrace (established in 1973 and started accepting students in the 1974–75 academic year). By 1973, the military regime had established five vocational and professional training schools throughout Greece, and more resources and money went into supporting special educational programs.

Such changes coincided with an attempted liberalization under civilian politician Spyridon Markezinis, as prime minister in 1973, whereby the military regime tried to gain some legitimacy based on a reformed constitution and a series of liberal legal documents, which it only partially applied, trying to combine pseudoliberalization with control, intimidation, and demobilization (Tortzis 2014). In higher education, the regime adopted a rhetoric of a constitutionally legitimate, self-administered university, which in reality was controlled and suppressed by the government, and a "modern" school system, which in reality was strictly supervised. This type of policy mix lacked credibility and led to the student uprising in the Law School in February 1973, when law students went on strike and barricaded themselves inside the buildings of the Law School of the University of Athens, demanding to cancel the law that imposed forcible drafting (conscription) of the so-called subversive youths, as eighty-eight of their peers had been forcibly drafted into the army. The regime responded by sending the police to suppress the uprising. The events at the Law School are widely considered the prelude to the subsequent, more impactful, Polytechnic uprising in November 1973. There, the student grievances at first concentrated on internal matters, such as democratic elections and free discussions regarding their educational curriculum, demanding their democratic rights to be respected as members of the Greek university community, but then quickly expanded to include open demands for the fall of the military junta. The Polytechnic uprising gained massive momentum and ended in bloodshed following the intervention of the police and the army; the image of the tank crushing the gate of the Polytechnic School has remained one of the most powerful images in the nation's collective memory, pointing to the shamefulness of the regime and the heroic defense of the students.

The Greek left-wing student movement that had developed after 1970 was not rigidly communist in orientation; the activities of those who supported the movement had adopted broader progressive ideological frames that proved resonant beyond the students and cut across the wider political and social spectrum. For the majority of them, the junta was singled out as being the fascist enemy in a common, national, antidictatorial struggle (Asimakoulas 2009). The Polytechnic student uprising signaled the beginning of the end of the military regime; it put an abrupt end to the regime's attempted "liberalization," and it brought about the immediate downfall of Papadopoulos's authority and his overthrow by the hard-line faction within the junta, establishing a more repressive regime and fierce suppression of any opposition.

During the period of the "invisible dictator" Brigadier Ioannidis, it had become obvious that higher education had become the strongest pillar of resistance, presenting the regime with the most serious source of opposition. In an effort to "address" the causes of revolutionary student mobilization, the Ioannides regime organized "On Youth," a series of (nine) ministerial councils between February 1974 and June 1974. Among the variety of opinions heard, some ministers tried to associate the student antidictatorial struggle with the revolutionary movements of Western Europe or the ills of consumerist society; others blamed unemployment; others, the decreasing influence of the Greek Orthodox Church and the "lack of ideals." Subsequent propositions to reform higher education varied from the reactionary and backward-looking options to the reformist and forward-looking; it is interesting to note that some of the latter views suggested the abolition of university chairs, student participation in the management of universities, the evaluation of the professor's work every seven years, the introduction of Marxist philosophy in teaching, the official use of Modem Greek language, or changes in technical education and the infrastructure of the university apparatuses (for the proceedings of the ministerial councils on educational matters, see the remarks of D. Sarafianos and A. Loverdos in *Anti* 442 [13 July 1990]: 54–56). None of these suggestions were ever implemented within the economically and politically doomed—for the military junta—climate of 1974, yet they revealed the divergence of opinions within the military regime, the conflicting nature of the suggestions, and the unavoidable need for change.

DEALING WITH THE AUTHORITARIAN LEGACIES OF THE MILITARY JUNTA IN EDUCATION

The downfall of the military regime on 24 July 1974 marked a new beginning for Greek politics and society by what is known as Metapolitefsi (μεταπολίτευση, regime change), with concrete steps to move away from the dictatorial traumatic experiences and to redress some balance in a polarized postauthoritarian political and social process. Nowhere is this more visible than in the field of education, which went through a period of catharsis and lustration, timidly at first, during the New Democracy government, and then more forcefully when PASOK (Πανελλήνιο Σοσιαλιστικό Κίνημα, Panhellenic Socialist Movement) came to power in 1981.

One of the most important priorities had to do with the cleansing of the educational apparatuses of those who had cooperated with the junta and were appointed in university positions, in what was termed as the "dejuntification" of education. A list of ninety-two professors and readers were charged by the Special Disciplinary Council and were either convicted or acquitted of the charges (see remarks of D. Daveas in *Politis* 2 [June 1976]: 23–28). All those who had been dismissed from their university posts during the junta period were automatically reinstated. All those who had been directly appointed to university posts by the regime without being elected to their posts by the faculties were dismissed (Wasser 1979: 87).

The extreme right-wing indoctrination and the anticommunist/antileftist propaganda, which had reached its apogee with the military regime, led to a postjunta, anti-right ideological bias, the rise of a "progressive," left-wing ideological discourse, and a suspicion toward the "reactionary" nature of the right. The demobilization of the youth and the suppression of the student movement by the junta resulted in a postjunta mobilized and party-politicized student environment (Karamanolakis 2015). It was no coincidence that the struggle against the dictatorship had produced a new collective hero in the Greek imaginary, in the form of the student community of the Polytechnic uprising, and bestowed on it a prominent role in subsequent political and social developments, particularly inside the universities themselves. Thousands of students flocked to general assemblies in their faculties, demanding that universities be cleansed of the academics who had served the dictatorship. A central component of the political forces that represented the student movement was the communist Left, as the youth sections of the two communist parties (the pro-Soviet KKE [Κομμουνιστικό Κόμμα Ελλάδας, Communist Party of Greece] and the Euro-Communist KKE of the Interior) accounted for nearly 50 percent of participation in student elections. At the same time, the forces of the extraparliamentary Left also acquired a significant presence.

The need for educational reform became urgent, and the New Democracy government adopted the 1976 reform aiming at the expansion of the educational system, the reorganization and administration of secondary education, and the introduction of vocational-technical upper secondary schools. The change in political power from the right-wing New Democracy to the socialist PASOK in 1981 brought about more daring reforms and allowed the realization of a series of demands that had emerged in the 1960s under Papandreou, including the broadening of higher education, democratization, and the active participation of the student movement in the administration of the universities or the abolition of the professor's chair. In general, PASOK promoted welfare policies and introduced progressive institutional changes to education aiming at increasing the number of students in higher education. For this reason, it established the Integrated Lykeio (a type of upper secondary comprehensive school) and modified the school curriculum, the content of textbooks, and the entry examination system to upper secondary and tertiary education. It upgraded the status of technical-vocational schools by abolishing KATE and introducing three-year TEIs (Τεχνολογικό Εκπαιδευτικό Ίδρυμα, Technological Higher Education Institutions) for those students who wished to obtain a vocational higher degree.

While the educational policies of the post-1974 democratic governments were not a reaction to the seven-year military rule alone but instead to a much longer historical need for change, the military junta dealt such a big blow to the freedom and liberal nature of education that it became a catalyst for radical change by the subsequent governments.

Among the most disdained memories of the junta period, the regime's repressive actions toward higher education in the Law School uprising and the much more aggressive intervention at the Polytechnic gave rise to the University Asylum Law, introduced in 1982. The aim of the law was to protect freedom of thought and expression on university campuses across Greece. The law made it illegal for police to enter universities without the permission of university rectors, and guaranteed sanctuary from arrest and state brutality for the students. The law became one of the most sacrosanct red lines for the majority of the student community, resulting over the years in some unintended consequences, including university campus infiltration, occupation, or disorder by extreme or nonstudent actors who could not be handled by the police.

For most people, the policies of the military regime maybe overlooked in a long series of reforms and counter-reforms, actions and reactions, continuities and ruptures that have tormented modern Greece's education story. However, for many Greek people with a living memory of the military junta and especially for those who were teachers and students of secondary or higher education at that time, the seven-year period is remembered as a time of control, student repression, and utmost ignorance of the rulers regarding educational matters, a big blow to the nation's soul and health.

Othon Anastasakis is the Director of South East European Studies at Oxford (SEESOX) and Senior Research Fellow at St Antony's College, University of Oxford. His most recent co-edited books include *Diaspora Engagement in Times of Severe Economic Crisis: Greece and Beyond* (Palgrave, 2022), *The Legacy of Yugoslavia: Politics, Economy and Society* (I.B. Tauris, 2020), and *Balkan Legacies of the Great War: The Past Is Never Dead* (Palgrave Macmillan, 2016).

NOTES

1. This chapter draws partly on archival material included in my PhD thesis, titled "Authoritarianism in 20th Century Greece: Ideology and Education under the Dictatorships of 1936 and 1967" (unpublished thesis, London School of Economics, University of London, 1992).
2. The seven-year military regime included seven successive governments, the first under Greek Attorney General Konstantinos Kollias as prime minister (April–December 1967), five under the leader of the military junta Georgios Papadopoulos (December 1967–October 1973), and the last one under Adamantios Androutsopoulos in the shadow of the "invisible" hard-line dictator Dimitris Ioannidis (November 1973–July 1974).
3. George Papandreou had served six times as minister of education (1930–32, 1933, 1947, 1951, 1963, and 1964–65); in two of these governments, he was also prime minister (1963 and 1964–65).
4. In May 1963, Grigoris Lambrakis, an independent left-wing MP and member of the Greek branch of Bertrand Russell's Peace Movement, was assassinated by right-wing extremists who had connections with the police. His death marked the beginning of DKNGL (Δημοκρατική Νεολαία Λαμπράκη, Democratic Youth Movement "Grigoris Lambrakis"), whose "repertoire of action included extensive riots and rallies, open discussions and peace walks, focusing mostly on educational and cultural issues" (Kornetis 2006: 60).
5. The 4 August Party was a radical right political formation founded in July 1965 by a group of young extreme nationalists named and inspired by the 4 August regime of Ioannis Metaxas (1936–41).
6. *Idionymon* was a term used in particular to refer to the crime established by Law 4229 of 1929 ("concerning safety measures for the social establishment and protection of freedom"), introduced by the liberal government of Eleftherios Venizelos, which imposed a penalty of six months imprisonment for anyone "who attempts to apply ideas that have as an obvious target the violent overthrow of the current social system, or who acts in propagandizing their application." This was specifically targeted against communists and anarchists.
7. The original leaders of the coup were Colonel Georgios Papadopoulos, Colonel Nikolaos Makarezos, and Brigadier Stylianos Pattakos, plus a "Revolution Council," which consisting of several dozen officers and army officials.
8. See remarks of A. Lentakis in *Anti* 17 (20 April 1975): 17 on the existence of financial and communication links between the party, ERE, and the student organization, EKOF. The former financed the latter's newspapers, paid its rents in Athens and Thessaloniki, and organized its indoctrination tours throughout the country.
9. Characteristic promotions of EKOF members to powerful posts included, among others, the case of Lakis Ioannides, who had been the president of EKOF in Thessaloniki during the period 1965–67 and had published student periodicals in which he had invited the opinions of people such as Konstantinos

Maniadakis, infamous and ruthless internal security chief of the 4 August 1936 regime. During the dictatorship of 1967, Maniadakis became an attaché at the Greek embassy in France, he published the periodical *Ideai*, and he was the president of the Cultural Movement of the Greek Youth in Western Europe. Another ex-member of EKOF, Pavlos Manolopoulos, president of the movement during the period 1960–63, became a prefect and in 1970 a minister of labor; see remarks of A. Lentakis in *Anti* 17 (20 April 1975): 20–22.

REFERENCES

Newspapers and Periodicals

Anti
Eleftheros Kosmos
Government Gazette
Greek Report
Hellenic Review
Makedonia
Politis
To Vima

Secondary Sources

Asimakoulas, D. 2009. "Translating 'Self' and 'Others': Waves of Protest under the Greek Junta." *The Sixties: A Journal of History, Politics and Culture* 13(1): 25–47.
"Athenian." 1972. *Inside the Colonels' Greece*. Translated by R. Clogg. London.
Bouzakis, S. 2011. "I ekpaideftiki metarrythmisi tou 1964–1965" [The educational reform of 1964–65]. In *Panorama istorias tis ekpaidefsis: Opseis kai apopseis* [Panorama of the history of education: Sides and opinions], vol. 2, *Neoelliniki ekpaidefsi, 1821–2010* [Modern education, 1821–2010], edited by S. Bouzakis, 223–40. Athens.
Clogg, R. 1972. "The Ideology of the Revolution of the 21st of April 1967." In *Greece under Military Rule*, edited by R. Clogg and G. Yannopoulos, 36–58. London.
Connelly, J., and M. Grüttner, eds. 2005. *Universities under Dictatorships*. University Park, PA.
Dimaras, A. 1988. *I metarrythmisi pou den egine* [The reform that did not take place]. 2 vols. Athens.
———. 1978. "Εκπαίδευση" [On education]. In *Istoria tou ellinikou ethnous* [History of the Greek nation], vol. 15, 489–94. Athens.
———. 2000. "Metarrythmisi kai anti-metarrythmisi (1964–1974)" [Reform and counter-reform (1964–74)]. In *Istoria tou ellinikou ethnous* [History of the Greek nation], vol. 16, 548–58. Athens.

Foukas, V. 2018. "Challenges in Greek Education during the 1960s: The 1964 Educational Reform and Its Overthrow." *Espacio, Tiempo y Education* 5(1): 71–93.

Frangoudaki, A. 1977. *Ekpaideftiki metarrythmisi kai fileleftheroi dianooumenoi: Agonoi agones kai ideologika adiexoda sto mesopolemo* [Educational reform and liberal intellectuals: Lost causes and intellectual deadlocks in the interwar period]. Athens.

Georgalas, G. 1970. *I ideologia tis Epanastaseos* [The ideology of the Revolution]. Athens.

———. 1971. *I krisis tis katanalotikis koinonias* [The crisis of the consumerist society]. Athens.

Georgiadis, N. 2007. "Educational Reforms in Greece (1959–1997) and Human Capital Theory." *Journal for Critical Education Policy Studies* 5(2): 342–68.

Grigoriadis, S. 1975. *I istoria tis diktatorias, 1967–1974* [The history of the dictatorship, 1967–74]. Athens.

Kapetanyannis, V. 1986. "Socio-political Conflicts and Military Intervention: The Case of Greece, 1950–1967." PhD diss., University of London.

Karamanolakis, V. 2015. "From the Fall of the Junta to 'Change': The Timid Transition of Higher Education in Greece (1974–1982)." *Espacio, Tiempo y educacion* 2(2): 33–48.

Kornetis, K. 2006. "Student Resistance to the Greek Military Dictatorship: Subjectivity, Memory and Cultural Politics, 1967–1974." PhD diss., European University Institute, Fiesole, Italy.

———. 2013. *Children of the Dictatorship: Student Resistance, Cultural Politics and the "Long 1960s" in Greece.* New York.

Kouvertaris, G. A. 1971. "Professional Self-Images and Political Perspectives in the Greek Military." *American Sociological Review* 36: 1043–57.

"Leading Greek Educationalist." 1972. "Traditionalism and Reaction in Greek Education." In *Greece under Military Rule*, edited by R. Clogg and G. Yannopoulos, 128–45. London.

Linz, J. J. 2000. *Totalitarian and Authoritarian Regimes.* Boulder, CO.

Linz, J. J., and A. Stepan, eds. 1978 *The Breakdown of Democratic Regimes.* Baltimore, MD.

McDonald, R. 1983. *Pillar and Tinderbox: The Greek Press and the Dictatorship.* New York.

Daloukas, M. 2013. "To chtypima stin psychedeliki neolaia" [The blow to the psychedelic youth]. *Istoria tis ellinikis neolaias* [History of the Greek youth] blog, 7 October. Retrieved 18 November 2019 from https://freedomgreece.blogspot.com/2013/10/blog-post_7.html.

Meynaud, J. (1966) 2002. *Oi politikes dynameis stin Ellada, 1946–1965* [The political forces in Greece, 1946–65]. Vol. 1. Translated by P. Merlopoulos and G. Notaras. Athens.

Noutsos, C. 1988. *Programmata mesis ekpaidefsis kai koinonikos elenchos (1931–1973)* [Programs of secondary education and social control (1931–73)]. Athens.

O'Donnell, G. 1988. *Bureaucratic Authoritarianism: Argentina, 1966–1973, in Comparative Perspective.* Translated by J. McGuire and R. Flory. Berkeley.

Papadopoulos, G. 1969. *To pistevo mas* [Our creed]. Vol. 2. Athens.

Payne, S. G. 1986. "Fascism and Right Authoritarianism in the Iberian World: The Last Twenty Years." *Journal of Contemporary History* 21: 163–77.

Pesmazoglou, S. 1999. *Ekpaidefsi kai anaptyxi stin Ellada 1948–1985: To asymptoto mias schesis* [Education and Development in Greece 1948–85: The inharmonious of a relationship]. Athens.

Polychronopoulos, P. 1978. *Paideia kai politiki stin Ellada* [Education and Policy in Greece]. 2 vols. Athens.

Rico, A. P., and J. L. H. Huerta. 2019. "Student Movements of the 'Long 1960s': Steps Towards the Cultural Revolution, Social Change and Political Transformation." *History of Education and Children's Literature* 14(2): 13–20.

Sanders, T. C. 1981. *Education and Authoritarianism in the Southern Cone*. American Universities Field Staff Reports: South America Series 12. Hanover, NH.

Tortzis, I. 2014. "1973: The *Metapolitefsi* That Never Was." *Byzantine and Modern Greek Studies* 38(1): 114–29.

Vovelle, M. 1990. *Ideologies and Mentalities*. Oxford.

Vrychea, A., and K. Gavroglou. 1982. *Apopeires metarrythmisis tis anotatis ekpaidesfsis, 1911–1981* [Attempts at reforming higher education, 1911–81]. Thessaloniki.

Wasser, H. 1979. "A Survey of Recent Trends in Greek Higher Education." *Journal of the Hellenic Diaspora* 6(1): 85–95.

Chapter 6

Can Dead Poets Speak Back?

C. P. Cavafy, Cold War Propaganda, and the Greek Dictatorship

Foteini Dimirouli

Culture has routinely been used as an instrument for political power and persuasion in the public sphere. In what we have come to refer to as "the cultural cold war," the realm of the arts and letters became part of the Cold War's propagandistic arsenal, including America's anticommunist overseas diplomacy.[1] If the undercover and invisible aspects of the United States' democratic "soft propaganda" have been the subject of much enquiry,[2] the cultural tactics favored by authoritarian regimes themselves, such as those backed or supported by the United States and the CIA in the second half of the twentieth century, have mostly been associated with the overt repressive tactics of censorship and persecution. Departing from this dichotomous paradigm, this chapter interrogates a case of inconspicuous cultural manipulation that occurred within right-wing authoritarianism: the Greek dictatorship's (1967–74) arrogation of the authority of C. P. Cavafy, one of the foremost figures of twentieth-century Greek literature, in its state discourse. A wide-reaching cultural point of reference, the poet, who died thirty-odd years before the junta seized power, did not emerge from, or subscribe to, dictatorial ideology. His poetry, however, was made to "speak" on its behalf—a process exemplary of the subtle ways in which emblematic cultural personalities can be enlisted for the purposes of authoritarian legitimation.

Two aspects of the seven-year Greek dictatorship's cultural politics have so far dominated critical investigation: first, the violence against, and silencing of, intellectuals, including the junta's infamous book bans; second, the appropriation of texts and imagery deriving from the great classics to promote the dictators' populist agenda (for early accounts of the junta's repressive strategies, see Clogg and Yannopoulos 1972; "Athenian" [Roufos] 1982).[3] But the use of prestigious modern texts to serve the junta's politics has remained an underinvestigated topic. If the regime's curtailment of the freedom of speech and routine aggressions are evidently illegitimate, how does one assess the legitimacy of literary appropriation, especially when it concerns a figure as highly esteemed as Cavafy? A hypothetical rejection of Cavafy's acclaimed poetry by the unenlightened and repressive Colonels would have, arguably, worked to further affirm the poet's literary value (at least in the long run). Equally, its endorsement by a set of problematic agents could easily be dismissed, a priori, as a usurping act that has little to do with the text itself or with its content.[4] By bringing forward examples of the use of Cavafy's well-known poems in the dictatorship's official public discourse, education apparatus, and affiliated scholarship, this chapter proposes that to better assess literature's aptitude to propaganda, it is necessary to turn to the poems themselves, question the ways in which they enable or resist political uses from within, and move beyond the methodological barriers posed by the notions of *misreading* or *misappropriation*. If these terms are commonly applied to denote politically questionable handlings of cultural material, they tend to merely describe the adaptation of texts considered "worthy" to ends considered to be "illegitimate" rather than to highlight the intricacies of interpretive tactics deployed for the accrual of political legitimacy.

Many are today drawn to Cavafy's work because it unsettles normative understandings of identity and ethnic purity. But what sustained the poet's uninterrupted popularity under the junta? Furthermore, what strategies of appropriation did the junta's ideologues use to ensure that Cavafy's poems appeared aligned with the regime rather than pitted against it? In pursuing these questions, this chapter traces the ideological tailoring that Cavafy underwent during the dictatorship, and discusses features of his poetry—including didactic content, symbolic dichotomies, idiosyncratic language, and a unique view of Hellenism—that facilitated his domestication. At the same time, the dictatorship's Cavafy-inspired propaganda is placed alongside other concurrent adaptations of the poet in politics: for anticommunist propaganda in the democratic United States and for antidictatorial protest in Greece. It is demonstrated in this way that poems by the same author can operate at once as a tool of oppression and a tool of resistance—a method of authoritarian legitimation and a way to manipulate popular opinion in democracies. By comparing the multivalent transnational and local receptions of Cavafy in the 1960s and 1970s, this chapter ultimately investigates whether dictatorial appropriation is unique in its tropes, and thinks about art's ability to resist its ideological co-options and speak back.

C. P. CAVAFY'S POETRY IN THE
IDEOLOGY OF THE REVOLUTION

Given the popularity Cavafy has enjoyed among writers and intellectuals affiliated with the Left, it appears striking, perhaps even paradoxical, to find his work included in the public rhetoric and education apparatus of a regime notorious for its right-wing ideology. The recent rise of postcolonial and queer studies has drawn fresh attention to aspects of the poet's work that are starkly at odds with social conservatism: his dealings with the marginalized Other, his emphasis on cultural crossroads, and his undermining of normativity and convention (see indicatively Jeffreys 2005; McKinsey 2010: 74–99; Halim 2013: 56–119). Equally, there is a long history of Cavafy being heralded abroad as exemplary of unpatriotic, unpartisan, and antiauthoritarian poetics. By the time the junta came into power, Cavafy's collected poems had been translated both in Britain and America; his reputation was steadily on the rise, and his poetic voice had been tethered to causes ranging from the liberal resistance to the Nazi threat, to the anti-American sentiment of the New Left in the face of the Cold War (Dimirouli 2022). In Greece, however, the first half of the twentieth century was marked by the reluctance of intellectuals on either end of the political spectrum to articulate their definitive support of the poet. Cavafy, who had spent the entirety of his adult life in Alexandria, Egypt, was a most contentious newcomer on the scene of Greek letters: his poetry had ignited long debates, during which he accumulated a host of fervent supporters but also bitter enemies. In this climate of embattled visibility, the Left remained cautious toward the Alexandrian, despite the publication of a landmark, albeit much contested, study of his poems as political allusion by the leftist intellectual Stratis Tsirkas in 1958 (Tsirkas 1958). This remained the case at least until 1963, when a special issue of a chief intellectual magazine of the Left, *Epitheorisi Technis*, included essays on Cavafy's work by prominent left-leaning thinkers. In the same year, the renowned Communist poet Giannis Ritsos (later exiled by the junta) published a small collection of poetry titled *12 Poems about Cavafy* (Ritsos 1963 [English translation, 1968]). It is only since these tributes that Cavafy, by then translated and widely celebrated abroad as a voice of dissent and a poet swiftly entering the canon of world literature, became mostly firmly accepted within intellectual factions of the Left in Greece.

The Greek military dictatorship seized power in 1967, capitalizing on decades of political instability, the largely manufactured idea of an impending communist threat, and a widespread sense that Greece was in a state of moral decline and political corruption. The Colonels marked the fourth anniversary of the coup in 1971 by publishing an authoritative statement of the regime's ideological program, *The Ideology of the Revolution: Ideals not Dogmas* (Georgalas 1971). The publication of this tract came at a critical time for the junta: while membership in NATO and American military aid had initially supported the regime as a bulwark against communism, Greece was forced to withdraw from the Council of Europe in 1969 to avoid expulsion due to the junta's human rights abuses (Keys 2012). The writer of *The Ideology of the Revolution*, ex-communist, propagandist, and deputy prime minister during the junta, Georgios Georgalas announced for the first time the dictatorship's enduring legitimacy as an ideologically driven revolutionary movement destined to protect Greece from a communist uprising.[5] In detailing the dangers of the communist threat, Georgalas, who had been born and brought up in Egypt, turned to the Alexandrian Cavafy, quoting extensively from two of his most popular poems, "Walls" and "The Windows," to elaborate the destructive nature of communist ideology.[6]

Cavafy's "Walls" features a first-person narrator lamenting a situation of enclosure and isolation:

> With no consideration, no pity, no shame
> they have built walls around me, thick and high
> and now I sit here feeling hopeless. (Cavafy [1975] 1992: 14)

The narrator's "fate" is both a form of personal torment and an impasse—it "gnaws my mind / because I had so much to do outside." The poem concludes with the realization that "Imperceptibly they have closed me off from the outside world," while the absence of clear, identifiable sensory signs leading to this suffocating imprisonment ("But I never heard the builders, not a sound") signals the unwitting loss of agency of someone who has either been left behind or become isolated. In "The Windows," Cavafy's narrator is similarly trapped within "dark rooms" searching in vain for windows. While the quest initially appears to prefigure a "great relief when a window opens," the poem ends with resignation to a different fate:

> perhaps
> it is better that I don't find them.
> Perhaps the light will prove another tyranny.
> Who knows what new things it will expose? (Cavafy [1975] 1992: 3)

In Cavafy's (1987: 165) own words, both poems were "allegorical," dramatizing the universal theme of "the Restricted Life" without openly referring to it. Georgalas (1971), in turn, added political inflections to this vague theme of restriction. Conflating the two poems' symbolism, he created his own allegory of the communist's tunnel vision:

> The dogmatist . . . harbors the illusion that whatever he perceives constitutes the only and absolute Truth. So, through unremitting deduction he arrives at his own absolute view of the World. This is his Dogma. Its follower ignores all other aspects of life. He views the World exclusively from his own point of view. He doesn't open any other window amongst the walls that surround him, which he has built and which "close him off from the outside world." And he doesn't open any because, as the poet says, "perhaps the light will prove another tyranny," since it would awaken him from the hedonistic self-deception that he exclusively owns the Truth. (Georgalas 1971: 12)

In Cavafy's isolated individual, Georgalas sees the dogmatic communist, who is willingly divorced from the outside world. The prison is of his own making and accrues a blinding, self-delusional quality that inhibits connections to reality.

A clear warning against the dangers of communism is most directly ascribed to Cavafy when Georgalas approaches the didactic, if ambiguous, final lines of "The Windows." By attributing them to their source—"as the poet says"—but explaining them in his own terms, Georgalas merges his own voice with that of the poem's narrator and with Cavafy's to bolster his message by association. Additionally, the use of the definite article—*the* poet—rather than Cavafy's name reminds the reader that a familiar and entrusted poetic voice is being summoned.

It is important to note that despite Cavafy's "outsider" position in Alexandria, his poetry had saturated Greek discourse. His collected poems may have only been published posthumously in Alexandria in 1935 and reprinted in Athens in 1948, but he had already been a focal point for discussion among the Athenian literati since 1918 (Karaoglou 1985: 19–21). Well-respected literary journals in Greece secured an early interest in his poetry, such as the prestigious *Nea Techni*, which dedicated an entire celebratory issue to Cavafy's work in 1924, and the established literary journal *Nea Estia*, which released a special issue about the poet in 1963. As I will discuss in one of this chapter's sections, a number of his poems had been included in Greek school textbooks—sometimes in bowdlerized form—and discussed in literary journals, while his archive and unpublished works were heated topics of debate among Greek intellectuals before and during the dictatorship (Savidis 1985a: 31–55).[7] Georgalas was therefore capitalizing on this preexisting symbolic authority, but also creating it anew through the poet's addition to the regime's ideological territory. This redeployment of shared cultural symbols and narratives is commonplace in propaganda: relying on the past means there is no need to craft new stories, but merely to tell old ones in new ways.

Faced with the possibility of noncompliance by poets who were contemporaneous with the junta, Georgalas benefitted from the fact that Cavafy was safely and silently out of the scene. Unlike Cavafy, the Nobel Laureate George Seferis, the most famous member of the so-called Generation of the 1930s and chief arbiter of taste and new directions in modern Greek poetry, was alive at the time of the coup, and publicly condemned the dictatorship in his statement "Toward a Precipice," aired by the Greek BBC service in 1969. This gesture, among others, tethered his name to the antidictatorial struggle and conveyed artists' collective dismay at the state of censorship and repression in Greek political life. It resulted, most notably, in the suspension of Seferis's diplomatic passport. However, the deceased Cavafy could neither react in person nor direct the interpretation of his work. His transformation into a mouthpiece for the Right was therefore lodged in the implicit understanding that he could never stand up for himself or for his poetry.

It was also convenient that—as Cavafy's editor G. P. Savidis (who in 1963 edited the first edition of Cavafy's poems to reach a wide audience) stated in the very same year that the junta seized power—nobody was privy to Cavafy's own "political convictions," which have remained an object of presumption and speculation to the present day (Savidis 1985b: 106). Even so, Cavafy's homosexuality and his homoerotic poems might be thought to interfere with the ideological program of the conservative dictatorship. But the junta eschewed this "problem" by altogether neglecting the erotic poems and, as we will see later, by erasing suggestive content in the nonerotic ones. Both strategies predated the junta. The erotic aspect of Cavafy's work had already been absent from public discourse, and his homosexuality was well known but hardly ever spelled out, offering convenient continuity to the dictatorship's purified version of the poet[8] and tallying with the regime's willful denial of the very existence of nonheteronormative sexualities in Greek society (for an overview of queer life in Athens during the dictatorship, see Papanikolaou 2014: 162). Cavafy could still function as a legitimizing intellectual authority insofar as only selected aspects of his work continued to be made visible by the official state discourse.

SELECTIVE READING AND ANTICOMMUNIST PROPAGANDA IN GREECE AND ABROAD

The ritualization of Cavafy's preeminence in public discourse before and during the junta was pivotal for Georgalas's appeal to "the poet" in *The Ideology of the Revolution*. But there were also internal features of Cavafy's poetry—binaries and dichotomous poetic structures, expressive minimalism, interpretive openness, and situational ambiguity—that offered ample ground for variable interpretations, and therefore for ideological co-option.

We see this at play not only in Georgalas's tract but also when, in 1966, Cyrus L. Sulzberger, a figure of mythical proportions in American journalism, appealed to the perennial symbolic popularity of Cavafy's "barbarians" to craft political content that overlapped with the junta's anticommunist discourse, albeit from beyond the borders of Greece.

Before moving on to Sulzberger's dealings with Cavafy's poem, it is helpful to remember that the Alexandrian had divided his poetry into three distinct categories—the sensual, the philosophical, and the historical. Despite its shortcomings, this distinction serves to draw attention to a certain form of existential aporia, which lacks fixity, in the so-called philosophical poems quoted by Georgalas in his dictatorial tract. Both "Walls" and "The Windows" construct through symbolism allegorical dualities (between the margins and the world, the self and others) but withhold from the reader the precise source or nature of the occurring alienation. This hermeneutic indeterminacy allows for a broad range of readings into the poem's structuring dichotomy between inside and outside. For instance, according to Seferis, "Walls" was an indication of Cavafy's "unbelievable loneliness" (Seferis 1993: 188)—an interpretation that hinted at his homosexuality and aligned with views most commonly attempted by Cavafy's critic Timos Malanos, who also read "The Windows" through the lens of the poet's sexual orientation (1980: 296).[9] Conversely, Tsirkas (1959: 9) claimed that "Walls" had nothing to do with sexuality; rather, at the time of its writing, it meant to express the poet's exclusion from the social life in Alexandria due to his status as a fallen bourgeois. For C. L. Karaoglou (1985: 42), "Walls" and "The Windows" put forward a more general sense of an *ars vivendi*, which made them popular in 1920s Athens among a generation of readers prone to disillusionment and the contemplation of failed ideals. In the 1970s, the American poet James Merrill argued for a strong sense of agency in "Walls." In his telling, the walls had to be of the narrator's "own making"; otherwise, the poem would be little more than an "exercise in self-pity" (Merrill 1975).

Like many others before and after him, then, Georgalas adapted Cavafy's symbols to his own outlook. By attributing the sense of stagnation and failure evoked in the poems to ideological restrictions, and narrowing down the individual predicament into a political category, Georgalas crafted a morality tale to warn against the communists' blinkered dogma. In this way, he created out of "the poet" an ally who enabled a portrayal of the dictatorship as a much-needed alternative to the shackles of communist fanaticism. In his reading, Cavafy's binary is unbalanced, with the "inside" presented as dangerous. The dictatorship, on the other hand, provides the unspoken answer to the predicament of Cavafy's imprisoned individual: in contrast to the delusional enclosure of "dogmatic ideology," it stands for the "outside world," for "Freedom," and for the authentic "Life."

Even if one abides the tendentious identification of Cavafy's narrator with a communist ideologue, the presumption that the world of the dictatorship might solve the narrator's aporia is a one-sided reading of the existential impasse that the poem puts forward. For Georgalas, the concluding line of "The Windows" ("perhaps the light will prove another tyranny"; Cavafy [1975] 1992: 14), speaks of the communist's unwillingness to confront any reality that "would awaken him from the hedonistic self-deception that he exclusively owns the Truth." However, in the context of Cavafy's admonitions on the futility of attaching hopes of salvation to hasty solutions, the line may suggest that any new reality presents nothing but a transient or superficial change. Elsewhere, in "The City," Cavafy warns that dreams of escape from one's reality may lead to disappointment, for it is impossible to escape one's own self. "Waiting for the Barbarians" similarly ends in the betrayal of expectations for external intervention. In Georgalas's hands, however, Cavafy's poetry conveys the dismal spirit of belief in dead-end ideologies. Through the employment of the anticommunist rhetoric of communist tyranny and dogmatism that was operative on an international arena, Georgalas inserted Cavafy in the dictatorship's campaign to exclude citizens of left-wing or communist persuasions from political and civic life in Greece.[10]

One might wish to detect a distinctly authoritarian strategy behind Georgalas's brazen domestication of Cavafy's symbolism for the sake of presenting the dictatorship as the ultimate resolution to mistakes of the past, and as a saving grace from the communist predicament. In a democratic public sphere in which the ideological use of cultural institutions is subject to open contestation, we might suspect that such a strategy would either have failed or, facing the inevitable prospect of failure, never have been initiated in the first place. Nevertheless, Sulzberger, who from 1944 to 1954 served as chief foreign correspondent of the *New York Times* and as head of its foreign service,[11] followed a similar line in his appropriation of Cavafy in an op-ed about Greece in the foreign affairs column of the newspaper. In "The Bourgeois 'Barbarians,'" Sulzberger projected upon the despairing tone of Cavafy's "Waiting for the Barbarians" his own view of the covert tactics of post–civil war communist infiltration in the Greek political scene, as well as the urgent need to contain them (Sulzberger 1966: 42). Even more pointedly than Georgalas, Sulzberger divested Cavafy's poetry of its open-endedness to illustrate a condition of perpetual emergency under the communist threat. Unlike Georgalas, however, Sulzberger did so from within a democratic regime and from within the pages of a well-respected newspaper.

In "Waiting for the Barbarians," a poem crafted in the form of a dialogue, Cavafy suggestively presents a city's decline and inactivity in the face of imminent invasion by a threatening Other. But the poem ends with an ironic twist, for the "barbarians" never arrive. Rather than offering relief, the news paralyzes the community. Dreams of salvation had been projected upon the arrival of the enemy: "Now what's going to happen to us without barbarians? / Those people were a kind of solution" (Cavafy [1975] 1992: 16). In his article, Sulzberger identifies the "barbarians" as the communists, whose role he initially treats as a blessing in disguise:

> The great Greek poet Cavafy once inquired: "And now, what will become of us without barbarians? They were a kind of solution." For postwar Greece the Communists for a long time served the role of the ancient "barbarians," a unifying menace. During a bloody insurrection the rest of the country joined against them with a display of unity rare for Greece. The uprising was squashed, the Communist party was banned and that "kind of solution" is gone. Greece is now lapsing into its customary discord. (Sulzberger 1966: 42)[12]

Quoting selectively, Sulzberger in his reading erases the themes of political decline and passivity present in Cavafy's poem to promote an idea of unity in the face of adversity. Such a reading dovetailed with Sulzberger's understanding of the dynamics of the Greek Civil War, a conflict which saw the Communist Party force "the rest of the country" to come together, according to his telling. Speaking of "unity" in the context of civil war is of course only conceivable once the enemy has been identified as external and the communists have been, presumably, stripped of their national identity. Sulzberger's rhetoric aligns with the conservative strategy of communist "othering," a practice that was at the heart of the Colonel's ideological politics, was present in Greece long before the coup, and had intensified after the Greek Civil War. Stereotypes about communists were expressed in a register of betrayal and fraudulence, bolstering the Greek dictatorship's claims of defending Western freedom against Soviet totalitarianism. They were also acted on with violent methods of repression, including torture in prisons for those presumed to be "communists" or opponents of the regime, but also the reopening of camps that had served as spaces of internal exile for "suspect" citizens during the latter half of the 1940s.[13]

Gradually escalating in its alarmism, Sulzberger's article returns to Cavafy's "Waiting for the Barbarians" and, at the same time, to the rhetoric of impending communist revolution that had fueled Cold War military interventions and the United States' support of right-wing dictatorships. No longer a mere threat, Sulzberger now reveals, the Greek communists have already, in fact, infiltrated the city's "gates" in "bourgeois" disguise:

"The barbarians" are no longer the "kind of solution" for Greece that they represented by inspiring their opponents to unite right after the civil war. Strictly speaking, the "barbarians" are still outlaws, but everybody knows that many are already within the gates and moving among respectable friends. With the Communists wearing bourgeois habits, their old Greek enemies inquire: "And now, what will become of us?" (Sulzberger 1966: 42)

Written only a few months before the coup, the op-ed carved out an ideological space in implicit support of any political act that would drag the country out of the "customary discord" that made it vulnerable to communist presence. Notably, the Colonels, and especially the regime's initial leader, dictator Georgios Papadopoulos, would resort to the very same reasoning in presenting the coup as a "revolutionary" act (Mikedakis 2007: 1). In a sense, Cavafy's poetry in the writings of Georgalas and Sulzberger worked as a transnational, symbolic landscape of ideological cohesion: Georgalas embedded Cavafy in Cold War anticommunist rhetoric, rather than just domestic politics, while Sulzberger drew the Greek case closer to American interests by utilizing the "insider" voice of a Greek poet for the dissemination of his anticommunist message.

The deployment of Cavafy's popular poems to galvanize anticommunist sentiment was therefore at work both in the state propaganda of a dictatorship ideologue and in the foreign affairs commentary of a *New York Times* journalist. Like "Walls" and "The Windows," Cavafy's "Waiting for the Barbarians" sets up binaries between Us/Them, Inside/Outside, Self/Other that are amenable to the vilification of any presumed "enemy." Structured upon a territorial metaphor bereft of geographical or historical specificity, it served Sulzberger's divisive portrayal of the communists as an existential threat to Greek civilization; a portrayal that, in turn, enabled the perpetuation of an exclusionary notion of Greek national identity and served the agenda of the Cold War. This is yet another instance where Cavafy's dichotomies and binaries lend themselves to elective adjustment, which amounts here to presenting two sides of the ideological spectrum and then siding with one of them. Even so, Sulzberger's reading still requires some resistance to Cavafy's tentative treatment of the binary between citizen and barbarian: in the end, the barbarians turn out to be something better than villains, and the citizens something worse than victims. Not only did Sulzberger bypass layers of signification, but he also created altogether new content about the enemy as an instigator of unity and as an inconspicuous infiltrator, neither of which are attributes of Cavafy's "barbarians" in the original poem. The similarities between Cavafy's manipulation by an American journalist of the Cold War and a key agent of the Greek dictatorship reveal the ways in which propaganda is masterfully played out at the level of the phrase.

It also prompts a reconsideration of the cultural strategies of the dictatorship, which have often been dismissed as preposterous and banal, rather than strategically geared to match the aspirations of reactionary politics in Greece.

CAVAFY'S RELIGION, HISTORY, AND LANGUAGE IN THE CONTEXT OF THE JUNTA'S DISCOURSE

The minimalism, symbolism, and formalism of Cavafy's poems facilitated his selective readings and monolithic interpretations by those prepared to weaponize poetry for their own agendas. Nevertheless, key thematic and linguistic features of Cavafy's poetic corpus also made him an attractive ally for the junta. It is important to dwell upon these, for they also illuminate Cavafy's presence in education, to which I will turn in the next section of this chapter. In his "historical" poems, which drew upon a vast timeline extending from classical antiquity through to the Byzantine Empire, Cavafy delved into core problematics in the formation of Greek identity: the tensions between paganism and Christianity, the rise and fall of political powers, and the redefinition of the Hellenic character in settings of ethnic mixture. There, also, Cavafy was masterful in posing questions without answers and leaving the reader in suspension. Was he a Christian sympathizer? Did he harbor nationalistic sympathies? A definitive interpretation of the belief system evinced in Cavafy's poetry has been as elusive as a definitive interpretation of many of his poems. If contemporary critical tendencies have perceived Cavafy's ironic musings on power as a scathing commentary on the expression of all kinds of nationalistic fervor, the cluster of his so-called Christian poems about the emergence and eventual dominance of the Christian doctrine routinely propelled interest in the poet's personal investment in tradition and religious custom in the first part of the twentieth century.

In 1932, the Greek philologist and historian Konstantinos Dimaras claimed that Cavafy's own "Christian faith . . . cannot be contested" (Dimaras 1932: 86). G. P. Savidis argued that three early poems of Cavafy attested to his piety, his belief in life after death, and in Jesus Christ. In an essay entitled "Was Cavafy Christian?," he urged the reader to "read with retrospective Christian enlightenment every poem by Cavafy that has to do with religion" (Savidis 1985c: 151). Savidis derived additional evidence for Cavafy's siding with Christianity from one of the poet's notes, which rejected "the philosophical ideas of harshness, of the right of the survival of the stronger." In the note, Cavafy had proposed that "not harshness, but Tolerance, Empathy, Allowance, Goodness (in good measure, and not exaggerated), constitute both the Power and the Wisdom" (Cavafy 1983: 49). Unlike Forster, who associated ideas of tolerance and inclusivity with Cavafy's anti-heroic/anti–grand narrative poetic perspective—what he termed Cavafy's interest in "the little men who can't be consistent or maintain their ideals"—Savidis considered the poet's siding with the vulnerable to have been influenced by "the foundational principle of liberal Christian ethics" (Forster [1951] 1983: 41; Savidis [1973] 1985c: 154).

This early, "traditional" version of Cavafy, which encompassed both poetic and personal reverence for Christian doctrine, no doubt resonated with the dictatorship's emphasis on religion as a quintessential marker of national identity. The notion of Christianity as a pillar of Greek national identity had first been introduced with the coinage of the term "Helleno-Christian" (*ellinochristianikos*) by Spyridon Zambelios, a pioneering nineteenth-century romantic historiographer.[14] The concept of Helleno-Christianity subsequently became dominant in Greek discourse, operating as a tool of power and anticommunist propaganda in post–World War II Greece and igniting patriotic sentiment anew by its conversion into the dictatorship's trademark slogan, "Greece for Christian Greeks." The robust association between Cavafy and Christian values intersected with a core tenet of the dictatorship's articulation of national pride and could be seen to account at least partially for Cavafy's enshrinement as an authorial voice appropriate for public discourse and pedagogy during the dictatorial rule.

Moreover, Cavafy's poetic expansion across the temporal landscape of Hellenism distinguished him from his contemporaries. The negotiation of Hellenic temporality and its periodic boundaries had long preoccupied Greek historiography. Zambelios was the first to approach Greek national history through the lens of continuity between classical, medieval, and modern Greek civilization, and to consider the Byzantine Empire as pivotal to this narrative. This restructuring of national time, first articulated in an era when Byzantium was considered incompatible with ancient Greece and the Greek version of the Enlightenment (Dimaras 1982: 376–77), was most influentially achieved later by historian Konstantinos Paparrigopoulos in his multivolume *History of the Greek Nation* (1860–74). The idea of a Hellenic continuum stretching from classical antiquity to modern times, as propagated by these figures during the nineteenth century, was strongly promoted by the dictatorship. Far from being a negligible feature of the junta's legitimizing ideology, it signposted a crucial ideological divergence from the interwar dictatorship of Ioannis Metaxas (1936–41) (for more on the differences between the two regimes, see Kourniakti 2018: 16).

The Metaxas dictatorship rested its nationalistic visions on the tripartite structure of the "Third Hellenic Civilization." This designated periods of Hellenic glory—classical antiquity, the Byzantine Empire, and Metaxas's own regime—but excluded the Hellenistic, Ottoman, and post-1830s periods as "lacking in splendor or grandeur" (Carabott 2003: 29, 31). In contrast, the dictatorship of the Colonels, rather than identifying periods of decline, sought to inculcate through the idea of continuity "a narrative of perpetual Hellenic military and cultural indestructibility" (Kourniakti 2018: 16). In the foremost ideological primer of the dictatorship that was also circulated at high schools during the dictatorship for educational purposes, Theofylaktos Papakonstantinou's *Education of the Citizen* (1970), the Hellenistic period was appreciated as a time of cultural flourishing during which

> the Greek language became a universal language, the Greeks came to play an international role and the sciences, particularly [the fields of] astronomy, mathematics, geography, medicine, and physics, principally advanced by Greeks, became enormously developed, the only comparable [development to which] made its appearance in Europe from the seventeenth century. (Papakonstantinou 1970: 430)

There is significant ideological and historiographic overlap between Cavafy's poetic dealings with the Hellenic continuum—ranging from poems inspired by classical Greece to poems about the Hellenistic and Byzantine eras—and the "well-established grammar of cultural continuity" that the dictatorship inherited from the nineteenth century (Kourniakti 2018: 26). Cavafy's leveling of different periods of Hellenic history served to enliven a long past, and the poet was known to have been inspired by Paparrigopoulos's historiography in doing so. In 1941, the critic Malanos (1990: 90 [Letter 38, 7 December 1941]) reminded Seferis that Cavafy was an avid admirer of Paparrigopoulos, whose influence was evident not only in the depiction of Julian the Apostate, but also in the overall "historical route in [Cavafy's] poetic expression": "Mythological, ancient, Macedonian (Hellenistic), Byzantine, and modern are one and the same Greece. Cavafy offers his own Greek history following the spirit of Paparrigopoulos" (for an early analysis of the Julian poems and their importance for Cavafy's craft, see Bowersock 1981: 89–104). It so happened that Cavafy's personal version of Greek history leaned upon the same source that had also inspired the dictatorship's promotion of an uninterrupted narrative of Hellenic achievement and worth (for the influence of the Byzantine heritage on modern Greek identity, see Ricks and Magdalino 1998).

If Cavafy's "Christian" poems displayed a thematic focus that intersected with the dictatorship's ideology—in Georgalas's (1971: 19) words, the "national-Helleno-Christian progressive Ideology"—the poet's interest in a broad spectrum of Greek history crucially converged with surviving ideas about the importance of indestructible Hellenic continuity. In this case, Cavafy's emphasis upon different periods of Greek history was not valued because, as in Forster's ([1919] 1983: 16) reading, it provided a refreshing alternative to over-rehearsed classicist clichés—the "tyranny of Classicism"— but for the very opposite reason: because the glorious classical past was preserved in its later manifestations. There is a paradox inherent in these contrasting approaches. In Forster's writings, as well as in recent criticism, Cavafy's sense of history has been valued for revitalizing Greek identity by resisting racial purity, nationalistic obsessions, and territorialism. For the dictatorship, the same expansive model functioned as an arena for the enhancement of nationalistic ideas of exceptionalism and national virtue, alongside similarly geared efforts to boost patriotic sentiment through extravagant appropriations of the classics.

The aptitude of Cavafy's work to serve the dictatorship's vision of Hellenism calls for a comparison between the poet's "own Greek history" and the question of "Greekness" as it emerged from major representatives of the Generation of the 1930s, namely, George Seferis, Odysseus Elytis, and George Theotokas. Redefining Greek identity was a major concern for these authors, whose promotion of an ethnocentric national paradigm has led critics to speak of "distinctly national, if not nationalist" preoccupations (Layoun 1990: 13). These authors, engaged as they were in reactivating the Hellenic tradition to redefine modern Greek identity, sensed weakness in Cavafy's work: the decadent space of Alexandria and Cavafy's own reclusive nature were considered to be ill-suited to robust and forward-looking notions of Greek identity. Such concerns informed the controversy surrounding Cavafy in Greece. Seferis (1993: 123) had initially perceived Cavafy's poetic enclosure as entirely stifling and lacking in vitality. This visceral response was later scrutinized by Robert Liddell (1945: 101), who speculated that the Athenian establishment's initial caution toward the poet could be attributed to the dismissal of Cavafy's "mixed language" by fervent supporters of the "demotic," as well as the poet's departure from the "idolatry of the ancients." Of course, factors of literary antagonism and, majorly, the Athenian literary establishment's distaste for Cavafy's sexual orientation contributed to his early rejection. But it is still true that Cavafy's decisive appearance on the scene of Greek letters in the 1920s threw into relief the partiality of Greek modernist authors for themes derived from classical antiquity, but also, crucially, their position in the decades-long and ideologically burdened dispute about which language would become the official language of the Greek state: the Katharevousa ("purist," archaized language) or the demotic (spoken, popular vernacular).

The embattled "language question" was at the center of competing visions of Greek national identity, as well as of competing claims to cultural authority and power prior to the independence of the Greek nation-state in the early eighteenth century and until the fall of the dictatorship in 1974 (Mackridge 2009: 5). Cavafy's work was pulled into these tensions when personalities central to the demoticist camp, such as Jean Psichari, dismissed his hybrid linguistic idiom as an anachronistic, and ultimately failed, experiment (for a list of the intellectuals who expressed a negative option on Cavafy's work in the 1920s, see Karaoglou 1985: 29–30). Cavafy's poetic idiolect—which mixed Katharevousa and demotic Greek—was regarded as artificial and obsolete, a perspective that found forceful articulation by Peter Vlasto, a supporter of the demotic. In 1933, he wrote dismissively of Cavafy as the embodiment of the "new race of undisciplined hybrids arising out of the clash of the orthodox followers of Psichari and of the puristic fossils" (Vlasto 1933; see also review by R. M. Dawkins [1934: 106–7], who disagrees with Vlasto's position). Yet Cavafy's mixed language, which Vlasto protested, suited the junta's program and its institutionalization of "purist," archaized language "as a sign of education, as a status symbol" (Anastasakis 1992: 221). Before the junta's ascent to power, the language controversy "remained a deeply contentious issue" with serious political implications. Demoticism was often regarded as synonymous with communism and was "demonized by nationalists" who, "claiming to be the sole guardians of national values," used the language issue "as an instrument of power and oppression" (Mackridge 2009: 289). By the 1960s, Katharevousa was still the language of officialdom and continued to be used in universities and schools, but the Colonels aggressively pursued a program of its restoration to general use. In doing so, Cavafy's idiolect, maligned by the Generation of the 1930s as it was, provided the junta with a model of cultural achievement in the Katharevousa.

This was not the first time that the entanglement of a dictatorship's political agenda with the primacy of Katharevousa would amount to a positive predisposition toward Cavafy's work in Greece. During the dictatorship of General Theodoros Pangalos (June 1925–August 1926), "authorities made a concentrated effort to link demotic and the demoticist movement with communism, and there was much debate in the press in 1926 between supporters of demotic and supporters of *katharevousa*" (Mackridge 2009: 290). At the same time, the Pangalos dictatorship awarded Cavafy the Silver Medal of the Order of the Phoenix for his contribution to Greek Letters. Picking up where Pangalos had left off, the Colonels' regime would reclaim the link between demoticism and communism, as well as the elevation of the archaized Katharevousa to the "true national language," despite the fact that in 1964 the centrist government of Georgios Papandreou had introduced demotic to all levels of education on equal terms with Katharevousa. The dictatorship reversed these reforms and enshrined the preeminence of Katharevousa in the constitution of 1968, meaning that it was now "not only the official language of the state but also (for the very first time) of education" (Mackridge 2009: 316). Apart from reinstating Katharevousa in general education, the junta also revived the teaching of the Greek classics in the original Ancient Greek (rather than in translation) in secondary schools. This return to traditionalist humanist education created a hospitable arena in which to accommodate Cavafy's language and poetic themes.

Cavafy's linguistic idiom, historical consciousness, religious focus, and didactic content formed a platform that suited core aspects of the dictatorship's ideological derivations from postwar ideology. Not only are these links implied in Cavafy's preferential treatment during the junta, but they must have been particularly effective: Cavafy's poetry, widely read even before the coup, was now presented through a lens that made the dictatorship's rhetoric about the uniqueness of Greek identity, its roots in the Christian tradition, and its definition in contrast to communism further intelligible to the Greek public. This two-way process rests, after all, at the heart of literary appropriation—the paving of new interpretive avenues from which the original emerges in a different light. As I demonstrate in the next section, this process of reinterpretation in accordance with political framing was further compounded by the teaching of Cavafy's poems "Ithaca" and "Thermopylae" in schools, where the celebration of themes and accomplishments derived from ancient texts and history informed overall school culture (Kalamatianos, Lagios, and Stathopoulou-Christofelli 1971: 264–66).

CAVAFY IN SCHOOLS: DEVELOPMENTALISM AND MILITARY CULTURE

The dictatorship reinstated school textbooks from the 1950s as part of their policy to methodically reverse the educational reforms of the Center Union that took place in 1964 and 1965 and to revive the educational apparatus of the anticommunist, postwar state ("Leading Greek Educationalist" 1972: 135–37; Kazamias 1974: vii–15). If Georgalas had forced symbols and extracts from Cavafy's poems into conformity with the message he intended to circulate, Cavafy's poems "Ithaca" and "Thermopylae," the two poems selected for secondary school textbooks before the junta, acquired new meaning under a range of educational policies fraught with militaristic performativity and the ideas about progress and development that the dictatorship was trying to entrench.

Cavafy's poem "Ithaca" rewrites the epic hero Odysseus's adventures in order to elevate the value of the great journey relative to the insignificance of the return to the island. Odysseus is told,

> To arrive there is your final destination.
> But do not rush the voyage in the least.
> Better it last for years.

The didactic premises of Cavafy's retelling of the story gains full force in the final lines of the poem, where the third-person narrator reveals that true value resides in the experience:

> If then you find her poor, Ithaca has not deceived you.
> As wise as you've become, with much experience, by now
> you will have come to know what Ithacas really mean. (Cavafy 2007: 39)

The poem's instructive tone in narrating the story of individual perseverance in the face of adversity, as well as its counsel to prioritize self-development above the attainment of an imagined goal, intersected with the ethos of strife that permeated the dictatorship's developmentalist discourse.

The ideological projections of the military dictatorship as a regime geared toward modernization and fighting for the country appealed to lower-middle-class aspirations of social ascent and emphasized the notion of hard work as the basis of building a prosperous country of the Western world (Poulantzas 1976: 14–15). They also foregrounded continuities with the classical past, by drawing upon archetypal images and scenarios that reflected the heroic mentality of personal development, and taught young people "that their moral debt to their ancient ancestors made industriousness and productivism patriotically necessary" (Kourniakti 2018: 150). In a statement delivered to journalists in 1967, the leading dictator Papadopoulos likened Greece's "progress" to an ever-continuing journey that had begun in ancient times and consisted of "handing over the baton from our generation to the coming [generation]." Centered around the imagery of a relay race, the metaphor conveyed an ongoing process, rather than the safe arrival "at a harbor" (Papadopoulos 1968, vol. 1: 17). Papadopoulos's statement is here particularly resonant with the language of Cavafy's "Ithaca," speaking to the ways in which its popularity had shaped the lexicon of everyday use and informed its adoption by populist rhetoric. Such messages, which articulated developmentalism in agonistic or militaristic language (the "battle for progress," in Georgalas's [1971: 23] words) were directed by Papadopoulos and his confederates toward the education of the younger generations.

The dictatorship's educational reversals retained only a number of core subjects among their offerings at secondary school, one of which was modern Greek literature, and through them aimed "to transmit political messages, national ideals and [to] influence, albeit indirectly, the political education and socialization of future citizens" (Karakatsani 2004: 265–66). In the context of the dictatorship's programmatic reform of secondary education to meet its political and propagandistic agendas, the didactic message of "Ithaca" became all the more pronounced as a conduit to ideal citizenship through interminable effort toward betterment, and in keeping with the ethos of the great predecessors. Conveniently for the junta's educators, two of "Ithaca's" lines that betray debts to the tradition of literary decadence had been censored in the textbooks that the dictatorship reinstated. Among the many instructions to Odysseus, the prompt for him to "acquire . . . sensuous perfumes of every kind / as many sensuous perfumes as you can" detracted from notions of robust masculinity, by bringing aesthetic pleasure and sensuality into focus. The erasure of these lines rendered the new, purified version of the poem all the more suited to the dictatorship's militaristic discourse (see high school textbook Kalamatianos, Lagios, and Stathopoulou-Christofelli 1963: 267–69).

Similarly, "Thermopylae" was apposite to the institutionalization of the militaristic ethos of the regime under the fascist ideological leadership of the dictatorship's hardliners Konstantinos Plevris and Ioannis Ladas (Meletopoulos 2008: 276–77). By dramatizing the famous stand of the Spartans against Xerxes's invading Persian army, the poem shared thematic grounds with the Spartan visions of the youth organization Corps of the Greek Alkimoi. Founded in 1924, Alkimoi had a long history as an anticommunist youth organization of the Far Right before it was brought under the supervision of the General Secretariat of Sports in 1968. By the 1970s, the Corps, which approximated an official dictatorial youth organization, counted twenty thousand members and participated in activities that became increasingly ritualized, including mass spectacles, mass swearing-in ceremonies in stadiums in downtown Athens, and commemorative trips to Thermopylae. After the fall of the dictatorship, it was discovered that the Corps had been supplied with thousands of firearms by the General Secretariat of Sport for the purposes of the formation of a paramilitary group (Kourniakti 2018: 144).

Published in 1973, the first *Book of the Initiate Alkimos* claimed the Corps' origins in the state of ancient Sparta, and went at length to outline the "leading role" that Sparta had played in combatting "the Persian invasion and the danger it posed" with "insurmountable heroism" (Soma Ellinon Alkimon

1973: 5). Cavafy's poem "Thermopylae" brought to life this milestone episode of Spartan bravery and resilience in the face of certain defeat.

> Honour to those who in their life
> set out and guard Thermopylae.
> Never wavering from duty;

Thus the poem begins, extending from a singular event to a celebration of the virtues of loyalty and dedication (Cavafy 2007: 11). Even as the poem proceeds toward a more sinister end, prefiguring betrayal and the inevitable defeat of the Spartans, the dimension of masculine heroic valor and a refusal to yield is significantly aggrandized when framed by the junta's coercion of students to participate in militaristic organizations and performances.

Unlike the selective poetic extraction undertaken by Georgalas, the inclusion of "Ithaca" and "Thermopylae" in school textbooks predated the junta, and therefore did not exclusively operate with strategic propagandistic intention. However, the poems acquired new implications as part of a strategy where taught subjects and materials were meticulously surveyed for their suitability to the dictatorship's revisionist program of militarized education and classical formalism (see, e.g., an analysis of the militarization of physical education during the dictatorship in Giannakopoulos and Albanidis 2015: 1366–67). In the context of a school culture that entailed a series of covert repressions, including the compulsory attendance of the regime's mass spectacles, as well as multivalent manifestations of the dictatorship's affliction of "ancestoritis" (the obsessive return to ancient ancestors) (Clogg 1972: 45), it can be safely surmised that Cavafy's poems were retained and taught partly due to a newly formulated conduciveness to the regime's educational aims and reforms. The selection of these particular poems also served to enhance the poet's image as a patriotic and moralistic Christian Hellene, enabling his other textual and symbolic uses during the dictatorship.

A POET OF BOTH SIDES: CAVAFY IN *EIGHTEEN TEXTS*

This chapter has so far investigated different components of Cavafy's propagandistic appropriation: the manipulation of poetic properties by propagators of both democratic and authoritarian anticommunist rhetoric, as well as the reframing of poems by the dictatorship's right-wing education apparatus. During the same period, Cavafy became the voice of dissent. His work occupied center stage in *Eighteen Texts*, the prime joint act of intellectual resistance against the dictatorship published in 1970 by prominent Greek intellectuals and writers. D. N. Maronitis was the author of an essay on Cavafy which, among seventeen other fictional, poetic, and essayistic works, shed light upon the country's dire state under the dictators. The collected volume is considered a milestone in antidictatorial discourse and has been monumentalized as the most subversive textual event in modern Greek history. It first circulated in three thousand copies, which were sold out within days, leading to numerous reprintings and translations in different languages (Bien 1973).

A university lecturer and literary critic, Maronitis made no secret of his antidictatorial sentiments. He had been made redundant from his university teaching position in 1968 and had been arrested on account of his political beliefs and activity. His essays, including the one on Cavafy, were often explicitly polemical against the junta, leading to his imprisonment in 1973. Maronitis's contribution to *Eighteen Texts* was titled "Arrogance and Intoxication" after a phrase extracted from Cavafy's poem "Darius" and subtitled, parenthetically, "The Poet and History." Ostensibly preoccupied with Cavafy's poetry, Maronitis's (1970) essay addressed the poet's role "at such a critical time" when "the daily word is paid for dearly," a phrasing clearly alluding to the dictatorship's curtailment of free speech.[15] In an inversion of Georgalas's rhetoric about the dictatorship's capacity to liberate Greece from the delusional enclosure of communism, Maronitis (1970: 136) likened the dictatorial background to a "prison" and paid tribute to those who despite the limitations of their captivity spoke out by using "a symbolic warning language, the prisoners' language"—a reference to discursive subtlety in conditions of repression that calls attention to the essay's own cautionary tropes.

Maronitis brings forward Cavafy's poem "Darius," whose poet-protagonist Phernazis remains preoccupied with his poetic craft and the flattery of those in power despite an impending war with the Romans. In Phernazis's behavior, Maronitis (1970: 153) detects an "inability to participate more actively in the historical event, caused by the self-centered psychology of man in general and the poet in particular." A thorough reading of Cavafy's poem by Maronitis reveals that "arrogance and intoxication" may not in fact refer just to King Darius—the subject of Phernazis's poetic interest—but to Phernazis himself. Even further, Maronitis's reader is led to suspect that the essay may not be only or even primarily interested in uncovering the dubious political and historical positioning of Cavafy's fictional poet, but in commenting upon political inactivity and apathy in the present moment of crisis.

The descriptive and seemingly innocuous title *Eighteen Texts* served to camouflage what was in reality "a piercing protest against dictatorship and repression" (Roberts 1977: 2). In the same vein, it is the analysis of Cavafy's poem in Maronitis's essay that sheds new light on the essay's title itself: "arrogance and intoxication" is part of a poetic line-turned-commentary both on the brutality of the dictatorship and the complicity of the apathetic citizen or writer. When Maronitis ultimately calls for Cavafy's poem to be "a good and clear mirror, where all of us—including our poets—can see our reflection," the dual function of his essay as a scholarly analysis of Cavafy's poem and a coded protest becomes fully apparent. And should it not be apparent—for the essay deliberately favors ambiguity, as it merges a disillusioned perspective on modern society with literary criticism—Maronitis (1970: 154) prompts those somehow "puzzled and unsatisfied" by his analysis to remember that "in every effort our first step is self-knowledge. Everything else follows." The transformation of Cavafy's poem into a reflective "mirror" for those living under the dictatorship alerts to an oppressive reality. In this evasive manner, the essay adopts "Darius" to highlight the responsibility of poets and intellectuals at difficult times, the need for collective action, and the power of symbolic language to mobilize dissent.

Maronitis (1970: 139) hastens to add that enlisting Cavafy, rather than any contemporary creator, to communicate "the deep wounds of our collective life" was a necessity: "In this instance, we need poems that do not deliberately belong to 'engaged' poetry, so as not to come against just or unjust prejudices; moreover, we need poems whose identity is known and easily perceived by all; finally, our very recent poetry cannot be deciphered without violent and hasty gestures, and it is useful to avoid these here." Here, the strategic appropriative practices of resistance overlap with those of the dominant discourse, in that by entrusting a recognizable poet of the past, who is safely removed from the murky waters of the present, the message can be projected without the interference of poetic intention or partisanship. All the appropriations of Cavafy considered so far ventured into these conveniently neutral grounds: the poet was dead, but his work was famous; his poems were external to the dictatorship and the Cold War, but lent themselves to didactic allegorizing. Maronitis's use of Cavafy as a prompt to counter oppression may appear apt and even expected today, for it is in keeping with the poet's antiestablishment reputation. This is, however, the very same reputation that has long obscured Cavafy's adoption by dictatorial ideology.[16] In the context of the poet's dictatorial afterlife as presented here, Maronitis's essay reads as a response not only to the dictatorship's repressions, but also, perhaps unwittingly, to the place that Cavafy symbolically deserves outside the "prison" of the Colonels' propaganda, or even as an intellectual weapon against it.

When considering this Cavafy-centered ideological warfare, it is important to note that opposite Maronitis stood not only the official state discourse of the dictatorship, but also scholars of different persuasions. Dimitris Tsakonas, an academic and researcher who enjoyed a symbiotic relationship with the dictatorial establishment, systematically presented Cavafy as emblematic of his proauthoritarian ideas. Considered to be one of the least unsavory of the dictatorship's ideological supporters, Tsakonas "tried to theoretically support the need for authoritarian government" through an idiosyncratic interpretation of the Hellenic past (Meletopoulos 2008: 243, 251). In his work on sociology, he attempted to prove how, unlike other Western countries, Greece had been prevented from undergoing a gradual passage from enlightened despotism to parliamentary democracy due to the Ottoman rule, and was therefore entirely unprepared for democratic governance. Insofar as Tsakonas's political vision entailed strict state control, military intervention, and the strong presence of the Greek Orthodox Church, it shared common grounds with the dictatorship and underpinned his collaboration with Georgalas on projects of anticommunist "national enlightenment" before the coup.[17] However, Tsakonas also distanced himself from the dictators' "official" line about the regime as an ostensible stepping stone toward the reinstatement of democracy, and from their reliance on capitalist and consumerist Western models as a means for progress (Poulantzas 1976: 120; see also Mouzelis 1978: 128–30). He proposed, instead, a system of community governance—an intellectually grounded Platonic Polity—drawing on the Christian Orthodox–inspired ethics of solidarity. For this and for other reasons, Tsakonas was initially sidelined by "the regime in whose favor he had preached," before rising to the positions of deputy minister in 1970 and minister of culture in 1973 (Meletopoulos 2008: 24).

In 1969, Tsakonas published the two-part article "C. Cavafy's Sociology" in a chief organ of prodictatorial ideology, the newspaper *Nea Politeia* (New Polity). In this piece, Cavafy's distance from Greece was considered an asset: the poet's experience as a fallen aristocrat in a decaying Alexandria, his Byzantine-infused spirit, and his measured, ascetic, semi-Europeanized temperament threw the Greeks' "provincialism" into relief. These aspects of Cavafy's life and work highlighted, for Tsakonas, Greece's regressive state, which he attributed to the limited understanding of European powers' intervention in Greek affairs, as well as illusions of grandeur and political mishandlings. According to him, Cavafy's enlightened and "scholarly" poetic language exposed Venizelism and the movement of demoticism (which Tsakonas considered to be interlinked) for what they were: bogus idealizations driven by naïve superstitions and folkloric obsessions that fueled the populist rhetoric of the Megali Idea (Great Idea)[18] and led the country to the Asia Minor defeat (Tsakonas 1969, part 2: 1–2).

The link between Venizelism and demoticism that Tsakonas iterated had become active following the Asia Minor defeat when Venizelist educational reforms reinstated the demotic in primary education. Controversy was ignited, with conservative anti-Venizelists claiming that "demotic was once again being imposed in education by coup d'état" and promoting the view that "there was an unholy alliance between Venizelos and demoticism" (Mackridge 2009: 289). Fueled by this long-standing connection, Tsakonas fashioned Cavafy into a dignified affiliate of Katharevousa, whose intellectual depth and national vision juxtaposed the superficial "chatter" of the demoticists, and as a proponent of an Aristotelian "middle ground," which revealed the "greed" of misguided Venizelist progressives. Not only did Tsakonas (1969, part 2: 1–2) see in Cavafy's cynical immersion a world of transitions and decline a superior, enlightened position, but he also projected on Cavafy's use of ancient words and grammatical forms that were not commonly used in everyday speech his own views on the catastrophic handling of Greek affairs by "barbaric illiterates" who promoted the Megali Idea and subscribed to the "crassness of Venizelism and Demoticism." By emphasizing the national value of Cavafy's linguistic idiom, Tsakonas's pieces reveal just how crucial the language question was for the junta's positive disposition toward Cavafy. In another publication of similar content for the Alexandrian newspaper *Filologikos Tachydromos*, published in 1972, Tsakonas once more describes Cavafy as a "national poet," who can only be adequately understood in connection to a reevaluation of the Greek past.[19] In this way, Cavafy became Tsakonas's own "mirror" for citizen awareness, on premises that were rhetorically commonplace in the dictatorship: the need to end unrest and rectify mistakes of the past, to redefine the Hellenic identity, and to condemn demoticism (and therefore communism) as dangerous and destructive. By hailing Cavafy as a warning voice against disasters of national scale and as a guide for a better future in Greece, Tsakonas, divergent as he was from the dictatorship in terms of his envisioned system of governance, further entrenched the poet in prodictatorial discourse.

Cavafy's assimilation by two scholars at opposite ends of the political spectrum exposes the adaptability of poetry to serve conservative social functions just as well as antiauthoritarian ones: the same art that is domesticated by the discourse of resistance can be turned upside down to assert dictatorial legitimacy, ignite nationalistic sentiment, and vilify opponents. Tsakonas, similarly to Maronitis, advocated through Cavafy an urgent need for social change and political awareness, albeit through a defense of authoritarianism, rather than a plea to resist the dictators. Also, like Maronitis, he instructed his reader to look at the poet and his work for intellectual guidance toward his own definition of sound judgment and citizen responsibility. Unlike Maronitis, however, he did not generate his social critique from the analysis of the ironies and plot twists of Cavafy's poetry. Rather, he found in Cavafy's "outsider" position, rather than in the poetry itself (which is never, in fact, directly quoted), an "enlightened" voice detached enough from the Greek national center and its "provincialisms" to function as an instructive plane for his personal perspective on history, politics, and society. Again, this may constitute evidence that sidestepping layers of signification is a unique feature of proauthoritarian readings. However, misguided or poorly substantiated readings of Cavafy, either more outwardly propagandistic or more obliquely ideological (and the two categories can be blurry), are not exclusive to the dictatorship's turbulent times. Both Seferis and Malanos had transposed their prejudices about homosexuality into the reading of Cavafy's poetry. Equally, the celebrated British author Lawrence Durrell had fictionalized Cavafy into a cipher of his own imperialist and Orientalist imaginings through selective quotation of his poems in *The Alexandria Quartet*. And even critics, Peter Jeffreys (2006: 1) notes, "are guilty of a certain amount of scholarly narcissism as they attempt to fashion Cavafy in their own ideological image and likeness." Even as a host of perspectives on the poet could be accounted for as misreadings or misappropriations, these are unlikely to ignite strong sentiment. "Political" only in a broader sense, their biases are restricted to literary debate. From this point of view, the study of poetry's place within the heated polemics of democratic dissolution is uniquely placed to reveal the political impact of different reading methods. For unless the context is as evidently distasteful as that of the Greek dictatorship, and the appropriators as universally disliked as those affiliated with it, the politics of poetic assimilation can go undetected, gaining momentum without being questioned.

CONCLUSION

The varied instances of appropriation examined here are inextricably tied to the visibility that Cavafy enjoyed through time. The poet's ever-rising posthumous acclaim provided a hospitable arena for readings that corresponded to the fraught ideological fabric of the Cold War and was powerful enough in its appeal to transcend regime type. Methods of selection, extraction, erasure, and adaptation of poetic content to communicate propagandistic messages operated similarly regardless of whether appropriation occurred within a far-right regime or a democratic setting: Sulzberger's anticommunist use of Cavafy was more heavy-handed and partial than Georgalas's dictatorial cooption, even as it was neutralized by its democratic framing and publication by a widely disseminated newspaper (a prime example of the public-facing avenues in which the clandestine mission of the cultural Cold War was couched). Similarly, the reading of Cavafy by Maronitis, a scholar committed to the antidictatorial struggle, instantly appears more legitimate than that of Tsakonas due to its very politics: it fulfills art's promise for the advancement of hope and for social betterment in conditions of dictatorial repression. However, precisely because in such cases textual manipulation is likely to be a priori considered rightful, the extent to which Maronitis appealed to literature in an inherently different manner to Tsakonas needs to be tested in its own right if we are to distinguish the internal workings of textual reception from the politics that best serve or affirm our preferred cause.

The poet Seamus Heaney's reflections on the age-old question of poetry's place in a world of both "governments" and "revolutionaries" are helpful here. In his collection of lectures *The Redress of Poetry*, Heaney embarked from the tumultuous backdrop of Northern Ireland to explore "the frontier of writing." By this, he meant the contested border that separates "the actual conditions of our daily life" from "the imaginative representation of those conditions in literature," and "the world of social speech" from "the world of poetic language" (Heaney 2010: 18). The question that emerges from Heaney's theorization of the frontier, and with which he grapples, is the difference between "applied" poetry, which intends to express a political position, and poetry that engages with the world indirectly:

> Poetic fictions, the dream of alternative worlds, enable governments and revolutionaries as well. It's just that governments and revolutionaries would compel society to take on the shape of their imagining, whereas poets are typically more concerned to conjure with their own and their readers' sense of what is possible or desirable or, indeed, imaginable. (Heaney 2010: 25)

Heaney is sympathetic toward a demand for poetry that would meet the immediate needs of "the field of force" of political activism. Indeed, this could be one way to approach the "redress of poetry"—meaning poetry's instrumental role in correcting imbalances and providing answers. However, he also warns that a balance-tipping could be effected when "engaged parties" expect poetry "to be an exercise of leverage on behalf of their point of view ... [and] the entire weight of the thing to come down on their side of the scales" (Heaney 2010: 18). In this case, poetry is valued less for its "distinctly linguistic means" and more for its immediate function, and is therefore at risk of losing its "artistic integrity" (Heaney 2010: 35).

Heaney's deliberations on the relation between engaged art and artistic autonomy presuppose authorial intention. Nevertheless, as Cavafy's case demonstrates (and as Maronitis points out by reaching for poems that "do not deliberately belong to 'engaged' poetry"), the question changes in nature when refocused on the textual politics of reception. What happens when "meaning" becomes constantly reinvented through the process of reading? In such cases, the poet does not seek to exercise "leverage on behalf of their point of view" (Heaney 2010: 25); it is, rather, appropriation that may divest poetry of its relative autonomy and ambivalence to serve conservative social functions just as well as progressive ones, authoritarian functions just as well as dissenting ones. If reality is a "labyrinth" whose "impassibility is countered by the poet's imagining some equivalent of the labyrinth and bringing himself and the reader through it" (and we may think here of Cavafy's "walls" and "windows" as such imaginings), then a partisan appropriation of poetry may strip it from this labyrinthine quality to best achieve its propagandistic aims (Heaney 2010: 27). If the "answer" of poetry needs to be offered in "its own language, rather than in the language of the world that provokes it," then surely the assimilation of poetic discourse in the language of politics or journalism may detract from its artistic potential (Heaney 2010: 428).

The terms introduced here—especially "leverage" vis-à-vis the poem's "artistic integrity"—have implications for our quest for optimal reception strategies. Much of the conflict between poetry and world, as Heaney understands it, plays out as blindness toward emotional complexity, and in favor of ideological structures. This is pertinent to Cavafy: his characters, often engrossed in conflicts against the world and history, can be flattened out by a failure to experience "antithetical pairings . . . as emotional dilemmas [rather] than as doctrinal cruces" (Heaney 2010: 44; for example, in poems inspired by the history and vocabulary of Christianity). Perhaps paradoxically, the conditions of strict dictatorial control under which Maronitis's essay was written necessitated encoding that preserved the poetic language. Even as the critic deploys Cavafy with an evident aim to unsettle power and protest censorship, the poem "Darius" is presented in its entirety and analyzed within a stand-alone section, separate to the one that connects the poem to current predicaments. As a result, the reader is guided, through historical and literary analysis, to independently unpick the layers of "Darius," as well as Phernazis's reckoning with power and the emotional journey he undergoes. This invitation for the reader's textual engagement undermines the primacy of Maronitis's outlook, for it does not altogether preclude other interpretative possibilities. It is then on grounds of the reader's guided immersion in the "equivalent labyrinth" of Phernazis's confusion amid social upheaval, rather than just the "labyrinth" of the dictatorship, that the poetry's "artistic integrity" is defended in ways that it is not in Tsakonas's writings.

Cavafy as the poet "of both sides" remains relevant in an era where walls are erected in the shape of "echo chambers"—vastly populated spaces of discursive circularity that fence off our belief systems from positions other than our own. The Alexandrian's case works as a forceful reminder that literature we feel attached to, and which we have come to think of as "canonical," exists diffusely in the world, a source that can be detached from authorial intention and oriented toward unpredictable directions in the public sphere. Free and unprotected, especially when their author can no longer speak on their behalf or safeguard their posterity, even the most treasured poems can take on lives that operate through politically variable distortions, transformations, and adjustments of the original. Employing the vicissitudes of the embezzlement of Cavafy's poetry by the junta to chart other instances of ideological reading strategies (some of which may equally fall into the categories of misreading or misappropriation) urges us to rethink reception on textual grounds, and to seek, on those grounds, indications of integrally flawed or biased interpretative practice. Since politics are open to contestation, and potential readings are infinite, textual criticism is ultimately tasked with testing not merely the political legitimacy of the claim, but also how much of the poetry survives after the "leverage" that burdens reception has been exercised.

Foteini Dimirouli holds a BA (Athens) and MA (Durham) in English literature, as well as a DPhil in comparative literature (Oxford). Her thesis, titled "Cavafy Hero: Literary Appropriations and Cultural Projections of the Poet in English and American Literature," engages with the politics of textual dissemination and cultural legitimation that underpinned C. P. Cavafy's rising literary celebrity during the twentieth century. A revised version of her doctoral dissertation is forthcoming as a monograph by Oxford University Press. Foteini's research interests lie in the fields of Greek, English, and American literature, as well as their intersections during the modernist period. She has taught extensively in the above areas at Oxford University and has published papers on related topics. She is currently early career development fellow at Keble College, Oxford.

NOTES

This chapter could not have been written without the support and expertise of Jessica Kourniakti. I am also indebted to Peter Mackridge, David Ricks, Mark Fisher, and Stratis Bournazos for their invaluable feedback on the early drafts of this work.

1. Saunders (1999: 1) provides a comprehensive account of America's cultural propaganda during the Cold War and argues that "a central feature of this program was to advance the claim that it did not exist" (see also Caute 2003; Iber 2019).
2. A recent strand of criticism has focused on the American cultural cold war and its connections with cultural diplomacy in Greece, mostly in the period leading to the dictatorship (for example, by scholars S. Bournazos, A. Adamopoulou, D. Lalaki, and G. Koutsopanagou). For an overview that includes the period of the dictatorship, see Laliouti 2019.
3. Scholarship about the junta's appropriation of the classics includes Van Steen 2015, which examines how the "Festivals of the Military Virtue of the Greeks" invested in the popular currency of the classical past, and Kourniakti 2018, which surveys how the classical past became a valuable resource to further the political ends of the dictators.
4. The first *Book Index* blacklisted Marxist texts and Russian literature, modern writers (ranging from Giannis Ritsos and Vasilis Vasilikos to Jean-Paul Sartre, T. S. Eliot, and Albert Camus), certain works of Aristotle, classical drama translated or staged by politically "suspect" Greek personalities, as well as a number of studies by classical philologists and historians (for example, those touching on the topic of ancient Greek homosexuality) (Van Steen 2015: 97–99).
5. Georgalas was born in 1928 in Cairo, Egypt. He was introduced to Marxism from a young age and was consistently involved in communist politics before gaining expertise in propaganda on behalf of the Communist Party in Hungary. He abandoned communism in 1956, after the Hungarian Revolution, and returned to Greece. From 1958, he became involved with the Greek armed forces on matters of propaganda, this time from a fiercely anticommunist, nationalist position. Between 1960 and 1964, he was the editor and main contributor of *Sovietologia* (Sovietology), an anticommunist monthly periodical dedicated to combatting the "red totalitarian forces." His official positions and public engagement posts for the Greek Armed Forces entailed the delivery of seminars on Sovietology, presentation of radio broadcasts, and specialization in matters of psychological warfare. During the military dictatorship, Georgalas actively took up initiatives in the sector of Press and Information. From June 1970 to August 1971, he became deputy prime minister on the side of Papadopoulos, the leading colonel of the junta. He was also a prolific author of books on Greek history and national ideology.
6. Georgalas had been brought up as a member of the Greek community in Egypt. This background, as well as his eventual siding with the dictatorship, introduces grounds for new research on Cavafy's symbolic role as a link between mainland Greeks and the Greek community of Egypt, especially given the latter's favorable predisposition toward the dictatorship and its governance.
7. In 1968, Faidros Barlas published a piece titled "Poor Cavafy!" in the predictatorial newspaper *Nea Politeia* on the occasion of the publication of Cavafy's unpublished poems by Savidis in 1968. His piece focuses on the ethics around

posthumous manipulation of archival material, and Barlas (1968: 3) indirectly criticizes Savidis (albeit without mentioning him by name) for attempting to partake of Cavafy's "glory" by setting his posterity at risk. Savidis resigned in 1971 from his university lectureship at Aristotle University of Thessaloniki, in protest against the dictatorship's interferences in academic matters. He returned in 1974, after the junta's fall.

8. In the 1920s, for instance, Cavafy's first translator, George Valassopoulo, had gone so far as to refuse to translate Cavafy's "erotic" poems, which he referred to as "lurid" in a letter to E. M. Forster almost two decades later; see Valassopoulo 2009 (Letter to E. M. Forster, 2 February 1944).

9. More recently, "Walls" was theorized in terms of the politics of the closet by Eve Kosofsky Sedgwick (2011: 56).

10. In 1949, Georgalas, who was at the time a communist, wrote the article "About Cavafy and His Work" ("Guro apo ton Kavafi kai to Ergo tou") in an Egyptian newspaper where he lauded Cavafy as a "great poet" despite his lack of interest in national themes. For him, "the poet of 'the Walls'" was a poet of "the mud," "the swamp," and "the rotten," whose creative gifts were lodged in the uniquely "human" outlook of the marginal and the outcast. It seems that Georgalas's affection for Cavafy persisted throughout his conversion from communism to fervent anticommunism, and eventually prodictatorial ideology. However, the tract shows that Georgalas's account of Cavafy's vision changed to accord with his own ideological transformation. Whereas initially he praised Cavafy for being attentive to the festering underbelly of society, in 1969 he was offering the dictatorship as a tangible answer, a promise of hope and national blossoming that Cavafy's poetic world altogether lacked. The piece was published in two parts under the pseudonym Giannis Aigalitis ("Για τον Καβάφη και το Έργο του" [About Cavafy and his work]," unknown Egyptian newspaper, 2 and 3 May 1949, ELIA archive). Identification of Aigalitis with Georgalas is documented by a few sources, among which is Daskalopoulos 2003; however, Daskalopoulos mistakenly records dates of publication as 3 and 4 May 1949.

11. A journalist and chief foreign correspondent for the *New York Times* during the 1940s and 1950s, Sulzberger was a member of the powerful family that owned the newspaper. Well-connected within political circles, he was known for his anticommunist sentiments, and in 1977 was accused by the journalist Carl Bern-stein (1977: 59) for complicity in Cold War operations and links to the CIA that went "far beyond those normally maintained between reporters and their sources." In 1942, Sulzberger married a Greek woman, Marina Tatiana Lada, and remained well acquainted with, and vocal about, Greek politics.

12. Note that the Communist Party of Greece (KKE) was outlawed in 1947 and remained banned until 1974.

13. The Greek variant of Cold War anticommunism, known as *ethnikofrosyni* (national mindedness), first gained currency in Greece during the interwar period but acquired a new dimension of organized hostility after World War

II and especially during and after the Greek Civil War. Its discursive fabric included spreading, through various practices, a "set of negative myths and stereotypes intended to portray the Greek Left as a segment of society divested of its 'Greekness' and thereby from the body of the Greek nation" (Kazamias 2014: 128).

14. The term is found in the introduction to a short Greek collection of folk songs published in 1852 (Dimaras 1982: 378).
15. References here are to the translated edition (Maronitis 1972: 117).
16. Outside Greece, for example, a generation of Anglophone poets of the 1960s and 1970s turned to Cavafy as they were seeking poetic expressions from the margins and voices of dissent (Dimirouli 2017).
17. Georgalas and Tsakonas were members of the nationalist "Greek Educational Society," which was founded in 1957 and circulated a number of anticommunist publications to schools and repressive institutions, such as the army and the police.
18. The Megali Idea (Μεγάλη Ιδέα, Great Idea) was an irredentist concept of Greek nationalism that aimed at claiming historically Greek-inhabited areas through territorial expansion. It was dominant in the mid-nineteenth century and in its most utopian form came to represent a revival of the Byzantine Empire through Greater Greece, with Constantinople (Istanbul in Turkish) as its capital. The Liberal Party politician and prime minister of Greece Eleftherios Venizelos (1910–20 and 1928–33), a charismatic figure who enjoyed widespread popularity, was credited with securing the expansion of the country's northern frontiers after World War I and for keeping alive the hope of pursuing the Megali Idea. The national imagining of a broader Greece came to a halt with the defeat of the Greek forces in Asia Minor in 1922 and the subsequent signing of the Treaty of Lausanne in 1923.
19. Tsakonas, "Ο Αλεξανδρινός Καβάφης και η Μεγάλη Ιδέα" [The Alexandrian Cavafy and the Great Idea], *Filologikos Tachydromos*, 1972, ELIA archive.

REFERENCES

Periodicals

Epitheorisi Technis
Filologikos Tachydromos
Kainouria Epochi
Nea Estia
Nea Politeia
Nea Techni
New York Times
Rolling Stone

Archives

Athens, Greece
Hellenic Literary and Historical Archive (ELIA)

Secondary Sources

Anastasakis, O. E. 1992. "Authoritarianism in 20th Century Greece: Ideology and Education under the Dictatorships of 1936 and 1967." PhD diss., London School of Economics and Political Science, University of London, UK.
"Athenian" [R. Roufos]. 1972. *Inside the Colonels' Greece*. Translated and with an introduction by R. Clogg. London.
Barlas, F. 1968. "Kaimene Kavafi!" [Poor Cavafy!]. *Nea Politeia*, 11 December 1968, 3.
Bernstein, C. 1977. "The CIA and the Media." *Rolling Stone*, 20 October 1977, 55–67.
Bowersock, G. W. 1981. "The Julian Poems of C. P. Cavafy." *Byzantine and Modern Greek Studies* 7: 89–104.
Bien, P. 1973. "Arrogance and Intoxication: A Review of Eighteen Texts." *Boundary 2* 1(2): 524–36.
Carabott, P. 2003. "Monumental Visions: The Past in Metaxas' 'Weltanschauung.'" In *The Usable Past: Greek Metahistories*, edited by K. S. Brown and Y. Hamilakis, 23–37. Lanham.
Caute, D. 2003. *The Dancer Defects: The Struggle for Cultural Supremacy during the Cold War*. Oxford.
Cavafy, C. P. (1975) 1992. *Collected Poems*. Translated by E. Keeley and P. Sherrard and edited by G. Savidis. Princeton.
———. 1983. *Anekdota simeiomata poiitikis kai ithikis* [Unpublished notes on poetics and ethics]. Athens.
———. 1987. "O Kavafis scholiazei kai analyei ta 'Keria' (1973)" ["Cavafy comments upon and analyzes 'Candles' (1973)"]. In *Mikra Kavafika* [Essays on Cavafy], vol. 2, edited by G. Savidis, 162–65. Athens.
———. 2007. *The Collected Poems of C. P. Cavafy, with Parallel Greek Text*. Translated by E. Sachperoglou and edited by A. Hirst and P. Mackridge. Oxford.
Clogg, R. 1972. "The Ideology of the 'Revolution of 21 April.'" In *Greece under Military Rule*, edited by R. Clogg and G. Yannopoulos, 36–58. London.
Daskalopoulos, D. 2003. "Note Δ980." In *Vivliografia K. P. Kavafi* [C. P. Cavafy's bibliography], 625. Athens.
Dawkins, R. M. 1934. "Review of Vlastos 1933." *Journal of Hellenic Studies* 54: 106–7.
Dimaras, K. T. 1932 "Merikes piges tis Kavafikis technis" [Sources for Cavafy's poetry]. *O Kyklos* 2(3–4): 69–86.
———. 1982. *Ellinikos Romantismos* [Greek Romanticism]. Athens.
Dimirouli, F. 2017. "A View on the Greek Dictatorship from the 'Lighthouse' of *The New York Review of Books* (1967–1974)." *Journal of Modern Greek Studies* 35: 369–96.

———. 2022. *Authorising the Other: C. P. Cavafy in the English and American Literary Scenes*. Oxford.
Forster, E. M. (1919) 1983. "The Poetry of C. P. Cavafy." In *The Mind and Art of C. P. Cavafy: Essays on His Life and Work*, 13–18. Athens.
———. (1951) 1983. "The Complete Poetry of C. P. Cavafy." In *The Mind and Art of C. P. Cavafy: Essays on His Life and Work*, 40–45. Athens.
Georgalas, G. 1971. *I Ideologia tis Epanastaseos: Ochi dogmata alla ideodi* [The ideology of the revolution: Ideals, not dogmas]. Athens.
Giannakopoulos, A., and E. Albanidis. 2015. "Attempts at the Militarization of Physical Education and Sport during the Dictatorship Period in Greece, 1967–1974." *International Journal of the History of Sport* 32(11–12): 1359–77.
Halim, H. 2013. *Alexandrian Cosmopolitanism: An Archive*. New York.
Heaney, S. 2010. *The Redress of Poetry: Oxford Lectures*. London.
Iber, P. 2019. "The Cultural Cold War." *Oxford Research Encyclopedias: American History*. Retrieved 19 November 2020 from https:/doi.org/10.1093/acrefore/97801 99329175.013.760.
Jeffreys, P. 2005 *Eastern Questions: Hellenism and Orientalism in the Writings of E. M. Forster and C. P. Cavafy*. Greensboro, NC.
———. 2006. "Cavafian Catoptromancy." Paper presented at Modern Greek First Online Roundtable: Cavafy, University of Michigan, Ann Arbor, February. Retrieved 19 November 2020 from https://lsa.umich.edu/content/dam/modgreek-assets/modgreek-docs/CPC_Jeffreys_Cavafiancatoptromancy.pdf.
Kalamatianos, G., I. Lagios, and M. Stathopoulou-Christofelli. 1963. *Neoellinika anagnosmata ST' Gymnasiou* [High school textbook]. 2nd ed. Athens.
———. 1971. *Neoellinika anagnosmata ST' Gymnasiou* [High school textbook]. 9th ed. Athens.
Karakatsani, D. 2004. "The History of Citizenship Education in Greece during the Post-war Period (1950–1990): Content and Aims." In *Childhood in South East Europe: Historical Perspectives on Growing Up in the 19th and 20th Century*, edited by S. Naumovic and M. Jovanovic, 265–76. Munster.
Karaoglou, C. L. 1985. *I Athinaiki kritiki kai o Kavafis (1918–1924)* [Athenian criticism and Cavafy (1918–24)]. Thessaloniki.
Kazamias, A. 2014. "Antiquity as Cold War Propaganda: The Political Uses of the Classical Past in Post–Civil War Greece." In *Re-imagining the Past: Antiquity and Modern Greek Culture*, edited by D. Tziovas, 128–46. Oxford.
Kazamias, A. M. 1974. *Education and Modernization in Greece*. U.S. Department of Health, Education, and Welfare, Office of Education, Bureau of Research, No. 7-1111. Washington, DC.
Keys, B. 2012. "Anti-torture Politics: Amnesty International, the Greek Junta, and the Origins of Human Rights 'Boom' in the United States." In *The Human Rights Revolution*, edited by A. Iriye, P. Goedde, and W. I. Hitchcock, 201–22. Oxford.
Kosofsky Sedgwick, E. 2011. "Cavafy, Proust, and the Queer Little Gods." In *The Weather in Proust*, edited by J. Goldberg, 42–68. Durham, NC.

Kourniakti, J. 2018. "The Classical Asset: Receptions of Antiquity under the Dictatorship of 21 April in Greece (1967–73)." DPhil thesis, University of Oxford, U.K.
Laliouti, Z. 2019. *O "Allos Psychros Polemos"* [The "other Cold War"]. Heraklion.
Layoun, M. H. 1990. "Introduction." In *Modernism in Greece? Essays on the Critical and Literary Margins of a Movement*, 9–20. New York.
"Leading Greek Educationalist." 1972. "Traditionalism and Reaction in Greek Education." In *Greece under Military Rule*, edited by R. Clogg and G. Yannopoulos, 128–47. London.
Liddell, R. 1945. "Cavafy." In *Personal Landscape: An Anthology of Exile*, edited by R. Fedden, 100–7. London.
Mackridge, P. 2009. *Language and National Identity in Greece, 1766–1976*. Oxford.
Malanos, T. 1980. *O Kavafis*. Athens.
Maronitis, D. N. 1970. "Yperopsia kai methi (O poiitis kai i istoria) [Arrogance and exultation (The poet and history)]. In *Dekaochto keimena* [Eighteen texts], 135–54. Athens.
———. 1972. "Arrogance and Intoxication: The Poet and History in Cavafy." In *Eighteen Texts*, translated and edited by W. Barnstone, 117–34. Cambridge, MA.
McKinsey, M. 2010. *Hellenism and the Postcolonial Imagination: Yeats, Cavafy, Walcott*. Madison, NJ.
Merrill, J. 1975. "Marvelous Poet." Review of *Cavafy, A Critical Biography*, by R. Liddell, and *C. P. Cavafy: Collected Poems*, translated by E. Keeley and P. Sherrard. *New York Review of Books* 22(12), 17 July.
Meletopoulos, M. 2008. *I diktatoria ton syntagmatarchon: Koinonia, ideologia, oikonomia* [The Colonels dictatorship: Society, ideology, economy]. Athens.
Mikedakis, E. 2007. "Renouncing the Recent Past, 'Revolutionising' the Present and 'Resurrecting' the Distant Past: Lexical and Figurative Representations in the Political Speeches of Georgios Papadopoulos (1967–73)." PhD diss., University of New South Wales, Sydney, Australia.
Mouzelis, N. P. 1978. *Modern Greece: Facets of Underdevelopment*. London.
Papadopoulos, G. 1968. *To pistevo mas* [Our creed]. Vol. 1. Athens.
Papakonstantinou, T. 1970. *Politiki agogi* [Citizen's education]. Athens.
Papanikolaou, D. 2014. "Mapping/Unmapping: The Making of Queer Athens." In *Queer Cities, Queer Cultures: Europe Since 1945*, edited by M. Cook and J. V. Evans, 151–70. London.
Poulantzas, N. 1976. *The Crisis of the Dictatorships: Portugal, Greece, Spain*. Translated by D. Fernbach. London.
Ricks, D., and P. Magdalino. 1998. *Byzantium and the Modern Greek Identity*. London.
Ritsos, Y. 1963. *12 poiimata gia ton Kavafi* [*12 poems about Cavafy*]. Athens.
Roberts, S. V. 1977. "With Military Junta Gone, Poetry in Greece is Reaching Floodtide." *New York Times*, 10 February.
Savidis, G. P. 1985a. "To archeio tou K. P. Kavafi (1963)" [C. P. Kavafi's archive (1963)]. In *Mikra Kavafika* [Essays on Cavafy], vol. 1, edited by G. Savidis, 31–35. Athens.

———. 1985b. "I politiki aisthisi ston Kavafi" [The political feeling in Cavafy's work]. In *Mikra Kavafika* [Essays on Cavafy], vol. 1, edited by G. Savidis, 101–24. Athens.

———. 1985c. "Itan Christianos o Kavafis? (1973)" [Was Cavafy Christian? (1973)]. In *Mikra Kavafika* [Essays on Cavafy], vol. 1, edited by G. Savidis, 147–54. Athens.

Seferis, G. 1993. *O Kavafis tou Seferi* [Seferis's Cavafy]. Edited by G. P. Savidis. Athens.

Soma Ellinon Alkimon. 1973. *To vivlio tou protopeirou Alkimou* [The book of the Alkimos novice]. Athens.

Stonor Saunders, F. 1999. *The Cultural Cold War: The CIA and the World of Arts and Letters*. New York.

Sulzberger, C. L. 1966. "Foreign Affairs: The Bourgeois Barbarians." *New York Times*, 7 October 1966.

Tsakonas, D. 1969. "I koinoniologia tou K. Kavafi" [C. Cavafy's sociology]. Parts 1–2. *Nea Politeia*, 7–8 August.

Tsirkas, S. 1958. *O Kavafis kai I epochi tou* [Cavafy and his time]. Athens.

———. 1959. "Ta teichi enos kritikou kai i techni tou Kavafi" [The walls of a critic and Cavafy's art] *Kainouria Epochi* (Winter): 1–14.

Valassopoulos, G. 2009. "Letter to E. M. Forster, 2 February 1944." In *The Forster-Cavafy Letters: Friends at a Slight Angle*, edited by Peter Jeffreys, 112. Cairo.

Van Steen, G. 2015. *Stage of Emergency: Theater and Public Performance under the Greek Military Dictatorship of 1967–1974*. Oxford.

Vlasto, P. 1933. *Greek Bilingualism and Some Parallel Cases*. Athens.

Chapter 7

Religion Enchained
The Church of Greece under the Military Junta

Charalampos Andreopoulos and Athanasios Grammenos

THE CHURCH OF GREECE

With the conclusion of the Greek War of Independence, the Greek people achieved political independence but were governed spiritually by the Ecumenical Patriarchate of Constantinople (Istanbul). The territory covered by the newly established Kingdom of Greece (1832) remained under the canonical jurisdiction of the Ecumenical Patriarchate and was ruled by local dioceses (metropolitanates). These ecclesiastical units were subjected to the canon laws of the Holy See and were conceived by and accountable to the Holy and Sacred Synod of the Ecumenical Patriarchate.

However, the Bavarian regency council, appointed to rule Greece until King Otto of Bavaria reached his maturity, orchestrated the wresting of those dioceses from the control of the Patriarchate—an act that led to the formation of an autocephalous Greek Orthodox Church in 1833 (Roudometof 2010: 21–38; Nanakis 2013: 261–64). Given the significance of the Orthodox faith for the people of Greece, the Bavarians aimed to keep the Church under their political control, and they did so with two more provisions: first, the king himself was named the Head of Church, despite the paradox that he was Roman Catholic; second, the Greek Holy Synod would be appointed by the king, and it would include a secular member—the royal commissioner—with executive responsibilities. Practically, that meant that the king had the power to veto the hierarchy's decisions. In addition to these measures, the election of the archbishop was also a privilege of the monarch.

The Holy Synod would submit three names of bishops to the monarch from which he would make his selection. Therefore, the creation of Greece's autocephalous Church was not only uncanonical, but it was also established in a manner that would facilitate political interventions by subsequent secular leaders. This framework did not benefit the Church; the ability of the Crown to influence the Church's leadership and make it partisan led to frictions, especially in the early twentieth century during the period of the National Schism (1915–17).

The Ecumenical Patriarchate reacted immediately to this violation of the Holy Canons by refusing to have communion with Athens. After almost two decades, however, the tensions were eased, and Constantinople accepted the fait accompli. On 29 June 1850, the Church of Greece was recognized as an autocephalous church, with a proclamation, or synodal tome, that provided the context for its administration (Geromichalos 1981). Shortly thereafter in 1852, the Greek state issued two laws that largely complied with the patriarchal proclamation (Stragkas 1969–87, vol. 2). According to these laws, the provisions set by the regency council in 1833, recognizing the king as the supreme authority of the Church, were no longer valid. From that moment on, the Holy Synod, consisting of five bishops, was running the Church. However, the critical role of the royal commissioner was maintained, along with the procedure of electing bishops by the king. In essence, the Church continued to operate under the restraints of the political authority.

In the twentieth century, the Church was the casualty of political intervention from every authoritarian regime that ruled the country, beginning with General Theodoros Pangalos and his short-lived regime (1925–26), followed by the dictatorship of Ioannis Metaxas (1936–41), who used the above provisions to put the Church under "general surveillance" (Andreopoulos 2017: 69–75) in his rather ambitious effort to launch the Third Hellenic Civilization (for the ideology of the regime, see Gazi 2011). This suggestion had its roots in the second half of the nineteenth century (Skopetea 1988: 133), when the irredentist concept of the Megali Idea (Μεγάλη Ιδέα) for the restoration of the Eastern Roman (Byzantine) Empire was very popular and remained alive in the beliefs and the manifestations of the conservative circles of Greek society into the twentieth century. The military junta of 1967–74 exceeded the degree of interference by the previous dictatorships, leading to an unprecedented control in the name of the "Church's salvation" (Konidaris 2014). While the Colonels attempted to exploit the Church for their political and ideological purposes, Archbishop Ieronymos I (Kotsonis) exploited and undermined his own authority by reforming the administration of the Church and its elected synod in a manner that violated canon law.[1]

THE IDEOLOGY OF THE MILITARY DICTATORSHIP

As already discussed in this volume, the Colonels enacted a coup on 21 April 1967 that was self-tasked with bringing order, promoting their notion of a Greco-Christian Civilization, and eliminating the communist risk (Vryonis 1969: 7). In principle, they thought of their intervention as a *salus populi* project. Colonel Georgios Papadopoulos, one of the coup leaders, declared the regime's ideology in a speech titled "Our Belief" (Andreopoulos 2017: 45–50), which was later published and distributed in a seven-volume edition with other political material. "Our Belief" became a central tool of propaganda that attempted to outline a solid ideological foundation for what they called the "Revolution" (Woodhouse 1985).

In the preface, Papadopoulos articulated his rather vague vision for Greece and its people, although it is highly doubtful whether the regime had a clear set of principles that could constitute a political platform (Close 2014: 115–17). The two ideological pillars in Papadopoulos's scheme were (a) anticommunism and (b) the rise of Greco-Christian Civilization, which echoed Metaxas's grandiose plans. Most of the Colonels had begun their military career when Metaxas was in power and were heavily influenced by his ideas. In addition, after World War II, they became members of IDEA (Ιερός Δεσμός Ελλήνων Αξιωματικών, Sacred Bond of Greek Officers), an ultraconservative secret group of officers that attempted a coup d'état against the elected government in 1952. Thus, the term "Greek Christianity" echoed not only the sentiments and youthful influence of Metaxas but also was ideal for expressing the ideology of the regime, since it was appealing to the emotions not only of the dictators but also of a significant part of Greek society, as well, including individuals and members of Christian organizations. Essentially, control over the Church would mean the ability to influence its constituents and expand the junta's outreach in a desired way. In this sense, Education Minister Konstantinos Kalampokias said that the Church is "the soul of the nation" (Stragkas 1969–87, vol. 7: 4902). As Richard Clogg (1972: 36–40) has critically argued, however, this was likely nothing but a "pseudo-ideology," roughly built by the Colonels in order to provide moral ground for the dictatorship and its practices.

Nonetheless, the Greco-Christian ideology was wrapped up with the motto "Greece of Christian Greeks" and the reawakening of the old triptych "Homeland-Religion-Family" in order to allow the dictatorship to appear as both the guarantors of the traditional values of the Greeks and the opponents of communist principles. With these inspirational slogans, the government sealed its political rhetoric, which idolized the past and glorified the present and future of the nation through the work of the army and the

Church (Mikedakis 2007). Above all, it sent a powerful signal of continuity of the post–Greek Civil War state ideology, which was predominantly anticommunist and anti-Left. At the same time, the junta also rejected the prospect of Greece as a European nation, which was an idea that had failed to unite and inspire the people, necessitating a new source of social motivation. Colonel Stylianos Pattakos (1968: 436), vice president of the government, argued that

> [Greece's former] leadership had ignored its own spring, ancient but always lifegiving spring, drinking from sources that have nothing new for Greece. It was imperative for the army to come to the political realm, to lead us again to the spring with the national wisdom.... The spirit of Greco-Christian Civilization's worldview defines the spirit of our Revolution, too.

The Greco-Christian Civilization, as a nationalist project, was extended to every Greek, living both within and outside of Greece. The junta leaders sought to capitalize on this vision by courting recognition and support from Greeks abroad. An ideal opportunity for them was presented in 1968, when the Greek Orthodox Archdiocese of North and South America decided to hold its biannual clergy-laity congress in Athens; in fact, the reason Archbishop Iakovos (Koukouzis) decided to go to Athens was due to Greek American interest in expressing their solidarity to relatives in Greece and giving them courage in a difficult time (Malouchos 2002: 74). The archdiocese was an eparchy of the Ecumenical Patriarchate, and given the size and the social status of the Greek American community, Istanbul relied heavily on it. The decision to hold the conference in Athens provided an opportunity for both the junta and the Greek Orthodox Church.

The Colonels, from their side, tried to capitalize on the benefits of this rare occasion, especially by gaining international publicity and presenting themselves as defenders of Orthodoxy. The Greek American delegation was welcomed at the airport by Archbishop Ieronymos and a number of high officials before Papadopoulos later greeted them in his office, surrounded by photographers and reporters. On 22 July, the official opening ceremony took place, and as Alexander Kitroeff points out in his chapter, Papadopoulos was there to receive the audience and make two proposals revealing the spirit of his ideology: first, he suggested that all future congresses be held in Greece because "the Greek Orthodox Church and the Greek Nation were identical" (see the contribution of Alexander Kitroeff in the present volume); and, second, to rename the congress as "the Assembly of the Nation."[2] Apparently, neither of these was possible, but Papadopoulos's maximalist ideas were an effort to display the junta as a guardian of any Greek Orthodox institution in or out of Greece.

THE JUNTA'S DESIGNATIONS FOR THE CHURCH

Within a month of the coup, the junta leaders put in motion their plan for occupying the Church in order to use it for their political and ideological purposes. Emergency Law 3/1967, issued on 10 May, suspended the active canonical law, distorted the spirit of the Church's Statutory Charter in the sense that it politicized ecclesiastical affairs, and imposed an authoritarian system of administration. The first victim of the new regime was Archbishop of Athens and all Greece Chrysostomos II (Chatzistayrou), a respected hierarch with a long humanitarian record who was already eighty-seven years old. The junta wanted to replace him with a puppet hierarch whom they could control. After Chrysostomos's robust denial to succumb to the demands of the regime and resign, the lawmaker ousted him ipso facto by tailoring a provision exclusively for this case, setting the age limit for holding that office at eighty years.

Following Chrysostomos's removal, the Colonels suspended the function of the Holy Synod (the main administrative body of the Church consisting of bishops) and substituted it with an extraordinary "small" council of eight bishops (from now on, the "small synod") who would be selected by the regime *ex merito* (ἀριστίνδην).[3] The first duty of the new small synod would be to elect bishops to fill all vacant positions in addition to finding a suitable replacement for the position of the archbishop. The bishops who were chosen to staff the small synod submitted three names to Kalampokias, and he chose Archimandrite Ireonymos, who was a professor of canon law at the Theological School of Aristotle University in Thessaloniki and royal chief priest at the Palace. Ieronymos enjoyed the support of both King Constantine II and Papadopoulos. The latter became closely associated with Ieronymos through a religious fraternity, the "Greek Light" (Ελληνικό Φώς) founded by King Paul, Constantine's father, in the army. Today, it is widely known that many similar groups were working in secret, but according to a CIA report written shortly after the coup, this one belonged to a much broader movement named Zoe, which had permeated Greek society (Papachelas 1997: 322–23). The CIA report details how Papadopoulos was so influenced by the nationalist and anticommunist teachings of that group that he was referring to Zoe's project of Greco-Christian Civilization quite frequently.

The operation of the small synod paralyzed the functioning of the Church, abolishing the democratic principle of decision-making (Andreopoulos 2007: 91), while a new Emergency Law (214/1967) was enacted that organized auxiliary Church courts, known also as Holy Courts, and empowered them to give judgment on "predicate offenses," such as the damage to one's reputation or the loss of "fine testimony from people on the outside." These changes aimed to cleanse the hierarchy from those who were not cooperative with the dictatorship, and several clergymen lost their seats without the right of appeal, suffering humiliation and defamation (Stragkas 1983: 4982). The Church leaders displayed a rather passive stance to the Colonels' designations and did not protest the regime's attack on canon law, as well as on their own freedom. However, some factions within the Holy Synod foresaw an opportunity to pursue their political priorities, in the context of the Greco-Christian principle, through their tight relationship with the state.

ARCHBISHOP IERONYMOS AND THE CANONICAL ORDER

In the first phase of the junta (1967–73), Archbishop Ieronymos made an attempt to circumvent aspects of two fundamental documents of the Greek Orthodox Church: (1) the proclamation, or synodal tome, with which the Ecumenical Patriarchate granted autocephaly to the Church of Greece in 1850, as discussed above; and (2) the Patriarchal and Synodical Act of 1928, with which Istanbul assigned the administration of the metropolitanates of Northern Greece to Athens, withholding for itself the "spiritual union." More precisely, the dioceses of Northern Greece—the so-called New Lands— belonged to the Ecumenical Patriarchate as part of the Ottoman Empire until the conclusion of the Balkan Wars in 1913. After the Greco-Turkish War of 1919–22, the Holy See decided for practical reasons to pass the territories' administration to Athens but still maintain oversight of their spiritual and canonical guidance (for more information, see Vlachos 2002). Thus, these documents were significant not only for symbolic reasons but also because they provided the framework of operation for these dioceses and their relations with the Holy See. With such uncanonical actions, Ieronymos, ironically a professor of canon law, attempted to cut the patriarchal knot, or at least ignore it. He sought to reduce the influence of the Patriarchate and keep all the power for himself. In the end, however, his actions had only the opposite effect: by asking the Holy See to intervene, Ieronymos gave it motivation to protect its own interests, which only served to limit the power that the Archbishop of Greece sought for himself.

Ieronymos, confident with the power granted to him by the junta, attempted to convert the Church from autocephalous to fully independent, trying to fulfill the vision of a purely national ecclesiastical body that would assist the rise of the Colonels' vision for a Greco-Christian Civilization. This "independence" meant that the Church of Greece would not have to obey the canons of the Ecumenical Patriarchate, especially the Acts of 1850 and 1928. For example, the new charter that Ieronymos introduced in 1969 made no mention of the above patriarchal documents because he did not think that a self-regulating organization should follow the provisions imposed by another church (Andreopoulos 2007: 211–16). As a result, he ignored the previous normative framework and established a new model that he thought he could manipulate completely. This is clearly seen in Ieronymos's decision to sidestep the traditional system of seniority to elect the bishops for the Holy Synod; in fact, the 1969 charter allowed him to appoint literally any bishop he wanted. He also altered the status of Northern Greece's dioceses and provided an opportunity for their participation in the archdiocese administration. By proposing what in principle was a centralized system, Ieronymos thought he could bolster his own influence.

However, these changes did not go unnoticed by Ecumenical Patriarch Athenagoras (Spyrou). When the draft charter went public, Athenagoras wrote two letters in response, one to Papadopoulos and one to Ieronymos, warning them that the scheduled reforms violated the Act of 1928 and disturbed canonical order. Ieronymos ignored the letter, leaving it unanswered. This did little to gain support for the archbishop among the hierarchy of the Church, which included many pro-Patriarchate bishops who were uncomfortable with the way that Ieronymos was ruling. This unofficial flank formed a block of resistance to the archbishop's designation in November 1972, when the existing small synod had completed its tenure and a new one had to be elected. Following the provisions of the new charter, as mentioned above, the supposed elections were nothing more than the direct appointment of Ieronymos's favored members, an act that provoked such tensions within the hierarchy that a deep schism was created. In response, Bishop Amvrosios of Eleftheroupolis challenged the new electoral process before the Council of State on 2 March 1973; the Council of State then annulled the results, not because the elections were considered uncanonical, but rather because they were determined to be illegal. This was the first victory of the pro-Patriarchate faction. Realizing that his attempt to accrue more power had failed and his authority had been undermined, Ieronymos submitted his resignation on 25 March 1973, on the religious feast day of the Annunciation as well as Greek Independence Day. The dictators were caught off guard by the resignation and were unprepared for what would follow. To buy some time and avoid a more significant crisis, Colonel Stylianos Pattakos convinced Ieronymos to remain in his position.

A few weeks later, on 10 May, the hierarchy convened again to elect a legitimate small synod. This time Ieronymos lost the vote. The Supreme Administrative Court's (Council of State's) decision had had a strong impact upon the hierarchy and resulted in Ieronymos's absolute defeat, as he failed to secure the support of his own faction. The majority of the bishops voted en bloc against the nominees of the archbishop, thus restoring canonical order. Simultaneously, the bishops sent a political message denouncing the interventions of the junta via Ieronymos that had kept the Church a hostage for so long. The following months were very pressing for Ieronymos, but Papadopoulos expressed his support and encouraged him to stay as long as possible, at least until he and the other junta leaders could orchestrate a smooth transition. In the meantime, however, an internal coup by Brigadier Dimitrios Ioannidis removed Papadopoulos from power on 25 November 1973. Ieronymos was now utterly isolated; he had lost his majority support in the Church hierarchy, and he now lost his strongest supporter within the junta leadership. With Papadopoulos's fall from power, Ieronymos's position as leader of the Greek Orthodox Archdiocese was untenable, and he submitted his resignation again on 15 December 1973.

OLD ARCHBISHOP, NEW ARCHBISHOP

The process of selecting a new archbishop fell to the senior hierarchy of the Church, known as the Πρεσβυτέρα Ιεραρχία, which consisted of thirty-five bishops who were elected before 21 April 1967, and thus their canonicity could not be disputed. These clergymen assembled on 12 January 1974 for the common purpose of electing the successor of Ieronymos, and they unanimously decided for Seraphim (Tikas), Bishop of Ioannina in Epirus. While the selection might have been interpreted as a fresh start for the Church leadership, this was not the case. First, Seraphim had known Ioannidis since World War II and the Resistance, when they were comrades. Second, the road for Seraphim to become the archbishop was paved by Ioannidis himself, when he facilitated Ieronymos's exodus. For Ioannidis, this was a good opportunity to distinguish himself from Papadopoulos, and he expressed his interest in having the Church return to some semblance of normalcy. In addition, Ioannidis sought to ally himself with Seraphim, not for any ideological reasons, but rather for tactical purposes. Both Ioannidis and a majority of bishops were tired of the friction that had plagued the Church under Ieronymos, and united to stand by Seraphim.

Ioannidis gave Seraphim unlimited freedom in order to reform the Church and restore order. However, Seraphim exploited his power to exact revenge against Ieronymos and his supporters. If the most damning stain on Ieronymos's record was his uncanonical election to office, for Seraphim it was the dismissal of twelve bishops from Ieronymos's bloc, without giving them the right to a trial or appeal. These priests had been promoted to the rank of bishop by Ieronymos, and they were considered his fellows. The new Church leadership cancelled their appointment without strong legal arguments, creating a dangerous precedent for the future that would be repeated in the 1990s (Konidaris 2016: 81–86).

In principle, the crisis in the Church was not over yet. Both Ieronymos and then Seraphim ruled with emergency laws, legislative decrees, and other irregular acts, deliberately overlooking canonical procedures. Just like democracy in Greece, the Church had also been derailed from its normal proceedings, fractured as it was among parties. Indeed, the polarization in the Church was so great that it would take external mediation to ease the tension. Such relief would eventually come with the fall of Ioannidis's regime after the crisis in Cyprus in July 1974, and the subsequent arrival in Athens of Konstantinos Karamanlis, who soon after was sworn in as prime minister, providing the ground for reconciliation and a fresh start. From his self-exile in Paris, Karamanlis had been very critical of the junta's interventions in the administration of the Church. In an interview with a Swiss newspaper, he called them "medieval theocratic notions, empty of content," while "the methods of the regime [were] anything but Christian"; more than that, the military dictatorship and its "contradictory and incoherent policy had created a tyrannical and illegal regime failing the entire country" (Tzermias 1990: 185).

When Karamanlis assumed his responsibilities, he coordinated efforts with other interested agents to unite the Church. Karamanlis was the leader of the conservative flank in Greece, and his political party, *Nea Demokratia*, was a conservative party equivalent to the Christian Democrats in Europe. Therefore, he was representing the social classes that were most concerned with religion and which were vital for him if he were to cut any ties between the Church hierarchy and the Colonels (Tzermias 1990: 185). For Karamanlis, what happened to the Church under the military dictatorship was simply a farce that went beyond any interpretation of religiosity and canonicity. His negative assessment of the dictatorship's performance was evident in his comments that "the Public Administration, Church, and Education had fallen into a dangerous decay" (Svolopoulos 1997: 170–71).

That being said, Karamanlis had realized that the Church had already had enough of political interventions, and that he would have to work with Seraphim, even if he was associated with Ioannidis. The two men made a gentlemen's agreement of noninvolvement in each other's affairs, working in a spirit of respect and cooperation to restore faith and confidence in church-state relations. Following that agreement, Karamanlis shielded the Church's autonomy by setting up "the establishment of a canonical foundation in order to allow the Greek Church to function alongside the state" (Anagnostopoulos 2017: 87). Seraphim, for his part, assured that no more intra-Church conflicts would emerge, and the canonical order would be respected.

AN ASSESSMENT OF IERONYMOS'S TENURE

Archbishop Ieronymos was a man with qualities and skills widely recognized by friends and enemies. Bishop Iakovos (Makrygiannis) of Elassona, who belonged to the opposite faction, described him as a "clergyman of exceptional scientific prestige . . . good and humble . . . worthy of being enlisted for Archbishop's candidacy" (see Andreopoulos 2007: 271n688). However, Ieronymos's efforts to ascend beyond the Church hierarchy during the formative years of his career were unsuccessful. In the early 1960s, Ecumenical Patriarch Athenagoras considered him for the position of titular Bishop of the Ecumenical Throne, but eventually he assigned to Ieronymos only the administrative duties ascribed to this position (Andreopoulos 2007: 105n126). In addition, Ieronymos was nominated twice in 1962 and once in 1965 to fill a potential vacancy, but neither of these nominations bore any fruit. His nomination was each time rejected by the majority of the bishops, not because they were not convinced of his credentials, but rather due to the political pressure exerted on them by King Constantine (Andreopoulos 2007: 271).

Once he became archbishop, Ieronymos worked with the junta to benefit the clergy on some long-standing issues. His good relationship with Papadopoulos helped him place the clergy on the public payroll, improving the lives of thousands of priests across the country. The decision was announced by Papadopoulos himself on 2 May 1968, hitting the headlines the next day.[4] In a gesture of gratitude, Ieronymos awarded him the apostle Paul's Golden Cross, making him the first premier to ever receive that prize. Sealing his support for the clergy, Papadopoulos proceeded to new "gifts," increasing the pensions and benefits of the clergy's insurance fund (*Church*, vol. 21, 1 November 1967, 641). Other achievements include his decisive support for Christian Solidarity (Χριστιανική Αλληλεγγύη), the archdiocesan institution serving the needs of elderly; his improvement of the theological education with the establishment of the Ecclesiastical Academy, which would train highly skilled clerics; and his foundation of the Interorthodox Center of Penteli, in Athens, as an international educational organization and convention center.

However, Ieronymos tarnished his leadership with the establishment of a synod that was not elected based on canon law. Ieronymos was perceived as abusing his power to solidify his position and leadership. His elevation to the position of archbishop, together with the election of twenty-nine bishops during the period of 1967–73, was considered problematic from a canonical perspective and became a wound that took a long time for the Church to heal. Ieronymos's achievements were obscured by his autocratic attitude and the abolition of the Holy Synod. His personal style and excessive confidence matched the junta's ethnocultural ambitions, distracting him from pursuing more important goals like modernizing or renewing the Church according to contemporary needs. Lastly, Ieronymos represented an inflexible school of thought and refused to compromise with his ideological competitors. In this way, Ieronymos undermined his own work and reputation, estranged himself from many other bishops, and, finally, lost allies who might otherwise have helped him. Ieronymos's attitude in the end created a bitter divide between his and the Patriarchate's supporters, which resulted in a divided and polarized Church administration.

CONCLUSION

As most of the scholarly literature suggests, authoritarian regimes tend to manipulate religious institutions for political gains, exploiting their bonds with the large community of faithful citizens in any given society (see, e.g., Johnston and Figa 1988; McCallum 2012; Koesel 2014; Sarkissia 2015). The military dictatorship removed a sitting archbishop, Chrysostomos, and gave his replacement, Ieronymos, free reign to make changes in the administration of the Church. Ieronymos's blatant disregard of the Church's legal framework and canonical tradition resulted in a growing frustration and anger among the bishops. The support from the junta was inadequate to bridge the gap, and Ieronymos's resignation became inevitable, making his vision for the Church's administration and its functions collapse.

The ecclesiastical problem was the only one in which both leaders of the military dictatorship, Papadopoulos and Ioannidis, applied almost identical policies: both leaders directly interfered in the internal affairs of the Church; they both violated internal concord by defying the Holy Canon; they both imposed a leader who would be loyal to the military regime; and, lastly, they both marginalized individuals who would undermine their legitimacy. Papadopoulos removed Archbishop Chrysostomos, who refused to succumb to the former's designations, while Ioannidis removed Ieronymos, who, beyond his connection with Papadopoulos, was also responsible for the Church crisis in the eyes of the public. The election of Seraphim was another political act in the ecclesiastical drama of the dictatorship. Even though he came to power to put an end to the turbulence, he still seized upon the opportunity to eliminate potential rivals from the Church administration. Once democracy was restored, however, Seraphim agreed to cooperate with the new prime minister for the common goal of reinstating canonical normalcy and stabilizing a fractured Church hierarchy that had become untenable under the junta.

Charalampos Andreopoulos studied in Greece, received his PhD in ecclesiastical history from Aristotle University of Thessaloniki, and is a member of the Ecclesiastical and Canon Law Association (in Athens). He serves as a teacher of religion in secondary education (high) schools. His research interests focus on the study of modern political and ecclesiastical historiography. He writes for the magazines *Nomocanonica* (a biannual review of canonical and law issues) and *Theology* (official journal of the Church of Greece). He is the author of the book *I Ekklisia kata ti diktatoria, 1967–1974: Istoriki kai nomokanoniki prosengkisi* [The Church of Greece during the dictatorship, 1967–74: A historical and nomocanonical approach] (Επίκεντρο Publications, Thessaloniki, 2017).

Athanasios Grammenos received his DPhil in international relations from the University of Macedonia in Thessaloniki. His doctoral dissertation was on the impact of the Greek diaspora on U.S. foreign policy, with a focus on the Greek Orthodox Church. He is currently postdoctoral researcher at the Theology School of Aristotle University of Thessaloniki studying the role of religion in international relations. He is research associate in the Friedrich Naumann Foundation for Freedom, working on the development of education projects for democracy, human rights, and freedom. He is a past recipient of the Library Research Fellowship Program at Sacramento State University (2019–20). He has published the book *Orthodoxos Amerikanos: O Archiepiskopos Voreiou kai Notiou Amerikis Iakovos stis ellinoamerikanikes scheseis (1959–1996)* [Orthodox American: Archbishop Iakovos of North and South America in Greek-American relations (1959–96)]. He is completing the editing of a book dedicated to the bicentennial of the Greek Revolution, which will be published in late 2021.

NOTES

1. The most important rival groups were formed on political grounds, traced back at the interwar period—namely, between the Royalists and the Liberals. There was also a bitter division between those who supported closer ties with the Ecumenical Patriarchate and those who opposed them.

2. "Η XIX Κληρικολαϊκή Συνέλευση της Ορθόδοξης Αρχιεπισκοπής Βορείου και Νοτίου Αμερικής στην Αθήνα" [The 19th Clergy-Laity Congress of the Greek Orthodox Archdiocese of North and South America in Athens], National Audiovisual Archive, Asset: D1199, Theme ID: T2584, retrieved 15 November 2019 from http://www.avarchive.gr/portal/digitalview.jsp?get_ac_id=1199&thid=2584.
3. An *ex merito* synod is not unknown in the ecclesiastical tradition. It is an uncanonical intervention by the government, which selects the supposedly excellent hierarchs according to its favors for an extraordinary occasion. It was invented by the state to have a say in the Church's internal affairs (*sacra interna corporis*), but it took effect only a small number of times.
4. The announcement covered the front page of many newspapers; indicatively, see the cover of *Makedonia* (printed in Thessaloniki) on 3 May 1968.

REFERENCES

Periodicals

Church
Makedonia

Secondary Sources

Anagnostopoulos, N. 2017. *Orthodoxy and Islam: Theology and Muslim–Christian Relations in Modern Greece and Turkey*. London.

Andreopoulos, C. 2017. *I Ekklisia kata ti diktatoria, 1967–1974: Istoriki kai nomokanoniki prosengkisi* [The Church of Greece during the dictatorship, 1967–74: A historical and nomocanonical approach]. Thessaloniki.

Clogg, R. 1972. "The Ideology of the 'Revolution of 21 April 1967.'" In *Greece under Military Rule*, edited by R. Clogg and G. Yannopoulos, 36–58. London.

Close, D. H. 2014. *Greece since 1945: Politics, Economy and Society*. London.

Gazi, E. 2011. *"Patris, thriskeia, oikogeneia": Istoria enos synthimatos (1880–1930)* ["Fatherland, religion, family": History of a slogan (1880–1930)]. Athens.

Geromichalos, A. 1981. *Ekklisiastiki istoria tis Elladas* [Church history of Greece]. Thessaloniki.

Johnston, H., and J. Figa. 1988. "The Church and Political Opposition: Comparative Perspectives on Mobilization against Authoritarian Regimes." *Journal for the Scientific Study of Religion* 27: 32–47.

Konidaris, I. M. 2014. "I Ekklisia kata ti diktatoria kai I metapolitefsi: I diktatoria stin Ekklisia" [The Church during dictatorship and restoration: Dictatorship in the Church]. In *I diktatoria ton syntagmatarchon kai i apokatastasi tis dimokratias*

[The Colonels' dictatorship and the restoration of democracy], edited by P. Sourlas, 170–74. Athens.

———. 2016. *Encheiridio ekklisiastikou dikaiou* [Manual of ecclesiastical law]. 3rd ed. Athens.

Koesel, K. J. 2014. *Religion and Authoritarianism: Cooperation, Conflict, and the Consequences.* Cambridge.

Malouchos, G. 2002. *Ego, o Iakovos* [I, Iakovos]. Athens.

McCallum, F. 2012. "Religious Institutions and Authoritarian States: Church–State Relations in the Middle East." *Third World Quarterly* 33: 109–24.

Mikedakis, E., "Renouncing the Recent Past, 'Revolutionising' the Present and 'Resurrecting' the Distant Past: Lexical and Figurative Representations in the Political Speeches of Georgios Papadopoulos (1967–1973)." PhD diss., University of South Wales, Sydney, Australia.

Nanakis, A. 2013. *The Ecumenical Patriarchate in the Late Ottoman Empire: From Genos and Ethnarchy to Nation.* Thessaloniki.

Papachelas, A. 1997. *I viasmos tis ellinikis dimokratias: O amerikanikos paragon, 1947–1967* [The rape of Greek democracy: The American factor, 1947–67]. Athens.

Pattakos, S. 1968. "Pros to neon ellinikon lykavges: 'Hellas Ellinon Christianon'" [Toward the Greek dawn: "Greece of Greek Christians"]. *Theseis kai ideai* 1(5): 436–38.

Roudometof, V. 2010. "The Evolution of Greek Orthodoxy in the Context of World Historical Globalization." In *Orthodox Christianity in 21st-Century Greece: The Role of Religion in Culture, Ethnicity and Politics*, edited by V. Roudometof and V. N. Makrides, 21–38. Farnham.

Sarkissia, A. 2015. *The Varieties of Religious Repression: Why Governments Restrict Religion.* Oxford.

Skopetea, E. 1988. *To protypo vasileio kai i Megali Idea: Opseis tou ethnikou provlimatos stin Ellada, 1830–1880* [The model kingdom and the Great Idea: Aspects of the national problem in Greece, 1830–80]. Athens.

Stragkas, T. 1969–87. *Ekklisias Ellados: Istoria ek pigon apsevdon, 1817–1967* [The Church of Greece: History from undisputable sources, 1817–1967]. 8 volumes. Athens.

Svolopoulos, K. 1997. *Konstantinos Karamanlis: Archeio, gegonota kai keimena* [Konstantinos Karamanlis: Archive, facts, and passages]. Vol. 7. Athens.

Tzermias, P. 1990. *I politiki skepsi tou Konstantinou Karamanli: Mia anichnefsi* [The political thought of Konstantinos Karamanlis: A detection]. Athens.

Vlachos, I. 2002. *Oikoumenikou Patriarcheiou kai Ekklisias Ellados* [The Ecumenical Patriarchate and the Church of Greece]. Pelagia.

Vryonis, C. 1969. *To ellino-christianikon ideodes tou agonos tis anexartisias: Kosmotheoritikon vothron tis 21is Apriliou 1967* [The Greco-Christian ideal of the struggle of independence: Worldview basis of the revolution of 21 April 1967]. Athens.

Woodhouse, C. M. 1985. *The Rise and Fall of the Greek Colonels.* London.

Part III

External Affairs

Chapter 8

Uneasy Alliances

Archbishop Iakovos and the Greek Colonels' Dictatorship

Alexander Kitroeff

In 1968, between 20 and 27 July, just a year after a group of colonels established a military dictatorship in Greece on 21 April 1967, the New York–based Greek Orthodox Archdiocese of North and South America held its biennial Clergy-Laity Congress in Athens. It was the first time in the archdiocese's five-decade history that this significant gathering would be held outside North America. The Greek Orthodox Church was the most important of all Greek American ethnic organizations, and its leader, Archbishop Iakovos, was considered the Greek American community's unofficial leader both in Washington, DC, and in Athens. And the Greek Americans were the wealthiest and most influential of all the Greek communities abroad in the second half of the twentieth century, both in terms of potentially influencing U.S. foreign policy toward Greece and offering material help to Greece. Thus, the archbishop's decision to hold the Clergy-Laity Congress in Greece represented a public relations victory for the military dictatorship in Athens, which had few friends abroad. But the congress in Athens represented the high-water mark of the relations between the regime and the leadership of the Church in America during its seven-year rule between 1967 and 1974. After 1968, relations between the two sides frayed steadily, although they never ruptured entirely in the years that followed.

By examining the dynamics of those relations from the vantage point of Archbishop Iakovos's actions, this chapter seeks to gain an understanding of the policies the 21 April regime adopted toward the Church in the United

States, as well as to assess the extent to which those policies reflected change or continuity in the relationship between Greece and the Greek diaspora in the post–World War II era. The Church may have not encompassed all Greek Americans by virtue of having by far the greatest membership of all community institutions, yet the Church's relations with the dictatorship are a good reflection of its policies toward Greek America. On the eve of the establishment of the dictatorship, a succession of Greek governments had treated the Church in America as a diasporic institution in the normative sense—that is, a community of immigrants and their offspring who maintained a close attachment to their country of origin (see definition in Cohen 1997: chap. 1). For its part, the Church was open to fostering a connection with the homeland because its historic roots were to be found on both sides of the Aegean Sea. Religions, as several scholars have pointed out, are by their very nature transnational in character and thus ideal domains for the study of homeland–diaspora relations. Since religions cross borders easily and can adapt to their host societies, several of their key elements, such as a reliance on rituals and traditions or language, anchor immigrant identities in the culture of the homeland (Vertovec 2009: 128–55). This is true of Greek Orthodoxy in the United States, where it plays an ever-increasing role in defining the identity of the Greek Americans, among whom many American-born understand their diasporic conditions are predicated on cultural characteristics such as religion, not as a relationship to a particular place—namely, Greece—as is the case with Greek-born immigrants (Jusdanis 1991; Roudometof 2000).

GREEK AMERICA AND GREEK ORTHODOXY ON THE EVE OF THE 1967 COUP

The relations between the Greek homeland and the Greek diaspora communities in the early 1960s reflected the changes wrought by the end of the Greco-Turkish War of 1919–22 and the end of the so-called Great Idea (Megali Idea), the vision of incorporating territories inhabited by ethnic Greeks and considered historically Greek within Greece's borders. The Great Idea, which drove Greek foreign policy from the mid-nineteenth century, dictated the state's efforts to enlist all the material and physical help it could muster from the Greek diaspora communities. When that vision collapsed, it brought a less instrumentalist relationship between the homeland and the diaspora, a looser one, with Greece turning inward to deal with the huge influx of refugees and not paying much attention to the Greeks abroad. Greece, nonetheless, continued to invoke the concept of a transterritorial

Hellenism that embraced the Greeks of Greece and those beyond the state's borders (Kitroeff 1991). But Greeks abroad quickly learned that they could not rely on any concrete support from Greece in their hour of need. The Greek government, for example, recommended that the Greeks in Egypt, who were facing pressures from the local nationalist movement, find ways to integrate themselves into Egyptian society (Kitroeff 2019b: 126–27, 185–92). And the diaspora communities continued to offer support to the homeland— for example, the aid for Greece after it entered World War II collected and sent by the U.S.–based Greek War Relief Association. There was also political support, such as that for the Greek Cypriot struggle against Britain in the 1950s, although, crucially, it was portrayed as the initiative of Americans of Greek descent concerned about their homeland, not as Greeks abroad operating under the instructions of the national center.

The Church in America—and especially its governing body, the Greek Orthodox Archdiocese of North and South America, which had been established in 1922—had played an important role in fostering close relations between Greek Americans and Greece throughout the twentieth century. Although in an ecclesiastic sense the archdiocese was under the jurisdiction of the Ecumenical Patriarchate of Constantinople, with its assent, the Greek government and its diplomatic representatives worked toward supporting Greek Orthodoxy in the United States. The Church's ethnoreligious character meant there was no contradiction in its functioning as an institution pursuing both national and religious goals. Therefore, it cultivated close ties with both the Greek government and the Greek Orthodox Church in Greece and the Ecumenical Patriarchate of Constantinople. But at no time did the Church surrender its autonomy, with the exception of its ecclesiastical adherence to the patriarchate's guidance in issues of ecclesiastical dogma. Indeed, the Church was also very active in establishing relations with the United States government and especially the president, portraying itself as a church representing immigrants and their children who were loyal Americans. The increasingly crucial role the United States played in shaping the political affairs of the Eastern Mediterranean region, of course, made those ties potentially very useful to Greece and Cyprus.

Moreover, from the 1930s onward, the Church was steadily evolving into the largest and most influential Greek American institution, and governments in Athens and Washington, DC, were not only open to establishing close ties with the Church, but also treated the archbishop unofficially as the leader of the Greek American community. This was the case especially with Archbishop Athenagoras, who served between 1931 and 1948, and Archbishop Michael, who served from 1949 to 1958. Both prelates had established cordial relations between the archdiocese and the White House and had gone on the record as supporting Greece's foreign policy goals. Athenagoras had enjoyed an especially close relationship with President Harry Truman, and it was largely thanks to the U.S. President's intervention that Athenagoras became Ecumenical Patriarch of Constantinople in 1948. And, in a highly symbolic moment, Athenagoras traveled to Istanbul to take his post on board Truman's presidential aircraft. Athenagoras's successor Michael enjoyed close relations with President Dwight Eisenhower. In January 1957, upon Eisenhower's invitation, Michael became the first Orthodox hierarch to take part in the inaugural ceremony of a U.S. president, by delivering the invocation. Earlier, in September 1956, President Eisenhower and First Lady Mamie Eisenhower had participated in the laying of the cornerstone of Saint Sophia Greek Orthodox Cathedral in Washington, DC. Michael, too, was outspoken in favor of Greece's rights in its disputes with Turkey, especially those over Cyprus (Constantelos 1990: 164–68). And as would be the case with Iakovos, both Athenagoras and Michael enjoyed a close and privileged connection to the Greek diplomatic authorities in the United States, and their insights into what the president thought about Greece were highly valued.

Iakovos, upon becoming archbishop in 1959, continued to foster good relations with the White House, as well as to speak out on issues relating to Greek national issues. Like his predecessors, he regularly conveyed messages to the clergy and the laity on the occasion of the dates of two important national celebrations in Greece. These were 25 March, which marked the day of the outbreak of the struggle for independence from the Ottomans in 1821 and coincided with the Feast of the Annunciation of the Virgin Mary, an important event in the Orthodox Christian calendar, and 28 October, which was the date in 1940 when Greece entered World War II on the side of the Allies. Iakovos's messages were longer than those of his predecessors and especially critical when referring to the Ottoman Turks. For example, his message on 25 March 1963 described the outcome of the Greek struggle in 1821 as "salvation from the reign of sin and death, and salvation from the yoke of slavery and tyranny" (Constantelos 1976: 1158). Iakovos, moreover, would go further than his predecessors in cultivating close relations with both the United States and Greek governments. He positioned himself not simply as a liaison between Athens and Washington but as a player in the foreign policy process.

Early on in his tenure as archbishop, Iakovos already enjoyed the respect of the White House. In March 1964, he accompanied President Lyndon Johnson's wife, Lady Bird, and former President Harry Truman as a member of the official delegation to the funeral of Paul, King of the Hellenes, which took place in Athens (Shreve and Johnson 2007: 58). That same year, Iakovos would become involved in the American response to the serious intercommunal violence between ethnic Greeks and Turks on Cyprus, which had gained its independence from British rule in 1960. In an encyclical addressed to the priests and the lay board members of each parish across the United States, he urged them to respond to the violence on the island by informing elected officials and the American public of those events and to take steps to offer relief to the Greek Cypriot victims. He spoke of the victims of "Turkish barbarism," adding that "as free and prospering people, we have a sacred obligation to face the dictates of our consciousness and our souls. . . . Thousands of souls are at this very moment in deadly peril in Cyprus and Turkey. . . . The ideals of freedom and justice are so flagrantly being violated by the Turks, tolerated unfortunately by us, as Greeks and Americans" (Costantelos 1976: 1167–68). But Iakovos was also in contact with the White House and many years later claimed that he was responsible for President Johnson's letter to Turkish president Ismet Inönü, in which he delivered a blunt warning that if Turkey got directly involved in the events on Cyprus, it risked an attack from the Soviet Union, in which case the United States would not support Turkey (Grammenos 2018: 123–25).

Iakovos made his views known to both American and Greek officials repeatedly, acting in many instances as their equal. There were also occasions when Iakovos's fervor over Greece's relations with Turkey made him adopt more radical positions than those in homeland Greece, whose official policies sometimes veered to circumspection rather than explicit condemnation of Turkey's actions. For example, at a meeting of the World Council of Churches held in January 1965, Iakovos proposed a resolution that deplored Turkey's interference in Cyprus's affairs and the mass expulsion from Turkey of most of the ten thousand–strong Greek minority in Istanbul in retaliation against Greek Cypriot actions against the Turkish Cypriots. It was an outspoken move that was in stark contrast to the more restrained reactions of the Greek government, which had sought the help of the United Nations in putting an end to the ongoing deportations (Alexandris 1992: 280–85). But at the World Council of Churches meeting, two bishops who were representing the Church of Greece did not support the resolution because they knew that the Greek Ministry of Foreign Affairs would think this was too radical a move. Informed of this, the Greek general consul in New York, Georgios Gavas, echoed the view that Iakovos's resolution could have had "negative consequences for our national issues."[1] The reigning in of Iakovos in this instance was emblematic of the relationship between the Church and Greece. There was no question that the Archbishop could and would function autonomously, and also position himself as best he could as a political power broker. On some occasions his initiatives might be stymied, but on others he might play an important role.

The military men that took power in April 1967 were inheriting a complex set of dynamics. They could not treat Iakovos and the Church as extensions of the national center; in fact, it is unlikely that they could issue any type of directive. Their ideological vision, a "Greece of Christian Greeks," could be construed as a religious-inflected concept of a transnational Hellenism. To put that into practice and mobilize the diaspora Greeks on their side, the regimes had to understand that the national center could no longer dictate policy as it did prior to 1922.

GREEK ORTHODOXY IN BETWEEN AMERICA AND GREECE

An important feature of Iakovos's early years as archbishop, which would influence his actions during the period of the junta, was his commitment to promoting the Greek language and culture. This included trying to find ways to establish closer ties between Greek Americans and Greece. This became apparent right away, at the Church's Clergy-Laity Congress held in Buffalo, NY, in 1960, which was the first that Iakovos presided over as archbishop. The congress was (and continues to be) a biennial gathering of clergy and laypersons from all the Church's parishes across the United States and was an occasion where the archbishop presented a report on the state of the Church that outlined its tasks ahead, which was discussed, amended, and approved by the delegates. Although the archbishop's address included an opening theological component, the rest of his presentation covered issues such as the changing demographics of the Greek Orthodox population in the Americas, the Church's finances, the state of Greek language education in the Church's schools, the philanthropic work of the Church's Ladies Philoptochos organization, the progress of the Church's theological school, Hellenic College Holy Cross, and any other of the broad range of activities in which the Church was involved.

In his address at the congress in Buffalo, Iakovos emphasized the need to strengthen the curricula and the quality of instruction and referenced the issue of ties with Greece for the 397 afternoon schools and twelve day schools administered by the Church. Those were the sum total of the Greek language schools that existed in the United States. Both the secular Greek American organizations and the Greek government had ceded the responsibility for Greek language education in the United States to the Church. Indeed, that meant that the Church was in regular contact with the Greek government in order to align as much as possible its school programs with those of the homeland. And at the Buffalo congress Iakovos announced a new initiative: summer trips to Greece for schoolchildren attending Greek language schools. He also recommended that teachers create a "pen-pal" system in which Greek American schoolchildren corresponded with their counterparts in Greece.[2]

Iakovos revisited the need for the Church to promote the Greek language and its educational ties to Greece at the Clergy-Laity Congress held in Boston in 1962 and even more significantly at the 1964 congress held in Denver. At the Denver congress, Iakovos also presented his view that the Church in America was no longer an insular immigrant church but one that was open to and interacted with American society. He said that Greek Orthodoxy in America was at the threshold of a new era that should entail an engagement with American society, saying, "Our Church has to move out of the margins and on to the arena of American life. To work, to struggle, to develop its spiritual life, to take its place among the other Church as a living entity, active, bold, ready to shoulder its responsibilities and eager to make sacrifices."[3] Yet at the same congress, the archbishop also dwelt at length on Greek education, as he had done at the Clergy-Laity Congresses at Buffalo and Boston. And if anyone was wondering whether the opening to America implied a distancing from cultivating ties with the homeland, their concerns would have been allayed a year later, when Iakovos issued another condemnation of the Turkish government's "oppression," as he stated, of the Ecumenical Patriarchate and the Greek minority in Istanbul (Constantelos 1999: 198–202).

THE ARCHBISHOP AND THE COLONELS

The coup of 21 April 1967 did not appear to deter Iakovos from taking steps to continue to be a power broker between Greece and the United States or strengthen the contacts of the Greek Americans with their homeland. In the eight years that had elapsed since he became archbishop, Iakovos had maintained cordial relations with both Greek prime ministers who had served between 1959 and 1965, the conservative Konstantinos Karamanlis and the centrist George Papandreou. And between July 1965 and April 1967, when political instability produced five short-lived administrations, Iakovos maintained a nonpartisan stance toward them. But the regime established on 21 April was a dictatorship. The Colonels had seized power, abolished the elected parliament, arrested or interned many political leaders and labor unionists and other public figures, and had placed the media under their control. While loudly proclaiming their Orthodox piety, the Christian character of their regime, and their respect for the Church, the Colonels forced Archbishop of Athens and Greece Chrysostomos to resign, and in May of

1967 they engineered the election of their own favorite prelate, Ieronymos Kotsonis, whose extreme right-wing and anticommunist views were well known. In 1966, the Church, which encompassed both North and South America. had held its Clergy-Laity Congress in Montreal, the first time it had been held outside the United States. In its aftermath, Iakovos began planning to hold the next congress in Greece, as a way of cementing the Church's ethnic character and ties to the Greek language and culture. The establishment of the dictatorship did not appear to deter him from that vision, and toward that purpose he held a meeting of the archdiocese's executive committee, the Archdiocesan Council, in Athens in August 1967, four months after the coup. The purpose of the archdiocesan meeting in Athens was to plan the Clergy-Laity Congress to be held in Athens the following year.

The Church was not the only Greek American institution that would hold its congress in Greece during 1967 and 1974. It was the same for the American Hellenic Educational Progressive Association (AHEPA), the Greek American Progressive Association (GAPA), and several of the large Topika Somateia fraternities, whose members originated from the same village, island, or region in Greece. Moreover, those organizations also visited Greece on several other occasions—for example, the celebration of the 150th anniversary of the Greek revolution in 1971—or simply for a summer vacation. The expectation was that the diaspora Greeks would return the welcome they had received by becoming "ambassadors" of the regime when they returned to their countries. And at a time when there was no television in Greece, the inclusion of most of those visits by Greek Americans in the short newsreels screened before every movie in cinema theaters in Greece was a boon to the regime's propaganda machine (Lambrinos 2013: 45–57). But it was the Church's congress along with AHEPA's which were the most politically significant because those were the two with the largest membership throughout the entire United States. And in terms of forging ties between the homeland and the diaspora, the Church carried the greater significance because AHEPA's members were almost all second- and third-generation Greek Americans.

The Archdiocesan Council's meeting held in the summer of 1967 in Athens was an example of how Iakovos wished to display his extensive political connections on both sides of the Atlantic. Iakovos brought with him two Greek American congressmen, John Brademas and Peter Kyros, and a Greek American business mogul, Tom Pappas, for whom he arranged meetings with Greek government officials. He spoke proudly about the two congressmen in the opening session of the council, which was public and attended by an array of VIPs who made short speeches: Georgios Christopoulos, Greece's deputy minister for foreign affairs; the Archbishop of Athens and Greece Ieronymos; the mayor of Athens, Amvrosios Plytas (all of them appointed by the junta); and several professors of the University of Athens, from where liberal and left-wing academics were being purged. Also present was the U.S. ambassador in Greece, Phillips Talbot. The choir of the Orthodox Cathedral in Athens participated in the opening prayer.

What in effect turned into a gala occasion took place in the city's best-known hotel, the Grand Bretagne, and received extensive media coverage. Iakovos, addressing his Greek hosts, studiously avoided references to politics. He stressed that the visitors to Athens were Americans of Greek descent proud to be returning to the homeland, but also proud of the success they had achieved in America, where they maintained their culture and their Greek Orthodox faith. For the archbishop, there was no contradiction in this composite identity, and the implications of this cultural hybridity were that the Church and the leading Greek Americans surrounding it were happy to bring Greece closer to the United States. He spoke of connection:

> I am possessed, as are all of us from America, by a deep and moving sense that is emotion, humility, thankfulness, joy, a skipping of the heart, a focusing of the mind and a new breath, a new beginning ... we feel we are somewhere in between a dream and reality, a reality that we hope will connect our soul with yours ... that is because we belong to each other. We are connected by the same descent, the same civilization, the same history, the same striving for the ideal, the same urgency to achieve perfection, for a new birth and a new beginning.[4]

Iakovos explained that by "new beginning" he meant setting out from Greece with a better understanding of the archdiocese's mission, which he described as "marrying the Greek-ness with the American-ness of our children in order to produce a new generation without psychological complexes, without a split personality, without divided loyalties."[5] Iakovos saw the ideal Greek American identity as a dynamic fusion of the two cultures, a way of balancing between America and Greece that was free of what he deplored—the ambivalence and ambiguity of the identity of foreign-born immigrants.

Thus, Iakovos maintained that the Archdiocesan Council's meeting in Athens in 1967, a few months after the Colonels' coup, did not entail a political statement or endorsement. But he certainly walked along a thin line between tacit criticism and an endorsement during his visit. In his opening speech, he did not explicitly support the dictatorship, even though most of the Greek guests he invited were the regime's appointees, but, when he spoke of the values shared by Greek Americans, he spoke of their "same passion for the truth, for freedom, for justice, for human decency" without referring openly to the Greek regime. After the council's meetings, Iakovos visited both Prime Minster Ioannis Kollias and Deputy Prime Minister (and Minister of Defense) General Gregorios Spandidakis. The archdiocese's press office issued a release for the two major Greek American newspapers, the *Atlantis* and the *Ethnikos Kiryx*, explaining Iakovos's visit to these two junta officials. It mentioned that the archbishop discussed the Greek American community's relationship with the homeland, and that he stated the community was concerned about the "national issues," using the general term that referred to whatever border or territorial conflicts Greece had at any given time with Turkey or any other of the countries with which it had a border; he did not take a political position and merely wanted to aid the homeland in this difficult time. And 98 percent of Greek Americans, he added, did not wish to be involved in Greece's internal affairs.[6]

For their part, the Colonels appeared to welcome Iakovos, but they stopped short of permitting him to play the role of intermediary between them and the Americans. Relations between the regime and the U.S. government were still somewhat strained in the months immediately following the coup. Thus the regime's officials had chosen not to attend a reception in Iakovos's honor given by Talbot, the U.S. ambassador, in the summer of 1967, because the regime was adopting a hard-to-get attitude toward the Americans.[7] It was a reminder that even Iakovos's capacity of acting as a go-between had its limits.

The council's meeting confirmed the decision to follow the Clergy-Laity Congress scheduled for July 1968 in Athens, and Iakovos stuck to that plan. In December 1967, King Constantine of Greece who had somewhat reluctantly gone along with the Colonels' coup back in April, decided he could no longer tolerate the regime. He staged a countercoup with the help of some military, but it ended in failure and with him fleeing the country. If anything, the failed coup exposed the nature of the regime in Athens as one representing the interests of the relatively small group of the officers around Georgios Papadopoulos who were in charge. All this did not deter Iakovos, and his determination to return to Athens in the summer of 1968 was bolstered by the largely tacit support that a significant segment of the Greek American establishment—that is, the major organizations and the wealthiest businessmen—maintained toward the Colonels' junta. Purged of some leading liberals and communists who had been deported during the McCarthy era, the Greek American community was becoming more and more politically conservative.

Looking back on those years forty years later, Greek American activist Dan Georgakas (2007) offered one of the most authoritative assessments of Greek American attitudes toward the junta:

I thought Greek Americans would be outraged by what had happened in the place they so frequently lauded as "the cradle of democracy." What I discovered, however, was that many Greek Americans knew almost nothing about the politics of contemporary Greece. Many imagined the junta was part of an anti-Soviet crusade and in any case, that Greece was so backward that it needed an occasional law-and-order dictatorship. Others did not want to jeopardize their present or future business and professional opportunities in Greece. Still others were fearful that being identified as anti-junta would bring harm to family members in Greece.

And, Georgakas (2007) added, "I was most shocked by the silence of the Greek American establishment, including the Archdiocese. Individuals, of course, worked behind the scenes, but for a myriad of reasons, most organizations would not speak out until the colonels murdered university students at the Polytechnic in 1973." Georgakas's assessment is very close to that of someone who also witnessed the Greek American attitudes toward the junta: Orestis Vidalis, a former military officer who was a supporter of the king and who was permitted to leave Greece and settle in the United States in 1968. There, he kept a diary of his efforts to persuade American officials and Greek American individuals and organizations to take a more actively critical attitude toward the dictatorship. He wrote in his diary that the Greek Americans believed the regime's assertions that it had saved Greece from communism. Aside from a few notable exceptions, he wrote, "the Greek-American community in general behaved in a way that helped the dictatorship in many ways," mainly by allowing "the U.S. administration to claim that the Greek-Americans considered the situation in Greece to be just fine." In doing so, "the Greek-American community was unable . . . to realize that the dictatorship was a problem" (Vidalis 2009: 396). All this meant that potentially the regime could endear itself to at least a segment of Greek Americans and transform their tacit support into something more productive. But to do so they had to deal with Iakovos.

THE CLERGY-LAITY CONGRESS CONVENES IN ATHENS

When Iakovos arrived in Athens in July 1968, the regime was very much in place, but a few things had changed. In the aftermath of King Constantine's failed countercoup, the ringleaders of the April 1967 takeover stepped forward and assumed the government positions in which they had originally appointed figureheads. Papadopoulos replaced Kollias as prime minister, and Stylianos Pattakos replaced Spandidakis as vice-premier. Spandidakis was also dismissed from his position as minister of defense, and Papadopoulos assumed that position. The archbishop would be meeting with the men who wielded the real power. And throughout the congress, while he would be seen standing next to several leading members of the regime who were present in both the ceremonial and the business aspects of the gathering in Athens, he refrained from making any explicit political statements. The tone of the congress had already been set by Father Nicon Patrinacos, the editor of the Church's monthly magazine, the *Orthodox Observer*, whose July 1968 cover anticipated the congress in Athens with a blue background, a drawing of an ancient Greek column, and the words "To the Land of Our Fathers." In the editorial, Patrinacos spoke about Greek Orthodoxy in America's return to its "ancestral land" but studiously avoided any mention of politics or the dictatorship. And wishing to draw the distinction between Greek Americans and the Greeks that reflected the Church's understanding of its character as a diaspora, he wrote, "The American-born Greek Orthodox stands by the side of his Greek-national counterpart in striking similarity but in striking contrast as well" (N. D. P. [Nicon Patrinacos] 1968: 3).

The opening of the Clergy-Laity Congress in Athens was heavy on pomp and Greek Orthodox symbolism, reflecting the Church's embrace of the homeland and, by extension, of the regime. The *New York Times* reported on the two-hour opening ceremony that took place at the foot of the Acropolis in the restored second-century Roman theater of Herod Atticus, close to Mars Hill, where the Apostle Paul had preached: "High above the ancient amphitheater the evening sunlight dimmed on the smooth white sides of the temple of the Wingless victory," while "a choir of Greek American clergymen sang the national anthems of the two countries . . . and the sky darkened into a deep blue and yellow spotlights played on the walls of the ancient backdrop." Outside, the report added, "and on all the city's major avenues Greek and American flags decorated the lampposts." Papadopoulos greeted the three thousand persons in attendance and formally opened the congress. Following various greetings by officials, Iakovos took the podium and set out the goals of the congress, including the strengthening of the cultural and religious ties of the Greek Americans to their homeland. He told his audience, "We want the Greeks in Greece to see the children and grandchildren of the immigrants are not just preoccupied with material gain. . . . We also want to discover the principles and ideals that we can share and work for a renewal of Orthodox theology throughout the world" (Fiske 1968).

Yet beyond all the ceremonial symbolism of a Church abroad returning to the homeland, the speeches of Papadopoulos and Iakovos evoked a different concept of homeland-diaspora relations. Papadopoulos quite bluntly suggested that all future Clergy-Laity Congresses be held in Greece and include clergy and laity from America and Greece. His reasoning was that the Greek Orthodox Church and the Greek nation were identical because Greek and Christian civilizations "were carving the same road" (Papadopoulos 1968). The dictator's suggestion made sense if one took seriously the regime's crude postulate that Greece was a nation of Greek Christians, a fusion of the concepts of Greekness and Greek Orthodoxy that remained as a slogan and was not elaborated upon, and in any case had no basis in either theological or even nationalist doctrines that drew distinctions (albeit fine ones) between Greek Orthodoxy and Greek nationhood. Papadopoulos embraced the pre-1922 idea of a unified Hellenism striving for the Great Idea. In fact, at least on one occasion he spoke about the Greeks abroad embodying the Great Idea (Lambrinos 2013: 138). In contrast, Iakovos evoked a diaspora that was both connected to Greece culturally but living in a different environment, similar but also different. It was a notion that reflected his belief that the Greek Orthodox people abroad were not merely an extension of Greece. He spoke of the Greek Americans and the Greeks being "of one accord, of one mind" (a phrase in the Apostle Paul's *Epistle to the Philippians*) in the sense that they were of the Orthodox faith, but he also reminded the Greeks in the audience that "you live in circumstances different than ours" (Iakovos 1968: 44).

The return-to-the-homeland theme featured prominently in Iakovos's main address to the congress, in which he carefully navigated between speaking about the similarities and the differences between the Greeks and the Greek Americans. The entire speech was geared to explaining the evolution of the archdiocese in America, describing its functions, and outlining the problems Greek Orthodoxy faced in the New World. Unlike all other keynote speeches, there was not a pronounced spiritual message framing it, although the archbishop addressed the theme of the congress, how the Greek Americans and the Greeks of Greece were coming together to become "of one accord, of one mind." The speech reads as a report that the archbishop was making to the Greek homeland, with him in the role of an independent narrator and interpreter. He opened with one of his favorite topics—how the communities had become parishes—a necessary introduction for the Greeks of Greece, who were more familiar with the older diaspora model in which the community organization was separate from and sometimes more powerful than the Church. The missions of each parish he described as religious; these were "instilling and perpetuating faith, ecclesiastical order, the Holy Canons, the Worship and Holy Tradition, and above all the educating of the new generations in the history of our people and our Church."[8] From there, Iakovos went on to describe the challenges the Church was facing in America, speaking at length about how social changes threatened the Church's values, especially because two-thirds of the members of the Church had been born in the United States. The archbishop painted a dark picture of American society, which would have certainly accorded with a conservative assessment of the 1960s. As part of it, the Greek Orthodox were "exposed to every imaginable danger" because, Iakovos continued ominously, "today's political, economic, social and spiritual climate in America is not at all conducive to favoring the normal development and shaping of the mind and the ethos of average man. . . . Everything: religion, language, family tradition, ethnic heritage, are under judgement . . . all these are being overturned."[9] Faced with this imminent catastrophe, the Church in America was drawing from its homeland and becoming of one mind with it, strengthening and broadening its front, making it impenetrable: "And Orthodoxy as a way of life and ethos shall persist."[10]

In talking about the Greek homeland, Iakovos was careful not to mention the 21 April regime by name, though he presented Greece as possessing regenerative qualities, perhaps as a gesture toward his belief that he would express again during the regime's tenure—namely, that Greece would overcome present problems and see progress in the future. He also emphasized that the connection with the homeland he sought was in the name of religion and nationhood, and that the Greek Orthodox people in America were not interested in becoming involved in the politics of Greece, which was another way of pointing to the distinctions between homeland and diaspora. The archbishop told his Greek audience that the Greek Americans had come "to seek together with you the sound from the blue heaven of Christian Greece, and to be moved with you by the thrill of new life when it comes with a rushing mighty wind to sweep away all that is decayed and old around us and within us." This all sounded very similar to the claims made by the regime about cleaning up Greek society and politics and its vision of a "Greece of Christian Greeks." But Iakovos made sure to cast the intended rebirth in spiritual terms, even though there were certain echoes of the regime's political rhetoric. And he described the Church of Greece as "the only truly free Orthodox Church," the implication being that it enjoyed freedom in Greece under a right-wing dictatorship, while the other Orthodox Churches under communist dictatorships in Eastern Europe were not free.[11] The connection with the homeland, the theme that persisted throughout the proceedings, Iakovos explained, was based on a shared Greek Orthodox identity and patriotism, the pursuit of the national interest: "Of course we have our political views too, but these refer to the politics of our new country. . . . We recognize the value of patriotism, but we are careful not to confuse real patriotism with the voicing of political expressions that are not truly national." It was the nation above everything else, Iakovos said: "Greece as a nation is more sacred to us than any political set-up. The politics of Greece are most important, but they are a matter that concern you," and he added that Greek citizens could have "the determining vote about them"—a strange thing to say since the regime had abolished democratic elections.[12]

The Clergy-Laity Congress was a balancing act on Iakovos's part: it conferred legitimacy on the regime by being held in Athens, but it emphasized Iakovos's own role as a leader of the Greek Orthodoxy who could connect Greek Americans to their historic homeland, and could act as an interpreter of America and the Greek Americans to an audience in Greece. Iakovos himself chose to overlook the favors he was doing to the regime, even though he saw that its propaganda outlets touted the congress as a sign that the Greek diaspora supported it.

TALKING TO ALL SIDES

After his retirement, in an autobiographical conversation with Giorgos Malouhos, a Greek journalist, that appeared in book form in 2002, Iakovos denied emphatically that he had any sympathy toward the Colonels. Rather, he maintained that his purpose was to use his good offices to persuade the Colonels to restore democracy in Greece and to signal to the Greek people the archdiocese's solidarity by underlining its presence by meeting in Athens. Iakovos explained that he was talking to all sides, keeping up a correspondence with the former prime minister Karamanlis, and was also in contact with King Constantine. Iakovos also referred to several letters he sent to the dictators. In the letters he appears to go along with their claims that the seizure of power was supposedly temporary and proposes ways they can guide the country back to becoming a democracy. But the regime, he also implies in the letters, did not to want to go along with his advice.

In a letter Iakovos sent to the regime's prime minster Papadopoulos in March of 1968, he spoke about his visit to Athens in February of that year—to plan the upcoming Clergy-Laity Congress—and how he had detected a change in the public mood compared to that in the summer of 1967. He said he discovered a sense of nervousness, concern, and fear, and he also said he detected that Papadopoulos himself had realized that pursuing his stated goals was much more difficult than he had originally anticipated. The archbishop advised the dictator that if he was truly interested in defending Greece's national interests, he should raise the peoples' morale by introducing a new, more just, and democratic order. The implication, of course, was that the dictator could and would somehow improve the failings of the system he had abolished and step aside to allow for a rejuvenated democracy to flourish in Greece (Malouhos 2002: 73–81, 225–63).

A year later, in February 1969, Iakovos was writing to Pattakos, who was at the time minister of the interior, and acknowledged that the suspension of constitutional liberties had been necessary in 1967, but said now was the time to restore those liberties. He also made sure, though, that even while he was urging the dictators to restore democracy, he and the Greek Americans he influenced would not criticize the regime publicly, not wishing to damage the standing of the Greek nation internationally (Malouhos 2002: 264–74).

While the archbishop was communicating privately with the regime's leaders and offering advice on how they could restore democracy to Greece, publicly the archdiocese and its churches maintained formal relations with the regime's diplomatic representatives in the United States. Greek diplomats were conspicuously present in church services and other events, such as banquets hosted by the archdiocese or local churches. And they appeared side by side with the clergy as honored guests at events organized by Greek American organizations. Needless to say, neither the archbishop nor the leading clergy appeared anywhere near the few pro-democracy demonstrations and meetings held by Greek Americans or others who were opposed to the dictatorship in Greece. Their stance understandably frustrated radical activists, such as Dan Georgakas, but also the more moderate opponents of the junta who were in the United States. Vidalis's diary attests to Iakovos's constant maneuvering and the ease with which—after communicating with the state department, exiled politicians, King Constantine, and the Colonels—he could suddenly claim he could not do something that might anger the Colonels. The reason Iakovos gave Vidalis was that he was not a political figure, nor were the Greek Americans he was asked to influence. Vidalis (2009: 45–48, 51–52, 284–87) patiently but unsuccessfully tried to persuade the archbishop to criticize the regime publicly. Yet there is no evidence to suggest that the regime in Athens showed any great appreciation for the archbishop's stance.

A CHANGE IN ATTITUDE

The turning point in Iakovos's attitude toward the dictatorship came in a series of developments in 1973, the year before the regime collapsed. Iakovos visited Greece in April 1973 and spent a few days in Thessaloniki and then in Athens. Things did not run very smoothly in the Greek capital due to indifference on the part of the government and the government-controlled media. Henry Tasca, the U.S. ambassador to Greece (1969–74), described the visit as falling "somewhat short of resounding success" because, among other things, Iakovos's lecture at the University of Athens that evening "was poorly attended by ranking government, military and university authorities," who were "conspicuously absent." Even when the regime made an eleventh-hour effort to make the archbishop feel more welcome, it fell short of the archbishop's expectations. Iakovos remarked that the "warmth of personal contacts in Thessaloniki" was a contrast to the "generally cold, impersonal reception" he had received in Athens.[13] One of the reasons for the apparent indifference toward the archbishop's visit was that part of the constituency that would have normally welcomed him—clerics, seminarians, and professors and students of the theological school—suspected that Iakovos was turning his back on the Greek language, which they considered one of the pillars of Greek Orthodox tradition. Those suspicions were triggered in 1970, when a controversy broke out within the ranks of Greek America following the Clergy-Laity Congress held that year in New York. At that congress, Iakovos announced that it would be permissible for the Sunday liturgy to be performed in English in parishes in the United States if the parish priest considered it appropriate because most of the congregation was American-born and had lost the use of the Greek language. A small but vociferous segment of the Greek American community made up of Greek-born immigrants and the Greek-language press based in New York misconstrued this move as the archbishop's wish to banish the Greek language from the Church. They embarked on a series of vigorous public protests that lasted for two years before eventually subsiding. The effect that the protest campaign had in Greece (where knowledge of the American environment was limited) was to replicate the fears of the Greek-born immigrants in the United States and to raise the specter of diluting Greek Orthodox tradition. The regime, via a statement made by Pattakos, reiterated its support for preserving the Greek-language liturgy, and a number of theologians echoed that view. Evidently, those fears still lingered and affected Iakovos's reception in Athens in 1973 (Kitroeff 2019a).

The real distancing between the archbishop and the Colonels came later that year, and at Iakovos's initiative. In the summer of 1973, the regime decided to put an end to its relationship with King Constantine, who had been in exile since his failed countercoup in 1967. The regime had not wanted to go as far as abolishing the monarchy and had appointed a "vice regent," army general Georgios Zoitakis, who had fulfilled the functions of head of state. But in May 1973, a Greek naval destroyer, the Velos, which was participating in a NATO exercise, did not return to its base in Greece, but instead it mutinied and made its way to a port in Italy, where its officers and crew declared their opposition to the dictatorship and requested political asylum. Wrongly assuming that the exiled king was involved in this protest, the regime moved against the monarchy and held the referendum on 27 July. Its result, a decision to abolish the monarchy, was a foregone conclusion given the lack of freedom of political expression in Greece.

Iakovos's reaction to the referendum came only after U.S. Secretary of State William P. Rodgers stated that the abolition of the Greek monarchy by the regime was an internal Greek matter. Iakovos had maintained regular contact with the exiled king as part of his power-broking contacts with all sides. He evidently felt so strongly about the American reaction that he not only sent a private letter to Rodgers, protesting his reaction to the referendum, but also leaked his letter to the secretary of state to Greek American *New York Times* journalist Nicholas Gage. In the letter, he described the Colonels' government as "a tyranny" (Miller 2009: 172). Gage (1973) went ahead and made the letter public, and in his report he included the State Department's response, which was to express surprise because until then it had "no hint of the Archbishop's feelings." The State Department's response was an accurate reflection of Iakovos's public stance toward the dictatorship up to that point. But evidently the archbishop's attitude toward the Colonels had now changed, and he felt strongly enough about the referendum that he leaked the letter on the eve of his departure for Greece, where he was traveling for a service in the memory of Ecumenical Patriarch Athenagoras, who had passed away in 1972. Maybe to protect himself from any retaliation from the regime, he had ended his letter to Rodgers by noting that "my motivation in addressing this letter to you Mr. Secretary is purely American, purely Christian and purely moral, for as a clergyman, I must at all times, stand for the freedom and the dignity of the God-made Man."[14] By underlining the fact he was writing as an American, he was not only making his intervention more effective in terms of how it would be received by the State Department; with an eye to Athens' reactions, he was also alluding to his view that the Church in America was autonomous from the Greek government.

Iakovos need not have worried about the reactions in Athens because evidently it was not in the interest of the regime to bring about a breach of its relations with the archbishop. Speaking to correspondents, Byron Stamatopoulos, the regime's chief spokesman, voiced shock and disbelief at reports citing the letter and Iakovos's characterization of the regime. The government, he indicated, could not react until it could obtain a verified copy of the letter. And he added somewhat mischievously that "Archbishop Iakovos, in the presence of witnesses at the Athens Hilton recently, over breakfast paid tribute to me personally as well as to the leaders of the revolution" (*Dayton Daily News* 1973)—the term "revolution" was what the regime called the coup of April 1967. Thus, their contacts continued even if the atmosphere had become more strained. When the next Clergy-Laity Congress came around (it was held between 30 June and 7 July 1974), the Greek ambassador to the United States, Constantine Panayotakos, was an honored guest and made a short speech. Iakovos responded, saying that the Church's ties with the homeland are strong, but qualified that statement by adding that "politically we may not belong to the homeland, but we belong in a national sense."[15] While the ambassador's presence and Iakovos's comment pointing to a degree of daylight between the Church and the homeland indicated that nothing much had changed in a year, there were other changes that had taken place, and others which were to come very soon. In November of 1973, a student uprising at the Athens Polytechnic School, which lasted three days, was put down violently by the army. It was the biggest demonstration of popular antidictatorship sentiment that the regime had experienced since it had seized power. Blaming Papadopoulos and his attempts at liberalizing the dictatorship, Dimitrios Ioannidis, one of the ringleaders of the coup in April 1967 who had then become the head of the military police, overthrew Papadopoulos and took charge. The regime automatically took on an even more repressive and nationalistic character. Vidalis (2009: 360–65) rushed to see Iakovos in order to persuade him to come out and publicly condemn the repression that was unfolding in Greece, but the always-cautious archbishop stalled for time, and Vidalis does not record whether Iakovos followed his advice.

There were more changes in the summer of 1974 that distanced Iakovos somewhat further from the dictatorship. Ioannidis engineered a coup on Cyprus that overthrew the government of Makarios, who managed to flee the island, and installed ultranationalist Nicos Sampson in power. The ultimate goal was to bring about the union of Cyprus with Greece, a nationalistic dream that had lived on even after Cyprus had become an independent state in 1960. But the coup gave an excuse to Turkey to invade the island in the name of its status as one of the guarantor powers of Cyprus's independence. When the Turkish operations were in their second day, Makarios arrived in New York in order to inform the United Nations and request their help, and Iakovos invited Makarios to participate in a special service for peace that was held at the Greek Orthodox Cathedral in New York. The invitation of Makarios was a clear rebuke to the regime in Athens, even though he sought to make clear in his address during the service that his church was impartial in the conflict between Makarios and the government in Athens that was trying to annex Cyrpus and effect its union with Greece. "The Greek Church in the United States," he said, "tries to abide by the American tradition of keeping the church and state two separate entities." And as if to drive the point home, he concluded by saying, "Most Greek-Americans are second and third generation citizens. They are not getting into any fights over what is happening thousands of miles away" (Coutros 1974). In retrospect, when the dictatorship collapsed soon after and Iakovos and the rest of the Greek American community would engage in lobbying efforts to persuade the United States to take measures against Turkey, his statement has an ironic ring to it. But at the time, it was close to evoking the distance that Iakovos liked to place in between the diaspora and the community—when it suited him.

CONCLUSION

The transnational character of Greek Orthodoxy means that, in theory at least, a Greek Orthodox Church located in the midst of a significant Greek diaspora community could play an important role in forging closer links between that community and the Greek homeland, but this did not happen between 1967 and 1974. Iakovos's decision to hold the 1968 Clergy-Laity Congress in Athens offered the dictatorship numerous potential benefits. These included, first of all, the legitimization of the newly established regime gained by having Athens as the venue of a major diaspora institution, which, moreover, was based in the United States, Greece's most important ally. Second, and more importantly in terms of this study, it provided the opportunity for the regime to forge a close relationship with Iakovos and, through him, the Greek American community. Third, given Iakovos's ties to the U.S. foreign policy establishment, constructing a close relationship with the archbishop would have offered the regime an opportunity to gain valuable access in Washington, DC. But the regime gained none of these benefits because it failed to follow up on the closeness that was on display at the Clergy-Laity Congress in Athens in 1968. Instead, the dictators and the archbishop drifted slowly but steadily apart.

The breakdown in the relations between the regime in Athens and Iakovos was the fault of the dictators and cannot be blamed on the archbishop. Iakovos continued to cultivate the ties he had established in 1968 and scrupulously avoided any public criticism until he ultimately gave in after the 1973 referendum and spoke publicly of a tyrannical regime. For its part, the Greek dictatorial government played along with the archbishop's efforts to offer advice, but at no time did they appear to make any concessions in adopting any of the measures he recommended. One reason was because they would have weakened the tight grip that the junta exercised over Greek society. Another reason has to do with the way the Colonels viewed the relationship of the homeland and the diaspora. Papadopoulos's message to the Clergy-Laity Congress was indicative. He recommended that the congress take place permanently in Greece because he subscribed to the view that the diaspora was a mere extension of the Greek nation. It was a view that would have been excusable prior to 1922, when the pursuit of the Great Idea sought to marshal the support of all Greeks the world over. To be sure, several Greek political leaders invoked the concept of a global Hellenism after 1922, but in practice government policies reflected a recognition of the diaspora's autonomy, even its assimilation into the host-society culture. But Papadopoulos frequently spoke about his vision of a "Great Idea" in which Greece was at the center of global Hellenism. It was an inward-looking and isolationist vision that discounted the circumstances in which the Greeks of the diaspora, and especially the second- and third-generation immigrants, were living (Vogli 2007: 50). And that type of homeland-diaspora relationship was not only unrealistic given the degree of assimilation into American society that the Greek Americans had achieved by the 1960s, but it also placed the diaspora on the receiving end of any decision-making process—something that would have been completely unacceptable to Iakovos.

Papadopoulos's and the regime's approach to homeland-diaspora relations represented a rupture in the policies of Greek governments in the post-1922 era—although not in the rhetorical sense, because the idea of global Hellenism was always on the lips of Greek politicians. The rupture was in dealing with the Greeks abroad through the lens of a form of revived Great Idea, which created the expectation that they would conform to the policies of the national center and use Greece, for example, as the permanent site of their congresses. The leaders' statements inviting the Greeks abroad to advertise the virtues of the regime in their host countries also fell within the ambit of considering the diaspora as an extension of Greece. And the assumption that visiting diaspora Greeks would return to their democratically ruled countries and act as "ambassadors" for a dictatorial government betrayed an ignorance or indifference toward the conditions in which the diaspora was living. The rupture in Greek government policy, finally, was most dramatically shown by the refusal of the regime to heed any of Iakovos's advice. Previous governments had treated Iakovos himself and his predecessors Athenagoras and Michael respectfully, and sought to gain from the access all three had enjoyed in Washington, DC. There is no evidence that anyone in the government between 1967 and 1974 considered Iakovos a valuable asset and treated him accordingly. A comment attributed to Ioannis Ladas, who was among the group that planned the coup of April 1967, was that Iakovos was a "devil-priest." Although it is difficult to verify, it reflects the frustration that the archbishop's sense of autonomy caused the dictators. There may also be something to be said about the provincialism of the military leaders of the dictatorship. The only model of church-state relations they knew was the one in Greece, where the Church was beholden to the government, and they acted accordingly. Had they had a more sophisticated understanding of the status of religion in the United States, they may have dealt with the Greek Orthodox archbishop of North and South America differently. It would be only after the military handed over power on 24 July 1974 that Iakovos's key role in shaping homeland-diaspora relations would be recognized by the Greek government.

Alexander Kitroeff is currently professor of history at Haverford College. He received his DPhil in modern history from Oxford University in 1984. His doctoral dissertation was on the history of the Greek diaspora in modern Egypt. He has published seven books on the Greeks in interwar Egypt, the Jews in Athens during World War II, the Greeks in the Americas, Greek identity and the modern Olympic Games, and a social history of the Athens-based sports association Panathinaikos. His sixth book, titled *The Greeks and the Making of Modern Egypt*, was published in 2019 by the American University of Cairo Press. His most recent work, titled *The Greek Orthodox Church in America: A Modern History*, was published by Northern Illinois University Press in 2020.

NOTES

1. Greek General Consulate in New York to Athens, Historical Archive, Greek Ministry of Foreign Affairs, KY 1965/18/4, 18 January 1965.
2. Greek Orthodox Archdiocese of America Archives, "Εκθεσις του Αρχιεπισκόπου Ιακώβου Ενώπιον της ΙΕ' Κληρικολαϊκής Συνελεύσεως εν Buffalo New York 19 Σεπτεμβρίου 1960" [Report of Archbishop Iakovos before the Clergy-Laity Congress in Buffalo New York, 19 September 1960], Folder DA Box L13.
3. Greek Orthodox Archdiocese of America Archives, "Report to the 17th Biennial Clergy-Laity Conference of the Greek Orthodox Archdiocese of North and South America by His Eminence Archbishop Iakovos," Folder KY Box L15.
4. Greek Orthodox Archdiocese of America Archives, "Συνεδρία του Αρχιεπισκοπικού Συμβουλίου της Ιεράς Αρχιεπισκοπής εν Αθήναις" [Meeting of the Archdiocesan Council of the Holy Archdiocese in Athens], 9 August 1967, Folder MU Box L17.
5. Ibid.
6. Vasiliades to *National Herald* and *Atlantis*, Telegram, New York, 3 August 1967, Folder AI Box L17, Archives, Greek Orthodox Archdiocese.
7. *Foreign Relations of the United States (FRUS), 1964–1968*, Vol. 16, *Cyprus; Greece; Turkey*, no. 297, "Letter from the Ambassador to Greece (Talbot) to the Country Director for Greece (Brewster)," 7 August 1967.

8. Greek Orthodox Archdiocese of America Archives, "Archbishop Iakovos' Message to the 19th Clergy-Laity Congress of the Greek Orthodox Archdiocese of North and South America," Athens, 22 July 1968, Folder AS Box 17, 30.
9. Ibid.
10. Ibid., 32.
11. Ibid., 33.
12. Ibid., 45.
13. Telegram, from United States Embassy Athens to State Department, 16 April 1973, retrieved 1 July 2019 from https://wikileaks.org/plusd/cables/1973THESSA00225_b.html.
14. Iakovos to Rogers, June 29, 1973, Pol 15 Greece DSCF, RG 59, NA; cited in Miller 2009, 172n49.
15. Greek Orthodox Archdiocese of America Archives, "Αντιφώνησις Σεβ. Αρχιεπισκόπου κ. Ιακώβου προς τον πρέσβυν της Ελλάδος κ. Κωνσταντίνον Παναγιωτάκον επί τη ενάρξει των Εργασιών της 22ας Κληρικολαϊκής Συνελεύσεως εν Σικάγω" [Response of His Eminence Archbishop Iakovos to Ambassador of Greece Mr. Constantinos Panayotakos at the opening of the proceedings of the 22nd Clergy-Laity Congress in Chicago], Folder DA Box L25.

REFERENCES

Periodicals

Atlantis
Dayton Daily News
National Herald
Orthodox Observer
New York Times

Archives

New York, NY
    Greek Orthodox Archdiocese of America Archives
Washington, DC
    National Archives
        Department of State Central Files, Record Group 59, National Archives (DSCF, RG 59)

Published Primary Sources

Foreign Relations of the United States (FRUS)

Secondary Sources

Alexandris, A. 1992. *The Greek Minority of Istanbul and Greek Turkish Relations, 1918–1974.* Athens.
Archbishop Iakovos. 1968. "Address by His Eminence Archbishop Iakovos." In *Praktika tis en 20–27 Iouliou 1968 20is Klirikolaikis Synelefseos ton Koinotiton tis Ellinikis Orthodoxou Archiepiskopis Voreiou kai Notiou Amerikis* [Minutes of the 20th Clergy-Laity Congress of the Communities of the Greek Orthodox Archdiocese of North and South America, 20–27 July 1969], 43–44. Athens.
Cohen, R. 1997. *Global Diasporas: A Definition.* Seattle.
Constantelos, D. J., ed. 1976. *Encyclicals and Documents of the Greek Orthodox Archdiocese of North and South America (1922–1972).* Thessaloniki.
———. 1990. *Understanding the Greek Orthodox Church: Its Faith, History and Practice.* Brookline, MA.
———. 1999. *The Complete Works of His Eminence Archbishop Iakovos.* Vol. 2, *The Torchbearer.* Pt. 1, *1959–1977.* Brookline, MA.
Coutros, P. 1974. "Makarios Makes Cyprus Vow in the Cathedral." *New York Daily News,* 22 July.
Dayton Daily News. 1973. "Primate's Rap Shocks Top Greeks." 30 July.
Fiske, E. B. 1968, "Orthodox Diocese of Americas Opens 19th Congress in Athens." *New York Times,* 22 July.
Gage, N. 1973. "Iakovos Criticizes Greek Government." *New York Times,* 27 July.
Georgakas, D. 2007. "Greek Americans against the Junta Then and Now." *National Herald,* 21 April.
Grammenos, A. K. 2018. *Orthodoxos Amerikanos: O Archiepiskopos Voreiou kai Noriou Amerikis Iakovos stis ellinoamerikanikes scheseis (1959–1996)* [Orthodox American: Archbishop Iakovos of North and South America in Greek–American relations]. Thessaloniki.
Jusdanis, G. 1991. "Greek Americans and the Diaspora." *Diaspora* 1(2): 209–23.
Kitroeff, A. 1991. "The Transformation of Homeland Diaspora Relations: The Greek Case 18th–19th Centuries." In *Proceedings of the First International Congress on the Hellenic Diaspora from Antiquity to Modern Times,* edited by J. M. Fossey, 233–50. Amsterdam.
———. 2019a. "Greek America's Liturgical Language Crisis of 1970." *Ergon: A Journal of Greek American Studies,* 26 February. Retrieved 1 July 2019 from https://ergon.scienzine.com/article/articles/liturgical-language-crisis-of-1970.
———. 2019b. *The Greeks and the Making of Modern Egypt.* Cairo.
Lambrinos, F. 2013. *Chounta einai: Tha perasei; Ta kinimatografika epikaira sti diarkeia tis diktatorias (1967–1974)* [It is a junta: Will it pass? The cinematic news during the dictatorship (1967–74)]. Athens.
Malouhos, G. P. 2002. *Ego, o Iakovos* [I, Iakovos]. Athens.
Miller, J. E. 2009. *The United States and the Making of Modern Greece: History and Power, 1950–1974.* Chapel Hill, NC.

N. D. P. [Nicon Patrinacos]. 1968. "Our Athens Clergy-Laity Congress" *Orthodox Observer* 34(589): 3.
Papadopoulos, G. 1968. "Omilia kata tin panygirikin enarxin tis Klirikolaikis" [Speech at the celebratory opening of the Clergy-Laity Congress]. In *Praktika tis en 20–27 Iouliou 1968 20is Klirikolaikis Synelefseos ton Koinotiton tis Ellinikis Orthodoxou Archiepiskopis Voreiou kai Notiou Amerikis* [Minutes of the 20th Clergy-Laity Congress of the Communities of the Greek Orthodox Archdiocese of North and South America, 20–27 July 1969], 26–28. Athens
Roudometof, V. 2000. "Transnationalism and Globalization: The Greek Orthodox Diaspora between Orthodox Universalism and Transnational Nationalism." *Diaspora* 9 (3): 361–97.
Shreve, D., and R. D. Johnson, eds. 2007. *The Presidential Recordings: Lyndon B. Johnson; Toward the Great Society*. Vol. 5. New York.
Vertovec, S. 2009. *Transnationalism*. New York.
Vidalis, O. E. 2009. *Confronting the Greek Dictatorship in the U.S. Years of Exile: A Personal Diary (1968–1975)*. New York.
Vogli, I. 2007. "O episimos logos tou kathestotos tis 21is Apriliou: To pistevo mas tou Georgiou Papadopoulou" [The official language of the 21 April regime: Georgios Papadopoulos's *Our creed*]. PhD diss., Panteion University, Athens, Greece.

Chapter 9

Uncle Sam Regrets

The United States and the Greek Coup of April 1967

James Edward Miller

> When the junta took over in 1967 . . . the United States allowed its interests in prosecuting the Cold War to prevail over its interests—I should say obligation—to support democracy, which was, after all, the cause for which we fought the Cold War.
>
> —President Clinton, Athens, November 1999

On the morning of 21 April 1967, the U.S. ambassador in Greece, Phillips Talbot, in condemning the "Rape of Greek democracy," began a cascade of statements of regret about the military coup by American officials. A few hours later, the Department of State's Greek specialist *par excellence*, Thessaloniki-born Daniel Brewster, director of Greek affairs, entered the office of Secretary of State Dean Rusk to brief his superior. Rusk remarked that he had dealt with nearly one hundred coups during his six-year tenure, and told his subordinate to calm down. The philhellene Brewster exploded: "This is different . . . [it's] the cradle of democracy," he told his superior. "That didn't impress," Brewster recalled. The coup was regrettable, Rusk explained, but the United States had more pressing issues to address and had only limited capabilities to effect change.[1]

Four years later, Robert Keeley, a very junior officer at the embassy in Athens in 1967, was still agitated. While on another assignment, he used his spare time to prepare a book-length manuscript analyzing the failure of

American diplomacy in Greece. Exercising prudence, Keeley shelved the document in favor of continuing his career, eventually becoming U.S. ambassador to Greece during the Andreas Papandreou era. Nearly a half-century later, he published his memoir, becoming, perhaps, the last American veteran of the Athens coup, including the CIA chief of station, to publicly express regrets and critique the embassy's performance (for the reactions, see Maury 1977; Miller 2009: 143, 146; Keeley 2010; see also American participant comments in Drew 1968; Couloumbis and Hicks 1976; Stern 1978).[2]

Regret is not an admission of guilt. It reflected two perceived failures: averting a coup and sacrificing support for democracy to Cold War priorities. Nevertheless, its expression by former U.S. officials added fuel to Greek conspiracy theories that survive nearly two decades after the release of a very full U.S. documentary record of a political crisis created and fueled by Greeks. Keeley dismissed the idea that the United States was behind the Colonels' coup or, for that matter, King Constantine's drift toward a "constitutional deviation." The issue regarding U.S. policy before April 1967 is whether and how Washington and its embassy in Athens might have intervened to spur on Greece's battling political factions toward a successful compromise, overcoming a political polarization that all those involved knew invited military intervention. After the coup, American policy was a Cold War–driven exercise in first accommodating the dictatorship and then embracing it. Keeley alone asked whether a U.S. show of force in the coup's immediate aftermath might have toppled the regime in its first days. His memoir has played a central role in stimulating this effort to rethink the events of 1964–68.[3]

THE LIMITS OF POWER

From 1945 to 2001, and again from January 2009 to January 2017, U.S. policy-making was grounded in a careful prioritization of its interests. Melvyn Leffler defined it as a strategy for maintaining U.S. "preponderance" through a combination of military power, economic aid, and alliance management. The consensus among senior officials working in successive U.S. presidential administrations was that the United States had limited capabilities and thus needed to prioritize its interests and seek out foreign allies in order to achieve its objectives. The strategy relied on international organizations, together with groups within individual nation-states that aligned with the United States on common objectives. These institutions and individuals served as multipliers of American power. Common sense dictated Washington's preference for working with other democracies, but given the threat posed by the Soviet Union, its dependent communist dictatorships (the Warsaw Pact states), and the Chinese Peoples' Republic, the United States frequently aligned itself with repressive noncommunist regimes, while downplaying criticism of their antidemocratic internal policies. The democracies constituted an inner circle of American allies. U.S. officials trusted that common institutions, together with shared cultural, economic, and political interests, would promote the "burden-sharing" that propped up American power and influence in order to pursue common objectives.

When Washington officials judged it possible, they supported the extension of democratic institutions in other parts of the world. "Nation Building" and its ideological twin, "Modernization," were efforts to expand the circle of democracies. President Harry S. Truman's March 1947 address to Congress, rallying public support for aid to Greece and Turkey, was the classic statement of this concept. The president explained that two strategically important states, although less than perfect democracies, were struggling to defend themselves against foreign and internal threats directed and supported by the USSR. Washington would intervene, within careful limits, in order to assist both nations. Ultimately, however, the fate of these two societies, and particularly a more endangered Greece, depended on the readiness of a majority of its people to confront communism (Leffler 1993).[4]

Given the importance of the Truman Doctrine as the first step in the successful roll-out of an overall strategy of "containment" of the Soviet threat, the United States faced a potential gap between its policy objectives and Truman's desire to restrain the commitment of American resources. In the Greek case, unlike many successive interventions, the United States avoided a "quagmire." The willingness of Greeks to fight and die for what they identified as being their national (and personal) interest allowed the United States to limit its involvement to supplying military aid and training, while fostering economic development with a generous outlay of Marshall Plan assistance. In early 1950, following a series of political and military errors, the Greek Communist Party (KKE) abandoned armed resistance and pulled its surviving forces out of Greece. Successes in military and political struggles against communist parties in Greece and Italy were early steps in the stabilization of Europe through a combination of Marshall Plan aid, NATO military coordination and training, and covert activities. The experiences provided the United States with a template for nation building that was then extended beyond Europe with less success.

Even before the Greek Civil War ended, American officials discussed the reallocation of resources from Greece and initiated a process designed to reduce Greek government reliance on U.S. assistance. The Marshall Plan officially terminated in 1952, although the actual passage of money and assistance allocated under this program continued through 1954. Thereafter, American officials expected Greece to implement its own modernization program. Cold War tensions modified this initial plan. Military assistance programs continued into the late 1950s, permitting the Greek government both to strengthen its defensive capabilities through aid grants, and also to reallocate significant budgetary outlays to support important economic development programs. However, the aid spigot was being turned off. The reallocation of U.S. resources away from Greece accelerated in 1953, when the Republican Dwight D. Eisenhower became the 34th U.S. president (on the reallocation, see Miller 2009: 23–43).[5]

U.S. aid reduction did not sit well with either the Greek public or their political representatives. Having been a central player in U.S. grand strategy from 1947 through 1949, and contributing significantly to the success of the U.S. containment efforts with their blood and resources, Greeks expected longer-term rewards in the form of more money in order to carry out a robust reconstruction, as well as continuing political support against their Balkan neighbors' political and territorial ambitions. Modern Greece's century-and-a-half history of client-patron relations with the European great powers was a poor preparation for dealing with the Americans. Adding to the Greeks' confusion and anger, Washington sent conflicting signals. As part of its effort to reallocate resources, Washington became enmeshed in Greek internal politics, pushing for a quick reordering of the Greek political system that would produce a government enjoying a parliamentary majority. The end result of U.S. involvement in writing Greek electoral laws—the 1952 election of a conservative government under General Alexandros Papagos—satisfied Washington's *desiderata* but stimulated Greek politicians of both the Right and Center-Left to double down on tactics designed to maintain American involvement in their political struggles. The Americans wanted influence on the cheap, and their Greek interlocutors wanted support, above all in the form of U.S. dollars. Shortly after assuming power, Papagos initiated an unsuccessful confrontation with the Eisenhower administration over aid. The pattern continued under his equally determined successor, Konstantinos Karamanlis (prime minister, 1955–63) (on the struggle, see Miller 2009: 66–72).

The sense that Washington was reneging on its commitments extended to Athens's foreign policy objectives. Seeking both protection and territorial expansion, Greece applied for NATO membership (1952) and participated in negotiations that led to the Second Balkan Pact (1953). The United States welcomed both moves, seeing them as useful contributions to Soviet containment. NATO membership brought with it a U.S. guarantee of Greece's territorial integrity. Expansion was another matter. The Truman administration's desire to reinforce the legitimacy of Civil War–era Greek governments led it to negotiate the transfer of the Dodecanese Islands to Greece (1947). Papagos, however, aimed to acquire the British colony of Cyprus, an island with a Greek majority population. He wanted the United States to leverage Britain off the island. The Eisenhower administration had no objections to unifying Cyprus with Greece but prioritized the desires of two more important strategic partners. Great Britain was initially determined to retain Cyprus, as it was critical to its Middle Eastern position. Continued British involvement in the Eastern Mediterranean was an American priority. Turkey, a frontline state in the Cold War confrontation with the USSR, declared its interest in Cyprus's ultimate disposition, citing, as justification, the presence of a large Turkish minority (approximately 19 percent of the Cypriot population). In the face of these objections, Washington urged Athens to avoid provocative actions that would damage NATO unity.

Greek Cypriots, with assistance from Athens, initially tried to peacefully protest in order to oust the British. When this protest proved ineffective, the Cypriot Greeks passed on to armed insurrection in order to force the British out and achieve enosis (unification) with Greece. The British deployed military force to crush the rebellion. Tensions between Greece and Turkey over Cyprus culminated in government-inspired, anti-Greek riots in Istanbul and Izmir (1955). Washington chastised both sides, a move that favored Turkey, and this violated most Greeks' sense of justice. Greece's status as being distinctly secondary in American policy calculations was on display. After the October–November 1956 Suez Crisis, the Eisenhower administration decided to dislodge the British from the island.

The British, rapidly losing their empire and great power position, while also deeply in debt, ultimately accepted the loss of Cyprus, but turned the retreat into a poison pill for enosis by making Turkey a full party to the negotiations for their departure. Lacking U.S. support, Karamanlis settled for a Greek voice in the negotiations. The London-Zurich agreements (January–February 1959) set up an independent, "bi-communal" Cyprus Republic and positioned Turkey to block the unification of Cyprus and Greece. Washington supported British management of a withdrawal that handed Turkey a coequal role in determining Cyprus's future. Disillusioned with American diplomacy, "the Greeks ... stoned American buildings, burned American flags, [and] attacked American citizens." The United States, meanwhile, was starting to hand over greater responsibility for Greece to its European allies, particularly Germany, which was the nation best positioned to meet Athens's economic requirements and shepherd its entry into the European integration process (Lee 1957: 107).[6]

FAMILY TIES

Despite the tensions created by Cyprus, and despite the resulting growth of anti-American sentiments among the Greek public and press, the relationship between the U.S. and Greek governments remained good throughout the early 1960s. Both Eisenhower and his successor, John F. Kennedy, considered Karamanlis to be a reliable NATO partner and respected his political acumen. Military aid continued to flow to Athens, although in smaller increments, and largely in the form of loans rather than grants of assistance. The United States appreciated the political difficulties inherent in Karamanlis's pragmatic management of the Cyprus issue. Dropping Eisenhower's noninterventionist approach to Cyprus, the Kennedy administration offered assistance to the republic's new president, Archbishop Makarios, with the objectives of reinforcing Karamanlis and also stabilizing NATO's "southern flank" by encouraging the new state to work with both Greece and Turkey in implementing the terms of the London-Zurich agreements.

As part of Cyprus's "nation building" strategy, Kennedy invited Makarios to Washington in June 1961, where he urged the Cypriot leader to foster cooperation between the island's Greek and Turkish communities in building a common homeland. However, Makarios had other ideas. He was under considerable internal pressure to "Hellenize" the island. Moreover, beginning in 1958, he discretely began expressing doubts about the utility of enosis. Unification, if it came, had to meet his terms. Meanwhile, Makarios, seeking foreign support, used military basing arrangements and requests for aid to keep both the United States and Britain involved in Cyprus.[7]

The Cyprus issue was a gift for Karamanlis's opponents. Greece's centrist parties, plagued by internal divisions, suffered political eclipse in the early 1950s. They returned to prominence in 1960, supported and encouraged by both the United States and Karamanlis. Reacting to the success of the communist-backed United Democratic Left (EDA) in the 1958 elections, Karamanlis and the Americans separately concluded that Greece needed a "legitimate" opposition to deflate the Left. Centrist politicians recognized the benefits of burying their feuds and uniting into a single party. George Papandreou, a reformer and skilled political tactician and master orator, dominated the negotiations that created a Center Union (EK) party. Signaling his good will toward Papandreou, while also reaffirming his longstanding commitment to Greek modernization, Karamanlis set up a largely U.S.-financed economic research center and invited a highly qualified economist, Andreas Papandreou, George's son, to lead the initiative. George Papandreou pocketed these family offerings but was mindful that his party was an ideologically incoherent coalition of former enemies, united almost exclusively by the desire for power, and concentrated on returning the center to government. In 1961, the EK came in at a distant second in parliamentary elections but succeeded in reducing support for the communist-dominated EDA. Washington and Karamanlis were gratified. George Papandreou, who had no interest in remaining as the opposition party, accused the government of voter fraud and demanded new and honest elections. He initiated a "ceaseless struggle" to highlight electoral corruption and force King Paul I to call a vote. Simultaneously, EK chiefs pressed the U.S. embassy to oust Karamanlis from power.[8]

Neither Karamanlis nor the United States appreciated Papandreou's maneuvers. U.S. policy continued its noninvolvement in Greek political maneuvering. This was a confusing approach because Washington was involved in Greek politics on another level. Since 1958, it had been financing a covert CIA "civic action" program designed to strengthen the electoral campaigns of both Karamanlis's ERE (National Radical Union) and the EK at the expense of the KKE-EDA. The Kennedy administration saw no reason to topple a valued ally such as Karamanlis in order to facilitate Papandreou's desire to be prime minister. Papandreou, with good reason, complained about voting irregularities that involved the Greek national police in rural areas and Greek army draftees. Although Washington kept quiet, the U.S. ambassador in Greece, Ellis Briggs, publicly endorsed the outcome of the 1961 Greek vote. Papandreou seized on Briggs's statement in order to amplify his call for new elections. Kennedy recalled Briggs as expeditiously as possible.

In November 1962, the EK leadership met with the new U.S. ambassador, Henry Labouisse, in order to reiterate their demands for Karamanlis's ouster. After Labouisse gave a tortured presentation about nonintervention to the political leaders his government was financing, Papandreou's longtime rival and current deputy, Sophokles Venizelos, squared the circle of circumlocution: "The Center Union did not seek American intervention in Greece's internal affairs. However, this did not mean that the embassy could not give 'advice' to the political leaders when the situation called for it. The United States was the leader of the Free World and its leadership . . . should be exercised." Labouisse avoided discussing the contradictions of U.S. policy by emphasizing that the EK should stay within legal boundaries in its maneuvers, and he promised further consultations. The United States would operate against the Far Left but was not going to become involved in political conflicts between the two democratic factions it supported.[9]

The monarchy, not the Americans, ousted Karamanlis in 1963. The main source of royal irritation was the prime minister's gradual whittling away of crown prerogatives and political influence. By 1962, Karamanlis was actively considering constitutional redrafting that would codify a reduction of royal powers. The king exploited Karamanlis's objection to a "private" London visit by Queen Frederika to force his resignation. In the small world of Greek politics, the king and queen had ample opportunity to take Papandreou's measure and that of his lieutenants. The royals concluded that, despite a tendency toward overheated rhetoric, the EK represented no major threat to their position. After ousting Karamanlis, King Paul granted Papandreou new elections that resulted in a plurality for the EK. Washington stood aloof. As Karamanlis's relationship with the royal couple deteriorated, his lieutenant Evangelos Averoff appealed to Secretary of State Rusk for support. Rusk declined, explaining that "while fully aware of . . . Karamanlis['s] great value to Greece and to the Alliance . . . one would not want to think of the future of a NATO country in terms of one life."[10]

Washington would soon regret Karamanlis's political demise but initially had little trouble adjusting to the EK victory. Not only did U.S. officials regard George Papandreou as being a reliable partner, but his son, Andreas, an American citizen with ties to the Democratic Party, would be at his side as an economic advisor and, Washington presumed, as a useful intermediary between the two governments. In February 1964, the younger Papandreou renounced his U.S. citizenship to run for parliament in his father's old electoral college. The EK's second electoral triumph gave it a substantial parliamentary majority to pursue major internal reforms and deal with the Cyprus issue.[11]

The U.S.-Papandreou relationship quickly soured over Cyprus. George Papandreou hoped to maximize his political standing by delivering unification rapidly. He underestimated Turkish resistance to Greek demands and badly misjudged Makarios's objectives. The Greek prime minister expected Washington to deliver enosis by leveraging Turkey into cooperation, arguing that it was the only way to stop Makarios from depriving the Turkish Cypriots of their rights under the London-Zurich agreements and to end the civil war that the president-archbishop's supporters had initiated in December 1963. Achieving enosis would solidify Papandreou's control over his party and its ambitious barons, while opening the way for Andreas to claim party leadership at the proper time.[12]

President Lyndon Johnson had other ideas. The new American president (1963–69) faced a November 1964 election. He wanted to avoid any commitment of U.S. power in the Eastern Mediterranean but was ready to function as a mediator of last resort. Instead of granting Papandreou's demands, Johnson initially passed the Cyprus hot potato back to the British and the United Nations. When both failed to pacify the island, he then sent his senior diplomats to the Eastern Mediterranean to secure a compromise. "Reasoning together" was the theme of LBJ's foreign and domestic policy. The United States would accept a deal for enosis, but it understood that Turkey required concessions from the Greek side, including some forms of territorial adjustment and military basing agreements, to make diplomacy work. Papandreou thought otherwise, however, pushing for insubstantial concessions to Ankara. He was secretly flooding Cyprus with Greek troops in violation of the London-Zurich accords and ultimately suggested that a Greek-organized military coup should end Makarios's rule.

In June 1964, after further clashes on the island and U.S. action to block a Turkish invasion, the American president invited the prime ministers of Greece and Turkey to Washington for joint discussions in order to resolve the crisis and save NATO's unity. Makarios pointedly was not invited. Turkey agreed to the initial U.S. meeting plan. George Papandreou balked at this. He had walked into a corner with his Cyprus demands because he could not, in his own words, "control" Makarios. Fearing a domestic backlash if he offered substantive concessions, Papandreou refused to meet with Turkey's prime minister, Ismet Inonu. The Turkish leader, a skilled international negotiator, signaled his desire for compromise in his separate talks with Johnson, thus increasing pressure on Athens. George and Andreas Papandreou arrived in Washington the following week. They remained intransigent. Both sides were frustrated. The Washington discussions became a turning point in U.S. relations with the Papandreous. Neither George nor Andreas ever regained American confidence. The elder Papandreou earned a reputation as being weak, emotional, and unreliable. Andreas had already clashed with the U.S. embassy and, by late 1964, was well on his way to becoming the *bête noir* of American diplomats serving in Athens.[13]

The Cyprus crisis of 1964 ended in September with a net defeat for American, Turkish, and Greek leaders. Makarios, who wanted neither enosis nor major changes to the status quo on the island, outmaneuvered them. He resented American-led efforts to impose a Greek-Turkish settlement on him. Well supplied by Athens, Greek Cypriot forces had surrounded the bulk of the island's Turkish Cypriot minority in village and urban enclaves. Makarios's next step, ethnic cleansing, could proceed at a more cautious pace. A United Nations peacekeeping force (dispatched in March 1964) served as a trip wire against a Turkish invasion, and the United States had demonstrated its determination to avert a clash between Greece and Turkey, even if the price was Makarios's continued rule. The president-archbishop, having survived American and Greek efforts to marginalize him, was the dominant player in Cypriot affairs.[14]

As the Cyprus confrontation went onto the back burner, Greek internal political divisions ignited. King Paul died in February 1964; his successor Constantine II was young, headstrong, and inexperienced, relying on advice from his reactionary mother and the court. The Papandreous suffered a major setback in Cyprus, while Andreas's initial forays into Greek politics had not gone well. His major weakness, a twenty-year absence in the United States, made Andreas an outsider within the EK, deeply resented by his father's internal rivals. To reverse his image problem, Andreas, always a fast learner, tacked leftward, becoming an outspoken critic of American policies, domestic and foreign. He built his own faction of younger EK politicians and found allies among EDA leaders. As Andreas stepped up his attacks on the United States and made friends on the Far Left, "Greek hands" in both Washington and Athens developed an obsession with the younger Papandreou that colored their analysis of Greek politics. They wanted the EK to weaken the EDA, but not an EK dominated by a skilled and untrustworthy demagogue. The Americans shared this "Andreas obsession" with large parts of the Greek political establishment: the leaders of the EK's right wing, the palace, the military, and, of course, the ERE. Their common antipathy for the younger Papandreou encouraged Greek conservatives of all stripes to demand bold moves against the prime minister and his son.[15]

When reports surfaced (May 1965) that Andreas had ties to a left-wing officers group, "ASPIDA," the king decided to oust his prime minister. The scandal involved the two most troubling institutions in Greece, its monarchy and its officer corps, and pushed the question of "who governs," elected officials or kings and generals, to the center stage. The great powers imposed a monarchy on newly independent Greece in 1832–33. It had rarely worked effectively as a stabilizing institution. The Greek army had played a critical role in the evolution of the new state since 1843. Beginning in 1909, its frequent interventions had created repeated periods of instability. Control of the army was central to the monarchy's position and difficult to achieve due to many officers harboring antimonarchy sentiments. ASPIDA rang alarm bells in Washington and at Greek army headquarters. A reputed left-wing conspiracy was bound to raise concerns in Washington, especially one connected with Andreas Papandreou.

Beginning in the late 1940s, a right-wing officers' organization, IDEA, had played a controversial role in Greek public life. Largely a movement of midlevel and junior officers with a few senior officers mediating its relationship to the high command, IDEA promoted its members' professional demands and involved itself at critical moments in politics. Its members' political views were right-wing, ultranationalist, and frequently antimonarchical. In May 1951, IDEA members staged an abortive coup in support of Papagos and against King Paul's actions. The marshal intervened to send the officers back to their barracks. IDEA's influence seemed to have declined under a Papagos government, and Karamanlis subsequently took over the defense ministry portfolio in an effort, apparently successful, to control his officer corps. Both U.S. military attaches and CIA officers had contacts with members of this group and its offshoots as part of their regular duties. (State Department officers normally avoided contacts with the military.)

Most of the officers involved in the 1967 coup had been IDEA members in the 1950s. The revival of military plotting took place in response to the king's ousting of Karamanlis. General Vassilios Kardamakis, the recently retired head of the Greek army, and reputed mastermind of the 1961 electoral abuses, in league with a number of midlevel officers, including the future mastermind of the 1967 coup, Georgios Papadopoulos, contacted American officials with a plan to maintain Karamanlis in power by force, if necessary. The embassy discouraged them. Karamanlis, informed by the Americans (and probably others), put an end to the plotting. By 1964, Papadopolous and other group members had coalesced around countering a new threat, the Papandreou government and its plans to gain firm control of the army and its intelligence services. The CIA had an informant inside the group, who reported regularly on their meetings. The discussions had a repetitive quality that seemed to have lulled American intelligence over the successive three years. The approximately two dozen malcontent officers who comprised the cell complained bitterly and talked vaguely of taking action. They did not do so because they were not in a position to act. The Greek general staff and government, well aware of their ambitions, shuffled the plotters into staff positions or into garrison duty, keeping them away from commanding units needed to actually launch a coup. The situation changed in December 1966 when the Greek army assigned Brigadier Stylianos Pattakos to command armored units at Athens's Goudi military reservation.[16]

Meanwhile, Greece's political stability dissolved. A government crisis, which both the Papandreous and Constantine embraced, came to a head in mid-July 1965 in a public exchange of letters between the prime minister and king. George Papandreou decided to force elections by telling the king he intended to step down. Constantine, who expected the move, immediately swore in a new government, led by EK defector George Athanassiades-Novas, without waiting for Papandreou to formally announce and submit his resignation. The Papandreous charged that the king had carried out a "coup" that demanded new elections. Both Constantine and the Papandreous (as well as most informed observers) thought that George Papandreou would win a new vote on a platform of breaking the power of the monarchy, the military, and the political Right. The investigation of ASPIDA ran aground due to a lack of evidence against Andreas, to the relief of American officials but not the Greek Right. The king refused to call elections, and the fragile EK gradually broke apart during a summer-long crisis over seating a new government. In spite of strong anti-Papandreou feeling at the CIA, Greek desk, and the embassy, Washington decided not to support the king. Washington expected that, using the lures of patronage and political rivalry, Constantine would peel away enough EK politicians to create a governing majority. In September 1965, EK-defector Stefanos Stefanopoulos put together a government of his fellow Center Union "apostates," with ERE support, thus staving off a return to the polls.[17]

A CONSTITUTIONAL DEVIATION

Between September 1965 and April 1967, the Greek political establishment engaged in a reckless battle that set the stage for a military intervention. From time to time, the king, party leaders, and George Papandreou tried to reach a compromise that would open the way to elections. A December 1966 deal that set up a nonpolitical "service" government cleared the way for a vote, but the EK demands for continuing Andreas Papandreou's parliamentary immunity from arrest after the king dissolved parliament upended cooperation. A minority ERE government assumed control of the voting process, violating the precedent of elections under a nonpartisan ministry. The Greek army planned to intervene if the vote produced a Papandreou victory. The ERE's move emboldened a group of officers to bypass the chain of command in order to prevent an election. The king, meanwhile, wavered between supporting free elections or backing a "constitutional deviation." He sought Washington's "blank check" for his ultimate decision. Ambassador Talbot discouraged a deviation and rejected a "blank check" option (see Pattakos 1990: 15, 30–32, 36, 52, 57–64, 73, 79–82, 102–25, on the Colonels' preparations for a coup).[18]

U.S. officials in Athens dithered over how firmly to deliver their anticoup message. The Athens station chief warned Constantine's chief advisor against a coup while formulating plans for a covert intervention to deny the EK a majority. CIA director Richard Helms met a Greek military representative in Washington and delivered the anticoup message. Washington's consistent but intermittent opposition to intervention failed to reign in an Andreas-obsessed embassy with the result that the American message to both politicians and military, a confusing "No coup but no Andreas," was a formula that left most Greek officials at their wits end. The Greek military certainly did not appreciate the direction, much less the subtleties, of the American message. During the night of 20–21 April, a well-organized dual coup took place against the government and the high command. Tanks and soldiers rolled into downtown Athens, arrested Greece's political and military leadership, surrounded the palace, and seized communications facilities. Greece awoke to a military dictatorship carried out by "unknown colonels."[19]

CAPITULATION

Alerted that something was amiss by a frantic middle of the night phone call from Prime Minister Panagiotis Kanellopoulos, Ambassador Talbot rushed to an almost-deserted embassy to inform Washington and gather his "country team" to confront the situation. American officials slowly assembled in the chaos created by the army's seizure of roads and telecommunications. In a 5:00 AM communication with the embassy, Constantine reported that tanks were moving toward his palace and he had no idea who was commanding them. He urged for an armed American intervention. The U.S. Sixth Fleet, however, was nowhere near Athens. A few hours later, after an initial meeting with a group of military men he scarcely knew, the king assessed them as being "incredibly stupid, ultra-rightwing bastards."[20]

While awaiting direction from Washington, Talbot took steps to strictly limit contact with the coup leaders, dispatching a military attaché to the Greek Pentagon to assess the military leadership's situation, while he met with the junta's civilian prime minister and front man, the royalist jurist Konsantinos Kollias. The meeting focused on respecting the human rights of political prisoners and pressing Greece's new rulers to speedily return to constitutional government. In reporting on the discussions, Talbot recommended that the United States take a "fairly starchy position" toward the junta, publicly "regret" the coup, and marshal support behind the king with the aim of restoring "normalcy" as quickly as possible. No senior embassy official suggested threatening the use of force against the junta, although CIA station chief Jack Maury urged a face-to-face confrontation with the coup's effective leader, Colonel Papadopoulos, as a way of heightening pressure on the military for a quick stand-down (Stearn 1978: 48).[21]

During the day, the king calmed down. He never again suggested the use of U.S. force against the coup makers. From his position at the bottom of the embassy pecking order, Robert Keeley argued that a show of force by the U.S. Sixth Fleet would topple the Colonels. He later recalled that Greeks went to the beaches near Phalarion, anticipating the arrival of rescuing American naval power. Keeley believed that Kollias's nervousness about American intentions, displayed in two separate encounters with Talbot, indicated that the junta would blink in the face of U.S. firmness. Kollias, however, was a figurehead, dragged out of bed to dignify the coup and represent its makers. Pattakos was confident enough to tell a U.S. military contact that "we are with you whether you want us or not." His steadiness impressed Talbot, who repeatedly reported to Washington that the junta was firmly in control (Stearn 1978: 48).[22]

Military intervention, in any case, was not on Washington's radar. It went ahead with a snap decision, made in response to the embassy's suggestion, to suspend the shipment of heavy military equipment as a signal of U.S. disapproval. Neither Rusk nor the president's chief foreign policy advisor, Walt W. Rostow, saw benefits in confronting the new regime. Since American officials believed that King Constantine, although erratic, was the best, and virtually only, lever to exert pressure on the Colonels for the speedy restoration of constitutional rule, they had to accept (while trying to avoid legitimizing) a government he had sworn in.[23]

Discarding force, the United States relied on its diplomatic tools to promote a return to constitutional government. One critical tool, economic assistance, was already off the table as a result of decisions made in the Eisenhower years. The Germans had more economic leverage, but as an export-driven economy they were loath to use this form of pressure. Furthermore, of course, Germany, only two decades removed from the Nazi experience, had reasons not to confront a former victim state. Rostow advised the president: "At some point . . . we should express regret—even if softly—that the Greek democratic process was suspended."[24] The president's advisor avoided stating the obvious: the U.S. government lacked domestic credibility to do much about Greece even if it had the desire. By 1967, Johnson's management of the Vietnam War had divided his nation, ignited a revolt inside the president's own (Democratic) party, sparked massive public protests, prompted congressional investigations, and limited LBJ to making his few public appearances on secure military bases. American public opinion, already shifting against the war, was unprepared to support a muscular response to situations such as Greece. Johnson and his critics agreed that the Greek situation was regrettable but not something justifying U.S. intervention. Western European leaders and their diplomats concurred with U.S. reluctance to take any action, arguing that Greeks had created the mess and, regrettably, would have to repair the damage by themselves.[25]

In practical terms, the NATO allies, with the exception of Denmark, Italy, and a few small NATO states, limited themselves to anodyne admonitions and statements of regret about the Greek situation. The big three, Britain, France, and West Germany, came to the same conclusions as Washington. The idea of suspending Greece's NATO membership got nowhere. The Alliance had a founding member that was a dictatorship (Portugal) and had looked the other way when Turkey's military toppled the elected Menderes regime (1960). Seven years later, Western priorities remained the same: maintaining as strong a military deterrent as possible, especially on its perennially troubled "Southern Flank." The alternatives to military rule, a return to conservative domination under the king, armed resistance, or some form of communist-dominated government, were as difficult to accept as the junta's continued reign. Restoration of constitutional government, the favored solution, was obviously a longer-term process, requiring unity among, and conciliation between, Greece's political factions.

Restoring Greek democracy became more difficult after December 1967. King Constantine's influence diminished as the junta retired senior officers loyal to the monarch. In August 1967, the king traveled to the United States, ostensibly for the America's Cup races, in order to sound out U.S. officials about supporting a countercoup. U.S. officials, including Johnson, tried to dissuade him, correctly judging that the officer corps largely would support the junta. Obsessed with his diminishing position, Constantine turned to Greece's former political leaders for support. Georgios Papandreou, Kanellopoulos, and other members of the ousted political elite signed on, but were powerless bystanders. As the king widened his preparatory contacts, the junta assembled details of his plans and positioned its police and military forces. The Colonels' bungling management of a November 1967 confrontation with Turkey over Cyprus set the stage for royal action. The Colonels permitted the king to launch his "lucky day" countercoup (13 December 1967), a strategy that allowed them to identify and round up Constantine's remaining military loyalists. The king delivered another gift to the junta by flying to self-exile in Rome hours after the coup failed. George Papadopoulos appointed himself prime minister and designated a senior general as regent, effectively terminating the monarchy.[26]

Ambassador Talbot's already dwindling influence was swept away in the countercoup. Although the king informed Talbot of his plan only on the morning of 13 December, the U.S. ambassador's observed presence at the palace the evening before, and on the morning of the countercoup, led the Colonels to call him in for questioning. Talbot's denials of involvement, while true, were an embarrassment that stripped him of credibility with the Greek government.[27]

NO MORE REGRETS

The king's failure and flight left the United States without effective leverage to promote its objective of returning Greece to constitutional government. Talbot had argued for months that the United States needed to gradually abandon its "starchy" stance. With Papadopoulos now head of the government and clearly the dominant figure in the junta, the ambassador promoted a strategy of bargaining with the senior Colonel for the gradual restoration of civilian rule. The first opening to the junta occurred in February 1968, when the U.S. Sixth Fleet hosted Greece's prime minister on a symbolically significant tour of the aircraft carrier *USS Franklin D. Roosevelt*. During 1968, a regularization of contacts between U.S. officials and Greece's new rulers proceeded. The Americans were on a slippery slope that led to a pragmatic relationship with the junta, and subordinated constitutional and human rights concerns to Cold War strategic imperatives.

Two events marked the transition. On 1 April 1968, Johnson announced that he would not seek reelection and instead devote the remainder of his term arranging a negotiated settlement to the Vietnam War. The president and his foreign policy became lame ducks. Repressive regimes such as the Colonels ignored feeble American efforts to promote democratic governance, waiting instead for a likely Republican president to institute policies more favorable to their interests. In August 1968, a Soviet crackdown on the Czechoslovak reform government of Alexander Dubcek put a premium on NATO unity, handing the Greek military greater leverage in its relations with the United States. Johnson grudgingly signed an order that reduced the categories of military assistance frozen since the April 1967 coup. In December 1968, following the victory of Republican Richard Nixon, the junta published and immediately suspended a new constitution, cementing rule by martial law. The Nixon administration speedily delivered what the junta wanted. Abandoning qualms about the nature of the Greek regime, it embraced Papadopoulos, enthusiastically endorsing the dictatorship as a model NATO ally. "Other (NATO) countries give us regiments of words," Nixon later declared, "Greece gives us regiments of troops." The decision, made in the early days of the new administration, required more than a year to implement in the face of domestic opposition, bureaucratic resistance, and legal requirements. However, the Nixon administration faced little opposition from the Greek American community. In addition to pro-junta Republicans, the U.S. Orthodox Church avoided any public disagreements with the Colonels. The first stage was to inform the Colonels of the new policy while disengaging from the king. Nixon's team carried out the operation during the funeral of former President Dwight D. Eisenhower (28 March

1969). In protocol terms, King Constantine, recognized by the United States as head of state, led the Greek delegation, meeting with the president. He was shunted off for a discussion with Vice President Spiro Agnew, who listened politely to Constantine while avoiding any commitments. The king was on his own. Meanwhile, Nixon and coup leader Pattakos met, and the president assured the Greek representative his administration would stay neutral on internal matters, focusing on NATO cooperation. The president promised a new Greece policy once he could resolve internal U.S. issues. Nixon was impatient to move forward on a policy designed to lift the arms freeze. However, the formal announcement of this decision awaited a series of maneuvers to prepare both U.S. public opinion and Congress, where Democrats controlled both chambers. On 14 November 1969, a National Security Decision Memorandum (NSDM 34) provided an outline of the policy. As part of the pantomime, about which the Greek junta was informed, Nixon appointed a right-wing career State Department diplomat, Henry Tasca, as ambassador and tasked him with providing a full assessment of the best U.S. policy.[28]

The Tasca Report (31 March), together with a classified analysis of the junta's internal structure, served as the basis of the policy outlined in NSDM 34. The United States would resume arms shipments, treat the junta as a full partner, emphasize its NATO contribution, and carefully nudge the Colonels in the direction of the restoration of democracy, but without linking this public effort with its major objectives.[29]

Tasca undertook the job of swaying the junta toward a democratic restoration with few tools save his own personality. He quickly developed and cultivated a relationship with Papadopoulos, whom he judged a relative moderate, amenable to a return to democracy. Over the next three and one-half years, the two men jousted over democratic restoration, while Tasca promoted Papadopoulos to Washington as the best hope for a change of direction in Athens. The State Department pressed for Greek action to restore democracy. The White House was largely indifferent to the issue. Tasca pressed Papadopoulos for action but then justified the Greek prime minister's inaction to his superiors. Neither the ambassador nor Washington tried to use the democratic opposition as a tool to leverage Athens into concessions (Miller 2009: 162–65). Tasca, in particular, was allergic to dealing with Greece's democrats, concerned such approaches would upset Papadopoulos's position inside the junta.

Failure to work with the opposition had another consequence that both Tasca and the White House could easily have foretold. When Greece restored democracy (1974), an emotional but equally understandable reaction led to an explosion of anti-Americanism, and that set the stage within a few years to the capture of power by the Greek politician the American government most feared, Andreas Papandreou.[30]

The junta was not only bad for U.S.–Greek relations but for the stability of the Eastern Mediterranean. The Nixon administration's anti-Soviet strategy recognized the importance of cooperation with Cypriot president-archbishop Makarios. Makarios, in turn, placed great reliance on American diplomacy to ward off the junta's ambitions to "unite" the island republic with the Greek state. Athens was ready to use assassination to remove Makarios and replace him with an extremist as the prelude to a declaration of unification (enosis). Unilateral action against Makarios would certainly bring a clash with Turkey, a fellow NATO state, breaching the alliance's "Southern Flank" to Soviet advantage. Keeping Athens at bay consumed American diplomats in the region and required stern interventions by Washington. Even the frequently obtuse Tasca, however tardily, intervened and pressed his "friend" Papadopoulos to refrain from attacking Makarios on various occasions. Neither Nixon nor his diplomatic Svengali, Henry Kissinger, wanted Greece confronting the Turks (Miller 2009: 181–82).

Greece under the junta was a difficult ally, but Nixon's fixation on its military potential drove a policy of tolerating the Colonels' threats to international stability, use of torture on domestic opponents, and flat refusal to turn power back to an elected government. The irony, revealed in full in 1974, but visible to outside observers much earlier, was that the Greek army was in a state of internal disintegration resulting from its role in the 1967 coup. Its officer corps was thoroughly politicized. Its chain of command had lost authority. The junta was deeply divided, and each faction had its own supporters among the officer corps. Neither the embassy in Athens, where Tasca stifled opposition to his reporting, nor the military attaches, nor the CIA (frequently the same individuals) were reporting on the disintegration of the fighting capabilities of the Greek armed forces.[31]

Papadopoulos's overthrow (25 November 1973) by the most radical element of the junta awakened Tasca to reality. The reorganized junta was a growing threat to regional peace. Democratic restoration was the only solution to its rule that could maintain the peace and extract the United States from its alignment with the "dictators." The ambassador, in his maladroit way, sought to awaken Washington to the threat and find democratic Greek interlocutors for himself and the United States (on the awakening of Tasca and his associates, see Miller 2009: 172nn52–53).

The Cassandra at the embassy in Athens could not convince his masters, especially Henry Kissinger. In a showdown meeting in Washington following the junta's July 1974 attack on Makarios, Kissinger, the mastermind of the 1973 overthrow of Salvadore Allende in Chile, piously told his ambassador that the "issue isn't between democracy and non-democracy. We conduct foreign policy here . . . we work with whoever is in power."[32] A few days later, he abandoned the junta to its fate, swinging his full weight behind Turkey's invasion after another military coup brought a more dangerous and repressive government into power in Athens (November 1973). Nixon and his lieutenant Henry Kissinger refused to change their course. In the summer of 1974, Greece's rulers provoked their own downfall by overthrowing Makarios, thus opening the way for Turkey to invade Cyprus and impose a partition.

American policy toward Greece in 1950–74 was a study of the difficulties inherent in any alliance strategy. Meeting Greek national objectives clashed with the broader U.S. strategic imperatives of containing the Soviet Mediterranean and Middle Eastern goals through cooperation with Britain and Turkey. The Cyprus issue fostered a widespread Greek mistrust of, and hostility to, Washington. The peculiar situation in which an "American" emerged as a leading figure in Greek politics and heir apparent to his prime minister–father's political movement could not have been anticipated and probably could not have been well managed once Andreas Papandreou determined that his road to power meant becoming Greece's most active critic of the United States. Nevertheless, embassy hostility to the younger Papandreou, a mix of reason and gut reaction, clashed with the more restrained views of Washington policy-makers who, however, struggled with a host of distractions, especially its disastrous Vietnam entanglement, and rarely focused on Greek issues. Far from seeking relief from the Greek problem through a coup, U.S. officials made efforts to encourage a political compromise, but without making commitments to the survival of the conservative forces involved in the confrontation. When a group of extremist officers moved to save their personal positions, Washington found it had no reliable political allies inside the new Greek establishment and, with regret, accepted a fait accompli.

James Edward Miller, the author of *The United States and the Making of Modern Greece* (University of North Carolina Press, 2009), was chairman of European Studies programs at the Foreign Service Institute and taught global and Mediterranean history courses at John Hopkins and Georgetown Universities. He has also published *Politics in a Museum: Governing Post-War Florence* (Praeger, 2002) and *The United States and Italy, 1940–1950: The Politics and Diplomacy of Stabilization* (University of North Carolina Press, 1986). He is currently at work on a book dealing with modernization in Southern Europe since 1700.

NOTES

1. Daniel Brewster, Oral History, Association for Diplomatic Studies and Training (ADST), Washington, DC. The collection is now online at ADST.org.
2. The ADST's "Country Reader" series of oral histories includes a number of expressions of frustration and regret by U.S. officials in Greece at the time of the coup and its aftermath.
3. On the coup in its international context and an excellent bibliography, see Klapsis et al. 2020. This volume of collected essays focuses largely on European reactions to the coup, a direction that has gained considerable attention in recent years.

   On U.S. involvement, see Klarevos 2006. For Keeley's views, see Keeley 2010: esp. 19–23. They largely correspond with my own in Lardner 2001 and Papachelas 2001. In discussing the agency's role, Keeley, a good diplomat, discreetly avoided mentioning that many of the surplus billets in the embassy's overinflated military section were assigned to CIA officers, including one who kept tabs on King Constantine.
4. The text of the Truman Doctrine, 12 March 1947, is available at avalon.law.yale.edu. On the roots of modernization and nation building theory in the Cold War United States, see Gillman 2003. The George W. Bush administration was the first serious deviation from this strategy and produced a major pair of disasters. Heedless of the recent past, the current American leadership has now plunged the world back into an era of international chaos, reminiscent of the two pre–World War eras. On the erroneous thinking behind the Bush deviation, see Mann 2004. Since the current U.S. administration is incapable of thinking in strategic terms, the best guide to its moves are the "tweets" of the egocentric demagogue Donald J. Trump; see also Allen 2008.
5. A good introduction to the question of U.S.–Greek relations in the Eisenhower era is Stefanides 2002. On the Kennedy era and the gradual shift of Greece into European hands, see Rizos 2006.
6. Two excellent studies of the American role in Cyprus and its decision to "hand off" Greece to Germany and Europe are Nicolet 2001; Pelt 2006.
7. Kennedy administration policy for Cyprus is detailed in *Foreign Relations of the United States* (*FRUS*), *1961–1963*, vol. 16, *Eastern Europe; Cyprus; Greece; Turkey*, 512–36. (Hereafter cited as *FRUS* with dates, volume, pagination). On Makarios's management of the Americans and British, see Miller 2009: 86–91.
8. On the need for a "democratic opposition," see "Dispatch 226 from Athens," 22 September 1958, 781.00/9-2258, Department of State Central Files, Record Group 59, National Archives, Washington (hereafter cited as DSCF, RG 59, NA) and an embittered Karamanlis's comments in a memorandum of conversation, 24 July 1961, 781.00/7-2461, DSCF, RG 59, NA. Two family memoirs that provide detail on George Papandreou's style of operations and his objectives are M. Papandreou 1970 and N. Papandreou 1996. On Karamanlis's support for Andreas's return to Greece, see Paraskevopoulos 1995: 14–15.

9. Memorandum of conversation, November 14, 1962, transmitted in Airgram A-396 from Athens, 14 November, 781.00/11-1462, DSCF, RG 59, NA. On U.S. covert activities and the rigging of the 1961 elections, as well as the "ceaseless struggle" campaign, see Miller 2009: 72–79, and the detailed notes thereto.
10. *FRUS, 1961–1963*, vol. 16, *Eastern Europe; Cyprus; Greece; Turkey*, 658–61, 675, 679–80. For the Queen's views, *FRUS, 1961–1963*, vol. 16, *Eastern Europe; Cyprus; Greece; Turkey*, 684–85.
11. American optimism regarding the new Papandreou team is reflected in "The Papandreou Style," Airgram A-1247 from Athens, 20 May 1964, Pol 15 Greece, DSCF, RG 59, NA.
12. *FRUS, 1964–1968*, vol. 16, *Cyprus; Greece; Turkey*: 17–37; vol. 33, *Organization and Management of Foreign Policy; United Nations*, 984–87. In editing the *1964–1968* volume on Greece, Cyprus, and Turkey, I exceeded my page limits and contrived a transfer of some of the materials relating to Cyprus to the volume (33) on United Nations issues, which I also edited, in order to expand coverage. See also Miller 2009: 97–101. Margret Papandreou's memoir, *Nightmare in Athens* (1970), was formed in the manner of a classic Greek drama, centered on Andreas's succession ambitions and his father's conflicting desires to retain control and arrange to pass the leadership to his son.
13. For documentation of the meetings, see *FRUS, 1964–1968*, vol. 16, *Cyprus; Greece; Turkey*, 137–66. Greek memoranda of conversation are in Papagiorgiou 1983, vol. 2: 44–67. In dealing with the embassy obsession with Andreas, Keeley (2010: 25–34) makes the critical point that Andreas's activities, although annoying, in fact were achieving a major U.S. goal by drawing Greek voters away from the EDA and into the EK.
14. The best commentary on Cyprus diplomacy is by three participants: Alexandrakis, Theodoropoulos, and Lagakos 1987. Nikos Kranidiotis, another participant in the diplomacy, provided a running commentary in Kranidiotis 1981, 1985, and 1986.
15. Keeley (2010: 44–58) lays out the case for seeing Andreas as a center-left reformer who was, in fact, debilitating the KKE-EDA. See Miller 2009: 112–34, on the development of anti-Papandreou sentiment and Greek efforts to exploit it. The Americans were not the only embassy that developed strong anti-Papandreou views, as both the British and the French held both men in contempt.
16. These comments are based on American intelligence sources, so they need to be carefully presented. Intelligence organizations are a crown jewel of national sovereignty and, despite close cooperation with the CIA and Pentagon, Greek officials never permitted Washington to "run" their intelligence services. The United States was involved with the creation of civil war Greece's military intelligence service. While filing reports on IDEA's activities during the 1950s, American officials seemed to regard it as a problem that only Greek officials could contain. The business of intelligence operatives, both CIA and military, was to maintain contact with their opposite numbers in foreign military/

intelligence offices. One of the eventual coup makers, Georgios Papadopoulos, served as an intelligence liaison officer with the CIA in roughly 1963–65. A. Papachelas (1997) provides some intriguing details about his informal contacts with the CIA, but nothing that points to anything going beyond the normal relationship of two cooperating intelligence agencies. Pattakos had American relatives and had attended military training in the United States. Neither man had any difficulty in telling the United States to stay out of Greek internal affairs once in power. I discovered a collection of reports on the coup makers from around 1964–66, while preparing the *FRUS, 1964–1968* volume on Greece, Cyprus, and Turkey. They were collected, without a folder, from part of a box of Athens embassy records, which suggests that the documents were hastily assembled in the aftermath of the coup. The lack of attention to the Colonels' plotting is discussed in Stern 1978, 35–46. When studying CIA documents for the coup period, I was surprised that in the immediate aftermath of 21 April, the Washington headquarters of the agency had little information on Papadopoulos and, apparently after contacting the station in Greece, produced a hastily assembled and not very informative biography for U.S. policymakers. On the 1963 plot, see *FRUS, 1961–1963*, vol. 16, *Eastern Europe; Cyprus; Greece; Turkey*, 664–68; Woodhouse 1982: 148–49. Andreas Papandreou (1970: 121) stated that the embassy informed his father in 1964 of the plotting. I suspect that he erred in his dating of the story by a few months.

17. At the time, I was preparing the *FRUS, 1964–1968* volume on Greece, Cyprus, and Turkey. The Office of the Historian at the U.S. Department of State was in the first stages of achieving full access to CIA files. At that point, I was reviewing the materials for the precoup period, selected by CIA historians, who did their best to assist us. We were not allowed to copy documents, nor were we provided with information on provenance. The documents were submitted for CIA review and rarely released. CIA historians explained that the files for the pre- 1968 period were in chaotic condition. However, we had our own set of minutes of meetings from the 303 Committee (covert operations), which I consulted at the Bureau of Intelligence and Research. The CIA denied release of the documents on the committee's decision to avoid involvement during the July–September 1965 events. As an alternative, I prepared a summary (editorial note) which was printed in *FRUS, 1964–1968*, vol. 16, *Cyprus; Greece; Turkey*, 430–31. During the final editorial process, the CIA objected to the publication of the editorial note. At this point, someone, presumably in the State Department, redrafted the note to meet CIA objections, and in the course of this managed to mix information on the 1965 and 1967 discussions so that the note is misleading. I was not informed of this action and was surprised and dismayed by the resulting note when it appeared in the print volume. Ironically, while the CIA was obstructing the release of the 303 Committee discussion of 1965, it declassified most of the minutes of the 303 Committee Greek discussion of 1967 in response to a freedom of information request. This error permitted us to print the 1967 document with a few excisions.

18. On efforts to restrain the king and army, see *FRUS, 1964–1968*, vol. 16, *Cyprus; Greece; Turkey*, 560–64, 567–77. Kanellopoulos, as head of the ERE, played a crucial role in setting the stage for the coup. His prevote maneuverings, which left the king exposed and nervous, were based on a belief that he could win the elections or at least force the Papandreous into some from of coalition, defanging the EK. See Kanellopoulos 1985: 184–87; 1987: 45–48.
19. Helm's meeting is discussed in Keeley 2010: 88, and based on a CIA insider's story. It took place in March 1967 at the request of the Greek generals, who were sounding out the United States through the CIA, which was an old habit. A long and extremely discursive discussion followed during which Helms, who was as much in the dark about the Colonels' plotting as his guest, extracted a promise to contact him before moving. Assuming that he had staved off a move by the generals, Helms was visibly very angry when the coup occurred. In addition to justifying the move, the Greek representative provided copious details of the general plan, which was a modified version of a NATO plan (Ierax 2) to respond to a Warsaw Pact invasion. A lengthy memorandum of conversation, prepared by Helms, is in the CIA files.
20. *FRUS, 1964–1968*, vol. 16, *Cyprus; Greece; Turkey*, 582–83. The irony of a reluctant coup-maker being the victim of more determined coup-makers escaped the overwrought king.
21. See also *FRUS, 1964–1968*, vol. 16, *Cyprus; Greece; Turkey*, 594–97.
22. See also *FRUS, 1964–1968*, vol. 16, *Cyprus; Greece; Turkey*, 594–97. Keeley (2010: 118–20) justifies his belief that a show of force would have been sufficient to topple the junta, including a very full summary of a 26 April second meeting between Talbot and Kollias in which he participated, and taking to task the editor of the *FRUS* series for failing to publish this document. However, the decision to avoid the use of force had already been made in Washington (*FRUS, 1964–1968*, vol. 16, *Cyprus; Greece; Turkey*, 586–87). On 23 April, Talbot reported that the chances of a Greek countercoup were nonexistent and the Colonels were in full control (*FRUS, 1964–1968*, vol. 16, *Cyprus; Greece; Turkey*, 587–88). After Talbot's first substantive meeting with Pattakos on 28 April, he reiterated that the conspirators had the ability to maintain their hold for the long term, as well as their readiness to work with the United States (*FRUS, 1964–1968*, vol. 16, *Cyprus; Greece; Turkey*, 594–98). Keeley's insistence that a determined U.S. show of force would have brought down the regime fails to meet the test of historical objectivity. In the first place, assembling a serious military contingent to make a show of force credible requires time for assembly and planning. At the time of the coup, the Pentagon reported that it would need thirty-six hours advanced notice simply to dispatch a helicopter to extract the king from his Athens palace (*FRUS, 1964–1968*, vol. 16, *Cyprus; Greece; Turkey*, 584n2) Without thorough preparation, the United States would be in the untenable position of making a threat it could not carry out. The Greek military was unlikely to be cowed by a hastily assembled show of force. The Colonels were, after all, vet-

eran intelligence officers who knew U.S. capabilities. They were also aware of the drawbacks involved in threatening, much less launching, a military assault on a major civilian population center such as Athens. Even if the U.S. military chose to mount a military operation in a less populated area, they would have faced the unwanted option of attacking an allied army. Moreover, U.S. capabilities were stretched thin during the height of the Vietnam War, something the Colonels could not have failed to note. The *New York Times* correspondent C. L. Sulzberger (1973: 324–27), a close friend to the king, met with the junta's leaders shortly after the coup and was impressed by their confidence and readiness to stand up to the Americans.

23. The United States had limited confidence in the king. Initial positive reviews of his management of the Cyprus crisis of 1964 gave way to reappraisals as he stumbled into confrontation with George Papandreou and played a major role in setting the stage for a coup.
24. *FRUS, 1964–1968*, vol. 16, *Cyprus; Greece; Turkey*, 580n3.
25. Daniel Brewster, Oral History, ADST, Washington, DC. See also *FRUS, 1964–1968*, vol. 16, *Cyprus; Greece; Turkey*, 580.
26. The chaotic nature of the king's action and its consequences are reported in *FRUS, 1964–1968*, vol. 16, *Cyprus; Greece; Turkey*, 703–16.
27. Keeley (2010: 152–57) reports on the reaction of U.S. officials and Talbot's diminished situation during, and in the wake of, the countercoup.
28. On the Greek American situation, see Kitroeff's contribution in this volume; INR, "Greece: Implications for US-Greek Relations of Junta's Continuation," 16 March 1971, Pol 17, DSCF, RG 59, NA; Memorandum of conversation, Palamas-Richardson, Greece, vol. 1, National-Security Files, Nixon Presidential Materials (hereafter, MERF, NSF, NPM), NA; on the formalization of a policy and domestic political considerations, see Miller 2009: 158–61.
29. Telegram 970 from Athens, 10 March 1970, memorandum to president, 23 May 1970, with attached Tasca Report, Greece, vol. 1, MERF, NSF, NPM, NA.
30. Kissinger to Nixon, 8 February 1972, Greece, vol. 2, MERF, NSF, NPM, NA.
31. *FRUS, 1973–1976*, vol. 30, *Greece; Cyprus; Turkey, 1973–1976*, 47–60. U.S. Congress, Greece, Spain, and the Southern NATO Strategy: Hearings Before the Subcommittee on Europe of the Committee on Foreign Affairs, House of Representatives, 92nd Congress, 1st session, Washington, DC, 1971.
32. *FRUS, 1973–1976*, vol. 30, *Greece; Cyprus; Turkey, 1973–1976*, 47–60.

REFERENCES

Periodicals

To Vima
Washington Post

Archives

Washington, DC
National Archives
Department of State Central Files, Record Group 59, National Archives (DSCF, RG 59)
National-Security Files, Nixon Presidential Materials, National Archives (MERF, NSF, NPM)

Published Primary Sources

Foreign Relations of the United States (FRUS)

Secondary Sources

Alexandrakis, M., B. Theodoropoulos, and E. Lagakos. 1987. *To kypriako* [The Cyprus issue] Athens.
Allen, D. 2018. "Trump's Foreign Policy Is Perfectly Coherent." *Washington Post*, 24 July.
Couloumbis, T., and S. Hicks, eds. 1976. *U.S. Foreign Policy Towards Greece and Cyprus: The Clash of Principle and Pragmatism*. Washington, DC.
Drew, E. 1968. "Democracy on Ice." *Atlantic Monthly*, April.
Gillman, N. 2003. *Mandarins of the Future: Modernization Theory in Cold War America*. Baltimore.
Kanellopoulos, P. 1985. *I zoi mou* [My life]. Athens.
———. 1987. *Keimena, 1967–1974* [Papers, 1967–74]. Athens.
Keeley, R. 2010. *The Colonel's Coup and the American Embassy: A Diplomat's View of the Breakdown of Democracy in Cold War Greece*. University Park, PA.
Klapsis, A., C. Arvanitpoulos, E. Hatzivassiliou, and E. G. H Pedaliou. 2020. *The Greek Junta and the International System: A Case Study of Southern European Dictatorships, 1967–74*. London.
Klarevos, L. 2006. "Were the Eagle and the Phoenix Birds of a Feather? The United States and the Greek Coup of 1967." *Diplomatic History* 30: 471–508.
Kranidiotis, N. 1981. *Dyskola chronia* [Difficult years]. Athens.
———. 1985. *Anochyroti politeia* [Defenseless state] Athens.
———. 1986. *Dyo krisimes faseis tou kypriakou* [Two critical phases of the Cyprus issue]. Athens.
Lardner, George, Jr. 2001. "History of U.S.–Greek Ties Blocked: CIA Opposes Disclosure of Proposed Covert Actions in '60s." *Washington Post*, 21 August. Retrieved 20 November 2020 from http://proxy.lib.csus.edu/login?url=https://www-proquest-com.proxy.lib.csus.edu/docview/409128050?accountid=10358.

Lee, C. P. 1957. *Athenian Adventure: With Alarums and Excursions*. New York.
Leffler, M. 1993. *A Preponderance of Power: National Security, the Truman Administration, and the Cold War*. Stanford.
Mann, J. 2004. *Rise of the Vulcans: The History of Bush's War Cabinet*. New York.
Maury, J. 1977. "The Greek Coup." *Washington Post*, 1 May.
Miller, J. E. 2009. *The United States and the Making of Modern Greece: History and Power, 1950–1974*. Chapel Hill, NC.
Nicolet, C. 2001. *United States Policy towards Cyprus, 1954–1974*. Manheim.
Papachelas, A. 1997. *O viasmos tis ellinikis dimokratias* [The rape of Greek democracy]. Athens.
———. 2001. "Jim Miller." *To Vima*, 26 August. Retrieved 20 November 2020 from https://www.tovima.gr/2008/11/24/politics/tzim-miler/.
Papagiorgiou, S. 1983. *Ta krisima ntokoumenta tou kypriakou* [Essential documents relating to the Cyprus issue]. 3 vols. Athens.
Papandreou, A. 1970. *Democracy at Gunpoint: The Greek Front*. New York.
Papandreou, M. 1970. *Nightmare at Athens*. New York.
Papandreou, N. 1996. *Father Dancing: An Invented Memoir*. London.
Paraskevopoulos, P. 1995. *Andreas Papandreou*. Athens.
Pattakos, S. 1990. *To aporrito imerologio tou Stylianou Pattakou* [The secret diary of Stylianos Pattakos]. Athens.
Pelt, M. 2006. *Tying Greece to the West: US–West German–Greek Relations 1949–74*. Copenhagen.
Rizos, S. 2006. *I Ellada, oi Inomenes Politeies kai i Evropi* [Greece, the United States, and Europe]. Athens.
Stefanides, I. 2002. *Asymmetroi etairoi* [Unequal allies]. Athens.
Stern, L. 1978. *The Wrong Horse: The Politics of Intervention and the Failure of American Diplomacy*. New York.
Sulzberger, C. L. 1973. *Age of Mediocrity: Memoirs and Diaries, 1963–1972*. New York.
Woodhouse, C. M. 1982. *Karamanlis: The Restorer of Greek Democracy*. Oxford.

Chapter 10

Britain, Europe, and the Greek Junta
"Business as Usual"

Alexandros Nafpliotis

The 1967 imposition of a dictatorial regime in a European country for the first time after World War II has been correctly identified as an anachronism (Rizas 2008: 445). One of the most important aspects of the junta's rule during the seven-year period is the conduct of its foreign policy, as well as the nature and quality of its international relations. This chapter aims at contributing to a better understanding of how the traditional ally Britain dealt with the rise, reign, and fall of the military dictatorship, by analyzing relations between Athens and London (in comparison with relations with other European capitals) within the context of international organizations such as NATO, the Council of Europe (CoE), and the European Economic Community (EEC). By analyzing archival documents from Greece, Britain, and beyond, a remarkable continuity of relations is discerned, with economic benefits outweighing political considerations for dealing with the junta in the case of Britain, as well as for other important Western European powers—namely, West Germany and France.

In the late 1960s, British governments were in a very weak position both financially and internationally, given the 1967 devaluation of the pound and London's decision to relinquish its traditional role in the region of the world that lies to the East of Suez. As a result, British governments had to follow policies that were meant to prove Britain's subordination to NATO and American interests. The Labour government under Harold Wilson (1966–70), after an initial reluctance in dealing with the junta, actively tried to establish a "good working relationship" with the Greek dictatorship, and to make sure that Greece would continue to fulfill its NATO obligations as a bastion of stability in a sea of turbulence in the sensitive area of the Eastern Mediterranean (Nafpliotis 2014).

The political orientation and democratic nature of the Wilson government meant that it was expected (domestically and abroad) to assume a critical position vis-à-vis a European right-wing dictatorship. This, in conjunction with economic and international restrictions mentioned above, brought the Labour government into a particularly difficult position, highlighted by differences between its rhetoric and actions, such as, for example, providing Greece with arms and condoning it within NATO, while at the same time Labour ministers openly criticized the junta's methods and urged it toward a "return to constitutional rule" in forums such as the CoE. British prime minister Wilson did not cut off relations with the Colonels; he decided to extend official recognition to their governments and kept trading with the junta, thus promoting a policy of "business as usual," but not caving into all their demands (keeping contacts, including visits, to a minimum, for example). It was only after Labour returned to power in 1974, following four years in opposition, that Wilson appeared adamant vis-à-vis the Greek dictatorship, in order to show that his policy was different from that of his predecessor, and to make good on Labour's pre-election promises of not condoning a right-wing regime (Nafpliotis 2016).

The Conservatives, on the other hand, due to their right-wing political orientation, appeared more realistic, following a pragmatic policy *par excellence*, thus giving precedence to defense cooperation and promoting trade with Greece over human rights protection and pushing for a return to democracy in the country. Edward Heath's government (in power from 1970 to 1974) concentrated on Greece's allegiance to the Atlantic Alliance, continuing and strengthening a "good working relationship," including actively promoting trade and maintaining peace in Cyprus, going well beyond their predecessors in conducting relations with the Colonels within a very warm climate. To achieve this, Whitehall pursued cooperation in all fields, and most importantly defense, with visits on both sides serving the purpose of bringing London closer to Athens. The four basic U.K. objectives of its policy toward Greece (NATO, Cyprus, bilateral trade, and a return to democracy in Greece) were changed in order to reflect "a new spirit" in relations, whereby the government in London would not twist the junta's arm over a return to constitutional rule and democratic liberties, as U.K. national archive documents show (Nafpliotis 2013: 93–94). The Conservatives strictly followed what I call the doctrine of *disconnected responsibilities* (introduced, however, in as early as 1969 by Labour), making it clear that the NATO and the CoE contexts were completely different and separate, and that developments in one would not spill over onto the other. However, the "familiar tightrope act" of Britain's relations with the junta (as it was termed by British diplomats at the time)[1] was also obvious under Heath, insofar as trade figures almost doubled and relations became warmer, with the British, however, failing to provide sufficient encouragement to the Markezinis experiment[2] and being somewhat constrained in approaching the junta by their participation in the European integration process. In relation to American influence, London—whether under Labour or the Tories—maintained a very close cooperation with Washington, keeping an "open line" on significant issues such as the official recognition of junta-led governments, NATO, and generally the degree of dealing with the regime, but also choosing to differentiate its policy from that of the superpower on a number of occasions, including arms sales and Cyprus (Nafpliotis 2013).

To better understand British decision-making regarding the dictatorship of the Colonels, it is essential to provide some context in terms of presenting a clear picture of what kind of relations the main allies had with the regime. The country at the top of the list of Greece's trade partners, West Germany, quickly decided that, despite the status of the regime and human rights violations on the part of the junta, it was in the interest not only of good Greek–German relations, but also of the Greek people, to avoid any movement that could have led the Colonels into isolation, pushing them toward nationalist tendencies and political neutrality.[3] Moreover, as the West Germans considered that the economic pressure on the regime would not have tangible political results but would, on the contrary, simply harm Greece, and as most of their allies agreed to continue commercial and economic relations with the Colonels, the Federal Republic of Germany (FRG) was determined not to lose its hegemonic position among Greece's trading partners. Bonn also clarified its attitude toward Greece's participation in NATO in a laconic way: "Since Greece is a member of NATO, it should be treated like any other member. Disagreements with the Greek government should not take place within NATO."[4]

Apart from West Germany, France was the other country that strongly opposed the condemnation of the regime in the EEC Council of Ministers, while underlining the strategic importance of Greece within NATO, especially given the Soviet presence in the Mediterranean (De Angelis and Karamouzi 2016). In addition, the French representatives of the European Commission expressed their opposition to freezing the European Investment Bank loan to Greece and of Athens' association with the EEC in general. Even more studious was France's attempt to develop trade relations with the junta after 1969, when French diplomacy reached the point of proposing to revitalize the relationship with the EEC so that other less conscientious countries would not benefit (Nafpliotis 2019). In general terms, the continuation (and in many cases the improvement) of bilateral economic relations with major Western countries (as well as the corresponding intensification of trade with Eastern European countries) allowed the regime to maintain the good course of the Greek economy for several years (at least until 1973).

This chapter is structured around three major themes, with sections on British policy toward the Colonels (and, to a lesser degree, other European countries, for comparison purposes) within the context of the CoE, NATO, and the EEC. The case of the CoE is quite indicative of London's handling of the so-called Greek issue (as the presence of a dictatorial regime in Greece was called at the time), especially when viewed in juxtaposition with policies adopted in NATO, where the stakes were much higher in geopolitical terms.

COUNCIL OF EUROPE

In September 1967, under severe pressure from their parliaments and from street protests, Denmark, Norway, Sweden, and the Netherlands demanded that the CoE take action against Greece over its breach of Article 33 of the European Convention on Human Rights (Fernández Soriano 2017). Greece was to be the very first instance where an interstate complaint against another member was to be investigated so thoroughly and a ruling made. By late 1969, Greece was forced to withdraw from the CoE, the second international setback the junta suffered after the freezing of the EC Athens agreement in 1967 (Pedaliu 2016). The British diplomats' reaction was to immediately stress the importance of not getting "drawn into unnecessarily provocative action by the Scandinavians."[5] The Foreign Office initially said that (a) it was absolutely *against* Greece's withdrawal, (b) it would try to avoid any discussion on a governmental level, and, if not successful, (c) it would try to "bury" the issue at the Council of Ministers.[6] Lord Hood (the deputy under-secretary for foreign affairs, with responsibility for Europe and the United Nations organization) agreed that the Greek humiliation in Strasbourg was barely tolerable, but a withdrawal would be a mistake and would provide ammunition to the junta's enemies to present the event as a victory against the regime.[7]

Whitehall did not want to assume any initiative, and its final stance would in any case depend on consultations with governments of allies. The Greek ambassador's personal impression was that the U.K. government would do everything possible (without, however, going out on a limb) to undermine Greece's expulsion. The junta thought that the United Kingdom had not yet formed a clear position on Greece's expulsion from the CoE and decided to provide information (under confidentiality) to persuade the United Kingdom and to help it intervene in other countries for the postponement of December 1969's decision, thus unofficially assuming the role of a mediator; and that is exactly what Britain did. It is also interesting to note that as late as in October 1969, British officials were going out of their way to comfort the Greek Colonels, saying that "Scandinavian countries like Sweden treated not only Greece in a foolish way but also even the United States and the United Kingdom (as was shown during [Michael] Stewart's Stockholm visit in July 1969, when a series of demonstrations on Biafra and Rhodesia took place)."[8]

It is important to note here the efforts also made by Paris and Bonn to influence other member states of the CoE in order to avoid an open condemnation of the Colonels' regime, notwithstanding the fact that there was a Labour government in the United Kingdom, and that the SPD had just assumed power in West Germany. For example, France and the Federal Republic of Germany worked eagerly, in September 1969, to encourage the Scandinavians to accept a proposal for friendly settlement. Clearly, Paris and Bonn worked actively to promote a friendly settlement and avoid Greece's exclusion. All this activity on the part of major European countries was not entirely irrelevant to a similar approach taken by the United States: as American diplomat Robert Keeley (2010: 198) has revealed, Washington provided "strong (but often behind-the-scenes) political support [to the Colonels' regime] by lobbying in their favor in organizations such as NATO, as well as in other bodies to which [the United States do] not even belong, such as the Council of Europe, where [it] discouraged friendly governments from taking any action that might annoy the Greek Colonels."

Nevertheless, the U.K. position changed in late October 1969. Due to opposing public opinion and parliamentary pressure at home, the government now turned to being in favor of avoiding a vote and in favor of having Greece withdraw. As time progressed and human rights violations reports (referring to incidents of torture and other police violence incidents in Greece) started circulating across Europe, it became increasingly difficult for even friendly governments to defend the actions of the Greek junta. Expressing his willingness to agree to the expulsion of Greece, Foreign Secretary Stewart said that "even big powers like Britain and France over Suez and the United States over Vietnam are obliged to take into consideration public opinion in their countries, as well as advice and pressure from other friendly and allied countries."[9]

Speaking of allied countries, however, it soon became clear that the United States was not pleased: in 1970, the new U.S. ambassador in Greece, Henry Tasca, said that Labour's "attitude to the Greek Government was mistaken and the part which the British Government played in the Council of Europe's decision [the previous] December had been mistaken and even irresponsible."[10] The FRG, however, agreed with the United Kingdom and underlined the opportunity to draw a clear distinction between the CoE and NATO, where all problems with Greece should be avoided (this foreshadowing the adoption of the doctrine of disconnected responsibilities by the United Kingdom). When it came to France, it was in an easier position, given that it was not part of the European Convention on Human Rights (ECHR). Nevertheless, it should be said that France recognized the role of the West German chancellor Willy Brandt as being key and mentioned the French parliament's hostile stance vis-à-vis the Colonels.[11]

Of all the big European countries, Italy was the closest to the Scandinavians' point of view but was more reserved, as it was interested in coordinating its actions with the British government in order to reach a common position (versus the Franco-German axis).[12] Rome followed the so-called *opzione del doppio binario* (i.e., the political isolation of Greece on a European level and tolerance toward Greece in the NATO context due to geostrategic interests; see Ghezzi 2014: 60), which echoes the doctrine of disconnected responsibilities pursued by London.

When it came to the Benelux countries, Belgium, the Netherlands, and Luxembourg had parallel positions. The Hague hesitated initially, as it would have preferred a joint Benelux action. The Dutch nevertheless decided to cooperate closely with the Scandinavians (Denmark, Sweden, and Norway) in submitting an application to the CoE. The Netherlands thus admittedly soon submitted a similar application to the Scandinavian one—with Belgium and Luxembourg expressing their sympathy with the applicant governments but not actually participating for formal reasons. In this respect, it should be noted that the United Kingdom doubted this was an effective way of bringing pressure on the junta.[13] Notwithstanding their previous position and active participation in the so-called Greek case being discussed in Strasbourg, the Dutch opted for a slightly more cautious approach, also stressing the importance of not linking the Greek case at the CoE to the country's membership in NATO. Having said that, The Hague did not relinquish its efforts to expel the Colonels' Greece from the CoE, mostly because of the pressure exerted on the government by the Dutch parliament.[14]

As far as Belgium was concerned, there were extremely critical reactions in parliament from the very beginning, asking for a break in diplomatic relations, and initiatives were taken in the context of both the CoE and the ECHR. Nevertheless, Belgian officials were quick to stress that events in the Middle East (see the Six-Day War) helped get the Greek issue out of sight slightly. More specifically, as regards the CoE resolution, Brussels thought it would be "better to appease" (*il vaut mieux apaiser*), to wait for events to become clear, and to give the junta a chance to fulfill its promises (on presenting a democratic constitution). The Belgian prime minister Pierre Harmel feared that the left-wing Socialists in Belgium would exploit the situation to develop a full-scale attack on NATO as a whole.[15]

On the other side of the dispute, the Greek junta's reaction to efforts to get Greece kicked out of the CoE was characteristic of its nature and way of governing. According to French officials, Athens reacted to the application in the context of the European Commission of Human Rights "(in the Greek tradition) in a nationalistic and hostile manner." The Greek press (or rather, the heavily censured outlets that kept publishing), under pressure from the regime, seemed very irritated by what was considered an unacceptable intrusion into Greek domestic politics, with a conservative Athens daily commentator declaring that it was time "to teach the idle leftists of the café called Europe a lesson, following their unacceptable attempt to meddle in the domestic affairs of an independent country."[16] As the Greek ambassador in London made abundantly clear: the regime's "'tolerance' cannot be sustained in view of the malevolent and one-sided stance of people in Strasbourg, which has caused general and uncontrollable indignation in Greece, where everyone is asking for a withdrawal from this instrument of the anti-Greek campaign."[17] Furthermore, the Greek junta made no secret of its expectations vis-à-vis the country's traditional allies: as Greek ambassador Ioannis A. Sorokos told U.K. officials, on the issue of the CoE, "We expect [Britain] to pursue a responsible policy and to influence other countries as well as to take into account European unity and the goodwill of the Greek people."[18]

By the end of 1969, however, the wave of dissatisfaction created in most European capitals (including London) by the Greek regime's abhorrent treatment of the population reached prodigious dimensions, as a secret report (in late November) written by the European Commission of Human Rights, which condemned the Colonels' "disregard for the rule of law and its practice of torture and imprisonment without trial," was leaked to the press (Woodhouse 1984: 69). This fact, in conjunction with America's unwillingness to press the British over Greece (the United States was, nevertheless, worried about the possible repercussions in NATO of action in the CoE),[19] resulted in Wilson's announcement on 9 December that his government would vote for expulsion. Nevertheless, Greek preoccupation over the CoE issue seemed to have subsided considerably after the decision to walk out of the organization, in view of the vote for Greece's expulsion in December 1969. The junta became increasingly "indifferent" to debates on Greece at the Consultative Assembly of the CoE, with the new Greek deputy minister for foreign affairs Christos Xanthopoulos-Palamas stating that "these types of debates do not interest the Greek government at all."[20] Overall, it is fair to say that the foreign policy of the CoE member states was shaped by individual foreign policy considerations, among which security considerations prevailed, due to the "soft" nature of the CoE, in contradistinction to a military organization such as NATO, where this approach is clearly illustrated.

NORTH ATLANTIC TREATY ORGANIZATION

When it came to the North Atlantic Alliance's stance toward the Greek Colonels' regime, international and regional events played a particularly important role. The junta, having declared its allegiance to NATO shortly after coming to power, was lucky enough to see Greece's geostrategic position significantly enhanced: the Six-Day War, whose outbreak occurred less than fifty days after the coup in Greece, considerably allayed the fears of Western officials in particular. The "widespread concern" that the U.K. defense secretary, Denis Healey, had admitted on 31 May, which all members of the NATO alliance felt, soon changed to a softer position toward the junta, due to its upgraded status as the only tried and tested Western ally in the wider region apart from Israel.[21] As Foreign Office officials—drafting notes for the prime minister's answer to a parliamentary question on NATO and Greece—wrote, "The Greek Government were helpful during the recent Middle Eastern crisis in connection with some of our evacuation arrangements . . . [so] it would be against our interests to cause trouble with them in NATO at this time, or to do anything which would disturb the uneasy situation over Cyprus."[22] It became evident that the United Kingdom (along with the United States, France, and Turkey) was very much opposed to a discussion of the Greek problem at the North Atlantic Council as suggested in 1968 by the Italian foreign minister, Amintore Fanfani. The NATO secretary general, Manlio Brosio, expressed his hope that Fanfani was not planning to raise the question at the Council. However, the Italian permanent representative made it known that his minister wished this to be discussed in a private meeting after the Council.[23] In general terms, Italy's stance vis-à-vis the regime was very close to London's doctrine of "disconnected responsibilities" and reflected the different opinions and goals within the Italian Center-Left; Fanfani's efforts to raise the Greek issue in NATO should thus be seen in the light of intraparty pressure exerted by figures such as Pietro Nenni and Italian society in general (Ghezzi 2014: 94–95; see also Soave 2014).

Brothers in Arms Policy

London's position in NATO in relation to the junta was epitomized by its arms policy toward Greece: in a seminal meeting of the Defense and Overseas Policy Committee in January 1969, it was decided that Britain "should in principle permit the supply to Greece of arms which she could reasonably be expected to acquire in order to fulfil her NATO role" and that "only the supply of those arms intended to repress the civilian population should be prohibited."[24] This decision was formulated following the previous example of the policy governing arms deliveries to South Africa in the 1960s.[25] This distinction between so-called straightforward items and U.S. policy on arms supply was the exact opposite of that of London: the British, as a matter of principle, did not provide the Colonels with military equipment that could be turned against civilians (items with a clear military use and thus could be exported) and items "which might be readily connected in the public mind" with repression and crowd control (which could not be exported) (Phythian 2000: 5). An agreement was also sought with major allies in NATO on a common policy for the supplies of arms and on export credits, with the United States being contacted first; however, it met with no substantial effect, as the Americans, traditional suppliers of weaponry to Greece, had chosen to terminate the delivery only of items of "high visibility," such as tanks and airplanes (Miller 2009: 152; Karakatsanis and Swarts 2018).

London's policy was largely directed by two major fears of British officials: first, the fear that if their country did not supply that kind of military equipment, its policy objectives would be placed in jeopardy because they would no longer be able to exercise the necessary influence with the Greek government in order to pursue them; and second, the fear that U.K. allies would rush to cash in. In connection to the last point, it should be noted that the United States (aircraft and minesweepers), France (patrol boats), and West Germany (submarines) had already signed contracts with the junta. Britain's poor economic condition (a very large deficit, which contributed to a series of sterling crises and which, in conjunction with international crises and dock strikes, eventually led to the devaluation of the pound in 1967) made it "exceedingly difficult to defend putting at risk export orders of this order of magnitude."[26] British prime minister Wilson asked to be informed on a regular basis regarding the American position on arms supplies, his point being that "the United Kingdom should not appear to give more support to the Greek régime, even in the NATO context, than the United States."[27] The primary suspect for providing arms to the Colonels' Greece was identified as being the French by not only the British, but also by King Constantine and the Americans, who shared the British fear of the junta "going French" (that is to say, buying most of Greece's new military equipment from France) (Miller 2009: 151; Karakatsanis and Swarts 2018: 69). It is important to note, however, that even the French themselves had similar concerns (voiced in the context of COREPER—the Committee of Permanent Representatives to the EC—almost at the same time; specifically, in early 1969) regarding "losing out to other, less scrupulous countries."[28] As Hervé Alphand (secretary general at the French Ministry of Foreign Affairs) stated in June 1969, "France is the third largest importer from Greece and fifth biggest exporter—we cannot stop being interested in this market with which we have a largely positive balance and which offers interesting prospects for the future."[29]

Disconnecting Responsibilities

It was during the same meeting on arms policy mentioned above that another major distinction in relation to the British government's stance on the Greek military junta (in the international context this time) was drawn; it was decided that actions to assist the defense of NATO and the British attitude toward Greece in the CoE were two different, albeit loosely related, issues. Foreign and Commonwealth Office (FCO) officials made their position clear:

> Our policies in the Council of Europe should be decided in the light of the moral and other issues involved, while questions of military co-operation should be treated in the NATO context. This distinction reflects the fact that whereas the Council of Europe has a democratic statute which its members are committed to observe, NATO is the product of a military alliance. *If a government is clearly in violation of the statute of the Council of Europe, a time must come when it can no longer be accepted as a member. But we remain firmly opposed to action against Greece in NATO, in which Greece occupies a key position on the South Eastern flank.* Any attempt to interfere with Greek participation in NATO would be strongly opposed by, among others, the United States, German and Turkish governments, and would have a politically divisive effect within the alliance in addition to its military implications.[30] (Emphasis mine)

The January 1969 meeting also revealed cracks within the Labour government, when it came to its stance on the Greek junta. Richard Crossman (secretary of state for social services) expressed his strong disapproval of the policy chosen primarily by Foreign Secretary Stewart and Prime Minister Wilson, which he characterized as a "combination of high-minded principle and arms sales" (Crossman 1978: 347 [30 January]). The Labour government was apprehensive from the very start of the "internationalization" of the Greek issue, reflected in the strong reaction of European and North American public opinion, and they struggled to assume a neutral position toward the Colonels. This (beneficial to the dictatorship) neutrality was exemplified by Britain's decision not to take the lead nor oppose moves to expel Greece from the CoE. Although the government in London was in "complete disagreement" with the dictatorial practices of the Colonels, British officials tried to promote a milder course of action vis-à-vis Greece in regional organizations, and to cultivate warmer relations by, for example, inviting the Greek minister of industry to the British capital. The solution given to the impasse by the ever-practical Wilson was the separation of the two regional "spheres": action in one forum (the CoE) would not influence policy in the other (NATO). Consequently, Whitehall, in an effort to palliate parliamentary criticism, chose to subscribe to the move to suspend Greece's membership of the CoE, and at the exact same time reassured the Colonels (and the Americans) that it would safeguard Greece's position in NATO. In this respect, Wilson's decision to "sacrifice" Greece's presence in a political organization of lesser significance was designed to function as a "safety valve," releasing pressure from the House of Commons and public opinion. Finally, the Wilson government also tried to influence its allies in treating the "special case" of the Greek junta in the same way: according to the Italian foreign minister's memoirs, Stewart's pressure on Nenni to drop his campaign to have Greece expelled from NATO reflected Britain's "deep indifference towards liberty's tragedies" (Nenni 1983; cited in Favretto 2006: 435).

Enter the Tories

When the Conservative Party won the June 1970 election in Britain, the support for the military dictatorship in Greece became even less reserved. The Conservatives immediately proclaimed that although they "had not been in full agreement with the way the previous British Government had handled the proceedings on Greece in the Council of Europe," they were in complete agreement regarding Greece's need to continue to play a full part in NATO.[31] The repercussions of the electoral outcome were not lost on the junta in Athens. The Greek ambassador in Britain, Sorokos, clearly stated that the United Kingdom "should remind [NATO] partners who forget their general responsibilities (for example, Denmark) that it is not possible to refer to issues of domestic politics."[32] Britain was involved in efforts made through the NATO general secretariat to promote dropping the Greek issue in the Atlantic Alliance, as well as in efforts to detach Norway from Denmark, and even to have Norway exert pressure on Denmark to stop creating problems for the junta. Moreover, the British ambassador in Denmark devised (and the Foreign Office examined) a plan to get Turkey involved in the issue and exert pressure on Copenhagen to ease up on the junta as well.[33]

In NATO's September meeting, Greece was the first item on the agenda. The British preparation for the meeting is characteristic of their view on the subject: "If in future the Scandinavians spoke in NATO against the Greeks, the British delegation should be prepared to underline the value of the Greek contribution to the Alliance."[34] The British government justified this position by claiming yet again that "discussion of Greek internal affairs would have a divisive effect within the Alliance, and the expulsion of Greece would open a critical gap in NATO's South Eastern flank."[35] As has been argued by a prominent historian of British foreign policy, "NATO was one of the forums where Britain chose to clearly demonstrate its continuing importance to the United States, thus countering the negative effect of London's withdrawal from East of Suez and Wilson's refusal to send troops to Vietnam" (Young 2009, vol. 2: 135). In the meantime, Greece's position in NATO had been reinforced by a new era in the junta's relations with the United States, triggered by international events, such as the evacuation of the U.S. Air Force base in Libya after Colonel Gaddafi's coup and the rise of anti-American sentiment in Turkey, and sealed with the appointment of a U.S. ambassador in Athens (following a hiatus of almost a year, due to Washington's hesitation in appointing a successor to Phillips Talbot). The main U.K. fear at the time was the danger that attempts by the Danes, Norwegians, and Dutch to discuss the internal situation within Greece, or even to question Greek membership of the Alliance, might trigger a Greek walkout (similar to the one at the CoE)—a "risk [that had] been aggravated by the death of [Foreign Minister] Panagiotis Pipinelis and by the increasing influence of hardliners in Athens."[36] The doctrine of "separated" or "disconnected responsibilities" (in the context of the CoE and NATO) served the British government very well, as it provided it with a defensive line in the face of criticism from both European and British liberals, as well as the Colonels.

It was exactly in that context that the first quid pro quo between London and Athens was put forward—that is, British support for an allocation of NATO funds to Greece for British use of the Souda base in Crete. The December NATO ministerial council revealed the priorities and the anxieties of not only the British but also of other Western Europeans. The most controversial issues up for discussion had to do with authoritarian Southern European regimes—namely, Portugal and Greece, which were members, and Spain, which was contemplating an informal association with NATO. The British generally thought that they "should not allow extraneous political controversy to interfere with the normal working of the Alliance." When it came to Greece specifically, they hoped that the matter would not be discussed at all because, although they accepted that they were looking forward to the restoration of Greek democracy, they also thought that "NATO [was] not the right forum to pursue this," and that it was particularly important that "NATO should present a united front in defence of its sensitive Mediterranean flank." This also explains why attacks by the so-called usual suspects (namely, the Scandinavians) were now received much more stoically in Athens. As the British ambassador in Greece admitted, "This greater confidence regarding their position in NATO on the part of the Greek Government reflected the development of the United States and British policy regarding defence co-operation with Greece during 1970."[37]

A Tale of Two Cities

Ever since the 21 April 1967 coup, Paris had followed a policy of noninterference in the domestic affairs of Greece, and relations with the junta were "particularly good."[38] Pipinelis's death in 1970 allowed for an even closer French connection with his successor (Gaullist) Xanthopoulos-Palamas. The watershed moment in that respect was the visit by the French foreign minister Jean de Lipkowski in 1972; this was the first official visit to Greece by a minister from a Western European democracy, and emphasis was placed on increasingly improving economic relations, favorable to French interests. British ambassador Sir Robin Hooper commented by saying that the "visit would leave the French one up on [Britain]" and thus bring them closer to the Colonels and to trade prospects.[39] This consequently led to the first (official) visit to Greece by a British minister (Lord Limerick, parliamentary under-secretary of state for trade and industry) in October 1972, with the FRG maintaining a similar stance. The British were keeping a watchful eye on visits by Western ministers to Greece, and were quick to learn from the "mistakes" of their allies: "We should . . . avoid the excesses which followed the recent visit by [the secretary of state at the German Foreign Ministry] Dr Frank, when the Greek press gloated over what they regarded as confirmation of Greece's international respectability."[40] And elsewhere: "The crux of the matter is whether Lord Limerick is to say anything to Greek Ministers about what HMG think about the nature of the régime here. . . . The French were able to say much less when M. Galley came in the summer and they got away with it very successfully. Galley, rather than Frank, would seem to be our best model."[41] Despite Greek reluctance "to be seen going other than American" (that is to say, not buying material exclusively from the United States), in case this should affect U.S. policy over military aid, West German and, especially, French exceptions were underlined as possible examples to be followed by the British and as possible future competition.[42]

As the years progressed and the Greek Colonels' regime did not show any significant signs of collapsing, London's defense of the junta's presence in NATO increased: Britain decided it should continue to resist attempts by the Danes and Norwegians for action against Greece in NATO, and try to dissuade other NATO governments from joining the Scandinavians' campaign. Whitehall appeared, therefore, to be taking a more proactive stance regarding Greece's position in the Atlantic Alliance, refusing to stand idly by and watch the developments unfold, and instead offering its assistance to the Colonels' cause. To cite only one example, British diplomats were told to "remind Dr Schmelzer of our views" when the Dutch foreign minister visited London in March 1972.[43] Furthermore, the British, of course, were interested in gaining in the process. As it was stated in another meeting, "If the Greeks really valued their relations with us and our efforts on their behalf in NATO and elsewhere, *they should see that some significant public contracts come our way*" (emphasis added).[44] It should be noted that Britain followed a very similar approach in its relations with Greece also within the framework of the EEC, which is the subject of the next section.

THE EUROPEAN ECONOMIC COMMUNITY

The Greek Colonels were very aware of the importance of British membership of the EEC (Britain joined in 1973) in the context of London's foreign policy. The personal involvement of Prime Minister Heath in this process, as well as the loosening of the special relationship with the United States, was acknowledged by the Greeks, who were also worried about developments in the EEC and their future in Europe in general. The British in turn acknowledged the Greeks' anxiety over the working of their Association Agreement with the EEC (initiated in 1961), which was bound to have repercussions on the relationship between Athens and London as well.[45] More specifically, the Foreign Office had the impression that "the EEC Commission was likely to persist in its hostile attitude towards Greece." As a result, FCO officials' fears were clearly manifested: "The Greeks are already looking for support and, on achieving full membership, we must expect further pressure from them. There is, however, little we can do, especially as Denmark and Norway—two of the Greeks' main European critics—will be joining at the same time."[46]

The difficulties presented on the relation between Athens and Brussels were far more complex than the discussion of the Greek issue within the NATO forum. That fact, in conjunction with the precarious status of the British within the organization (they were not an important founding member as in NATO, and they had been declined entry on two occasions), meant that London was initially not particularly keen on taking up the Greek cause within that context. However, the British ambassador, Hooper, remarked that Britain's accession to the EEC did "inevitably [bring the British] into a new relationship with Greece." More specifically, he said,

> The question of British support for Greek objectives in the EEC will be one which will be in the forefront of Greek preoccupations in the coming year; and how we are to confront and, if possible, turn to our own advantage the pressures to which we shall certainly be subjected will be one of the major problems—if not the major problem—of Anglo-Greek relations in 1973.[47]

In terms of commercial dividends, the British reasserted (in the EEC context this time) their expectation: "If we were to give the present Greek regime overt political support in the EEC we might expect to get over a period of time a share of the civilian public contracts." Commercial dividends were extremely significant, as Whitehall was particularly worried about Britain's sliding position in Greece's foreign trade list and about the success of its rivals:

> The French are, with the United States, the natural Western partners for the Greeks to choose in any major and sensitive (e.g. defence or aerospace) contract, and while the Greeks may be worrying about the perfidy of Albion in regard to arms contracts, they do not seem to have drawn similar conclusions from French behaviour towards Israel after the Six Days' War.[48]

It should be noted that comparable British figures for investment and credits were expected to be little above a tenth of the French level. Hooper suggested taking the French line of conducting contacts discreetly and with tact, in order to serve British hopes of "substantial, national commercial dividends" in Greece.[49] On the issue of the Colonels' proposed quid pro quo, whereby they would award contracts in the public sector to foreign companies for a more favorable attitude from EEC member states (including the British), London was slightly apprehensive but largely accommodating: "Unpalatable though this may be, we shall stand a better chance of getting such contracts if we appear reasonably forthcoming . . . we might, if we thought it right, do something to meet the Greeks."[50] The example of Greek wine exports to the EEC is telling: the U.K. representative at COREPER expressed himself to be in favor of the compromise proposals the Greeks were prepared to accept, and the British (who, however, had only a slight direct interest in the subject in view of the very small consumption of Greek wine in Britain) were expecting to be able to support the Greeks in the Council of Ministers as well.

London, however, was facing a dilemma: on the one hand, it was finding it increasingly difficult to upgrade its "good working relationship" with the junta; and on the other, it could not downgrade (let alone cut off) relations with Athens, as that would entail a big blow to British commercial prospects and would thus prove utterly counterproductive. Nowhere was this stalemate more obvious than in matters concerning the Greek association with the EEC. The British understood that appearing to freeze Greece's Association Agreement would harm their primary objectives vis-à-vis Greece, but were equally aware that lifting any restrictions on Greece would most likely remove "the one real incentive" for the Colonels to normalize the political situation. To exemplify this point, an official of the European integration department of the FCO wondered (while referring to the "freezing" of the Agreement) whether "we really want to thaw it without securing some kind of quid pro quo from the Greeks"; he continued, "I see no reason to throw this card away for nothing. Are we not in favour of some kind of return to democracy in Greece?"[51]

In mid-1973, nevertheless, it was agreed that the current British policy should continue, and that it was "presentationally important" for London to help the Colonels in Brussels, making clear to them that their troubles there were not of Britain's making. As part of the quid pro quo suggested by the junta, the British thought that, while remaining careful not to give empty promises, "it should nonetheless be possible to extract some advantage from such help as [the United Kingdom] might be able to give."[52] More specifically, Hooper suggested a "helpful and sympathetic attitude" toward the Greeks and their problems, believing that this would safeguard British interests, including prospects of obtaining public sector contracts, and would "ensure that [Britain's] principal competitors (the French and Germans) do not have the advantage." He clarified his point further, leaving little doubt about Britain's policy on this sensitive subject: "We should take full credit and extract what return we can whenever we speak up for the Greeks. We can support them on such matters as may arise within the Community affecting their interests but not impinging on important interests of other member states."[53]

It should be stressed, however, that Whitehall was left in no doubt about Athens' "exaggerated expectations" with regard to progress in Greece-EEC relations, and grudgingly viewed Georgios Papadopoulos's effort to use what leverage he had at his disposal ("notably the award of contracts in the public sector") to obtain a more positive attitude from member states, including Britain.[54] This is particularly interesting when viewed in comparison to the recent argument by Neovi M. Karakatsanis and Jonathan Swarts (2018: 197, 209) that "the colonels' regime exercised a great deal of agency and exerted a significant degree of influence over the United States, often forcing policy makers in Washington to concede to its demands."

In May 1973, nevertheless, the arrest of Ioannis Pesmazoglou (former Greek chief negotiator with the EEC) led to pressure in the House of Commons (even in the form of parliamentary questions on Greece by Conservative MPs). Britain was now giving signs that it would not hesitate to use the EEC if it decided to pressure Athens. It was, therefore, intense domestic criticism (Papadopoulos had even complained about this to the British ambassador in 1971)[55] in conjunction with London's desire not to rock the European boat upon its entry that played a significant part in Whitehall threatening Athens about reconsidering its stance toward the regime. The abolition of the monarchy in June, along the subsequent recognition issue, represents a clear example of the Europeanization of the United Kingdom's policy regarding the Greek military dictatorship—that is to say, an area of policy where coordination of views with important European partners took first place. The fact that Britain was now (after two failed attempts) a member of the EEC, as well as the fact that this process was institutionalized in a forum other than NATO, heavily influenced British policy vis-à-vis Greece. More specifically, Foreign Secretary Alec Douglas-Home informed the embassy in Athens that no decision on the recognition of the new government should be taken prior to consultation with Britain's EEC partners. The same coordination of views occurred in two more instances: (a) the reaction to the 1973 referendum on the proposed new Greek constitution (a message of congratulations was sent to Papadopoulos); and (b) the reception of Spyridon Markezinis's government and the issue of foreign recognition arising again in late 1973. The last incident especially had deep implications for FCO practice insofar as it sparked a reassessment of its recognition policy toward the direction of aligning it with that of the other EEC members (the so-called states not governments formula). After recognition, London decided to adopt a policy of "wait and see," letting the EEC lever work in favor of the restoration of democracy in Greece.[56]

Nevertheless, during the so-called Markezinis experiment in September 1973 (when for the first time since the coup, a civilian politician headed the junta regime; see Tzortzis 2019), Britain's "helpful and sympathetic" attitude toward Greece in the EEC context was reaffirmed, and it was agreed that Britain should neither take the lead nor be left behind in ratifying the enlargement protocol that would extend the Greek-EEC Association Agreement to the Community's new members. However, when hard-liners of the regime (under the leadership of the head of the feared Military Police, Brigadier Dimitrios Ioannides) decided to topple the civilian-led government of Markezinis and put an end to Papadopoulos's "liberalization" attempts, things took a different turn.[57] The new Labour government (in power since March 1974, again under Wilson) was more determined to adopt a harder line, but Whitehall realized that "acting alone or even in conjunction with those of our NATO and EEC partners (e.g. the Dutch and the Scandinavians) who think likewise we can exercise *very little influence* in this direction" (emphasis mine).[58] It was stated that the process should start in Washington, for only the U.S. government possessed sufficient means—strategic advantage, military aid, and financial and political involvement—to make pressure effective.[59] The Americans, however, had already relinquished that responsibility, and had made that fact clear to their European allies; as the U.S. ambassador said to Nenni, "If there were any limitations on our position ... it stemmed ... from a conviction that we could not be effective in exerting pressure on the regime. Our levers were inadequate."[60] Finally, the British were surprised by the reticence of their Greek interlocutors over the issue of the EEC.[61] However, this did not "unduly distress" the British because the Wilson government was at the time mainly preoccupied with reassessing and renegotiating Britain's membership in the regional organization, a process that culminated in the 1975 British referendum on EEC membership.[62]

THE VIEW FROM ATHENS

This chapter on Western European countries and the junta would certainly not be complete without referring to the Greek side of the relationship. Almost as soon as they came to power, the Greek Colonels appeared willing to pull out all the stops to reassure Western bloc countries of Greece's belief in, and allegiance to, Western institutions in general and NATO in particular. Numerous efforts were made to convince Westerners (especially those who, like the British, were not constantly condemning the regime) that no change in Greece's foreign policy orientation was forthcoming, and that NATO's position in their country and thus security in the organization's southern flank were guaranteed. That would have an effect, however, only as long as the Westerners were willing to sustain the Colonels, who, according to their own view, were protecting Greece from communist infiltration and were acting as a buffer against a domino effect in the region. This is a perfect illustration of what John Lewis Gaddis (2007: 129) has called "a compelling form of Cold War blackmail," as the Greek "domino" was indeed "advertising its propensity to topple."

In other words, the military regime was trying to persuade the West (including Britain) that the West needed the Colonels as much as (if not more than) the Colonels needed its (even tacit) support to hold on to power. In this context, therefore, the military leaders decided to appoint former generals to be Greek ambassadors in the important posts of London and Paris. Moreover, the junta actively pursued a rapprochement with France after 1970 with the aim to exert pressure on the United States and other Western allies, such as the British and the Germans: as British ambassador Stewart noted, the Colonels seemed "to be taking the necessary measures to foster the sense that Greece [could] afford to adopt a more independent line than hitherto," and there were numerous "indications that the [Greek] Government [was] seeking to diversify their arms supplies in order to avoid excessive dependence on the goodwill of the United States."[63]

In a statement that seemed to encapsulate the very spirit of Greek foreign policy and the Greek officials' perception of foreign relations at the time, Palamas said that "since Greece has left the Council of Europe, bilateral relations with its members had improved. This showed that *governments were really interested in their own relations with Greece–not in general democratic ideals and principles*."[64] It is also worth mentioning Stewart's observation that the junta's "grumpiness" in respect of the role of Westerners (especially the Scandinavians and British) in international organizations was "typical of the ignorance of the nature of international politics and relations which characterise[d] most of the present military rulers of Greece."[65] It is also important to note that the junta's blackmail was quite effective, as big Western European capitals strongly believed that an alternative to the triumvirate of Papadopoulos, Pattakos, and Makarezos would only be worse for their interests, and presumably Greece's interests as well; as a Foreign Office official wrote in 1971:

> In the event of another crisis (whether a minor one, like the CoE in December 1969, or a major one, like Cyprus in November 1967), [British ambassador Stewart] added, "It is very likely that only Mr. Papadopoulos will stand between the further estrangement of Greece from Western Europe, which is good for neither Greece nor Europe, or some ignorant or violent reaction urged upon him by his nominal subordinates."[66]

It can therefore safely be said that here was an important difference of approach between the British, whose objectives were primarily commercial and concerned mainly with bilateral trade, and the Greeks, whose objective was predominantly to secure U.K. support, after it entered the EEC, in achieving their aims there. What is also interesting to note is that the Greeks were not willing to recognize the existence of a political barrier in their relations with the EEC because of the nature of their regime. Greek ministers thought of that "as *of little consequence* and as an issue which it is inappropriate to raise in 'an economic organisation.'"[67] The junta, conversely, was more than willing to use any leverage it had in order to gain international support and legitimacy, for which it desperately longed. It is in that context that the Greeks explicitly proposed another quid pro quo to the British:

> The Greeks no doubt wished to suggest that our chances of getting a greater share in public sector contracts here depend upon the degree of political support we can give them in the EEC.... The sympathetic noises about showing consideration to Britain were presumably subject to *the implicit proviso that we are "on probation"* until the Greeks see what practical help we can give them in their European policies.[68] (Emphasis mine)

CONCLUSION

Greece's efficiency as a NATO ally was consistently the most marked and publicized objective of Whitehall vis-à-vis the Greek Colonels. It is unambiguous that the British condoned the junta in NATO, despite severe criticism from other members of the alliance. Both parties in power struggled (albeit with varying degrees of ardor) to convince critics at home and abroad of the necessity of recognizing the regime that had effective control of the country as the official government of Greece. This bipartisan recognition for the junta (as if these were normal, democratically elected governments) is obvious in the careful handling of the Greek issue in the aftermath of Greece's withdrawal from the CoE (so that it did not spill over into NATO), in the doctrine of "disconnected responsibilities" introduced by the Labour government and followed by the Conservative government as well, and in the general stance adopted by the British in relation to condemning the Greeks in the forum of the Atlantic Alliance.

Britain was a nation heavily dependent on trade and investment overseas, and that meant that it was more vulnerable than, for example, France or West Germany to the sudden loss of export markets.[69] Arms sales in particular were deemed important to Britain not only because of their contribution to total exports (almost 500 million GBP per year), but also because they bore a substantial share of the overhead costs of British defense industrial capacity, which was required to support the armed forces. As a general directive, Britain, in its effort to strike the right balance, might have to restrict the sale of arms that could be used for internal repression (such as small arms, armored cars), but not those with strictly external use (such as submarines, air defense missiles). Having said that, the amount of trade between the two countries was rather small (Britain's market share was around 8 percent, with its exports to Greece averaging around 60 million GBP per annum from 1967 to 1973), and, therefore, the importance of Greece was not due to its standing as a trading partner but mostly due to its strategic position in both the NATO and Eastern Mediterranean contexts.

In relation to the EEC, London was hoping to extract some advantage from its helpful (to the Greeks) attitude, by initiating a quid pro quo with the junta whereby the British would be awarded contracts in the public sector (e.g., for a nuclear power plant or the Athens metro system and/or the Athens airport) for an exchange of a more favorable attitude toward Greece in the regional organization. The British government, led by Heath, decided not to change its main policy toward Greece but to "go a stage further"[70] and add another element (that was to be subordinate to other British interests in the country) to its dealings with the Athens regime—namely, the promotion of a return to democracy in Greece. London decided to do so not because it was suddenly hit by the realization that its policy was not moral enough, but because it estimated, in view of domestic developments (i.e., intense parliamentary criticism) and international ones (i.e., the EEC and, to a certain extent, Cyprus), that its interests would be better served by adopting such an approach. The prospect of Britain's membership of the EEC functioned as a trump card in the hands of the British, who, although not very capable of acting in favor of the Colonels within the regional organization (the Greeks were primarily interested in seeing their Association Agreement with the EEC active again and the flow of Community funds toward Athens reinstated), could use it as leverage to push the Greek leadership toward a more liberal direction, crucially without assuming sole responsibility for that initiative, and without taking the heat alone. Through the use of such tactics, Whitehall could revert to its "familiar tightrope act" in pursuing its objectives toward Greece under a military dictatorship.

When it came to other EEC member states, West Germany agreed with the United Kingdom and underlined the opportunity to draw a clear distinction between the CoE and NATO. Italy reluctantly followed suit, shaping its own *opzione del doppio binario* (double track option), and also drawing a distinction between action in NATO and other less important forums. Benelux countries, led by the Netherlands, developed similar positions (although Brussels, where the NATO headquarters are situated, appeared slightly more pragmatic and willing to give the junta the benefit of the doubt), with The Hague closely cooperating with Scandinavian countries on the CoE, but stopping short of linking the Greek case there with membership in NATO. Important developments in the wider region, such as the Six-Day War in 1967, the crushing of the Prague Spring the following year, the removal of allied bases from Libya, and anti-American demonstrations in Italy and Turkey in the last quarter of 1969 significantly augmented the junta's geostrategic importance, thus also significantly raising the cost of a Greek walk-out from the Atlantic Alliance. As a consequence, the bigger states of Europe (most prominently the United Kingdom, France, and West Germany) decided to cordon off NATO and thus keep it safe from actions against the Greek dictatorship, especially as part of a spill-over effect from the Colonels' condemnation in Strasbourg. Furthermore, the three big capitals vied for the top place in the list of Greece's trading partners, in many cases ignoring public outcries in their countries in order to accommodate the Colonels (usually in the form of a quid pro quo suggested either by them or by Athens itself) to the point of obsessing over which one would sell more material to a military dictatorship in a European country, as exemplified by the back-to-back visits of French, British, and West German trade ministers to Athens in 1972.

For their part, the Greek Colonels displayed an inability to understand the difficulties that some Western European governments were facing in dealing with a dictatorial regime within democratic international organizations. The junta aggressively responded to applications in the context of the CoE, and even more so to raising the issue in NATO, often repeating the mantra that other countries should not interfere in Greece's domestic politics. More importantly, the regime used formal and informal means of blackmail to get big European countries (such as Britain, the FRG, and France) to support its cause within those organizations and even influence more recalcitrant countries (the Scandinavian ones) into agreeing to Greece's continuing participation, despite its well-documented human rights abuses and the lack of democracy in the country. The main instrument to achieve that goal was to use contracts in the public sector as bargaining chips in order for the junta to gain much-needed legitimacy abroad and, in turn, persuade its domestic critics that important liberal democracies were on its side. In some cases, Western European governments, most prominently both the Labour and Conservative governments in Britain (fretting that others would rush in to take advantage), decided to oblige the Colonels, who were in turn quite successful in playing big European countries against each other and thus attaining coveted benefits.

Alexandros Nafpliotis holds a PhD in international history from the London School of Economics and Political Science (LSE). He studied English language and literature at the University of Athens, as well as history and international relations at the LSE. He was previously a research associate at the Hellenic Foundation for European and Foreign Policy (ELIAMEP) and the National Hellenic Research Foundation, as well as a visiting fellow at the Hellenic Observatory at LSE, and has also worked for the British Embassy in Athens, the Council of the European Union in Brussels, and the High Commission of the Republic of Cyprus in the United Kingdom. More recently, he conducted research on contemporary European history at Maastricht University and the University of Luxembourg. His first book, *Britain and the Greek Colonels: Accommodating the Junta in the Cold War* (I. B. Tauris, 2012), which examines diplomatic, economic, cultural, and defense relations between subsequent British governments and the junta, was published in paperback by Bloomsbury in 2020. He has presented his research at conferences and seminars in Europe and the United States and won a dissertation prize from the London Hellenic Society. Alexandros has taught on various aspects of twentieth-century international history at the LSE for a number of years. His research interests lie in the field of contemporary European history.

NOTES

1. The National Archives of the United Kingdom (hereafter TNA), Foreign and Commonwealth Office files (hereafter FCO), 9/1233 Palmer to Goodenough, 30 October 1970.
2. That is how Papadopoulos's (limited) liberalization efforts in 1973 (which all but failed and led to the imposition of the harsher Ioannides regime) are known in Greece.
3. *Akten zur Auswätigen Politik der Bundesrepublik Deutschland* (hereafter *AAPD*), "Aufzeichnung des Ministerialdirigenten Böker," vol. IA4, 82.00/94.08, no. 308, 24 August 1967, 1221.
4. Ibid.; see also Pelt 2006.
5. The National Archives of the United Kingdom (hereafter TNA), Foreign and Commonwealth Office files (hereafter FCO), 9/228 H. A. F. Hohler (Assistant Under-Secretary for Foreign Affairs), London to A. E. Davidson (Head of Chancery/Counsellor [Political], NATO), 14 September 1967.
6. Greek Ministry of Foreign Affairs Archives (hereafter GMFAA), London Embassy files (hereafter LE)/1969/5.1, part 1, no. 7153/ΣΤ/2 Verykios to MFA, 21 December 1968.
7. Ibid.

8. GMFAA, LE/1970/4.4, no. 6374/ΣΤ/2 Sorokos, London to MFA, 15 October 1969.
9. GMFAA, LE/1970/4.4, no. 6532/ΣΤ/2 Sorokos, London to MFA, 18 October1969. This view was certainly opposed by British Conservative MPs, who said that the "CoE should be careful lest Greece's expulsion and snub to Portugal turn it unwillingly into a communist instrument" (GMFAA, LE/1970/4.4, no. 6775/ΣΤ/Z Sorokos, London to MFA, 29 October 1969).
10. TNA FCO 9/1213, Letter from Sir Michael Stewart (Ambassador in Athens) to R. Secondé (Head of Southern European Department, FCO), 20 July 1970.
11. Archives Ministère des Affaires Etrangères (hereafter AMAE), Europe Series 1961–70, no. 254, "Compte-rendu de l'entretien du Ministre avec M. Markopouliotis, Ambassadeur de Grèce le 11 Novembre 1969, 14 November 1969"; cited in Varsori 2010.
12. TNA FCO 9/854, tel. no. 1129, Sir P. Hancock, (Ambassador in Rome) to FCO, 11 December 1969, confidential.
13. TNA FCO 9/120, "The Political Situation in Greece," Foreign Office brief, BMV(67)14, 8 November 1967.
14. *AAPD*, no. 194, "Arnold an Auswärtiges Amt," Z B 6-1-13097/69, 9 June 1969, 694–95.
15. TNA FCO 9/120, "The Political Situation in Greece," Foreign Office brief, BMV(67) 14, 8 November 1967.
16. *Documents diplomatiques français* (hereafter *DDF*) 1968, vol. 1, Baeyens à Couve de Murville, no 117/EU, Athens, 8 February 1968, 247.
17. GMFAA, LE/1969 5.1, part 1, no. 7153/ΣΤ/2, Verykios, London to MFA, 21 December 1968.
18. GMFAA, LE/1970/4.4, no. 6532/ ΣΤ /2, Sorokos to MFA, 18 October 1969.
19. TNA FCO 9/883, Speaking notes by J. Snodgrass for Calvocoressi's call on the Chancellor of the Duchy of Lancaster, 1 December 1969.
20. *DDF* 1971, vol. 1, no. 43, La Grèce et le Conseil de l'Europe, Durand, Athens to Schumann, Minister of Foreign Affairs, Paris, 27 January 1971.
21. See Hansard, col. 87/7, and TNA FCO 9/148, Oral answer from Healey to Gardner, 31 May 1967.
22. TNA FCO 9/165, Speaking notes on Greece and NATO: Parliamentary question by Winnick (n.d.).
23. *DDF* 1968, vol. 1, Note, Entretien avec M. Brosio; Secrétaire General de l'OTAN, Paris, 12 January 1968, pp. 78–79. See also TNA FCO 9/179, Grèce-Reconnaisance du Govt Hellenique, Paris to EXTER 40, 5 January 1968.
24. TNA FCO 9/880, FCO Memorandum on arms for Greece, NV (69) A24, 20 February 1969.
25. In 1963, the British (Conservative) government decided that there would be a distinction between "straightforward" items with a clear military use (which could be exported) and items "which might be readily connected in the public mind" with repression and crowd control (which could not be exported). After Labour came to power in 1964, the issue regained prevalence as Wilson, who

had pledged not to sell arms to the African country, was now having second thoughts. In late 1967, the South African arms controversy divided the Cabinet and took a severe toll on both Wilson's government and his reputation.

26. TNA FCO 9/870, Memorandum by Foreign and Defence Secretaries, OPD (69) 3, 24 January 1969.
27. TNA FCO 9/871, Letter from E. Youde (Private Secretary [Foreign Affairs] to the Prime Minister) to J. Graham (Principal Private Secretary to the Foreign Secretary), 28 July 1969.
28. Historical Archives of the European Union (hereafter HAEU), FEM, b. 80, Secretary General's note to members of the Commission, 6 February 1969, confidential; cited in Varsori 2010.
29. AMAE, Europe Series 1961–70, no. 254, tel. circular no. 274 Ministry of foreign affairs (Alphand) to various diplomatic representations, 13 June 1969.
30. TNA FCO 9/885, Memorandum on policy towards Greece, WSG3/548/25, 16 June 1969.
31. TNA FCO 9/1206 and 9/1234, Record of the conversation between the Chancellor of the Duchy of Lancaster and the Greek Ambassador, London, 16 November 1970.
32. GMFAA, LE/1970 4.4, 3835/ΣT/2, Sorokos, London to MFA, 18 August 1970.
33. Ibid.
34. TNA FCO 9/1206, Notes on FCO meeting entitled "Policy Towards Greece," 30 September 1970.
35. TNA FCO 9/1215 FCO, Memorandum on Greece, 6 January 1970. See also Woodhouse 1984: 78, 83.
36. TNA FCO 9/1206, Brief for NATO ministerial meeting, 24 November 1970.
37. TNA FCO 9/1388, "Greece: Annual Review for 1970," no. 16/71, Stewart to FCO, 1 January 1971.
38. France was the third most important trade partner of Greece and, with the United States, the natural Western partner for the Greeks to choose in any major and sensitive (e.g., defense or aerospace) contract.
39. TNA FCO 9/1532, R. Hooper (Ambassador in Athens) to C. Wiggin (Assistant Under-Secretary for Foreign and Commonwealth Affairs [Western and Southern Europe]), London, 19 January 1972.
40. TNA FCO 9/1534, "General Political Brief," attached to A. Brooke Turner (Head of Southern Europe Department) to T. Brimelow (Deputy Under-Secretary for Foreign and Commonwealth Affairs [Europe]), 12 October 1972.
41. TNA FCO 9/1534, E. Powell-Jones (Counsellor, Embassy, Greece), to Brooke Turner, 5 October 1972.
42. TNA FCO 9/1530, "Defence Report," Brigadier Baxter (Defence Attaché, Athens), 2 March 1972.
43. TNA FCO 9/1728, "Greece," Record of office meeting in parliamentary undersecretary's office, 11 February 1972.
44. TNA FCO 9/1728, "Greece," Record of office meeting in parliamentary undersecretary's office, 6 September 1972.

45. The Greek Association Agreement (the first between the EEC and a third country) came into force in 1962 and provided for the gradual establishment of a full customs union between the Community and Greece, after a twelve-year transitional period. Soon after the April 1967 coup, the EEC decided to freeze the agreement, the most serious of the feasible alternatives short of the abrogation of the agreement (Coufoudakis 1977).
46. TNA FCO 9/1526, B. Hitch to A. Goodenough, 2 June 1972.
47. TNA FCO 9/1709, "Greece: Annual Review for 1972," no. 27/73, Hooper to Foreign Secretary, A. Douglas-Home, 2 January 1973.
48. Ibid.
49. TNA FCO 9/1734, Hooper to Brooke Turner, 3 January 1973.
50. TNA FCO 9/1734, M. Butler (European Integration Department [External]) to J. Wright (Deputy Under-Secretary [Economic and Consular]), 30 January 1973.
51. TNA FCO 9/1733, Wiggin's note, 6 November 1973, attached to A. Goodison (Head of Southern Europe Department) to Wiggin, 1 November 1973.
52. TNA FCO 9/1732, Record of meeting on Greece, 4 April 1973.
53. TNA FCO 9/1732, Hooper's comments attached to Goodison to D. Logan (Deputy Permanent Representative to NATO), 30 March 1973.
54. Ibid.
55. TNA FCO 9/1401, Hooper to Secondé, 30 June 1971.
56. TNA FCO 9/1732, Goodison to Hooper, 6 July 1973.
57. For a thoroughly researched investigation into the Polytechnic uprising of November 1973 that led to the new coup d'état, see Kornetis's (2013) seminal work *Children of the Dictatorship: Student Resistance, Cultural Politics, and the "Long 1960s" in Greece*.
58. TNA FCO 9/2005, Hooper to FCO, tel. no. 57, 14 March 1974.
59. Ibid.
60. United States National Archives (USNA), Rome to State, Confidential, tel. 2837, 5 October 1969, POL 23-9, 1967-69 SNF, RG 59; cited in Karakatsanis and Swarts 2018: 195.
61. TNA FCO 9/2013, Hooper to Baker, 3 May 1974. As Verney and Tsakaloyannis (1986: 187) have noted, "It was only after the Ioannides coup that any discussion of Greece's relations with the EC was stopped again."
62. GMFAA, LE/1974/5.11, 4111.4/10/AS867, Broumas (Ambassador in London) to Athens, 18 April 1974.
63. TNA FCO 9/1229, "Greece as a Military Ally," diplomatic report no. 441/70 by Sir Michael Stewart, 11 September 1970.
64. TNA FCO 9/1233, Record of conversation between the foreign and commonwealth secretary and the Greek under-secretary for foreign affairs, 20 October 1970.
65. TNA FCO 9/1385, "Greece: Sir Michael Stewart's despatch of 25 January," Palmer, 3 February 1971.
66. TNA FCO 9/1385, "Greece: Sir Michael Stewart's despatch of 25 January," Palmer, 3 February 1971.

67. TNA FCO 9/1534, Hooper to FCO, tel. no. 581, 3 November 1972.
68. Ibid.
69. TNA FCO 9/2019, "Relations with Politically Sensitive Countries" memorandum for OPD (74) 18, Hunt, Smith and Roberts, 3 June 1974.
70. TNA FCO 9/1733, Goodison to J. Denson (Counsellor in Athens), 9 October 1973.

REFERENCES

Archives

Athens, Greece
  Greek Ministry of Foreign Affairs Archive (GMFAA)
  London Embassy (LE)
Florence, Italy
  Historical Archives of the European Union (HAEU)
London, United Kingdom
  House of Lords Hansard Archive (Hansard)
  The National Archives of the United Kingdom (TNA)
  Foreign and Commonwealth Office (FCO)
Paris, France
  Archives Ministère des Affaires Etrangères (AMAE)
Washington, DC, United States
  United States National Archives (USNA)

Published Primary Sources

Akten zur Auswätigen Politik der Bundesrepublik Deutschland (AAPD)
Documents diplomatiques français (DDF)

Secondary Sources

Coufoudakis, V. 1997. "The European Economic Community and the 'Freezing' of the Greek Association, 1967–1974." *Journal of Common Market Studies* 16(2): 114–31.
De Angelis, E., and E. Karamouzi. 2016. "Enlargement and the Historical Origins of the European Community's Democratic Identity, 1961–1978." *Contemporary European History* 25(3): 439–58.
Fernández Soriano, V. 2017. "Facing the Greek Junta: The European Community, the Council of Europe and the Rise of Human-Rights Politics in Europe." *European Review of History/Revue européenne d'histoire* 24(3): 358–76.

Favretto, I. 2006. "The Wilson Governments and the Italian Centre-Left Coalitions: Between 'Socialist' Diplomacy and *Realpolitik*, 1964–70." *European History Quarterly* 36(3): 421–44.

Gaddis, J. L. 2007. *The Cold War: A New History*. London.

Ghezzi, F. 2014. "Contro un 'malinteso realismo': La politica estera di Nenni e la Grecia dei colonnelli." *Contemporanea* 17(1): 59–82.

Karakatsanis, N. M., and J. Swarts. 2018. *American Foreign Policy toward the Colonels' Greece: Uncertain Allies and the 1967 Coup d'État*. New York.

Keeley, R. V. 2010. *The Colonels' Coup and the American Embassy: A Diplomat's View of the Breakdown of Democracy in Cold War Greece*. University Park, PA.

Kornetis, K. 2013. *Children of the Dictatorship: Student Resistance, Cultural Politics and the "Long 1960s" in Greece*. London.

Miller, J. E. 2009. *The United States and the Making of Modern Greece: History and Power, 1950–1974*. Chapel Hill, NC.

Nenni, P. 1983. *I conti con la storia: Diari, 1967–1971*. Milan.

Nafpliotis, A. 2013. *Britain and the Greek Colonels: Accommodating the Junta in the Cold War*. London.

———. 2014. "'A Gift from God': Anglo-Greek Relations during the Dictatorship of the Greek Colonels." *Historical Review/La revue historique* 11: 67–104. Retrieved 20 October 2020 from https://doi.org/10.12681/hr.329.

———. 2016. "Oi ellinovretanikes scheseis kata ti diarkeia tis 'Metapolitefsis' (1974–1975)" [Anglo-Greek relations during the "Metapolitefsi" (1974–75)]. In *I metapolitefsi '74–'75: Stigmes mias matavasis* [The Metapolitefsi '74–'75: Snapshots of a transition], edited by V. Karamanolakis, I. Nikolakopoulos, and T. Sakellaropoulos, 93–104. Athens.

———. 2019. "I dytiki Evropi kai I diktatoria ton syntagmatarchon" [Western Europe and the Colonels' dictatorship]. In *I diktatoria ton syntagmatarchon: Anatomia mias eptaetias* [The dictatorship of the Colonels: Anatomy of a seven-year period], edited by S. Vlachopoulos, D. Keridis, and A. Klapsis, 303–24, Athens.

Pedaliu, E. G. H. 2016. "Human Rights and International Security: The International Community and the Greek Dictators." *International History Review* 38(5): 1014–39.

Pelt, M. 2006. *Tying Greece to the West: US–West German–Greek Relations 1949–1974*. Copenhagen.

Phythian, M. 2000. *The Politics of British Arms Sales since 1964*. Manchester.

Rizas, S. 2008. *I elliniki politiki meta ton emfylio polemo: Koinovouleftismos kai diktatoria* [Greek politics after the civil war: Parliamentarism and dictatorship]. Athens.

Soave, P. 2014. *La democrazia allo specchio: L'Italia e il regime militare ellenico (1967–1974)*. Soveria Mannelli.

Tzortzis, I. 2019. *Greek Democracy and the Junta: Regime Crisis and the Failed Transition of 1973*. London.

Varsori, A. 2010. "L'Occidente e la Grecia dal colpo di stato militare alle transizione alla democrazia (1967–1976)." In *Democrazie : L'Europa meridionale e la fine delle dittature*, edited by M. Del Pero, V. Gavin, G. Guirao, and A. Varsori, 5–94. Florence.

Verney, S., and P. Tsakaloyannis. 1986. "Linkage Politics: The Role of the European Community in Greek Politics in 1973." *Byzantine and Modern Greek Studies* 10(1): 179–94.

Woodhouse, C. M. 1984. *Modern Greece: A Short History*. London.

Young, J. W. 2009. *The Labour Governments, 1964–1970*. Vol. 2, *International Policy*. Manchester.

Chapter 11

West Germany's Policy toward Greece during the Junta Period in the Context of "Burden-Sharing"

Mogens Pelt

West Germany's interests in Greece were rooted in the crisis-ridden 1930s and conditioned by the Cold War. During the last interwar decade, Berlin left little doubt that it had economic and political ambitions there: it saw the economies of the two countries as complementary and wanted to arrange the division of labor between them in a way that would give Germany the role as the manufacturer of industrial and capital goods in exchange for agricultural products and minerals from Greece. In the realm of politics, Berlin desired a regime in Athens that would not oppose its efforts to undo the European order established by the Paris peace treaties in the immediate aftermath of World War I.

To a great extent, Berlin achieved both goals. Germany's trade with Greece rose by leaps and bounds, increasing the role of the Greek market as an outlet for Germany industry. It also made Greece more dependent on Germany. Furthermore, in the Greek dictator Ioannis Metaxas (1936–41), Berlin believed it had someone who would not want to obstruct German interests in southeastern Europe and who was willing to keep his country neutral in case of war between Germany and Great Britain. It was Mussolini's ultimatum to Greece on 28 October 1940 rather than fundamental disagreements with Greece or claims on Greek territories that triggered the series of events that would make Hitler give up his policy of "peace in the Balkans" and decide to occupy Greece (Pelt 1998: 255–63). In spite of the fact that the Axis occupation of 1941–44 was extremely brutal and killed more than half a million people if we include the effects of disease, malnutrition, and famine, West German relations resumed only five years after the last German troops had left Greece.

Among other factors, this must be explained by the fact that the occupation was followed by a civil war that unfolded in the context of the Cold War, in which both the officially recognized Greek government and West Germany were on the same side. Anticommunism and the fear of the Soviet Union created strong mutual interests between Bonn and Athens, which were enhanced by the fact that both governments were dealing with a troublesome other. In the Greek case, it was the losers of the Greek Civil War, who were identified as communists and so-called fellow travelers, as well as any legacy that would legitimize their struggle. In the West German case, the "other was the rival social and political system in the Soviet camp, East Germany." The position of West Berlin as an isolated island in the Soviet-controlled zone and the fact that Greece had no common borders with Western Europe were evoked as symbols of the common fate that connected these two countries on the postwar European stage (Pelt 2006: 116–18).

Within this context, the expansion of Bonn's economic relations with Greece followed a strategy that, on the one hand, wanted to regain old markets and, on the other, was designed to tie Greece to the West. In effect, this meant that West Germany took over some of the goals and expenditures that originally had been defined by the Truman Doctrine and the Marshall Aid program to contain communism, mainly in the field of reconstruction and economic development. With these as West Germany's paramount interests in the region, their policy thus resulted in a kind of a "burden-sharing" with the United States.

Although "burden-sharing" as a term is often used in relation to Washington's demands from its European allies to shoulder a larger share of the expenditures related to a common defense against the Soviet Union, I am using the term in a wider sense to analyze U.S.–West German–Greek relations beyond issues strictly confined to defense matters. In the context of the Cold War, the fight against communism and the Soviet Union was not considered a question limited to issues of arms and military force only. The fact that West Germany stood out as economically the strongest state in Europe west of the Soviet Union made Bonn's productive power crucial to Washington as a means to bolster Western Europe against local communism and threats from the East; an expansion of trade and financial dealings with West Germany, it was believed, would promote reconstruction and development. Economic growth, in turn, would enable the European states to shoulder an ever-increasing share of the defense burden, while enhanced prosperity would contribute to political and social stability, and thus strengthen Europe's overall defense capabilities. All this would serve to bolster the position of the West in the Cold War.

The aim of this chapter is twofold: first, to discuss how West Germany appraised its original postwar goals of tying Greece to the West after the establishment of the military dictatorship in 1967; and, second, to examine the way in which it handled the dilemma of keeping up this policy, not least its burden-sharing, at the same time that domestic opposition and some of Bonn's Western partners were demanding human rights and the prioritization of the constitutional issue in Greece. In discussing these topics, we shall first turn our attention to the role of reconstruction and development as methods of fighting communism and containing the Soviet Union, including the role of burden-sharing in the period prior to the establishment of the military dictatorship. Then, we shall consider both how West Germany and the United States responded to the establishment of the Colonels' regime and the impact the Greek coup d'état had on public opinion, where the illiberal aspects of the Greek state and its practices had been an issue for some time. The central part of the chapter discusses how the West German government walked the thin line between its traditional policy of nonintervention in domestic affairs of other countries, and demands from the streets and the parliament to revise this policy. Equally central is the discussion of how the West German government handled the dilemma created by the harsh criticism of internal Greek affairs by its Danish, Dutch, and Norwegian allies at the juncture when Bonn wanted to stick to its traditional policy of nonintervention and at the same time honor its crucial role in burden-sharing. It is the argument of this chapter that the West German government adhered to its traditional policy in spite of the harsh reactions in the streets and parliament as well as from its allies, but that it was forced by a majority in the parliament to cut the volume of its sensitive arms deliveries to a minimum.

The chapter relies mainly on published and unpublished documents from the German Ministry of Foreign Affairs. The scholarly literature on Germany's relations to Greece during the period of the military dictatorship is sparse. I have dealt with certain aspects of it in my book *Tying Greece to the West: US–West German–Greek Relations 1949–74* (2006), while Dimitrios K. Apostolopoulos, in the epilogue to his monograph *Die griechisch-deutschen Nachkriegsbeziehungen* (2004), offers a more comprehensive overview of the period. In addition, there exist some important contributions dealing with the multilateral aspects that involved West Germany. Regarding the issue of human rights abuses by the military regime and the issue of expelling Greece from the Council of Europe, there is Barbara Keys's essay "Anti-Torture Politics: Amnesty International, the Greek Junta, and the Origin of the Human Rights 'Boom' in the United States" (2012), as well as Kristine Kjærsgaard's "Confronting the Greek Military Junta: Scandinavian Joint Action under the European Commission on Human Rights, 1967–70" (2016). Finally, we should mention Effie G. H. Pedaliou's important contribution in *Diplomacy and Statecraft* from 2011, titled "'A Disconcordant Note': NATO and the Greek Junta, 1967–1974."

RECONSTRUCTION AND DEVELOPMENT AS MEANS TO FIGHT COMMUNISM AND CONTAIN THE SOVIET UNION

While the idea that the United States should participate in the reconstruction of Greece can be traced back to 1942–43, when private U.S. organizations such as the Near East Foundation got in contact with leading Greek businessmen to discuss plans for rebuilding Greece (Pelt 2006: 71–74), the initial attitudes toward the reconstruction of Germany were very differently represented by the so-called Morgenthau Plan; the plan proposed, among other things, that the Ruhr Area "should not only be stripped of all presently existing industries but so weakened and controlled that it cannot in the foreseeable future become an industrial area."[1] The Joint Chiefs of Staff Directive (JCS 1067) issued on 10 May 1945, governing the U.S. occupation of Germany until July 1947, contained elements from the Morgenthau Plan that aimed to prevent the overall living standards from rising to a level that would enable Germany's re-emergence as an aggressive power (Wend 2001: 27).

The declaration of the Truman Doctrine on 12 March 1947 became a turning point for both Greece and Germany in relation to their position in the Western camp. In the Greek case, it meant that the United States took over from Britain the military and financial support of the Greek government and its fight against communist insurgents. In the case of Germany, the United States gave up any intentions of the Morgenthau Plan that were left in the governing directives for occupied Germany. These trends were enhanced by the launching of the Marshall Plan the following year, which favored a policy that aimed at rebuilding Germany, while the Soviets continued to want a weak Germany that posed no military danger (Zubok and Pleshakov 1996: 49–53). In the end, the two powers would introduce their own social systems to their zones of occupation, leading to the establishment in 1949 of the Federal Republic of Germany and the German Democratic Republic.

America's policy toward West Germany was summarized by the National Security Council in a policy statement dated 17 August 1953, the so-called NSC 160/1 document. According to NSC 160/1, West Germany was potentially the strongest power west of the USSR, making "its reliable cooperation with other free European nations . . . indispensable for a strong and stable Europe." NSC 160/1 recommended an enhancement of West Germany's role in the defense of Europe, both because its defense could not be separated from its economic and political strength and because defense was a comprehensive undertaking that included Europe's will to solve its political, economic, and social problems.[2]

BURDEN-SHARING

Less than a year after the establishment of the Federal Republic in 1949, West Germany became the most important destination for Greek exports. In the following seventeen years Greek–West German relations expanded dramatically: in a series of agreements dating from 1953 onward, West Germany consented to assist the financing of several industrial projects, taking over the financing of a substantial part of the Greek development plan originally to have been funded by U.S. nonmilitary aid, which began to decline at this time. From 1957 onward, West Germany became the most important source of Greek imports; in 1958, Bonn granted a 200 million DM state loan to Greece—the first of its kind since the crisis-ridden 1930s; between 1959 and 1961, West Germany played a very active part in the process that resulted in Greece's association with the EEC; in 1963, Bonn granted Greece a new credit of 200 million DM; from about the same time, West Germany became an ever more important source of invisible assets generated by the increasing amount of remittances from Greek *Gastarbeiter* (migrant workers) (Pelt 2006: 355–63).

In the same period, it was on the agenda that Bonn should take over from the United States the burden of military aid to Greece. However, the political impact of the recollections of Germany's occupation of Greece turned out to be prohibitive. Instead, it was decided that NATO should take over from the United States, while Bonn was to provide a substantial part of that aid. Between 1963 and 1967, Bonn agreed to three tranches of military aid, totaling 101.3 million DM (Apostolopoulos 2004: 306–11). At the beginning of 1967, 92 million DM had been provided, while 9.3 million DM was still in the pipeline. At that time, a fourth tranche was also planned (Apostolopoulos 2004: 306–11). Regarding the specific nature of the West German aid, some was delivered in the shape of investment goods, some in the shape of military hardware, and some in the shape of surplus equipment from the Bundeswehr. In addition to this, since 1962 private West German firms were also in play, signing individual contracts with the Greek Armed Forces.[3]

UNITED STATES AND WEST GERMAN REACTIONS TO THE COUP D'ÉTAT IN APRIL 1967

Washington's immediate reaction to the coup d'état in April 1967 was to suspend the shipments of "selected major items of equipment in the grant aid program" to Greece and make future delivery dependent on constitutional progress. The intention of withholding this aid was to provide "practical evidence [of] U.S. concern for extra-constitutional developments in Greece." This also meant that the items selected for suspension were only those with a considerable degree of visibility, such as high-performance aircraft and tanks. The policy maintained a great degree of flexibility, and control of private transactions was not a criterion.[4] In other words, the main goal was to appear concerned. West Germany, Greece's second largest supplier of arms, chose a similar policy. Auswärtiges Amt (Federal Foreign Office of Germany) recommended the continuation of military aid that had been allocated within the framework of NATO. Bilateral military relations between Germany and Greece were also to be continued. However, the ministry warned, Bonn should be cautious regarding those contacts that attracted most publicity, such as the exchange of military officers. Like Washington, the Auswärtiges Amt wanted Bonn to leave the impression that it was concerned about the new situation in Greece. Regarding economic relations, again according to Auswärtiges Amt, sanctions had never been able to influence the political development in a country in the direction of democracy, and Bonn should therefore continue developing its economic relations with Greece.[5]

In this way, Auswärtiges Amt advocated business as usual, and that Bonn should base its relations with the junta on continuity. This was reflected in Bonn's negative stance on the decision by the European Investment Bank not to release a 10 million USD loan for road construction in Crete—a decision that was connected to the so-called freezing of the Greek association by the EEC.[6] At the same time, Bonn made clear that it was of the opinion that the new Greek government was undemocratic and blemished the reputation of the Western Alliance; to ameliorate this state of affairs, they argued, the federal government should urge the Greek government and the royal palace to restore a constitutional state. There were also voices in the state maintaining that one should not discredit the fact that the new regime seriously intended to fight communism.[7] In any event, the main goal toward the new regime was to avoid forcing the Greek government into isolation. Such a move would only encourage national socialist tendencies in the government or enhance the danger of Greek neutralism—and in that way play into the hands of the Soviet Bloc. Therefore, as long as Greece was a member of NATO, it should be the policy of West Germany that Greece be treated like any other member country.[8] The importance of continuity was demonstrated in practice in relation with a joint-NATO maneuver in Thrace planned to take place in late August 1967. The coup d'état in Greece made the Belgian minister of foreign affairs Pierre Harmel doubt if it was proper to go ahead with the exercise. While his British and Italian colleagues were hesitant too, the foreign ministers of West Germany and the United States, Willy Brandt and Dean Rusk respectively, both expressed their wish for the exercise to take place as planned.[9]

Along the same lines, only some six months after the coup d'état, in October 1967, a private German firm, Howaldtwerke-Deuschte Werft in Kiel, concluded an agreement with the Royal Hellenic Navy about the delivery of four U-boats of 900 tons.[10] Thus, security concerns made both Bonn and Washington decide to continue its military relations with the Colonels' Greece more or less under business as usual. However, at the same time, a new factor was beginning to make itself felt in Greek–West German relations: public opinion.

THE POWER OF PUBLIC OPINION

The 1960s have been called a phase of fermentation and transition, or even a *Zeitwende* (turning point), in which a number of impulses for change confronted traditional structures and norms. The postwar order came under pressure from calls for reform in both domestic and foreign policy, calls often followed by resistance and reaction. This confrontation was international, but with great variations in intensity and outcome from country to country. In Germany and other northern European countries, the economic boom created possibilities for mass tourism to southern Europe, including Greece, and for the transfer of Greek labor to northern Europe (Herbert and Hunn 2000: 273–310). As we shall see, this functioned as a kind of transmission belt that would bring Greek political issues to the attention of the British, Dutch, Germans, and Scandinavians, creating appeals for solidarity with the ordinary Greek citizen.

The first powerful instance of the internationalization of internal Greek affairs was the reaction by the British public to Queen Frederica's May 1963 private visit to London. She was met by demonstrations demanding the release of Greek political prisoners who had been incarcerated since the Greek Civil War.[11] The case caught the attention of the British public and of Parliament, and made the royal couple—not least the fact that German-born Frederica had been a member of the Nazi youth organization Bund Deutscher Mädel—the subject of much criticism. About a hundred MPs (Members of Parliament) supported the protests against Greece's holding "political prisoners, many of them veterans from the anti-Fascist resistance."[12] The international attention to the internal political situation in Greece increased as a reaction to the assassination in Salonika on 22 May 1963 of a deputy of the left-wing party, EDA (Ενιαία Δημοκρατική Αριστερά, United Democratic Left), and well-known peace activist, Grigoris Lambrakis, a professor at Athens University. The opposition alleged that he had been killed in revenge for the humiliation of Queen Frederica in London.[13] In this way, the Lambrakis case also affected an official visit by the royal couple to London planned for July 1963 and the internal political stability in Greece. On 11 June, after several abortive attempts to convince the king of the wisdom of staying at home as well as to avoid protest demonstrations, Prime Minister Konstantinos Karamanlis decided to resign.[14]

The royal visit to London resulted in massive demonstrations. Among the protestors were prominent public figures, such as the leader of the British Labour Party and future prime minister Harold Wilson and the philosopher Bertrand Russell. The demonstrations were depicted as the largest in London since the 1930s (Murtagh 1994: 69). In Greece, the killing of Lambrakis unleashed massive demonstrations, too, and gave birth to the so-called Z-generation with the emergence of the Lambrakis Youth as a Greek equivalent to the New Left in the West. In the wake of the so-called July events in 1965, when King Constantine instigated the fall of George Papandreou's government, this generation was active in organizing strikes and demonstrations against a system that was seen as illegitimate and repressive (Kornetis 2013: 19–36).

The Lambrakis case and the July events only strengthened the impression of Greece as a textbook example of Western hypocrisy, as the ideals of freedom and democracy, which the West professed to defend, appeared to be held cheaply in Greece. It was the Lambrakis case that first made "us aware that something was wrong in Greece," recalls Mogens Camre (2011: 111–12), who was a young Social Democrat and an early and central figure in directing attention in Denmark to the illiberal and repressive aspects of the Greek political system. These perceptions culminated with the Colonels' coup. Now the Greek case would also interact with and be energized by other issues that had reached the global public and the antiestablishment protest movements of the 1960s. In Germany, in the immediate wake of the coup, the General Students' Committee organized a demonstration against the military dictatorship. At the same time, the opponents of the dictatorship strived to get the Extra-Parliamentary Opposition (*Außerparlamentarischen Opposition*) to support their various protests and demonstrations. The Extra-Parliamentary Opposition was a loosely organized but central part of the West German student movement that originated from the opposition against the so-called Grand Coalition government (1966–69), which united the two biggest parties, the Conservatives (CDU) and the Social Democrats (SPD) under Chancellor Kurt Georg Kiesinger, with Willy Brandt as vice chancellor and minister of foreign affairs.

While Kiesinger was the first and only member of the Nazi party to be elected chancellor, Brandt had been an active participant in the anti-Nazi resistance (Herf 1997: 343–44). Because of the collaboration between two such different profiles, and with a share of more than 90 percent of the seats in the Bundestag (the parliament), the Grand Coalition threatened democracy, the Extra-Parliamentary Opposition claimed; there existed no opposition in parliament to address society's unwillingness to deal with its Nazi past and to fully recognize the crimes committed by that regime. This gave the question "What did you do during war, Dad?" a dimension that concerned the very fundament on which West Germany rested, because the Extra-Parliamentary Opposition accused their parents' generation of suppressing the past in their pursuit of reconstruction and economic security. It also connected its activities to the worldwide protests against the U.S. war in Vietnam (Hilwig 1998: 323–25).

In this way, the protests against the military regime in Athens—framed as fascist—began to align with the major issues that defined the relations between the Extra-Parliamentary Opposition and the government. These reached a level of crisis after the police killed Benno Ohnesorg, a young student who participated at a demonstration held on 2 June 1967 protesting against the Shah of Iran's visit to West Germany. On 16 to 17 December 1967, the opposition to the Greek junta held a conference at Bergneustadt. It was organized by the Greek-German committee for cooperation. The committee was comprised of SPD, the trade unions, Friedrich Ebert-Stiftung, and the West German and Greek branches of the Center Union and Social Democratic Union. The initiative to organize the conference came from SPD. The Greeks present at the conference had two demands: the isolation of the junta and an immediate cessation of the supply of arms.[15]

This must also be seen against the background of reactions in Scandinavia, where the Social Democratic Parties constituted the driving forces in turning the official policy of these countries against the Greek junta. It was evident from almost the same moment when the news of the Colonels' coup reached the world. Perhaps it was even the result of interaction and exchange of views of what should be done between the parties in Scandinavia and West Germany.

During the early hours of the coup d'état in 1967, the Colonels imprisoned Andreas Papandreou, who was arrested along with an estimated 6,700 other people during the first days of the new regime.[16] At that moment, Mogens Camre was in Athens. He had arrived on 17 April, invited by Andreas Papandreou to discuss collaboration between the Danish Social Democrat Party and the Center Union. After the coup and his return to Denmark on 23 April, Camre began to work for the release of Andreas Papandreou with support of the Danish prime minister Jens Otto Krag.[17] Because of this and as a result of the coup, on 5 May the Danish government brought up the Greek issue in NATO, sending a written declaration to the NATO ambassadors, expressing its regret about the recent developments in Greece and hoping that the country would return to democracy as soon as possible. The Norwegian government had sent a similar message.[18] From early on, Krag made clear that he wanted to use a multilateral approach to support the return of democracy to Greece on the grounds that what happened in Greece was the concern of all members of Western associations of which Greece was a member.[19]

On 10 May, the Scandinavian prime ministers' meeting in Oslo decided to summon the ministerial committee of the Council of Europe to discuss the coup d'état in Greece (Camre 2011: 137). According to a report dated 24 August 1967 by an American observer in Sweden, the "intensity of interests in Andreas Papandreou's case in Scandinavia is difficult to imagine."[20] According to the same observer, the case was covered in detail in the press and had become an important political issue, as well as a subject of concern to ministers and members of parliament in all the Scandinavian countries. Thus, a major item on the agenda of a planned Scandinavian foreign ministers' conference was a possible formal protest regarding the Papandreou case under the European Convention on Human Rights.[21] On 20 September 1967, Denmark, Norway, Sweden, and the Netherlands filed complaints concerning violations by Greece at the European Commission for Human Rights.[22] On 27 January 1968, Amnesty International concluded that the number of people detained without trial in prison establishments on the islands of Leros and Yaros was 2,777, and that numerous individuals were held without trial in prisons and police stations throughout Greece. Furthermore, it stated that "torture as a deliberate practice" was carried out by the Security Police and the ESA (Ελληνική Στρατιωτική Αστυνομία, Greek Military Police).[23]

BURDEN-SHARING UNDER PRESSURE

On 28 February 1968, pressure from the Social Democrats in the Bundestag forced the government to terminate bilateral military aid to Greece. However, military aid within the framework of NATO that already been allocated was to be continued.[24] This made the SPD convention held from 17 to 21 March 1968 pass a resolution demanding that West Germany suspend its military aid program within the framework of NATO and that no more arms be delivered to Greece.[25] It was at the same convention that Brandt launched one of the political cornerstones of his Ostpolitik, the recognition of the Oder-Neisse border—that is, the new postwar eastern borders which left large tracts of prewar German territories to Poland. In this way, the SPD convention had addressed two issues that linked West Germany's past and identity to current international affairs (Soutou 2018: 378).

Burden-sharing was now no longer simply a matter of supporting any Greek government that would keep the country tied to the West; it had become a contentious practice that was challenged by the public and in the parliament because of the junta's breach of human rights and its suspension of parliamentary rule. The shooting of the student leader Rudi Dutsche by a right-wing extremist on 11 April 1968 further polarized the relations between the government and the Extra-Parliamentary Opposition—and it increased the likelihood that any support of the Greek regime would also have the potential to question the moral character of the Western successor state to prewar Germany. The discussions of burden-sharing could no longer be confined to the triangle of Athens-Bonn-Washington. They would instead play out on a number of new stages. In addition to the streets, SPD, and the Bundestag, there were NATO and the Council of Europe, where the Scandinavian countries were becoming more and more hostile toward the junta.

It was against this background and on the grounds that the Greek government was making no progress in returning Greece to constitutional rule that in 1969 the Council of Europe was to decide if Greece was to be expelled as the Scandinavian countries and the Netherlands demanded. On 12 September 1969, the West German ambassador confided to the French government that Bonn regarded the legal arguments of the case against Greece to be well founded but feared the political consequences of an expulsion—namely, that it would make the Colonels "slip" and fall into the arms of the arms of the Soviet Union.[26] In other words, it was the Cold War aspects of the Greek case that concerned the West German government. That the priority of Cold War concerns made a case for continuity is clear from a conversation that Brandt held with the recently appointed SACEUR (Supreme Allied Commander Europe), General A. J. Goodpaster.

BATTLEGROUND NATO

Brandt told Goodpaster that the situation in Greece had created many problems. Personally, he felt forced to give up any hope that the junta would soon return Greece to constitutional rule. Such lack of constitutional progress in turn frustrated his efforts to resume the West German military aid program to Greece because the Bundestag had made this a proviso for full resumption. However, Brandt felt sure that public opinion in the Federal Republic would accept a recommencement of aid should NATO officially take over the task from West Germany and define West German military aid to Greece as "direct NATO aid."

The main problem about this procedure, according to Brandt, was that such a decision required the consent of the NATO council, which in a final analysis would make it dependent on the will of the individual member countries. Among such nations, opinion was divided: some countries gave priority to the military security of NATO's southeastern flank, while others were primarily concerned about the political situation in Greece.[27] What Brandt was suggesting was that NATO should assist Bonn in covering up military aid from West Germany as direct NATO aid. In this way, it would be possible to evade the objections by the Bundestag, Brandt believed. While the United States agreed to ease Bonn's burden, it intensified NATO's role as a battleground in the confrontations regarding the Greek regime at a juncture when the Danish, Norwegian, and Dutch governments were bringing increasing pressure to bear on Greece at the Council of Europe.[28]

It was in this situation that Washington instructed the U.S. embassies to urge restraint on its allies regarding the proposal to expel Greece from the Council of Europe. On 6 December 1969, U.S. foreign secretary William Rogers raised the issue with Brandt, now chancellor, expressing the hope that it would be possible to opt for something less drastic than an expulsion of Greece from the Council of Europe. The worst-case scenario, according to Rogers, would be if Greek membership in NATO should come into question. Here Rogers obviously attempted to use the specter of Greece's expulsion from NATO as a means to move the German chancellor. Brandt, in turn, promised to do whatever possible to avoid the case of Greece being forced to leave. However, should the case come up in such a way, Bonn had no choice but to vote for expulsion.[29] On 11 December 1969, the day before the future of Greek membership in the Council of Europe was to be decided, the West German cabinet reached the conclusion that whatever happened to Greece at that meeting, it should not affect, "if at all possible," the membership of Greece in the Atlantic Alliance or its association with the common market.[30]

Before the final vote on 12 December 1969, the junta decided to take Greece out of the Council of Europe on its own volition rather than being expelled. This forced West Germany to balance her interests carefully: on the one hand, a regard for public opinion as well as West Germany's position as a leading European country made the question of solidarity with her European partners crucial, a regard that had weighed heavily on the issue of the Council of Europe; on the other hand, as a major supplier of military aid to Greece and committed to burden-sharing with the United States, Bonn was compelled to pay attention to security considerations. From Bonn's point of view, this position was all the more important at a juncture when the junta was publicly condemned by the Commission of the EEC[31] and not least because it was under mounting pressure in NATO, primarily due to condemnation by Denmark, Norway, and the Netherlands.

REACTIVATING BURDEN-SHARING

It was in this situation that the U.S. Embassy in Bonn urged Washington to enhance the coordination of its arms supply policy with West Germany: if Washington wanted to ensure West German support for the U.S. point of view that "the need for NATO unity and for reinforcement of NATO's military strength should override measures in the NATO forum evidencing distaste for the Greek regime," it was now the time to inform the Germans of the developments regarding U.S. arms supply policy. For that reason, the embassy suggested, Washington should also accept West German sales to Greece of U.S.-made Hawk missiles and spare parts for M47 Patton tanks.[32]

In response, Rogers authorized representatives of the United States to discuss a mutual military sales policy with the West Germans, meaning that Washington was now taking steps to coordinate its own arms supply policy regarding Greece with Bonn.[33] At this juncture, Washington had already decided to lift its ban on the delivery of heavy weapons to Greece but still had to made the official announcement (Pedaliou 2007: 107). The trouble was the timing in order to avoid as much as possible raising a new wave of criticism. While the decision was taken in November, on 8 May 1970 Sisco informed the French government that an announcement would not be made until after the NATO meeting because of fear of the Scandinavians.[34] On 15 May 1970, the Danish minister of foreign affairs Poul Hartling told the Danish parliament that he intended to reject anything that could serve to strengthen the government in Athens.[35]

Rogers now turned to Bonn in an alarmed mood, warning that such attitudes would cause a split in NATO.[36] This and the fact that the Danish stance threatened to undermine the priority of Washington and Bonn that NATO's military strength should always be the supreme concern made Bonn swing into action. On 23 May, just prior to a NATO meeting in Rome, the German minister of foreign affairs, Walter Scheel, assured Rogers of his support of Washington's stance: "I share your concern.... Today I sent the [Danish] Minister of Foreign Affairs, Hartling, a letter in which I directed his attention to the severe consequences that any discussion at the meeting of the internal situation in Greece could have and I have asked him to abstain from any criticism of the internal politics of the Greek regime."[37] Nevertheless, Hartling did bring up the issue and voiced criticism against the junta. Hartling was supported by the Norwegian and Dutch ministers of foreign affairs.[38]

The American embassies in Copenhagen and Oslo received instructions from the State Department to stress to the Danish and Norwegian foreign ministers that "the United States consider unacceptable the attitude of the Danish and Norwegian Governments on the above issue"—that is, military aid to the junta.[39] In a memorandum dated 11 August 1970 to National Security Adviser Henry Kissinger, the State Department summarized the impasse in the following manner: "In sum, Denmark has stalled NATO approval of a routine report recommending that Allied governments provide military assistance for Greece.... In retaliation Papadopoulos threatened that Greece would not participate further in NATO's Defence Planning Committee if the matter remains unresolved when the DPC meets again 18 September 1970."[40]

In the end, Washington decided to couple the announcement of the full resumption of military assistance to Greece with the civil war in Jordan, the so-called Black September, and President Nixon's trip in late September to the Eastern Mediterranean.[41] On 21 September, the U.S. ambassador to Denmark, Guilford Dudley, informed Hartling of the decision. Hartling retorted that "the Danish Government did not like to see the embargo lifted and that he would have to make [a] public statement saying so."[42] Dudley, in turn, claimed that the Junta would get arms from one place or another, pointing at France who had already taken steps to supply tanks to Greece.[43]

Immediately after the resumption of full military aid to Greece, on 7 October 1970, Washington began to reevaluate the possibility of selling a squadron of F-4 Phantom aircraft to Greece. The Phantom was regarded as a "major, highly visible and highly publicized article of military equipment."[44] This decision must be seen in the context of competition with France, a major rival in the international arms market. Furthermore, the fact that Washington was beginning to consider homeporting in Greece made it even more important to find a *modus vivendi* with the junta. To this end, an accommodation with the Colonels in the so-called Phantom case was crucial—in particular because the case was expected to feature high on the agenda of U.S.-Greek military relations for years to come.⁴⁵ The Greek government expressed dismay at the cost of the Phantoms, claiming that France was ready to reduce the price of their Mirage aircrafts. However, Washington rejected any thought of price reductions.⁴⁶

With the financing of the purchases as the crucial issue, Washington decided to make an attempt "in a low-key fashion" and "informally" to make West Germany participate in the "F-4 transaction, particularly in view of potential financing problems."⁴⁷ Washington obviously wanted Bonn to undertake burden-sharing vis-à-vis the junta. These efforts must also be seen as an attempt by the Nixon administration to evade control from Congress, which was becoming increasingly critical of U.S. policy toward the junta.⁴⁸

At the same time, public criticism of the junta in West Germany was reaching new heights, something that made it practically impossible for the West German government to participate in the "Phantom transaction."⁴⁹ While Bonn's proposed role in the deal was kept secret, the United States and Greece finally signed an agreement concerning the sale of thirty-six Phantoms on 29 March 1972. Total costs were estimated at 150 million USD.⁵⁰ It is also clear that the Phantom sale happened at the expense of France. Paris had to give up the prospect of a large order of Mirage F-1 aircraft, believing that they lost the order because of massive U.S. government subvention. In fact, previously France had lost an order of Mirage III to the United States, while the last success in arms trade with Greece dated to 1970–71.⁵¹ These orders, in turn, could well have been a substitute for West German arms deliveries.

RISING OPPOSITION HOME AND ABROAD

The issue of military aid to Greece continued to be a most sensitive one for the German government. A decision by the Federal Security Council taken 1 March 1971 to resume military aid to Greece,⁵² followed by a decision by the government on 16 June 1971 that export of weapons and other war materials to NATO members should not be restricted,⁵³ was met with considerable resentment in the Bundestag. The position of the SPD had hardened since its 1968 resolution: an SPD convention held from 11 to 14 May 1970 now exhorted the SPD members of the Bundestag and the government to bring about a suspension of military aid to Greece.⁵⁴

Reacting to prospect of a resumption of military aid to Greece, SPD delegate in the Bundestag and member of the foreign affairs commission

Peter Conterier expressed his doubt that the SPD group would approve: the junta had taken no steps to restore freedom in Greece and had remained deaf to appeals for the release of political prisoners.[55] This transpired in the Bundestag at hearings concerning a proposed resumption of bilateral military aid to Greece by the granting of 40 million DM to Greece.[56] It was a highly unpopular issue among the Free Democratic Party (FPD) and SPD delegates in the foreign affairs and budget committees of the Bundestag. It also caused rifts within the government, even among the SPD ministers.

According to information Washington had obtained from a source at the German Ministry of Defense, it was a well-known fact that the minister of defense, Helmut Schmidt, supported Minister of Foreign Affairs Scheel, who was in favor of military assistance to Greece, while it was unclear what Brandt would finally decide.[57] Scheel urged the Social Democrat delegates to vote in favor of the government's proposal to resume military aid to Greece: it was imperative to follow a foreign policy "void of ideology." Such a policy was the cornerstone of West Germany's Ostpolitik, Scheel said, and he personally disapproved of the internal political conditions in the Eastern Bloc just as much as he disapproved of the internal political conditions in the Western countries under authoritarian rule.[58]

The efforts to resume military aid to Greece had turned into a complex battle fought on two main fronts. On the one front, the government had to cope with internal opposition in the SPD and from SPD and FPD delegates in the Bundestag; at the same time, it had to confront those of its NATO partners who insisted on bringing up the regime issue in Greece at the NATO councils. The struggle on that front continued to be uphill: an SPD convention held from 10 to 14 April 1973 reiterated its position that its members of the Bundestag and the government should continue to work to bring about a suspension of West German military aid to Greece.[59] Furthermore, at the NATO Council of Ministers' meeting in December 1973, the foreign ministers of Norway, Denmark, and the Netherlands explicitly raised the Greek case. It was the first time it was done at the same time, while the foreign ministers of Belgium, Canada, and Italy each spoke of the need for all members of NATO to carry out their commitment to the basic principles of democracy, individual liberty, and the rule of law. Furthermore, there were expectations that at the June 1974 meeting the new British government and Portugal perhaps would also follow that line.[60] As a result of all this, the decision to resume military aid to Greece was postponed. On the other front, Bonn was facing a regime in Athens that it feared might leave NATO and whose lack of military equipment would severely weaken NATO's southeastern flank.

BONN AND THE JUNTA

As mentioned above, Bonn was at pains to assure the junta that it followed a "foreign policy void of ideology." On 1 June 1973, in the wake of an abortive insurrection in the Royal Greek Navy taking place during the night between 23 and 24 May 1973, which among others invoked the name of King Constantine, the West German ambassador to Greece, Dirk Oncken, took up this theme in a conversation with Papadopoulos. While the Greek regime was considering abolishing the monarchy and turning Greece into a republic, Oncken assured Papadopoulos that Bonn had no intention of tampering with internal Greek affairs. In relation to the naval insurrection, the main concern to West Germany was that it did not impair the capabilities of the Greek armed forces and their contribution to the defense of the West. Otherwise, Bonn had no intention whatsoever of interfering in the situation: "The Federal government," Oncken wrote, "would allow its policy vis-à-vis Greece to be influenced only by foreign policy considerations."[61]

At the same time, it was also clear that Bonn wanted to avoid any high-profile public gestures that could be seen as a sign of support for the regime in Athens in this situation. The West German government decided to call off any further planning of a visit to Greece by the West German minister of foreign affairs, informing the Greek government on 13 June 1973 that "unfortunately the Minister of Foreign Affairs will not be able to visit Athens in the fall, as originally intended."[62] In the wake of the brutal quelling of a student uprising by Papadoulos's regime in November 1973 and the palace revolt that toppled the original junta, the West German ambassador to Greece advised restraint as the best position to be taken by the West vis-à-vis the new regime and for "business as usual" to be serve as the guiding principle: "I take it for granted that a reduction of the Greek Association Agreement with the EEC will not be on the table, nor Greek membership of NATO."[63] At the same time, Auswärtiges Amt instructed its ambassador to Norway to convey a démarche to the government in Oslo, asking it to abstain from bringing up the Greek case at the next NATO ministers' meeting. The British and American governments took similar steps.[64] In spite of this, and in tune with their well-known stance on the Greek dictatorship at the NATO meeting of ministers of 10–11 December 1973, the Norwegian and Danish ministers of foreign affairs once again expressed their concern regarding the internal situation in Greece, exhorting the Greek government to reestablish democratic conditions in the shortest possible time. The Greek minister of foreign affairs rejected the demands as a flagrant violation of the principle of nonintervention in internal politics.[65]

The November Polytechnic uprising in Greece caused the SPD group in the West German parliament to react and harden its position further. It now urged the government to abstain from granting military assistance to Greece not only within the framework of NATO but also in the shape of commercial transactions. Furthermore, the group called the government to use its influence to see to it that the Greek problem was put on the agenda of the NATO council meeting. The resolution was passed without opposition in the group.[66] According to the head of Auswärtiges Amt's department of treaties, Peter Hermes, the demands were without substance because West Germany had not provided any NATO military aid to Greece since the coup d'état of 1967.[67] While this was true, Bonn had delivered spare parts for M47 tanks worth 30 million DM, meaning that West Germany was still delivering military equipment.[68]

Concerning commercial transactions, Hermes warned that a prohibition would entail a complete standstill of armaments exports to Greece and contradict usual practice: since April 1967, West Germany's policy on exports of armaments to Greece was based on the premise that Greece was a member of NATO; that in order for Greece to fulfill its obligations in the defense of the southeastern flank of NATO, it needed efficient armed forces; and, for these reasons, since 1967 Bonn had allowed the commercial exports of war material to Greece.[69] In other words, Auswärtiges Amt was reiterating its well-known stance of "business as usual" and of the primacy of keeping Greece tied to the West.

However, against the backdrop of rising public and political pressure to cut arms deliveries to Greece, and at a time when the new regime's standing with the public was reaching a new low, the Federal Security Council decided on 3 April 1974 to hold back large deliveries of arms (hand guns, machine guns, and ammunition) to Greece, pending a decision to be made at its next meeting.[70] On 9 April 1974, the Federal Chancellery decided that West Germany should deliver only surplus material from the Bundeswehr.[71] The decision was made less than four months before the Greek military regime collapsed in the wake of its abortive attempt to unify Cyprus with Greece and the Turkish invasion of the island. At that juncture, Bonn's policy of supplying Greece with war materials had run its full course.

BRANDT AND BONN'S POLICY TOWARD GREECE DURING THE JUNTA

This policy was formulated and practiced with Brandt at the helm, both in his capacity as minister of foreign affairs and later as chancellor. We know that Brandt demonstrated an active interest in the Greek case from early on, and, only a few days after the coup, he got briefed in Copenhagen Airport about the new situation by Camre (2011: 135), who had just returned from Greece, where he had stayed during the coup as a guest of the Papandreou family. In May 1969, Brandt took the opportunity to demonstrate his distaste for the military regime by refusing to leave his aircraft during a stopover in Athens to avoid meeting with representatives of the junta. His role was said to have been crucial in the conversion of the death penalty to live imprisonment of Alexandros Panagoulis (Apostolopoulos 2004: 333–34). According to Horst Ehmke, who was in charge of the negotiations that led to the release of the political prisoner Professor Georgios-Alexandros Mangakis and his wife, it only happened because of Brandt's insistence on the release of political prisoners in exchange for military aid.[72]

In spite of these efforts, Bonn's overall policy toward the Junta was to go on as usual on crucial issues like foreign and security policy. This is worthy of notice for two reasons: first, in contrast to Kiesinger, his partner in the great coalition, Brandt represented the "other" Germany; and second, Brandt wanted to earn credibility among the Extra-Parliamentary Opposition. To this end, the Ostpolitik was symbolically useful because to some extent it addressed the demands that West Germany recognize its Nazi past. However, and in contrast to the Eastern Bloc countries, Greece was an allied partner of West Germany and crucial for the defense of the West, something the Ostpolitik could not change.

Thus, the main concern also with Brandt at the helm was to avoid forcing Greece into isolation—an action, it was feared, that would play into the hands of the Soviet Bloc—meaning that Bonn continued its traditional Cold War priority of tying Greece to the West. Brandt made this clear in an address on 25 March 1973 at an SPD convention: Bonn should not attempt to make Greece a stranger in NATO, and it should continue its relations with Greece;[73] his personal experience had taught him that it would take a war to make regimes like the Greek junta collapse; nothing else would work: "I don't know of any place where Fascist regimes or regimes akin to Fascism have collapsed because of pressure from other countries," he said.[74] His speech was well received by the junta-friendly papers and castigated by the opposition press. *Athens News* wrote that if France and Italy became dictatorships, "Herr Brandt and the Nazi left-overs who surround him will be very happy to see a United European dictatorship."[75]

It was public opinion, opposition from its NATO partners Denmark, Norway and the Netherlands, internal resistance in the SPD, and—most crucial—the refusal by SPD and FPD delegates in the Bundestag to give their vote that forced the federal government to postpone its deliveries to Greece.

It effectively and substantially reduced the actual turnover of transactions within the framework of NATO and bilateral aid so that the final arms deliveries were much less than planned. However, it was not the result the government's own policy line but something that was forced on it. The guiding political principles of the West German government remained: it should not allow its policy vis-à-vis Greece to be influenced by anything else but foreign policy considerations, and it had no intention of tampering with internal Greek affairs. The emphasis was clearly on the primacy of continuity. In relation to its partners in NATO, Bonn followed the line of the United States—namely, that "the need for NATO unity and for reinforcement of NATO's military strength should override measures in the NATO forum evidencing distaste for the Greek regime." In this field, too, the stress was very much on "business as usual," which in this case came in the shape of burden-sharing.

Mogens Pelt, PhD and DPhil, is director of the Danish Institute at Athens, associate professor in international history in the History Section at the Saxo Institute, University of Copenhagen (on leave), member of the board of the Centre for the Study of Nationalism at the Saxo Institute at the Faculty of Humanities, University of Copenhagen, and codirector (with Professor Catharina Raudvere) at the Centre "Many Roads in Modernity: South-Eastern Europe and Its Ottoman Roots" ToRS at the Faculty of Humanities, University of Copenhagen. He was a Stanley J. Seeger Fellow at the Program in Hellenic Studies, Princeton University in 2008–9, attached to the commission established by the Danish Parliament to investigate the Danish Security Intelligence Service in 2007–8, was a member of the working group of the Volkswagen Foundation–funded international network *Captive States, Divided Societies: Political Institutions of Southeastern Europe in Historical Comparative Perspective* (see www.cap-lmu.de/ projekte/fge/captivestates/ index.php) in 2005–7, was a visiting fellow at the Department of Near Eastern Studies, Princeton University in 1999, and was deputy director of the Danish Institute at Athens, 1993–96. His recent books include *Military Intervention and a Crisis of Democracy in Turkey: The Menderes Era and Its Demise* (I. B. Tauris, 2014); *Tying Greece to the West: American–West German–Greek Relations, 1945–1974* (Museum Tusculanum Press, 2006); (with Morten Heiberg) *Los negocios de la Guerra: Armas Nazis para la república española* (Editorial Crítica, 2005); and *Tobacco, Arms and Politics: Greece and Germany from World Crisis to World War, 1929–41* (Museum Tusculanum Press, 1998).

NOTES

1. *Foreign Relations of the United States (FRUS), 1933-1945, 1941,* vol. 13, *Conference at Quebec, 1944,* no. 91, Washington, DC, 9 September 1944, Top Secret, Roosevelt Papers, Briefing Book Prepared in the Treasury Department.
2. *FRUS, 1953-1960, 1952-1954,* vol. 7, *Western European Security,* no. 214, Washington, DC, 17 August 1953, Top Secret, Statement of Policy by the National Security Council, NSC 160/1.
3. 7 December 1973, Aufzeichnung des Ministerialdirektors Hermes, *Akten zur Auswärtigen Politik der Bundesrepublik Deutschland (AAPD),* 1973, no. 404.
4. Washington, DC, 27 February 1970, NEA State Department to Embassy Bonn, Athens and US Mission NATO USCINEUR, United States National Archives (USNA), RG 59, Def. 12-5 Greece.
5. Bonn, 24 August 1967, Auswärtiges Amt, Aufzeichnung: Betr.: Die deutsche Haltung gegenüber Griechenland, Politisches Archiv des Auswärtigen Amts (PAAA), vol. IA4, no. 415.
6. It meant that the EEC should break off negotiations over the agricultural policy, while the European Investment Bank blocked loans amounting to 55 million USD (Apostolopoulos 2004: 319).
7. Bonn, 24 August 1967, Auswärtiges Amt, Aufzeichnung: Betr.: Die deutsche Haltung gegenüber Griechenland, PAAA, vol. IA4, no. 415.
8. Ibid.
9. Paris, 11 August 1967, Note pour le directeur politique, Delegation francaise auprès l'OTAN a direction d'Europe, Europe Meridionale, Ministère des Affaires Étrangères (MAE), 189QO/234.
10. 5 May 1969, Aufzeichnung des Ministerialdirigenten von Staden, *AAPD,* 1969, no. 143.
11. Athens, 2 May 1963, British Embassy to FO, Greek Political Prisoners Agitation, British National Archives (BNA), FO 371/169067.
12. Ibid.
13. PAAA, vol. 2, ref. 206, no. 153.
14. Athens, 15 January 1964, Greece: Annual Review for 1963, BNA, FO 371/174806. Regarding contemporary documents from Karamanlis's office and his own later account of his resignation, see Karamanlis 1994: 15-34.
15. 21 December 1967, Papport från Greklandskonferencen i Bergneustadt den 16-17 december 1967, Mogens Camre Papers.
16. Athens, 1972, the Royal Danish Embassy, Den indrepolitiske og retslige udvikling i Grækenland siden militærkuppet den 21 april 1967, Mogens Camre Papers.
17. 4 May 1967, Copenhagen, Report by Mogens Camre, Mogens Camre Papers.
18. Paris, 6 May 1967, MAE, 189QO/234.
19. 16 June 1967, Copenhagen, Jens Otto Krag to Bodil Koch, Minister of Culture, Mogens Camre Papers.

20. 24 August 1967, Report from Sweden on Andreas Papandreou, Lyndon B. Johnson Library (LBJL), Confidential File CO 94, Greece.
21. Ibid.
22. The complaints were filed in September 1967 (*AAPD*, 1969, no. 145n4).
23. London, 27 January 1968, "Situation in Greece: A Report by Amnesty International," Amnesty International, index no. EUR 25/001/1968.
24. *AAPD*, 1969, no. 273n8.
25. 7 December 1973, Aufzeichnung des Ministerialdirektors Hermes, *AAPD*, 1973, no. 404n4.
26. Paris, 12 September 1969, Note pour le ministre, MAE, 189QO/237.
27. Bonn, 29 August 1969, Gespräch des Bundesministers Brandt mit dem Oberbefehlshaber der alliierten Streitkräfte in Europa, Goodpaster, *AAPD* 1969, no. 273.
28. In January 1971, U.S. Ambassador Tasca in Athens explicitly asked Washington to inform the West German government that the "the U.S. would consider German aid to Greece as [a] part of FRG [West German] contribution to NATO defence" (Athens, 7 January 1971, Embassy to Secretary of State, Subject: Visit of to US of German Under Secretary of Defence, USNA, RG 59, Pol. 7 Ger.W, XR DEF 12-5 Greece).
29. Bonn, 8 December 1969, Aufzeichnung des Staatssekretärs Bahr, Bundeskanzleramt, Geheim, Betr. Gespräch des Herrn Bundeskanzlers mit dem amerikanischen Außenminister am 6. Dezember 1969, AAPD 1969, 391.
30. Bonn, 29 January 1970, Embassy to Secretary of State, Subject: FRG Arms Sales Policy to Greece, USNA, RG 59, Def.12-5 Greece.
31. London, 1 August 1970, US Embassy London to State Department, USNA, RG 59, Pol.17 Greece–UK.
32. Bonn, 2 February 1970, Embassy to Secretary of State, Secret, USNA, RG 59, Def.12-5 Greece.
33. Washington, DC, 27 February 1970, NEA State Department to Embassy Bonn, Athens and US Mission NATO USCINEUR, NA RG 59, DEF 12-5 Greece.
34. Washington, DC, 8 May 1970, Reprise des livraison americaines d'armements lourds a la Grece, MAE, 189QO/234.
35. Copenhagen, 15 May 1970, Ambassador to Minister of Foreign Affairs, Danemark et la Grèce, la question de livraison d'armes, MAE, 186QO/97.
36. 23 May 1970, Walter Scheel to William Rogers, USNA, RG 59, Pol. 23-9 Greece.
37. Ibid.
38. Rome, 27 May 1970, Duckwitz z.Z. Rom an das Auswärtige Amt, Betr.: NATO-Ministerkonferenz in Rom am 26./27. Mai 1970; hier: Aussprache der Minister am ersten Sitzungstag, *AAPD* 1970, no. 240.
39. London, 1 August 1970, US Embassy London to State Department, USNA, RG 59, Pol. 17 Greece–UK.
40. 11 August 1970, Memorandum for Henry A. Kissinger, the White House, subject: Issue of Military Aid to Greece May Provoke Confrontation in NATO, USNA, RG 59, XR DEF 19-8 Greece, DEF 4 NATO.

41. 2 November 1970, Intelligence Note, Bureau of Intelligence and Research, Greece: Rapprochement with US, USNA, RG 59, Pol. Greece–US.
42. Copenhagen, 21 September 1971, Dudley to Secretary of State, Confidential, USNA, RG 59, DEF 12-5 Greece.
43. Ibid.
44. Washington, DC, 26 May 1970, Department of State, Theodore L. Eliot Jr., Executive Secretary, Memorandum for Mr. Henry A. Kissinger, the White House, Secret Nodis, USNA RG 59, DEF 12-5 Greece.
45. Ibid.
46. Washington, DC, 4 February 1972, NEA to Embassy Athens, Subj: F-4's for Greece, Confidential, USNA, RG 59, DEF 12-5 Greece.
47. Bonn, 7 February 1972, US Embassy to Secretary of State, Subject: FRG Participation in Greek F-4 Buy, Secret, USNA, RG 59, DEF 12-5 Greece.
48. Washington, DC, 8 February 1972, the Secretary of State, Memorandum for the President, Subject: Waiver of Prohibition on Assistance to Greece, USNA, RG 59, XR DEF 19-8 US–Greece; see also Washington, DC, 4 February 1972, Department of State, Action Memorandum to the Secretary, Presidential Determination, Greece.
49. Bonn, 7 February 1972, Embassy to Secretary of State, Subject: FRG Participation in Greek F-4 Buy, Secret, USNA, RG 59, DEF 12-5 Greece.
50. Washington, DC, 30 March 1972, USNA, RG 59, DEF 12-5 Greece.
51. Paris, 11 September 1973, Vente de matériels d'armement à la Grèce, MAE, 189QO/277.
52. *AAPD*, 1971, no. 122.
53. *AAPD*, 1974, no. 91n5.
54. 7 December 1973, Aufzeichnung des Ministerialdirektors Hermes, *AAPD* 1973, no. 404n7.
55. Bonn, 13 January 1972, MAE, 189QO/278.
56. Bonn, 7 February 1972, Embassy to Secretary of State, Subject: FRG Participation in Greek F-4 Buy, Secret, USNA, RG 59, DEF 12-5 Greece.
57. Bonn, 17 April 1972, Embassy to Secretary of State, Subject: FRG Military Assistance to Greece, Confidential, USNA, RG 59, DEF 12-5 Greece.
58. 7 March 1972, *AAPD*, 1972, no. 48.
59. 7 December 1973, Aufzeichnung des Ministerialdirektors Hermes, *AAPD*, 1973, no. 404nn7–8.
60. 5 June 1974, European Action Committee of Greece to Jean Sauvagnargues, Minister of Foreign Affairs, MAE, 189PQ/294.
61. Athens, 1 June 1973, Ambassador Oncken to Auswäriges Amt, *AAPD*, 1973, no. 172.
62. Ibid., no. 172n5.
63. Ibid., no. 172n16.
64. Ibid.
65. 11 December 1973, *AAPD*, 1973, no. 413.
66. *Bulletin: European Atlantic Action Committee on Greece*, 31 January 1974.

67. *AAPD*, 1973, no. 404.
68. Cf. *AAPD*, 1972, no. 48.
69. *AAPD*, 1973, no. 404.
70. *AAPD*, 1974, no. 91n17.
71. Ibid., no. 117n3.
72. *AAPD*, 1972, no. 102n7.
73. Bonn, 28 March 1973, PAAA, 14598.
74. Bonn, 2 April 1973, PAAA, 14598.
75. Bonn, 28 March 1973, PAAA, 14598.

REFERENCES

Periodicals

Athens News

Archives

Berlin, Germany
    Politisches Archiv des Auswärtigen Amts (PAAA)
Copenhagen, Denmark
    Mogens Camre Papers
London, United Kingdom
    British National Archives (BNA)
Paris, France
    Ministère des Affaires Étrangères (MAE)
Washington, DC
    Lyndon B. Johnson Library (LBJL)
    United States National Archives (USNA)

Published Primary Sources

Akten zur Auswärtigen Politik der Bundesrepublik Deutschland (*AAPD*)
Bulletin: European Atlantic Action Committee on Greece
Camre, M. 2011. *Knus Tyrannerne: Erindiger*. Odense.
Foreign Relations of the United States (*FRUS*)
Karamanlis, K. 1994. *To archeio: Gegonota kai keimena* [The archive: Facts and texts].
    Vol. 6, *Periodos dokimasias, 1963–1974* [Trial period, 1963–74]. Athens.

Secondary Sources

Apostolopoulos, D. 2004. *Die griechish-deutschen Nachkriegsbeziehungen*. Frankfurt.
Herbert, U., and K. Hunn. 2000. "Gastarbeiterpolitik in der Bundesrepublik: Vom Beginn der offiziellen Anwerbung bis zum Anwerbestopp (1955–1973)." In *Dynamische Zeiten: Die 60er Jahre in den beiden deutschen Gesellschaften*, edited by A. Schildt, D. Siegfried, and K. C. Lammers, 273–310. Hamburg.
Herf, J. 1997. *Divided Memory: The Nazi Past in the Two Germanies*. Cambridge, MA.
Hilwig, S. J. 1998. "The Revolt against the Establishment: Students versus the Press in West Germany and Italy." In *1968: The World Transformed*, edited by C. Fink, P. Gassert, and D. Junker, 321–49. Washington, DC.
Kornetis, K. 2013. *Children of the Dictatorship: Student Resistance, Cultural Politics, and the "Long 1960s" in Greece*. London.
Murtagh, P. 1994. *The Rape of Greece: The King, the Colonels and the Resistance*. London.
Pedaliou, E. G. H. 2007. "'A Disconcordant Note': NATO and the Greek Junta, 1967–1974." *Diplomacy and Statecraft* 22(1): 101–20.
Pelt, M. 1998. *Tobacco, Arms and Politics: Greece and Germany from World Crisis to World War 1929–41*. Studies in 20th and 21st Century European History 1. Copenhagen.
——. 2006. *Tying Greece to the West: US–West German–Greek Relations 1949–74*. Copenhagen.
Soutou, G.-H. 2018. *La guerre froid de la France, 1941–1990*. Paris.
Wend, H. B. 2001. *Recovery and Restoration: U.S. Foreign Policy and the Politics of Reconstruction of West Germany's Shipbuilding Industry, 1945–1955*. Westport, CT.
Zubok, V., and C. Pleshakov. 1996. *Inside the Kremlin's Cold War: From Stalin to Khrushchev*. Cambridge, MA.

Chapter 12

The Greek Military Regime and the Cyprus Question

John Sakkas

The Cyprus crisis in the early 1970s has been studied quite extensively from the Greek and Turkish points of view. Each side usually follows a sort of interpretation that is a by-product of a more general interpretation of the Cyprus issue, which views conflict as a situation emanating from domestic actors—for example, between two hostile groups or communities (Papadakis 1998: 149–65). In his recent study, Niyazi Kizilyürek (2016), a Turkish Cypriot political scientist at the University of Cyprus, sheds light on the interethnic, intraethnic, and interstate aspects of the Cypriot conflict with special attention to violence. Considerable attention has also been paid to the determining political influence of external actors, particularly of the United States and Britain, one of the three guarantor powers for Cyprus (for an excellent introduction to the Cyprus question, see Coufoudakis 2006; for the U.S. policy in Cyprus, see especially Bolukbasi 1988; Salem 1992; O'Malley and Craig 1999; Nicolet 2001; Rizas 2004; Pelt 2006; for British policy in Cyprus, see Faustmann and Peristianis 2006; Mallinson 2007; Morgan 2010; Nafpliotis 2013; Burke 2017). More recently, Neovi Karakatsanis and Jonathan Swarts have provided us with a clear understanding of the factors that influenced the formulation of American policy toward the dictatorship in Greece, arguing that under the Nixon administration the security importance of maintaining a loyal strategic ally in Greece overshadowed democratic concerns entirely. And Konstantina Maragkou has deftly presented the dilemmas and tasks facing three successive British governments during the period of Greece's military dictatorship and addressed the perennial conflict between pragmatism and principles (Karakatsanis and Swarts

2018; Maragkou 2018). Another important study, titled *The Greek Junta and the International System*, discusses the military dictatorship in Greece as a case study in order to point to continuities, as well as to the structural changes, in the international system during this period (Klapsis et al. 2020).

However, much less attention has been placed on the specific objectives of the Greek junta (1967–74) in Cyprus and the different approaches of its leaders to the issue. In addition, minimal consideration has been given to Turkey's strategic designs on the island and the influence and the degree of involvement of the superpowers in the evolution and manipulation of the Cyprus conflict in relation to their wider interests in the Eastern Mediterranean. As Vassilis Fouskas (2005: 55) asserts, "The Cyprus crisis of 1974 was not a matter of Greek-Turkish conflict alone . . . . It was a conflict with global dimensions seen in the context of a generalized Middle Eastern situation in which the security and defense of Israel was of paramount importance for the United States" (see also the conflicting views of John Sakkas and Ian Asmussen in Calandri, Caviglia, and Varsori 2016).

This chapter argues that the Greek military rulers sought enosis (unity) with Cyprus mainly for reasons of national and political concern. They gave special attention to the Cyprus issue, and a solution that would satisfy the Greek national pride—and the Americans—was deemed essential to their ability to remain in power. Like their predecessors, they were prepared to achieve enosis by making concessions to the Turks, but, unlike them, they were determined to move against Archbishop Makarios, the Cypriot president, who was opposed to such a solution, and neutralize him by either peaceful or even violent means. Furthermore, there were serious divisions on the Cyprus issue within the regime itself, between the pragmatists and the ultranationalists. The former advocated a friendly approach to Turkey and supported the intercommunal talks in Cyprus, while the latter were fervent opponents of Makarios and wanted to remove him from power, even at the risk of a confrontation with Turkey. Makarios's dedication to independence and maintaining the dominant Greek Cypriot position on the island was opposed not only by Athens but also by the nationalist Greek Cypriot faction led by General Grivas, who had fought the British in the late 1950s (the EOKA movement) and was now asking for immediate enosis.[1]

The chapter also demonstrates that Turkey's and the superpowers' policies toward Cyprus were driven mostly by geopolitical necessities. Turkey was seeking to protect its minority on the island and prevent enosis, but it was also concerned with the balance of power in the Eastern Mediterranean. If Cyprus were united with Greece, Turkey would be encircled, but if it were divided, Turkey would block Greek aspirations on the island while bringing the region under its control. Likewise, the United States and the Soviet

Union were concerned with the geostrategic significance of Cyprus and the island's effect upon the balance of power in the Near and Middle East. For the Americans, Turkey was the most vital ally in the region; for the Soviets, it was a key country in their policy of peaceful coexistence with the West.

The archives in the Greek Foreign Ministry for the period under consideration have yet to be opened. In 1988, Greece adopted the British thirty-year rule for the review and declassification of foreign policy documents. However, the declassification of the documents covering the dictatorship has not yet been completed. This chapter is primarily based on U.S. and British documents, as well as on the memoirs of some protagonists in the Cyprus question.

CYPRUS AFTER INDEPENDENCE

In August 1960, the Republic of Cyprus was proclaimed, bringing an end to the bitter anti-British struggle of 1954–59 (Crawshaw 1978; Holland 1998; for the London and Zurich agreements of 1959 that came into force in the form of the Treaties of Alliance, Establishment, and Guarantee, see Kyriakides 2009). However, three years later, a new crisis broke out when Makarios submitted "a thirteen point" plan aimed at amending key sections of the constitution. Turkey rejected it, and the tension between the two communities deteriorated into fierce intercommunal fighting (see Weston-Markides 2001 for one of the most important studies of the early history of the Republic of Cyprus). It soon became apparent that this crisis presented a threat to regional peace and stability; it could no longer be kept within the jurisdiction of an imperial power or the parties directly involved. The power vacuum created by British withdrawal had pushed Cyprus to the top of the Cold War agenda (for a comprehensive analysis of the 1963–64 Cyprus crisis, see James 2002).

In mid-1964, the United States attempted to reconcile the opposing demands of Greece and Turkey (enosis versus partition) by proposing to them a double-enosis along ethnic lines (the so-called Acheson plan), which would bring Cyprus firmly into the NATO sphere, making the whole island available to Western defense purposes, as it had been under British rule. The method of implementation and the exact areas to be turned over to Turkey varied with the different versions of the plan. All versions, however, involved partition and thus elimination of the independent state under Makarios. The liberal Greek prime minister, George Papandreou, was opposed to partition or federation. Partition, in his opinion, would lead the Greek part of Cyprus into becoming another Cuba, while federation would lead to civil war. He believed that the only possible solution was unrestricted independence, to be followed by a plebiscite and enosis.[2] When Dean Acheson presented his plan, Papandreou at first thought a version of it was worthy of discussion, but later, succumbing to pressure from his son Andreas and Makarios, he rejected it (Papandreou 1970; Brands 1987: 356–57; Rizas 2000).

At the time, Papandreou was dissatisfied with both the United States and Makarios. He gave high priority to U.S. Cold War concerns and was willing to entertain a NATO solution that gave Turkey a limited military presence on the island. Nevertheless, he was stubborn in his refusal to negotiate under the threat of a Turkish invasion of the island. When he insisted on an American guarantee that NATO preclude the threat of Turkish invasion, he was reminded of Turkish military superiority, and his demand was rebuffed. Papandreou was also annoyed with Makarios's reluctance to follow the instructions of his government (of Athens, the "national center") to be more pro-NATO and less pro-aligned. Although the ailing Greek prime minister was committed to rendering all possible assistance to Cyprus, he had no wish to see Makarios pursue an overly independent policy that might endanger Greece's national interests. He also suspected that after independence the archbishop was less committed to enosis than he had been in the 1950s. In order to enhance the island's defensive capability, as well as keep Makarios under his control, he sought the support of Grivas, who in June 1964 returned to Cyprus with the tacit approval of the Americans in order to organize and command the Cypriot National Guard and unify all irregular Greek Cypriot forces (Hatzivassiliou 2006: 164). For his part, Makarios knew about Acheson's diplomatic mission and was fully aware of the way in which Greece and Turkey were secretly discussing the possibility of dividing Cyprus between them. Makarios was against enosis in the form of double-enosis, even with a minimum of concessions to the Turkish Cypriots, insisting that Cyprus must be a completely independent and unitary state with democratic majority government and communal rights suitably entrenched in the constitution (Mayes 1982: 176).

In July 1965, following a major conflict with the king over the control of the army, Papandreou stepped down. In an atmosphere of protracted constitutional crisis, the caretaker governments that succeeded Papandreou in 1965–66 were reluctant to take any decisive steps toward a settlement in Cyprus. The Turks, on the other hand, were now willing to consider enosis in return for more territorial concessions which the Acheson Plan provided. Athens was prepared to concede only a British base, but Makarios rejected even that idea and instead proposed a NATO base manned by Turkish troops. In mid-December 1966, the Greek government fell, and the Greek-Turkish dialogue on Cyprus remained inconclusive (Mayes 1982: 183–85).

THE CYPRUS QUESTION, 1967–72

The Colonels were more dependent on the United States and more accommodating in their handling of the Cyprus question than their predecessors. They established closer ties with the U.S. administration (especially with the Pentagon and CIA) and increased military purchases from Washington at the expense of providing military facilities for the American navy in Greek ports. With respect to Cyprus, they publicly advocated enosis, but behind the scenes they worked for a solution based on the partition that was part of the Acheson Plan. Their main concern, however, was not Cyprus per se, but their relations with Makarios. They regarded him as being a cunning and guileful priest, who undermined Hellenic nationalism and thereby the cause of enosis by allying himself with the enemies of the Greek nation. They particularly deplored his policy of cultivating cooperative relations with the Soviet Union, his role in the nonaligned movement, and his opposition to Athens as a "national center" that should be dictating policy to Nicosia.

Georgios Papadopoulos, the junta leader, thought that removing Cyprus from Greek domestic and foreign policy would increase his prestige at home and diminish the regime's international isolation (Coufoudakis 1987: 233). Therefore, as soon as he assumed power, he hastened to forge a deal with the Turks behind Makarios's back and without his consent. In September, Greek and Turkish delegations met at the Evros border to discuss the Cyprus problem. The Greek side offered Turkey full sovereignty over the Dhekelia base and certain administrative autonomy to the Turkish Cypriots in exchange for enosis. The Turks rejected the Greek proposals out of hand. They were prepared to discuss federation, or a cantonal regime in Cyprus, or a Greek-Turkish condominium, but not enosis (Kuneralp 1998; Göktepe 2005: 435). In addition, they brought four conditions to the table. First, Cyprus should not be annexed unilaterally by either Greece or Turkey; second, neither Cypriot community should dominate the other; third, the 1959 Cyprus Treaties should not be revised unilaterally; and finally and most importantly, the balance of power established by the Lausanne Treaty (1923) in the Mediterranean between Greece and Turkeys should be preserved (Göktepe 2005: 435; Dodd 2010: 80–81).

Two months later, a disappointed Grivas launched an all-out assault on two Turkish Cypriot villages that controlled the main road linking Limassol to Nicosia. Turkey threatened to retaliate with military intervention unless Grivas left the island together with the ten thousand Greek mainland troops who had been illegally infiltrated into Cyprus since 1964. However, unlike 1964, this time the American pressure was directed toward the Greeks, who recoiled at the risk of a war with a stronger military power and accepted practically all of Turkey's demands (Markides 1977: 137; Göktepe 2005: 438–41). It was a humiliating diplomatic defeat for Papadopoulos that caused much frustration among hard-liners such as Dimitrios Ioannides, director of the Greek Military Police; Konstaninos Aslanides, general secretary for sports; Ioannis Ladas, general secretary of public order; and Antonios Lekkas, general secretary of industry.[3] This group of officers wereparticularly worried about the weakening of Cyprus's defense capability without any concessions on the part of Turkey. They also feared that the withdrawal of the junta-controlled troops and the return of Grivas to Athens would open the way for Makarios to reassert his authority and keep Cyprus under his firm control (Mayes 1982: 186–93; Rizas 2000: 77).

After 1967, the military regime continued making pro-enosis statements for public consumption and, at the same time, encouraged the two communities in Cyprus to negotiate and solve the internal constitutional problem themselves. However, the intercommunal talks led nowhere, and the blame for the failure was placed on Makarios's intransigence. Papadopoulos hoped to lay the foundation for enosis by cooperating with the Turks, but the archbishop insisted on Greek Cypriot majority rule, precluding any form of federalism or enhanced Turkish Cypriot local autonomy.[4] The junta leader could exert heavy pressure on Makarios through the Greek officers in the National Guard and the threat of the officers' withdrawal from the island leaving him at the mercy of the Turks. Nonetheless, he was reluctant to proceed with a coup against him. The archbishop was very popular in the Hellenic world, and the Colonels had not yet consolidated their position.[5]

The regime's conciliatory attitude toward the Cypriot leader had also been heavily influenced by the pragmatic American approach. After 1967, Washington grudgingly came to accept an independent Cyprus as the solution that best favored its interests. Makarios was seen as being an astute diplomat exploiting the balances of the international system and as a source of overall regional stability (Kissinger 1999: 197; Miller 2009: 177–78, 181). Besides, the costs and risks of his violent removal had risen considerably. The strategic importance of Cyprus had increased following the Six-Day War in the Middle East, while the Soviet Union was enhancing its military presence in the Eastern Mediterranean.[6] Subsequently, the Americans were prepared to tolerate Makarios for the time being and accept any solution to the Cyprus problem that did not endanger NATO's southern flank and kept out the Soviets.[7]

The military regime was also obliged to take into account the Soviet goals in Cyprus and the Eastern Mediterranean. A fundamental assumption in the Soviet strategic considerations was that Cyprus should remain unified, independent, and demilitarized. After 1964, the Soviets still considered

Makarios a legitimate political leader, but they also kept open their lines of contact with Ankara by recognizing the legal rights of the two national communities, which might lead to federation as a form of government on the island. In essence, the Cyprus dispute offered the Soviets the opportunity to reduce the cohesion and effectiveness of NATO and detach Turkey from the firm embrace of the Western alliance, a prospect that seemed as important to them as maintaining Cyprus as nonaligned.[8]

By late 1969, the rift between the Colonels and Makarios had intensified, but Papadopoulos still did not wish to see the archbishop forcibly removed from power. However, some of his ultranationalist colleagues, as well as members of the Greek Intelligence (KYP), were becoming increasingly impatient with the Cypriot leader and were devising plans to isolate or even eliminate him.[9] It is uncertain whether Papadopoulos had advanced knowledge of these plans for Makarios, but these colleagues and KYP members had close links to a terrorist organization in Cyprus, called the National Front, which demonstrated its opposition to Makarios and his supporters with bombings, attacks on police stations, and the assassinations of left-wing individuals. The tension between Athens and Nicosia reached its apex in March 1970, when the National Front attempted to kill Makarios himself.[10]

Despite its public declarations of its support for an unconditional enosis, the junta continued to be centered on the improvement of Greek-Turkish relations and a negotiated settlement of the Cyprus question. In an interview in the Turkish daily *Millet* in May 1971, Papadopoulos (1968–72, vol. 6: 92–95) bluntly stated that the Cyprus problem must be worked out between Greece and Turkey, and that "it should be made clear to the two Cypriot communities" that Greece and Turkey "are not willing to disturb their relations, let alone fight, for their sake." A short time later, Greek diplomats met with their Turkish counterparts in Lisbon and Paris in connection with NATO meetings being held there. Without reaching formal agreements, the Greek and Turkish interlocutors expressed the view that if no agreement were reached in Cyprus soon, the two countries would consult "on how to handle the problem" (Dodd 2010: 96; Mayes 1982: 213, 215).[11]

Shortly after these meetings, the junta began applying overt political pressure on Makarios. Its objective was to force him to make substantial concessions to the Turkish Cypriots or otherwise resign.[12] Papadopoulos warned Makarios to go along with the Greek government's suggestions, otherwise the government "will find itself in the awkward necessity to take these steps dictated by the national interests . . . however bitter these measures may be." Then, the Foreign Ministry passed a complementary but confidential note to Makarios, pointing out that "Athens, as the national center, draws and plans both policy directions and tactics." Makarios calmly replied that in matters concerning its survival and national future, Cypriot Hellenism had to have the last word (Kranidiotis 1985: 210-13).

Realizing that he could not persuade the archbishop to adapt to the national guidelines, Papadopoulos decided to take the "bitter measure" he had threatened. He would use Grivas as a threat to, and constraint on, Makarios, as well as a check on the growth of communism on the island. Makarios was not pro-communist, but he relied increasingly on the Cypriot Communist Party (AKEL) for internal backing against machinations from the mainland (Kissinger 1999: 199). For quite different reasons, both opposed NATO and union with Greece. In the elections of July 1970, AKEL secured nine out of thirty-five Greek Cypriot seats. The strength of the communist vote—at around 30 percent—shocked and angered Athens, and the conclusion was reached that something had to be done about Cyprus.[13]

In September 1971, Grivas supposedly escaped from house arrest in Athens and returned secretly to Cyprus. There, he set up and led the anti-Makarios EOKA-B, replacing the National Front, whose campaign had largely disintegrated. The new organization was in close contact with Greek officers in the National Guard and engaged together in sabotage activities against the government. It is interesting to note, however, that Grivas was not completely subject to the Colonels' objectives and desires. He had not forgiven them for letting him down after his attacks against Turkish Cypriot villages in November 1967 and for expelling the king after his abortive coup against the junta the following December. He also disagreed with Papadopoulos's policy of rapprochement with Turkey and his attempt to manipulate him in order to implement a policy of partition, which contradicted his lifelong goal of enosis with no concessions to Ankara. For their part, the Colonels did not conceal their annoyance with Grivas's extremism, fearing that the intracommunal struggle was risking direct foreign involvement.[14]

At the beginning of 1972, the shipment of Czech weapons for the Cypriot police gave Athens the opportunity to unleash a diplomatic offensive in order to force Makarios to succumb to its demands. The archbishop was asked to hand over all imported arms to the UN peacekeeping force and form a government of national unity on the Right and Center—even though AKEL and EDEK, the communist and socialist parties, had the backing of close to one in two Greek Cypriots—including representatives of Grivas, his main enemy in Cyprus (O'Malley and Craig 1999: 136). He was reminded again that Athens was the center of Hellenism, and that Cyprus was only a small part of the Greek nation. The Cypriot leader ignored these demands and arguments, making only a few concessions to the junta. It appeared to him that both Papadopoulos and Grivas were using the arms issue as a pretext to make him resign and precipitate partition in collusion with Turkey. This was no doubt a correct assessment.[15]

However, Makarios could still count on the United States, which continued to discourage any scenario of a forcible change that might have the effect of provoking civil war in Cyprus and offering the Soviet Union a chance to intervene.[16] Although the Americans viewed with concern Makarios's increasing ties with the nonaligned bloc and the support he received from AKEL, they knew that he was fiercely anticommunist and would never allow the Cypriot communists to have access to power.[17] Therefore, the Americans did not oppose him. In his memoirs, Henry Kissinger wrote, "At no time during my period in office did we take any measure to reduce his hold on power. We maintained an aloof, respectful, and wary relationship with him" (Kissinger 1999: 199). On the other hand, the United States was aware that a deal between Greece and Turkey on Cyprus, permitting double-enosis, would not be acceptable to Makarios as long as he maintained his own agenda. Under these circumstances, Papadopoulos had no other alternative than to lessen his pressure on Makarios by withdrawing his demand for resignation. The American administration's satisfaction with their "client" was evident. Papadopoulos "had helped to keep the Cyprus situation from breaking into flames." "No Greek government," concluded the Americans, "is likely to be more moderate over Cyprus than the present one."[18]

THE CYPRUS CRISIS, 1973–74

The year of 1973 was a crucial one for both Greece and the Cyprus issue. For his own reasons and under foreign pressure, Papadopoulos decided to move in the direction of a limited liberalization of his regime. He announced a general amnesty, the lifting of martial law, the formation of a civilian government under Spyridon Markezinis in October, and the holding of parliamentary elections in 1974. With regard to Cyprus, he denounced Grivas for the first time, fully aligning his policy with that of Makarios. These initiatives, however, alarmed and alienated Papadopoulos's former colleagues and important sectors of the military without winning the approval of the old political establishment or conciliating the students.[19] The hard-liners were anxious about the direction in which Papadopoulos was leading the country and accused him of betraying the ideals of the 1967 coup. In November, a few days after the Athens Polytechnic uprising and the army intervention to quell it, Ioannides toppled Papadopoulos in a successful coup and assumed control as the new head of the junta.[20]

Ioannides was intensely nationalistic and very suspicious of Turkish goals in Cyprus and the Aegean.[21] His chief aim was not the annexation of Cyprus to Greece, but the removal of Makarios in order to facilitate "an understanding" with Turkey on the future of the island.[22] He felt a bitter antipathy toward Makarios, considering him opportunistic and procommunist; he usually called him "the red priest."[23]

Both Ioannides and Makarios viewed the Cyprus conflict from a strictly ethnocentric perspective and misjudged the goals of the external agents in Cyprus and the degree of their involvement in the evolution and even manipulation of the conflict. Ioannides believed that the United States would condone, or at least tolerate, a move against Makarios and restrain Turkey, even at the eleventh hour, as it had done in 1964 and 1967.[24] For his part, Makarios was reasonably certain that the new Greek rulers would act rationally because "they were weak" and the Western allies and/or the Soviet Union would thwart a move by Athens that would then prompt an intervention by Turkey (Mayes 1982: 238; Miller 2009: 188). However, their estimation of the exogenous political designs was wrong, as in 1974 the circumstances were quite different from those that had existed in the 1960s. By 1974, the Americans were in favor of the Turkish goals in the Eastern Mediterranean, and in Cyprus in particular, and had no intention to intervene effectively to deter "the weak men" in Athens from moving against Makarios, while the Soviets had already tilted their preference to Turkey with a view to disengaging Ankara from U.S. influence.

Furthermore, in 1974 Bülent Ecevit was far more assertive than İsmet Inonu or Süleyman Demirel, and the Turkish army had all the means necessary to accomplish a successful military operation by land, sea, and air (Bolukbasi 1988: 179). When Ioannides staged a coup against Makarios on 15 July 1974, Turkey decided to intervene on the grounds of protecting the island's Turkish Cypriot minority. But its invasions in Cyprus a few days later and in August, after the collapse of talks in Geneva, were based not only on legal grounds but also on strategic priorities. Greece's attempt to accomplish enosis was seen as a dangerous revival of the Megali Idea, designed to encircle Turkey by adding Cyprus to the chain of Greek islands surrounding the Turkish coasts. This should be avoided by restoring the balance of power in the Eastern Mediterranean through a Turkish occupation of a substantial portion of the island. Certain factors, such as the weakness of the Greek junta, the diplomatic isolation of the Greek and Cypriot regimes, the rapprochement between Turkey and the Soviet Union since the late 1960s, and détente between the two superpowers, made it easier for Turkey to proceed unhindered in forcibly implementing its plan on Cyprus.[25]

The United States remained apparently inactive or indecisive during the 1974 crisis in Cyprus. As Kissinger states emphatically in his memoirs, "There was no sense of imminent crisis"; the United States "did not believe the situation was approaching a critical point" (Kissinger 1999: 203, 205–6). The State Department had ample warning about Ioannides's intentions in Cyprus from various sources, but it disregarded the possibility of a coup, and State Department officials—with the notable exception of Thomas Boyatt, director of Cyrus affairs—felt no urgency for action.[26] Accordingly, the American ambassador in Athens, Henry Tasca, who detested the new, obscure dictator, never met directly with him and conveyed Washington's opposition to the use of violence in Cyprus. Instead, he made representations at lower levels of the Greek government that ultimately proved ineffective (Kissinger 1999: 205).

In his memoirs, Kissinger (1999: 218) blamed Ecevit for the crisis after the Greek coup because although he asked Joseph Sisco, assistant state secretary for Near Eastern affairs, to deliver a sharp warning to Ankara, the Turkish prime minister "proved impervious both to American warnings and to the Greek concessions." The invasion was inevitable because "Turkey was not interested in a negotiated solution; it was determined to settle old scores" (Kissinger 1982: 1191). Kissinger (1999: 218, 228) also blamed America's domestic crisis because the Turkish invasion coincided with the terminal phase of Richard Nixon's presidency. However, evidence from U.S. documents seems to imply that although the Nixon administration was aware of Turkey's military plans and territorial goals, it was unwilling to intervene in order to influence the course of events as long as peace in the region was not endangered.[27]

The United States did not intervene to stop the Turks because of its strategic considerations.[28] The Arabs' ability to plan, coordinate, and execute a successful military attack on Israel, Soviet assistance to the Arabs, and Britain's and Turkey's refusal to allow the United States to use the intelligence facilities in Cyprus to support Israel led the Americans to realize the urgency of filling the existing power vacuum in the area. As the British were preparing to reduce their forces stationed on Cyprus,[29] and the Soviets were increasing their naval presence in the Eastern Mediterranean, Washington came to support the idea that the Turks should be allowed, or even encouraged, to reverse the negative balance of power in the region by settling the Cyprus problem in their favor. The division of the island would not only satisfy Turkey, which might then attempt to restore its relations with the United States, but it would also transform the island into a Western carrier serving the security and defense needs of Israel, as well as Kissinger's diplomacy in the Middle East.[30]

The coup against Makarios in July 1974 provoked the strong reaction of the Soviet Union, which took the opportunity to reaffirm its support to Cyprus and to condemn the machinations of "Greek militarists" (*Pravda*, 16 July 1974). *Pravda* (18 July 1974), the official newspaper of the Communist Party of the Soviet Union, accused the Greek junta of being a fascist regime, a simple pawn of imperialist powers that sought to dismember Cyprus and create a NATO stronghold in the Eastern Mediterranean.

Although the Soviets had been informed by the Turks of their plans regarding Cyprus, they took to action in order to forestall them (Cutler 1985: 60–89; Aslim 2016: 249–61). They even indicated that they were ready to accept a limited Turkish action provided that Cyprus's military and international status was preserved. On 20 July, they heard with satisfaction the Turkish declaration that the invasion aimed at the "restoration of constitutional procedures" and the return of president Makarios to power (*Pravda*, 25 July 1974). Reflecting the official view, *Pravda* justified the Turkish invasion as a logical reaction to the Greek intention of suppressing the Turkish Cypriot minority and annexing Cyprus. Arguing that NATO was using Cyprus to consolidate its military-strategic positions in the Eastern Mediterranean and the Middle East, the newspaper linked NATO's machinations around Cyprus to Israel's "aggression" against Arab countries. It was evident that the Soviets, like the Americans, were much more concerned about the balance of power and stability in the region than the fate of Cyprus itself (*Pravda*, 21 and 28 July, 4 August 1974).

CONCLUSION

The Colonels' Cypriot policy differed very little from that of their predecessors. This continuity is reflected in their demand for an almost unconditional enosis and their pursuit of a secret settlement with the Turks on a double-enosis scheme with American consent. Like their predecessors, they believed that Athens must direct a combined Greek and Greek-Cypriot strategy and used General Grivas as a tool in order to undermine or even eliminate Makarios and force the Turkish Cypriot community to accept Greek Cypriot dominance by whatever means necessary.

However, in contrast to their civilian counterparts, the Colonels were more cooperative with the United States and more eager to impose a version of the Acheson Plan on Makarios. In addition, they feared that Makarios might turn the island over to communist rule or, even worse, provide a base from which democratic opponents of their regime could operate. With every act of defiance by Makarios, they came to regard him not just as a danger to Greece's national interests but also as a popular threat to their power.

Papadopoulos, like most junta officers, sought a modus vivendi with Turkey that would facilitate enosis, even at the cost of some territorial concessions. Makarios was opposed to such a solution, but Papadopoulos was hesitant about moving openly against him because of the archbishop's high national and international prestige and the threat of Soviet involvement in case of a crisis in Cyprus. Ioannides, on the other hand, was more emphatic about asserting Greek rights against Turkey and more adventurous in dealing with regional issues than Papadopoulos had been. He believed that his inflexibility with Turkey and insistence upon enosis would help consolidate his internal military support, as well as distract popular discontent away from his regime. He regarded Makarios and the Cypriot Communists as the primary obstacles to the achievement of his objectives. Yet, unlike Papadopoulos, who sought to force Makarios into submission through the use of political pressure, manipulation, and threats against his life, Ioannides had no inhibition against using large-scale military force in order to remove his rival from the political scene. What he failed to appreciate, however, was that Turkey was regarded by the Americans as even more important than Greece to their strategic interests in the region.

Broadly speaking, the Colonels' Cyprus policy had two major consequences. As soon as they assumed power, they adopted a nationalist approach and tried, especially under Papadopoulos, to serve American interests in the belief that they thus furthered their own cause. Although they publicly advocated enosis and supported the intercommunal negotiations, they transformed the Cyprus dispute from being a Hellenic problem to a narrowly Greek issue. As such, the dispute would be solved in cooperation with Ankara and with the concurrence of Washington and London at the expense of the Cypriots' wishes and expectations. Furthermore, Ioannides's coup against Makarios offered the Turks an excellent legal pretext to fulfill a long-standing policy aimed at the division of the island along ethnic lines and the exclusion of Greece from the Eastern Mediterranean.

The Turkish invasion resulted in the occupation of about 37 percent of the island's territory, creating a huge refugee problem, as some 250 thousand Cypriots were forcefully displaced. It also forced the humiliated and demoralized junta to resign, and democracy in Greece was then restored under the leadership of Konstantinos Karamanlis. The Greek public blamed the new national catastrophe—second only to the Asia Minor catastrophe—on the military regime and the Americans who had backed it, and, in the late 1970s, anti-American popular feeling was widely exploited by Andreas Papandreou and his socialist party, PASOK. It was not until the late 1980s that

Greek anger against the United States would subside, and subsequent Greek governments realized that restoring relations with the United States was still in the national interest of Greece.

John Sakkas is professor of modern history at the University of the Aegean, Greece. He received his PhD from Hull University in 1993. His doctoral dissertation was on British public opinion and the Greek civil War, 1944–49. His research focuses on the Cold War period, with an emphasis on the Mediterranean and the Middle East. His book, *The Cyprus Crisis, 1967–74: The Greek Dictatorship, the Superpowers, and the Middle East*, will be published in 2022 by Harrassowitz Verlag. He is a member of the executive board of the European Defense and Security College and its Doctoral School at Brussels, and participates in the design, evaluation, and monitoring of European research programs at the European Commission.

NOTES

1. Grivas was a Greek Cypriot–born nationalist, who in the mid-1950s organized the clandestine military struggle of EOKA against the British colonial authorities. In the 1960s, he remained faithful to his dream of enosis and was transformed into one of the most bitter enemies of Makarios. His role in Greek and Cypriot politics during the dictatorship remains obscure and complex; his memoirs are confined to only his early political career up to the 1950s (Grivas 1964; for EOKA, see Novo 2010; French 2015).
2. *Foreign Relations of the United States* (hereafter *FRUS*), *1964–1968*, vol. 16, *Cyprus; Greece; Turkey*, no. 75, Memorandum of Conversation (Under-Secretary George Ball with Papandreou in Washington), 24 June 1964.
3. When the coup took place in April 1967, Ladas was in charge of the Greek Military Police and ordered the arrest of several prominent politicians and military personnel who were regarded as inimical to the "revolution." He was a right-wing extremist and in favor of the execution of Andreas Papandreou after his arrest. After the coup, he was replaced by Ioannides and transferred to the Ministry of Public Order. In the major reshuffle of July 1971, he was appointed undersecretary-governor of Thessaly, and his influence within the regime was considerably reduced. In the same reshuffle, other military leaders, such as Lekkas, an admirer of the dictator Metaxas (1936–41), were also removed from government posts and marginalized, thus revealing a serious split within the group of coup makers.
4. National Archives and Records Administration (hereafter NARA), Central Intelligence Agency (hereafter CIA), Intelligence Report: "Cyprus–An Old Problem," 24 September 1973, retrieved 23 March 2020 from https://www.cia.gov/library/readingroom/document/cia-rdp85t00875r001100160020-7; see also Kranidiotis 1985.

5. Foreign and Commonwealth Office, United Kingdom (hereafter FCO), 9/1216, Record of a Meeting on Greece, 16 March 1970; NARA, CIA, National Security Council, Memorandum for Kissinger from Harold Saunders and Rosemary Neaher, "The Cyprus Situation," 10 February 1972, retrieved 12 February 2020 from https://www.cia.gov/library/readingroom /document/loc-hak-20-4-15-8.
6. Although the communications facilities on Cyprus had been much reduced, it was "important for the Americans that the two British bases remain in friendly hands." *FRUS, 1969–1976*, vol. 30, *Greece; Cyprus; Turkey, 1973–1976*, no. 75, "Study Prepared by the Interdepartmental Group for Near East and South Asia," 6 May 1974; on the significance of these facilities and bases for U.S. and NATO interests in the Middle East, see O'Malley and Craig 1999 and Mallinson 2016.
7. FCO, 9/1162, Peter Ramsbotham (Higher Commissioner to Cyprus, 1969–71) to FCO, 25 November 1970; National Security Council (hereafter NSC), State Department to American Embassy, Ankara, 6 January 1972, no. 2359, Country File: Turkey, vol. 3, box 633.
8. NARA, CIA, Special Report: "Soviet Policy and Tactics in the Cyprus Dispute," 12 February 1965, retrieved 17 December 2019 from https://www.cia.gov/library/readingroom/document/cia-rdp79-00927a004800010002-9; for the Soviet policy in Cyprus in 1967–74, see Stergiou 2007; Sakkas and Zhukova 2013.
9. FCO 9/1209, Michael Steward (British Ambassador to Greece) to FCO, 23 February 1970.
10. FCO 9/1209, Views of Cleridis, President of the Cypriot House of Representatives and Chief Negotiator in the Intercommunal Talks, Ramsbotham to FCO, 23 March 1970.
11. In his memoirs, the Greek deputy foreign minister Christos Palamas (1979: 241) rejects outright the claim that "a NATO plan" was discussed by the Greek and Turkish representatives in Lisbon.
12. NARA, CIA, National Security Council, Memorandum for Kissinger from Harold Saunders and Rosemary Neaher, "The Cyprus Situation," 10 February 1972.
13. *FRUS, 1964–1968*, vol. 16, *Cyprus; Greece; Turkey*, no. 295, Circular Airgram from the Department of State to the NATO capitals, 12 July 1967 ("Existence of AKEL Threat to Hellenism as a Whole"); *FRUS, 1969–1976*, vol. 29, *Eastern Europe; Eastern Mediterranean, 1969–1972*, no. 383, Letter from Councilor of Embassy in Cyprus (Crawford) to the Officer in Charge of Cyprus Affairs (Boyatt), 19 November 1971.
14. NARA, CIA, Intelligence Report, "Cyprus–An Old Problem," 24 September 1973, retrieved 23 March 2020 from https://www.cia.gov/library/readingroom/document/cia-rdp85t00875r001100160020-7; Mayes 1982.
15. NARA, CIA, National Security Council, Memorandum for Kissinger from Harold Saunders and Rosemary Neaher, "The Cyprus Situation," 10 February 1972.
16. NARA, CIA, "Washington Special Actions Group Meeting," 14 February 1972, retrieved 22 November 2019 from https://www.cia.gov/library/readingroom/document /loc-hak-310-2-2-2.

17. According to Kissinger, one of the principal U.S. concerns was that AKEL not achieve predominance; however, "as long as Makarios is there, AKEL seems under control." *FRUS, 1969–1976*, vol. 29, *Eastern Europe; Eastern Mediterranean, 1969–1972*, no. 359, "Memorandum from Kissinger to Nixon" (n.d.). When Makarios visited the White House in October 1970, he assured Nixon that "by history and tradition and conviction we belong to the West" and "we will not become like Cuba." Then, he told the U.S. president that he "had never appointed a left-wing person to any significant post," and that he "accepts their support because it is a good way of keeping them under control" (*FRUS, 1969–1976*, vol. 29, *Eastern Europe; Eastern Mediterranean, 1969–1972*, no. 360, "Memorandum of Conversation," 25 October 1970; Camp 1980: 52–53). In the mid-1960s, the United States had tried to strengthen noncommunist labor organizations and to prohibit AKEL (Coufoudakis 1976: 246, 249).
18. *FRUS, 1969–1976*, vol. 30, *Greece; Cyprus; Turkey, 1973–1976*, no. 5, National Intelligence Estimate, 19 July 1973.
19. NSC, Analysis of the New Greek Military Regime by H. Tasca (American Embassy Athens) to State Department, 8 February 1974, no. 842, Country File: Greece, vol. 4, box 595. General Bonanos (1986: 115), the commander-in-chief of the Greek Armed Forces, was first informed that Ioannidis was making plans to overthrow Papadopoulos sometime in mid-August 1973. According to General Gizikis, Ioannidis's emissary, Captain Thanopoulos, informed him of a planned coup on 17 September 1973 (Hellenic Parliament, 1998, vol. 4: 295).
20. In his recently published study, Ioannis Tzortzis (2020) offers a detailed and multilayered analysis of the long-term consequences of the failure of the so-called Markezinis experiment.
21. *FRUS, 1969–1976*, vol. 30, *Greece; Cyprus; Turkey, 1973–1976*, no. 15, Interagency Intelligence Memorandum, 21 June 1974.
22. "Cyprus Coup: Meeting General Ioannides," 16 July 1974, accessed 17 September 2019, https://wikileaks.org/plusd/cables/1974ATHENS04528_b.html.
23. NCS, American Embassy in Athens to State Department, 14 June 1974, no. 3705, Country File: Greece, vol. 4, box 595; on Ioannides, see Miller 2009: 176–200.
24. In an interview in jail a short time before his death, Ioannidis argued that he had been deceived by the Americans about their real intentions. They had assured him that they would not allow Turkey to intervene. He had got this idea from his contacts with CIA officials in Athens. See *Adesmeftos Typos*, 25 July 2010, where he claims, "I was deceived by the Americans."
25. NSC, Joseph Sisco (Assistant State Secretary) to Kissinger, 21 July 1974, no. 4742, Country File: Greece, vol. 5, folder 2, box 595; see also Bolukbasi 1988: 187–90; Birand 1984: 24–36.
26. The State Department had been inundated by reports of an imminent coup against Makarios since March 1974. These reports came from Boyatt, the American embassies in Greece, Cyprus, and Turkey, and even from Sisco.
27. Regarding the fact that the Americans knew in advance of the Turkish invasion, see Mallinson 2016: xii; Kissinger (1999: 229) told President Ford on 10

August 1974 that the Turks "have about 15 percent of the island and want 30 percent. They might try to grab it."
28. The role of the United States in the Greek coup against Makarios and the Turkish invasion has been the subject of great controversy in the literature on the 1974 crisis. Some authors attribute the chain of events on Cyprus to secret decision-making by American policymakers in order to achieve strategic U.S. goals. O'Malley and Craig (1999) explicitly refer to their argument as a "conspiracy by America." Other major proponents of this theory include Christopher Hitchens (2002: chapter 7 on Cyprus), Lawrence Stern (1977), and William Mallinson (2007: 40), the last of whom has accused Kissinger of having had foreknowledge of, and having condoned, the invasion of Cyprus. On the other hand, others argue that the conspiracy theories are unsatisfactory explanations of the events leading up to the crisis in 1974 (Lindley and Wenzke 2008; Asmussen 2011). They point out that while it is certainly the case that the U.S. government merits criticism for its inactivity and focus on its own reputation and interests, no grand scheme existed to encourage a Greek coup or Turkish intervention in order to institute partition on Cyprus. Rather than driving the events on the island, the United States was in a reactive position, where the only consistent goals were to prevent a war between NATO allies and to promote negotiations as a means of resolving the issues and creating stability. Both U.S. and British policy on Cyprus had little to do with organized and carefully planned strategic policy (see also Constandinos 2009). As Miller (2009: 189) wrote about Kissinger's stance during the Cyprus crisis, "Incompetence, not malice, characterized his maneuvers."
29. On 21 March 1974, a British defense review was announced by the newly elected Wilson government involving considerable cuts in defense spending overseas, including Cyprus (Her Majesty's Stationary Office [HMSO], London, Cmnd 5976, Statement on the Defense Estimates 1975, March 1975: 1, 7, 14–15). With regard to the British bases, Kissinger considered them very important and pressured Britain into keeping them (see Mallinson 2016: xxviii).
30. Turkey's geopolitical position in the Middle East was greatly enhanced after the Yom Kippur War, and this, as some scholars claim, affected the U.S. attitude toward the Turkish invasion in 1974 (Sakkas 2016: 141–54; for the importance of Israel in U.S. foreign policy in the Eastern Mediterranean, see Fouskas 2005)

REFERENCES

Periodicals

Adesmeftos Typos
Pravda

Archives

London, United Kingdom
  Her Majesty's Stationary Office (HMSO)
  Foreign and Commonwealth Office, United Kingdom (FCO)
Washington, DC
  National Archives and Records Administration (NARA)
  Central Intelligence Agency (CIA)
  National Security Council (NSC)

Published Primary Sources

Foreign Relations of the United States (FRUS)

Secondary Sources

Aslim, I. 2016. "The Soviet Union and Cyprus in 1974 Events." *Athens Journal of History* 2(4): 249–62.

Asmussen, J. 2016. "The Post-Cold War Legacies of US Realism. The 1974 Cyprus Crisis in Perspective." In Calandri, Caviglia, and Varsori 2016: 155-169.

Asmussen, J. 2011. "Conspiracy Theories and Cypriot History: The Comfort of Commonly Perceived Enemies." *Cyprus Review* 23(2): 127–45.

Bolukbasi, S. 1988. *The Superpowers and the Third World: Turkish-American Relations and Cyprus*. Exxon Education Foundation Series on Rhetoric and Political Discourse 15. New York.

Bonanos, G. 1986. *I alitheia* [The truth]. Athens.

Brands, H. W. 1987. "America Enters the Cyprus Tangle, 1964." *Middle Eastern Studies* 23(3): 348–62.

Burke, J. 2017. *Britain and the Cyprus Crisis of 1974: Conflict, Colonialism and the Politics of Remembrance in Greek Cypriot Society*. London.

Calandri, E., D. Caviglia, and A. Varsori, eds. 2016. *Détente in Cold War Europe: Politics and Diplomacy in the Mediterranean and the Middle East*. London.

Camp, G. D. 1980. "Greek-Turkish Conflict over Cyprus." *Political Science Quarterly* 95(1): 43–70.

Constandinos, A. 2009. *America, Britain and the Cyprus Crisis of 1974: Calculated Conspiracy or Foreign Policy Failure?* Milton Keynes, England.

Coufoudakis, V. 1976. "U.S. Foreign Policy and the Cyprus Question: An Interpretation." *Millennium: Journal of International Studies* 5(3): 245–68.

———. 1987. "Greek Foreign Policy, 1945–1985: Seeking Independence in an Interdependent World—Problems and Prospects." In *Political Change in Greece: Before and After the Colonels*, edited by K. Featherstone and D. Katsoudas, 230–52. London.

———. 2006. *Cyprus. A Contemporary Problem in Historical Perspective*. Minneapolis.
Crawshaw, N. 1978. *The Cyprus Revolt: An Account of the Struggle for Union with Greece*. London.
Cutler, R. 1985. "Domestic and Foreign Influences on Policy Making: The Soviet Union in the 1974 Cyprus Conflict." *Soviet Studies* 37(1): 60–89.
Dodd, C. 2010. *The History and Politics of the Cyprus Conflict*. London.
Faustmann, H., and N. Peristianis, eds. 2006. *Britain in Cyprus: Colonialism and Post-Colonialism, 1878–2006*. Mannheim.
Fouskas, V. 2005. "Uncomfortable Questions: Cyprus, October 1973–August 1974." *Contemporary European History* 12(1): 45–63.
French, D. 2015. *Fighting EOKA: The British Counter-Insurgency Campaign on Cyprus, 1955–1959*. Oxford.
Göktepe, C. 2005. "The Cyprus Crisis of 1967 and Its Effects on Turkey's Foreign Relations." *Middle Eastern Studies* 41(3): 431–44.
Grivas, G. 1964. *Memoirs of General Grivas*, edited by C. Foley. London.
Hatzivassiliou, E. 2006. *Greece and the Cold War: Frontline State, 1952–1967*. London.
Hellenic Parliament. 1997. *To kypriako sti vouli ton Ellinon* [The Cyprus issue in the Greek Parliament]. Vol. 4. Athens.
Hitchens, C. 2002. *The Trial of Henry Kissinger*. London.
Holland, R. 1998. *Britain and the Revolt in Cyprus, 1954–1959*. Oxford.
James, A. 2002. *Keeping the Peace in the Cyprus Crisis of 1963–64*. London.
Karakatsanis, N. M., and J. Swarts. 2018. *American Foreign Policy towards the Colonels' Greece: Uncertain Allies and the 1967 Coup d'État*. New York.
Kissinger, H. 1982. *Years of Upheaval*. Boston.
———. 1999. *Years of Renewal*. New York.
Kizilyürek, N. 2016. *A History of Resentment and Violence: The Fight for Status and Ethnic Conflict in Cyprus*. Istanbul.
Klapsis, A., C. Arvanitopoulos, E. Hatzivassiliou, and E. Pedaliu, eds. 2020. *The Greek Junta and the International System: A Case Study of Southern European Dictatorships, 1967–74*. London.
Kranidiotis, N. 1985. *Anochyroti politeia: Kypros, 1960–1974* [Unfortified state: Cyprus, 1960–74]. Vol. 1. Athens.
Kuneralp, Z., ed. *A Footnote to Turco-Greek History: The Kesan-Alexandroupolis Talks, September 9–10, 1967*. Istanbul.
Kyriakides, K. A. 2009. "The 1960 Treaties and the Search for Security in Cyprus." *Journal of Balkan and Near Eastern Studies* 11(4): 427–39.
Lindley, D., and C. Wenzke. "Dismantling the Cyprus Conspiracy: The US Role in the Cyprus Crises of 1963, 1967, and 1974." Poster presented at the University of Notre Dame, 20 May 2008.
Mallinson, W. 2007. "US Interests, British Acquiescence and the Invasion of Cyprus." *British Journal of Politics and International Relations* 9(3): 494–508.
———. 2016. *Kissinger and the Invasion of Cyprus: Diplomacy in the Eastern Mediterranean*. Newcastle upon Tyne.

Maragkou, K. 2018. *Britain, Greece and the Colonels, 1967–74. Between Pragmatism and Human Rights*. London.
Markides, K. 1977. *The Rise and Fall of the Cyprus Republic*. New Haven.
Mayes, S. 1982. *Makarios: A Biography*. London.
Miller, J. E. 2009. *The United States and the Making of Modern Greece: History and Power, 1950–1974*. Chapel Hill, NC.
Morgan, T. 2010. *Sweet and Bitter Island: A History of the British in Cyprus*. London.
Nafpliotis, A. 2013. *Britain and the Greek Colonels: Accommodating the Junta in the Cold War*. London.
Nicolet, C. 2001. *United States Policy towards Cyprus, 1954–74: Removing the Greek-Turkish Bone of Contention*. Mannheim.
Novo, A. 2010. "On All Fronts: EOKA and the Cyprus Insurgency, 1955–1959." PhD diss., Oxford University, England.
O'Malley, B., and I. Craig. 1999. *The Cyprus Conspiracy: America, Espionage and the Turkish Invasion*. New York.
Palamas, C. 1979. *Diplomatiko triptycho* [Diplomatic triptych]. Athens.
Papadakis, Y. 1998. "Greek Cypriot Narratives of History and Collective Identity: Nationalism as a Contested Process." *American Ethnologist* 25(2): 149–65.
Papadopoulos, G. 1968–72. *To pistevo mas* [Our creed]. 7 volumes. Athens.
Papandreou, A. 1970. *Democracy at Gunpoint: The Greek Front*. New York.
Pelt, M. 2006. *Tying Greece to the West: US–West German–Greek Relations, 1949–74*. Copenhagen.
Rizas, S. 2000. *Enosi, dichotomisi, anexartisia, 1963–1967* [Union, partition, independence, 1963–67]. Athens.
———. 2004. *Oi Inomenes Politeies, i diktatoria ton syntagmatarchon kai to kypriako zitima, 1967–1974* [The United States, the dictatorship of the Colonels, and the Cyprus issue, 1967–74]. Athens.
Sakkas, J. 2016. "Conflict and Détente in the Eastern Mediterranean: From the Yom Kippur War to the Cyprus Crisis, Oct. 1973–April 1974." In Calandri, Caviglia, and Varsori 2016: 141–54.
Sakkas, J., and N. Zhukova. 2013. "The Soviet Union, Turkey and the Cyprus Problem, 1967–1974." *Les cahiers Irice* 10: 123–35.
Salem, N., ed. 1992. *Cyprus: A Regional Conflict and Its Resolution*. New York.
Stergiou, A. 2007. "Soviet Policy toward Cyprus." *Cyprus Review* 19(2): 83–106.
Stern, L. 1977. *The Wrong Horse: The Politics of Intervention and the Failure of American Diplomacy*. New York.
Tzortzis, I. 2020. *Greek Democracy and the Junta: Regime Crisis and the Failed Transition of 1973*. London.
Weston-Markides, D. 2001. *Cyprus 1957–1963: From Colonial Conflict to Constitutional Crisis. The Key Role of the Municipal Issue*. Minnesota Mediterranean and East European Monographs 8. Minneapolis.

Conclusions

The 1974 Moment of Rupture and the Legacies of a Discredited Past

Othon Anastasakis and Katerina Lagos

The Greek military junta lasted for a full seven years and three months, leaving a haunting memory in the Greek collective consciousness and no achievements to its credit.

It is hardly surprising that no one came out as a winner during this period in Greece. The army ended up discredited in the eyes of the Greek people and internally divided, an institution that was unable to protect the country from external threats. Political elites lost their standing, for they not only were unable to prevent the advent of the military regime in the first place, but also failed to bring about its downfall; having said that, it is to their credit that they refused to cooperate at any stage during the military regime's rule. Greek civil society was another significant victim of the junta's reign, exposed to human rights abuses, police repression, and governmental incompetence. The United States, because of its heavy-handedness and dubious position vis-à-vis the regime, struggled to gain the trust of the majority of the Greek people and in some cases earned many enemies; the U.S. Embassy in Athens had to place itself under constant protection for fear of citizens' protests and demonstrations. The monarchy, however, lost the most during these years, and while the king had already gone into self-exile from December 1967 onward, his fate was effectively sealed when Karamanlis conducted a referendum immediately after the fall of the junta and the overwhelming majority voted for the abolition of the institution. If one adds the dismal economic performance during the oil crisis, by 1974 the country's politics, economy, society, and foreign policy were all descending into chaos at high speed. The culmination of this disarray occurred in July

1974, when the regime, under the leadership of hard-liner Dimitrios Ioannidis, sponsored a coup d'état for the island of Cyprus. The failure of the overthrow was only compounded by the Turkish invasion and partition of the island that remains to this day, leaving Cyprus as the ultimate casualty of the junta in Greece.

With the military in tatters, the collapse of the junta and the return to civilian rule was a major opportunity for the political class to clean up their act and face up to their responsibilities toward parliamentarism, as well as a wake-up call to never repeat the mistakes of the pre-1967 period. As it transpired, the country sailed through its transition to democracy, and despite the ups and downs in the internal and external affairs of the post-1974 period, Greece could boast that its democracy transitioned successfully toward consolidation, where competitive party politics and alteration of power became the norm and the military returned to its barracks where it belonged. Nevertheless, the legacy of the 1967–74 dictatorship was noticeable for years to come, and the democratic elites had to reverse the negative effects of the military rulers in most areas of government policy.

Legacies, as individual and collective memories, are important referents of the past, and they may be related to historical *periods* or historical *moments*. As a historical period, the seven-year authoritarian experience is remembered as a period of ineptitude and repressive practices, but also as a period against which the political elites and many citizens had an opportunity to prove their democratic credentials and resistance. Among the several threshold moments, the 21 April 1967 coup d'état is remembered as a time of political disgrace, recriminations, and blame. The November 1973 Polytechnic uprising is another threshold moment that showed that the attempted liberalization by the junta was impossible and unacceptable. Finally, the July 1974 moment of the breakdown of authoritarian rule retained a dual conflicting significance in the subsequent intergenerational memory, as a moment of national tragedy, on the one hand, and a moment of celebration for the victory of democracy over the dictatorship, on the other, as well as the start of a new epoch in Greek politics. The latter two moments, which in their own ways brought about the discrediting and downfall of the regime, continue to be commemorated annually, and often stir controversy.

The junta legacies, however, haunted not only the Greek politicians and citizens; they extended into the wider international community, especially when one bears in mind that the military regime took place at the height of the Cold War and was the outcome of Western anticommunist practices during the 1950s and 1960s. One of the points that this book has tried to highlight is that despite the rhetorical condemnation coming from the Western democracies, some of them continued to work with the military regime with a "business as usual mentality," guided either by their own economic interests and/or by the exigencies of the Cold War and competition with the Soviet Union. While the focus of most historians of the Cold War period has centered around aspects of totalitarianism behind the Iron Curtain in the Eastern bloc, the West has its own ghosts in the form of authoritarian regimes that flourished in southern Europe and Latin America. Some of them, such as Spain and Portugal, go back to the interwar years, while others, such as Chile, came to power in the latter half of the twentieth century. All of these regimes were in working relationships with the democracies of the West; for the latter, financial interest and Cold War politics prompted them to turn a blind eye to many undemocratic abuses in order to maintain beneficial trade relations.

In the context of continuities and discontinuities with the past, a theme that has been prevalent throughout this book, the 1974 moment became the signifier of *real rupture* with the illiberal past of Greece. The collapse of the military regime marked a new beginning for Greek politics and society—what came to be known as the Metapolitefsi. Against the background of the foreign policy debacle in Cyprus, the change of guard from military to civilian rule was surprisingly peaceful and swift, an elite-based compromise dominated by the political personality of Konstantinos Karamanlis, who returned from his self-exile in Paris as the supposed savior of democracy.

Karamanlis brought back to politics the political class, which had been marginalized during the years of dictatorship, and with his newly formed New Democracy Party, he achieved a record electoral victory of 54.37 percent in the 17 November 1974 elections, on the first anniversary of the Polytechnic uprising. As prime minister of Greece, he took some quick and decisive steps to ensure a steady transition to democracy by legalizing the Communist Party of Greece (KKE), which had been outlawed since 1948, and freeing all political prisoners. He also conducted a referendum on the question of the monarchy, where an overwhelming majority (69.2 percent) voted for its abolition and the establishment of a republic. In addition, he oversaw a series of trials against the military conspirators, known as the trial of the instigators of the 21 April 1967 coup, which resulted in the death penalty for Georgios Papadopoulos, Stylianos Pattakos, Nikolaos Makarezos, and Dimitrios Ioannidis on the grounds of high treason. Yet Karamanlis was loathe to repeat the mistakes of the past and commuted their sentences to life imprisonment. These first moves were important signals that the new democracy was ready to stand on its constitutional feet, over and above any extra- or para-constitutional interventions, including the military, which from then on was subsumed firmly under civilian rule. The postdictatorial

Constitution of Greece, which was enacted in 1975, introduced the Third Hellenic Republic, confirmed the separation of powers, and also secured civil and political liberties. Under the new constitutional practice, the military was placed under strict civilian control and never attempted to impose its influence or challenge domestic politics. This was a major break with the past, given that since the mid-nineteenth century, the military had been an influential factor in politics. However, with the fall of the dictatorship, Greek democracy would no longer allow such interventionist practices to be repeated ever again.

At the same time, Karamanlis removed the country from the military wing of NATO to show his displeasure toward the inaction of Greece's allies vis-à-vis the Turkish invasion in Cyprus and as a symbolic reaction to the heavy-handedness of the United States in Greek internal affairs. He then made the most important strategic decision of his time in power—namely, to commit to the accession of Greece into the European Economic Community (EEC) at a time when a large part of the Greek population viewed the West with some suspicion. The role of the United States, in particular, remained for years one of the most controversial influences on Greece, with the country becoming one of the most anti-American nations in Europe. Karamanlis anchored his entire political strategy on rapid and full entry into the EEC and openly claimed that his decision rested on political rather than economic grounds.

However, even the role of the EEC in the liberalization and final breakdown of the military regime is sometimes exaggerated from a positive perspective. The actual freezing of the EEC-Greek relations was not as overwhelming as it may sound; during the junta, progress toward Greece-EEC free trade continued, with the dismantling of tariff barriers occurring on schedule. While EEC assistance was frozen after 1967, financial assistance from Western sources came through NATO within the framework of the Cold War. The essays in this book have shown some examples of this ambivalent practice. The freezing of association itself was not motivated by pure idealism but was due to more complex and ambiguous reasons. Individual EEC governments cooperated with the military regime for strategic, geopolitical, and security reasons. In some ways, such individual national stances toward the military regime help to explain the reluctant Greek attitudes regarding the issue of Greece's membership in the EEC. Indeed, consensus was missing from Greek politics and society during the preaccession period. Moreover, the preparation of the country during the late 1970s to become a member was a cause pursued by the right-wing New Democracy Party, with PASOK (Πανελλήνιο Σοσιαλιστικό Κίνημα, Panhellenic Socialist Movement) and the parties of the Left being strongly against it.

Despite the domestic and external achievements of New Democracy as the first postjunta government in Greece, there was a sense among many Greeks that the political process was still based on elites whose continuity with the pre-1967 political class had not been totally disrupted, and that those who had been excluded for so long had not yet spoken. The voices of those who were marginalized or overlooked were successfully captured by the charismatic Andreas Papandreou, the once radical politician of the Center Union Party of the 1960s, and were translated into a victorious political discourse that would bring his PASOK party to the forefront of Greek politics. In 1981, PASOK, a center-left party that had been formed from fragmented resistance movements during the period of the dictatorship, came to power and dominated the 1980s and beyond. The victory of Papandreou's party constituted another decisive moment in the country's postauthoritarian political trajectory, a peaceful electoral alteration from a conservative to a socialist party, under the banner of change. PASOK won a convincing victory of 48.1 percent of the national vote, which then brought about a new political class, with a more inclusionary and equitable message and a promise for a radical break with the pre-1974 past. In sum, one cannot understand the actions of New Democracy and PASOK during the 1970s and 1980s without recourse to the years of military rule in Greece. For some politicians, civil servants, academics, and others, their resistance to military rule became a badge of honor to be used when circumstances required.

With time, the impact of the military regime faded, giving way to the gradual consolidation of democracy in Greece and the country's Europeanization. Yet one can still trace important links with this discredited past. The so-called 17 November Group and its offspring terrorist organizations are a legacy of anti-Americanism and civic resistance that started in the junta years and have continued ever since. The law on the asylum policy in Greek universities, barring the presence of the police in campuses and remaining in force until August 2019, became one of the sacred red lines for many students and faculties, a legacy of the junta's police intrusions in the universities. The commemoration of the Polytechnic uprising continues with the same passion every year, including a march ending outside the U.S. Embassy in Athens, as a symbol of respect for those who fought for intellectual and civic freedoms, and at the same time is consistently exploited for political and media purposes. The division of Cyprus, the continuing presence of the Turkish army in the north of the island, and all the failed attempts to resolve this problem remind us of the fatal and irresponsible decisions taken by the military regime in its final year. Last but not least, within the fringes of the political system, there are still some supporters who continue to reminisce with nostalgia about the years of the military junta.

The above legacies show that there is resilience in some aspects of Greece's dictatorial past, and despite its fading away with time, it remains a part of the collective memory.

Yet the most important legacy and commemoration from those years is Greece's 1974 constitutional moment, gathering mythical proportions as a cut-off point with an illiberal past and as a model of democratic transition for many other subsequent European postcommunist countries on their way to the European Union. This belief, widely held in the Greek national consciousness, was challenged for the first time in recent times due to Greece's unprecedented peacetime, post-2008, decade-long economic crisis—not just by those who voted for the neo-Nazi Golden Dawn, allowing it to occupy third place in the parliament with 7 percent of the vote in the 2015 elections—but also from citizens protesting in the streets against the ills of the two-party system that had brought the country to a state of economic bankruptcy and even against the European Union, which had imposed severe economic austerity. During the darkest and most difficult moments of the crisis, there were even some international observers wondering whether Greek democracy could survive this massive economic shock and the challenge to its political status quo. As it happened, the Greek democratic political system survived the difficult decade, proving that despite the deep political and societal polarizations that thrived during the crisis, the democratic foundations remained solid, confirming the positive legacy of the 1974 moment.

Othon Anastasakis is the Director of South East European Studies at Oxford (SEESOX) and Senior Research Fellow at St Antony's College, University of Oxford. His most recent co-edited books include *Diaspora Engagement in Times of Severe Economic Crisis: Greece and Beyond* (Palgrave, 2022), *The Legacy of Yugoslavia: Politics, Economy and Society* (I.B. Tauris, 2020), and *Balkan Legacies of the Great War: The Past Is Never Dead* (Palgrave Macmillan, 2016).

Katerina Lagos is a Professor of History at California State University, Sacramento and the Director of the Angelo K. Tsakopoulos Hellenic Studies Center and Hellenic Studies Center. Her most recent publication is *The Fourth of August Regime and Greek Jewry, 1936-1941* (Palgrave, 2023).

Index

Note: Page references noted with an *f* are figures.

Academy of Athens, 152
Acheson, Dean, 323
Acheson Plan, 322, 323, 324, 332
Agnew, Spiro, 256
agriculture, 155
Akheloos River dam, 105
The Alexandria Quartet (Durrell), 187
allegories, 184
Allende, Salvador, 258
Alphand, Hervé, 275
American Hellenic Educational Progressive Association (AHEPA), 222
American Society of Travel Agents (ASTA), 118
anarchism, 148, 149
Anastasakis, Othon, 4, 6, 7
Anastassopoulos, George, 115
Ancient Greek, 147, 179
Andreopoulos, Charalambos, 5, 7, 51
Androutsopoulos, Adamantios, 79
Angelis, Odysseas, 45, 149
Angelopoulos, Demetrios, 115
anticommunism, 28, 143, 158, 169–74, 185, 187, 201, 296
anti-Greek campaigns, 272
anti-Left, 201
antileftist propaganda, 158
Apostolopoulos, Dimitrios K., 297
Arab League, 123
archbishops, selections of, 205–7. *See also* Greek Orthodox Church
Archdiocese Clergy-Laity Congress (1968), 8
Aristotle University, 155, 202
Arnaoutis, Michael, 56
artistic integrity, 189
Ash, Roy, 121
Asia Minor catastrophe (1922), 5, 15–21, 38, 186, 332
Aslanides, Konstaninos, 325
Asmussen, Ian, 321
ASPIDA, 249, 251
Association Agreement (with EEC), 104, 107, 131, 279, 281, 283, 286, 311. *See also* European Economic Community (EEC)
Athanassiades-Novas, George, 250250
Athenagoras, Archbishop, 217, 232, 235
Athens, Greece, 17, 18, 199, 224, 225–29, 230, 234, 235
Athens Merchants' Association, 115
Athens Pedagogical Institute, 146
Athens Polytechnic uprising (1973), 59, 233, 328, 341

Atlantic Alliance, 267, 277, 278, 279, 306
Atlantic Maritime Enterprises Company, 123
Atlantis, 224
austerity, 345
Auswärtiges Amt (Federal Foreign Office of Germany), 300
authoritarianism, 92, 140, 142, 143, 164; in education, 157–59; regimes in Latin America, 342
autocephalous Greek Orthodox Church, 198. *See also* Greek Orthodox Church
Averoff, Evangelos, 247
Axis occupation of Greece, 22, 296

Bakirdzis, Euripides, 22, 24
Balance of Payments, 109, 110*f*
Balkan Wars (1912–13), 16, 37, 203
Baltazzis, Georgios, 17
Bank of Greece, 93, 109
Barlos Brothers Company, 114
Bauxites Parnasse S.A., 113, 114
Belgium, 271, 272, 310
Berlin, Germany, 295. *See also* West Germany
Bermeo, Nancy, 92
bilateral trade, 267
Bodosakis-Athanasiadis, Prodromos, 111, 112
Bonn, Germany, 296, 299, 300, 306, 307, 311, 312–14. *See also* Brandt, Willy; West Germany
book bans, 164
"The Bourgeois 'Barbarians'" (Sulzberger), 171
Brademas, John, 222
Brandt, Willy, 9, 301, 302, 306, 312–14
Brewster, Daniel, 240
Briggs, Ellis, 246
British Foreign Office, 22
Brosio, Manlio, 273
Buffalo, New York (USA), 220
Bund Deutscher Mädel, 302

Bundestag (West Germany), 309
burden-sharing, 296, 299–300, 305, 307–9
bureaucratic-authoritarianism, 92
Butler, Frank P., 120
Byzantine Empire, 51, 174, 176

Camre, Mogens, 302
Canada, 310
canonical order, 203–5
canon law, 199
capital imports, 85
capitalism, 145
capitulation, 252–54
Castro, Fidel, 149
Cavafy, C. P., 7, 164–65, 190; anticommunism propaganda, 169–74; in context of junta's discourse, 174–79; in *Eighteen Texts,* 182–87; ideologies, 166–69, 185; in schools, 179–82. *See also* poetry
censorship, 150–51
Center Union (EK) party, 7, 44, 146, 179, 245, 246, 249, 304, 344
Central Powers, 38
Centre for Planning and Economic Research (CPER), 79
Chile, 258
China, 112
Christian Democrats, 206
Christianity, 51, 174, 175, 206, 228. *See also* Greek Orthodox Church
Christian Solidarity (Χριστιανική Αλληλεγγύη), 207
Christopoulos, Georgios, 222, 223
Christou, Panagiotis, 142
Chrysostomos II, 7
Chrysostomos II (Chatzistayrou), 202
CIA (Central Intelligence Agency), 27, 41, 241, 246, 250, 251, 324
civil wars, 18
Clergy-Laity Congress (1966), 222
Clergy-Laity Congress (1967), 215, 220, 221

Clergy-Laity Congress (1968), 224, 225–29, 234, 235
Clergy-Laity Congress (1970), 231
Coca-Cola, 122–27
Cold War, 3, 5, 24, 187, 241, 244, 255, 257, 284, 295, 297, 305, 322, 341, 342; anticommunism and, 28; anticommunism propaganda, 169–74; containment of Soviet Union, 298–99; military ideology of, 35; onset of, 27; propaganda, 164–65. *See also* Soviet Union
Colonels, the, 5, 6, 7, 8, 9, 35, 36, 304; anniversary of the coup, 166; Brandt, Willy, 312–14; Cyprus policy and, 331 (*see also* Cyprus); dictatorships, 54; economic policies under, 73–74 (*see also* economic policies); European Economic Community (EEC), 279–83; expulsion of Greece from CoE, 269–73; foreign investment under, 103 (*see also* foreign investments); Great Britain and, 268; Greco-Christian Civilization, 203; growth and, 91 (*see also* growth); Iakovos, Archbishop, 215–16 (*see also* Iakovos, Archbishop); ideologies, 172, 200 (*see also* ideologies); NATO (North Atlantic Treaty Organization), 273–79; Phantom case, 309; propaganda, 184; relationships with the West, 283–85; revolution and, 51; rise of, 40–48; UK support of, 274; United States and, 241 (*see also* United States of America); and West Germany, 307 (*see also* West Germany); West Germany policies toward, 295–98 (*see also* West Germany); West Germany relationship with, 311–12. *See also* coup d'état (1967); junta

Commission on Education (1957), 145
Committee on Higher Educational Matters, 155
Common Agricultural Policy (CAP), 92
communism, 41, 50, 149, 242, 296; advocates of, 52; containment of Soviet Union, 298–99; fear of, 23; risk of, 200; warnings of dangers of, 168
Communist Party, 3, 42, 172
conservatism, 41
Conservatives (CDU), 302
Conservatives (Great Britain), 267, 276, 282, 285
Constantine I (King), 16, 17, 37, 38, 46, 50, 202, 207, 224, 229, 230, 231, 241, 252, 254, 256, 274, 302, 311; countercoup, 56–58; leaving Greece, 58
Constantine II (King), 28
constitution (Greece), 251–52
Constitution of 1968, 152
construction, 84–86
Conterier, Peter, 310
continuity, economic policies after 1967, 78–84
COREPER (Committee of Permanent Representatives), 275, 280, 281
Council of Europe (CoE), 266, 267, 269–73, 275, 276, 285, 287, 307
Council of Ministers, 269, 281
countercoup (King Constantine), 56–58, 225
coup d'état (1967), 1, 10, 34, 278, 304, 341; economic policies after 1967, 78–84; Greek America on eve of, 216–20; military actions in, 58; start of, 48, 49; United States of America and, 240–41 (*see also* United States of America); United States of America reaction to, 300–301; West Germany reaction to, 300–301
coup d'état (1974), 9

coups: attempts (1935), 19, 20; countercoup (King Constantine), 56–58; Gaddafi, Muammar, 277; Goudi Revolt (1909), 15, 35, 37, 57; Ioannides, Dimitrios, 90
credit policies, 83*f*; credit conditions, 86; private sector lending, 87; real credit growth, 85*f*
Crete, Greece, 277, 300
crises: Cyprus, 80, 320–21, 328–31 (*see also* Cyprus)
The Crisis of the Consumerist Society (Georgalas), 148
Crossman, Richard, 275
Cuba, 322
currencies, reliability of, 77, 89
Cypriot Communist Party (AKEL), 327, 328
Cypriot National Guard, 323
Cyprus, 9, 43, 44, 75, 217, 219, 233, 286; after independence, 322–23; crises, 80, 81, 90, 206, 328–31; Cyprus question (1967–72), 324–28; Greek unity with, 321; intervention and, 245; opposition to partition of, 323; Turkey invasion of, 323

Dafnis, Grigoris, 19
Danish Social Democrat Party, 304
Darius (King), 183, 184
Daveas, D., 158
Dawkins, R. M., 178
debt, 92. *See also* credit policies
Defence Planning Committee (DPC [NATO]), 308
Defense and Overseas Policy Committee (1969), 274
deficits, trade alliances and, 88*f*
Dekemvriana (Δεκεμβριανά, December Events) of 1944, 24
Delphi Bauxites, 114
Demertzis, Constantine, 20

democracy, 229, 241, 242, 278; Greece as birthplace of, 1; New Democracy government, 344
Democratic Army (DA), 6, 26, 40
Demoticism, 186
demotic (spoken) language, 145, 178
Denmark, 269, 271, 276, 277, 279, 307, 311
Denver, Colorado (USA), 221
despotism, 185
dictatorships, 1, 34, 140, 154, 164–65; anticommunism propaganda, 169–74; the Colonels, 54; economic policies under, 73–74 (*see also* economic policies); education and, 181; Goudi Revolt (1909), 35; Iakovos, Archbishop, 215–16 (*see also* Iakovos, Archbishop); ideologies of military, 200–201; military, 34; West Germany policies toward, 295–98 (*see also* West Germany). *See also* authoritarianism; junta
Die griechish-deutschen Nachkriegsbeziehungen (Apostolopoulos), 297
Dimirouli, Foteini, 7
Dokopoulou, Evangelia, 107
domestic policy, 301
drachmas, 89. *See also* currencies
drug smuggling, 113
Dubcek, Alexander, 255
Durrell, Lawrence, 187
Dutsche, Rudi, 305

Eastern bloc, 342
East Germany, 296. *See also* West Germany
economic aid, 241, 243
economic austerity, 345
Economic Development Financing Corporation, 107
Economic Development Plan for Greece (1968–72), 79

economic imperialism, 103
economic policies, 73–74; after 1967, 78–84; economic development, 76–78; gross domestic product (GDP), 74, 75; growth legitimation, 84–90; investments, 81–84; long-term view of economy, 74–76; stability and, 80–81
economic stagnation, 5
economies, 2, 154
Ecumenical Patriarchate of Constantinople, 198, 199, 201, 203, 204, 218, 220, 221
EDA (Ενιαία Δημοκρατική Αριστερά, United Democratic Left) party, 43, 44, 302
EDES (Εθνικός Δημοκρατικός Ελληνικό Σύνδεσμος, National Republican Greek League), 23
EDHN (Εθνική Δημοκρατία Νεολαία, Greek Democratic Youth), 149
education: authoritarianism in, 157–59; Cavafy in schools, 179–82; censorship, 150–51; control of, 152–54; and dictatorships, 181; Greek National Army and, 140–42; indoctrination, 150–51; policies, 141; propaganda, 150–51; pseudomodernizing/pseudoliberal facade, 154–57; reaction and counter-reform in, 144–48; as a threat, 142–44; traditional humanist, 179; youth demobilization, 148–50
Education Act (1964), 146
Education of the Citizen (Papakonstantinou), 176
EENA (Εθνική Ένωσις Νέων Αξιωματικών, Union of Young Greek Officers), 45, 47
EES (Εταιρεία Ελληνικών Σπουδών, Society for Greek Studies), 79
Egypt, 112, 217

Ehmke, Horst, 313
Eighteen Texts, 182–87
Eisenhower, Dwight, 105, 218, 243, 245, 255
Eisenhower, Mamie, 218
EKOF (Εθνική Κοινωνική Οργάνωσις Φοιτητών, National Social Organization of Students), 154
ELAS, 23, 25, 26
Eliopoulos, Athanassius, 112, 113, 114
Eliopoulos, Elias, 112, 113, 114
Eliopoulos, George, 112, 113, 114
Elytis, Odysseus, 177
Emergency Law 3/1967, 202
Emergency Law 129/1967, 146
Emergency Law 214/1967, 202
ENA (Ένωσης Νέων Αξιωματικών, Union of Young Officers), 25
Epistle to the Philippians (Apostle Paul), 227
ERE (Εθνική Ριζοσπαστική Ένωσις, National Radical Union), 43, 149, 246
Erhard-Markezinis agreement (1953), 112
Ethnikos Kiryx, 224
Ethnosotirios Epanastasis, 34–36; countercoup (King Constantine), 56–58; Greek military (pre-World War II), 36–40; in power, 48–55; rise of the Colonels, 40–48
eudemonism, 148
Europe: authoritarian regimes in, 342; and the junta, 266 (*see also* junta)
European Commission of Human Rights, 272
European Convention on Human Rights (1967), 269, 304
European Economic Community (EEC), 1, 8, 77, 78, 80, 88, 92, 104, 107, 266, 268, 279–83, 286, 299, 343; Association Agreement with, 279, 281, 283, 286, 311; Greece's relationships with, 283–85

European Union (EU), 345
executions of the Six, 18
exports, 75, 88f
Extra-Parliamentary Opposition (Außerparlamentarischen Opposition), 303
extreme right-wing indoctrination, 158

F-4 Phantom aircraft, 308
Fanfani, Amintore, 273
Federal Republic of Germany (FRG), 268, 271, 278, 298, 299, 306. *See also* West Germany
Federal Security Council (West Germany), 309
Federation of Greek Industries (FGI), 116
Federation of Greek Industry (SEB), 80
Fiat, 119, 120
financial repression, 77
Finlay, George, 150
fiscal policies, 82f
Five-Year Economic Development Program Committee, 115
Foreign and Commonwealth Office (FCO), 275, 281
foreign capital, 84–86
foreign direct investment (FDI), 85, 89, 109, 111, 117
foreign exchange, 88
Foreign Investment Committee, 114
foreign investments, 103–4; American economic assistance, 104–6; Coca-Cola, 122–27; Gerber, 127–30; Greek manufacturers and, 111–17; Litton Industries, 117–22; Nutricia, 127–30; Pepsi-Cola, 122–27; protecting economic establishment, 107–11
foreign policy, 243, 301, 311, 322, 324
Fouskas, Vassilis, 321
France, 148, 254, 268, 273, 275, 278, 285, 287
Frangatos, Gerasimos, 142

Frederika (Queen), 247, 301, 302
Free Democratic Party (FPD), 310
Free-Thinkers Party (Κόμμα των Ελευθεροφρόνων), 39
French Revolution, 36

Gaddafi, Muammar, 277
Gaddis, John Lewis, 383
Gage, Nicholas, 232
Galley, M., 278, 279
Gantonas, Nikolaos, 142
Garoufalias, Petros, 46
Gastarbeiters (guest workers), 90, 299
Gavas, Georgios, 219
general education, 147. *See also* education
Generation of the 1930s, 169
Georgakas, Dan, 224, 225, 230
Georgalas, Georgios, 35, 36, 49, 50, 53, 148, 167, 168, 169, 170, 171, 173
George I (King), 15
George II (King), 20, 21, 23, 39
Gerakinis, Christos, 28
Gerber, 127–30
German Democratic Republic (GDR), 298
Germany, 295. *See also* Federal Republic of Germany (FRG); West Germany
Gerolymatos, André, 2, 5, 36
Golden Dawn, 345
Gonatas, Stylianos, 19
Goodpaster, A. J., 305, 306
Goudi Revolt (1909), 15, 35, 37, 57
Gounaris, Dimitris, 17, 38
Grammenos, Athanasios, 5, 7, 51
Grand Bretagne (Athens, Greece), 223
Grand Coalition government (1966–69), 302
Great Britain, 44, 254; Conservatives, 282, 285; Council of Europe (CoE), 269–73; and Cyprus, 244, 320 (*see also* Cyprus); European Economic Community (EEC), 279–83; government in the 1960s,

266; Greece's relationships with, 283–85; House of Commons, 276, 282; and the junta, 266 (*see also* junta); Labour government, 267, 268, 275, 276; MPs (Members of Parliament), 302; NATO (North Atlantic Treaty Organization), 273–79; policies toward Greece, 274; United States's relationship with, 272
Great Idea (Megali Idea), 216, 235
Great Powers, 18
Great Synthesis (Μεγάλη Σύνθεσις), 36
Greco-Christian Civilization, 200, 201, 203
Greco-Christian ideals, 51, 143
Greco-Turkish War (1897), 5, 15, 37
Greco-Turkish War (1919–22), 203
Greece: Association Agreement (with EEC), 279, 281, 283, 286, 311; Athens (*see* Athens, Greece); Axis occupation of, 22, 296; as birthplace of democracy, 1; Brandt, Willy, 312–14; Christianity in, 228 (*see also* Greek Orthodox Church); Clergy-Laity Congress (1966), 222; Clergy-Laity Congress (1967), 215, 220, 221; constitution, 251–52, 343; Council of Europe (CoE), 269–73; coup d'état (1967), 1 (*see also* coup d'état [1967]); and Cyprus, 320–21 (*see also* Cyprus); democracy, 229, 278; dictatorships, 164–65 (*see also* dictatorships); economic policies, 75; European Economic Community (EEC), 279–83; foreign policy and, 243; *Gastarbeiter* (migrant workers), 299; history, 151; isolation of government, 301; Johnson, Lyndon B. and, 247–48; Kennedy, John F. and, 245–47; Kingdom of Greece, 198; migrations, 75; military involvement in politics, 2; monographs on political history of, 2; NATO (North Atlantic Treaty Organization), 268, 273–79 (*see also* NATO [North Atlantic Treaty Organization]); politics and, 341; post-World War II, 3, 216; public opinion and, 301–4; reconstruction of, 298–99; relationships with the West, 283–85; trade partners and, 268; United States of America aid to, 4; West Germany policies toward, 295–98 (*see also* West Germany); West Germany relationship with, 311–12. *See also* Colonels, the; junta
Greek America: on eve of coup d'état (1967), 216–20; policies, 216
Greek American community, 201
Greek American Fascism, 111
Greek American Progressive Association (GAPA), 222
Greek Civil War (1946–49), 2, 5, 24–28, 25, 36, 40, 41, 45, 48, 103, 154, 172, 201, 296
Greek Communist Party (KKE), 242
Greek Constitution, 49, 55
Greek Cotton Textile Manufacturers Association, 116
Greek Cypriot forces, 323
Greek Foreign Ministry, 322
Greek Holy Synod, 198, 199, 202, 203, 204
Greek identity, 52, 174, 177
Greek Independence Day, 204
Greek Industrial Development Bank, 119
Greek Light (Ελληνικό Φώς), 202
Greek Ministry of Foreign Affairs, 219
Greek National Army, 5; Asia Minor catastrophe (1922), 15–21; and Cyprus, 320–21 (*see also* Cyprus); and education, 140–42 (*see also* education); Greek Civil War, 24–28 (*see also* Greek Civil

War); intervention in elections, 251; morale of, 26; in politics, 15; training of Greek officers (USA), 40; World War II and the occupation, 21–24
Greek Orthodox Archdiocese, 205, 215; archbishop selections, 205–7; autonomy of, 206
Greek Orthodox Church, 5, 7, 51, 185; dictatorships and, 207; on eve of coup d'état (1967), 216–20; fundamental documents of, 203; Greek-language liturgy, 231; Iakovos, Archbishop, 215 (*see also* Iakovos, Archbishop); ideology of military dictatorship, 200–201; Ieronymos, Archimandrite, 203–5, 207–8; influence of, 157; junta's designation of, 202–3; under the military junta, 198–99; symbolism and, 226; in the United States of America, 217, 232, 233, 234
Greek Rally Party, 42
Greek Right, 251
Greek-Turkish War (1919–22), 216
Greek War Relief Association, 217
gross domestic product (GDP), 74, 75, 81, 86, 87, 111
growth, 82*f*; legitimation, 84–90; real credit, 85*f*
Guevara, Che, 149
Guillaume, Pierre, 118

Halyvourgiki Steel, 115
Harmel, Pierre, 272
Hartling, Poul, 307, 308
Hatzianestis, Georgios, 17
Hatzipetros, Alexandros, 45
Hawk missiles, 307
Healey, Dennis, 273
health, 155
Heaney, Seamus, 188, 189
Heath, Edward, 267, 279, 286
heavy industry as engine of growth, 74

Hellacana Trading Co.–Spyropoulos Bros., 127
Hellenic Company of Chemical Products and Fertilizers Ltd., 112
Hellenic Industrial Development Bank (ETVA), 107, 108
Hellenic Review, 151
Hellenism, 53
Helms, Richard, 251
Hermes, Peter, 312
hierarchies in religion and government, 199
Higher Council of Education, 147
hippy movement, 148
history: Cavafy, C. P., 174–79; Greece, 151
History of the Greek Nation (1860–74 [Paparrigopoulos]), 150, 175
History of the Greek Revolution (Finlay), 150
Hitler, Adolf, 296
Holy Courts, 202
Holy See, 198, 203
Holy Synod. *See* Greek Holy Synod
Homeland-Religion-Family, 200
homosexuality, 169, 187
Hood (Lord), 269
Hooper, Robin, 278, 279, 281
Hoppers, Vernon, 125
House of Commons (Great Britain), 276, 282
Howaldtwerke-Deuschte Werft, 301

Iakovos, Archbishop, 8, 201; change in attitude, 230–34; Clergy-Laity Congress (1968), 224, 225–29; and the Colonel's dictatorship, 215–16, 221–25; as devil-priest, 235; on eve of coup d'état (1967), 216–20; promotion of Greek language and culture, 220–21; relationships with American presidents, 218; sympathy toward the Colonels, 229–30

Iakovos (Makrygiannis) of Elassona (Bishop), 207
IDEA (Ιερός Δεσμός Ελλήνων Αξιωματικών, Holy Bond of Greek Officers), 3, 25, 26, 27, 28, 45, 55, 200, 249, 250
ideologies, 141, 143; Cavafy, C. P., 166–69, 185; Colonels, the, 172; of military dictatorship, 200–201
The Ideology of the Revolution: Ideals not Dogmas (Georgalas), 49, 167, 169
Ieronymos, Archimandrite, 7, 203–5, 207–8
Ieronymos I (Kotsonis [archbishop]), 199
imports, 75; capital, 85; trade alliances, 88*f*
independence, Cyprus after, 322–23
indoctrination, 144, 150–51, 158
Industrial Development Corporation, 107
industry, 74, 155
inflation, 77, 80, 89*f*, 90
Inonu, Ismet, 248
intellectuals, 143, 164, 166
Interorthodox Center of Penteli (Athens, Greece), 207
interwar period, 16
investments, 3, 82*f*; economic development and, 76–78; economic policies, 81–84; foreign, 103–4 (*see also* foreign investments); public, 84
investor intentions, 109
Ioannides, Dimitrios, 9, 90, 142, 157, 205, 233, 328
Iron Curtain, 342
Israel, 273, 330. *See also* Middle East
Italy, 271, 273
"Ithaca" (Cavafy), 179, 180, 181, 182

Jefferys, Peter, 187
Jesus Christ, 174
Johnson, Lady Bird, 218
Johnson, Lyndon B., 218, 247–48, 253, 255

Joint Chiefs of Staff Directive (JCS 1067), 298
Julian the Apostate, 176
junta, 34, 46, 81, 115, 131, 141, 169; authoritarianism in education, 157–59; Brandt, Willy, 312–14; burden-sharing, 309 (*see also* burden-sharing); Cavafy in context of junta's discourse, 174–79; collapse of, 73; designation of Greek Orthodox Church, 202–3; ethnocultural ambitions of, 207; European Economic Community (EEC), 279–83; expulsion of Greece from CoE, 269–73; Great Britain and, 266, 267, 268, 269; Greek Orthodox Church under the military, 198–99 (*see also* Greek Orthodox Church); ideology of, 144; leaders, 53, 54, 59; legacy of, 340–45; lending and, 87; NATO (North Atlantic Treaty Organization), 273–79; November Polytechnic uprising (1973), 312; politics of, 164, 165; practices of, 8; relationships with the West, 283–85; UK support of, 274; and the United States, 253, 257 (*see also* United States of America); West Germany and, 307; West Germany policies toward, 295–98 (*see also* West Germany); West Germany relationship with, 311–12; and youth, 148–50. *See also* Colonels, the; coup d'état (1967); Greek National Army; military

Kakridis, Andreas, 5, 6, 108
Kalamnpokias, Konstantinos, 141, 200
Kalergis, Dimitrios, 15
Kalogerakos, Nicholas, 6, 85
Kanellopoulos, Panagiotis, 252, 254
Karakatsanis, Neovi M., 282, 320

Karamanlis, Konstantinos, 81, 43, 105, 106, 206, 229, 245, 246, 247, 302, 332, 340, 343
Karaoglou, C. L., 170
Kardamakis, Vassilios, 250
KATE (Κέντρα Ανωτέρας Τεχνικής Εκπαιδεύσεως, Centers of Higher Technical Education), 155, 159
Katharevousa, 52, 145, 148, 177, 178, 179
Katsambas, Christopher, 116, 117
Keeley, Robert, 240, 241, 252, 253, 279
Kemal, Mustafa, 38
Kennedy, John F., 105, 245–47
KET (Κέντρο Εκπαιδεύσεως Τεθωρακισμένων, Armored Training Center), 48
Keys, Barbara, 298
Kiesinger, Kurt, 9, 302, 313
Kingdom of Greece, 198
Kissinger, Henry, 257, 258, 308, 328, 330
Kitroeff, Alexander, 7, 201
Kizilyürek, Niyazi, 320
Kjærsgaard, Kristine, 298
KKE (Greek Communist Party), 45, 158
Kollias, Ioannis, 224, 225, 253
Kollias, Konstantinos, 78, 252
Kondylis, George, 20
Korais, Adamantios, 51
Krag, Jens Otto, 304
Krokidas, Sotirios, 19
Krushchev, Nikita, 42, 43
ΚΥΡ (Κεντρική Υπηρεσία Πληροφοριών, Central Intelligence Service), 27, 41, 326
Kyros, Peter, 222

labor unions, 77
Labouisse, Henry R., 45, 246
Labour government (Great Britain), 267, 268, 275, 276. *See also* Great Britain
Ladas, Ioannis, 53, 325

Lagos, Katerina, 2, 5, 6
Lambrakis, Grigoris, 302
languages: Cavafy, C. P., 174–79; demotic (spoken), 145, 178; Greek-language liturgy, 231; Katharevousa, 52, 148, 177, 178, 179 (*see also* Katharevousa); Modern Greek, 146, 147; role of, 51, 52
Larymna nickel mines, 112
Latin America, 34, 91, 141; authoritarian regimes in, 342; military regimes, 143
Lausanne Treaty (1923), 324
Law 93/1969, 149
Law 129/1967, 147
Law 509, 42
Law 553/68, 153
Law 652/1970, 155
Law 2687/53, 85, 111, 126
Law 4379/1964, 145
Law Decree 672/70, 153
Law Decree 746/70, 156
laws, 84; canon law, 199; and religion, 199
Law School, 156, 159
Leffler, Melvyn, 241
left-wing politics, 3
Leonidas (King), 53
liberalism, 84, 140
Liberal-KKE (Κομμουνιστικό Κόμμα Ελλάδας, Communist Party of Greece), 20
Liberal Party *(Eleftheros Kosmos)*, 149
Libya, 277
licenses, 128
Life magazine, 113
Limerick (Lord), 278
Linz, Juan, 142
Lipkowski, Jean de, 278
literature, 164. *See also* Cavafy, C. P.
Litton Industries, 85, 117–22
London-Zurich accords, 248
long-term view of economy, 74–76, 76*f*

M47 Patton tanks, 307
Makarezos, Nikolaos, 37, 47, 128, 284
Makarios, Archbishop, 9, 248, 257, 258, 321, 322; coup against (1974), 331; Cyprus crisis (1973–74), 328–31; diplomacy of, 325; relationship with Cyprus, 324; relationship with United States, 328; Soviet Union and, 325, 326
Makedonia, 39
Malouhos, Giorgos, 229
Mandakas, Emmanuel, 24
Mangakis, Georgios-Alexandros, 313
Mao Zedong, 149
Maragkou, Konstantina, 320
Marinopoulos, Demetrios, 116, 127, 128, 130
Markezinis, Spyridon, 79, 112, 156, 328
Markezinis experiment (1973), 268, 282
Maronitis, D. N., 183, 184, 188, 189
Marshall Plan, 40, 103, 104, 242, 298
Marxism, 149, 157
Maury, Jack, 252
Mavromichalis, Kyriakoulis, 37
McCarthy, Joseph, 42
McGrew, William, 120, 121
McNamara, Robert, 55
Megalopolis Power Station Project, 106
Melistas, Nikos, 81
ΜΕΟ (Μυστική Επαναστατική Οργάνωσιν, Secret Revolutionary Organization), 21
Merrill, James, 170
Metapolitefsi, 34
Metapolitefsi (regime change), 342
Metaxas, Ioannis, 20, 21, 22, 34, 38, 39, 54, 111, 175, 176, 199, 295; ideologies, 200 (*see also* ideologies); propaganda, 54
Meyer, Frank A., 127, 129, 130
Michael, Archbishop, 217, 235
Middle East, 45, 123, 271, 273, 330, 331
migrant workers *(Gastarbeiter),* 299
migrations, 75

military, 266; aid and United States of America, 279; the Colonels (*see* the Colonels); and Cyprus, 320–21 (*see also* Cyprus); dictatorships, 34 (*see also* dictatorships); and education, 140–42 (*see also* education); Greek military (pre-World War II), 36–40; increase in expenditures, 21; involvement in Greek politics, 2, 15; junta (*see* junta); regimes (Latin America), 143; revolts, 15; royalist-dominated officer corps, 20, 21; United States control of Greek, 26
Military Academy, 54
military coups, 1. *See also* coup d'état (1967)
Military League, 15, 37
Miller, James Edwards, 3, 5, 8
Millet, 326
mining, 113
Ministry of Agriculture, 127
Ministry of Coordination, 87, 93, 118, 120, 121, 123, 124, 128, 129
Ministry of Defense (Germany), 310
Ministry of Education, 145, 153
Ministry of Finance, 127
Ministry of Foreign Affairs (Germany), 297
Ministry of National Economy 2001, 93
Ministry of Press, 150
Modern Greek language, 146, 147
modernization, 40, 242, 243
Monetary Committee, 78, 87
monetary policies, 80, 83f. *See also* economic policies
Monthly Statistical Bulletin (Bank of Greece), 93
Montreal, Canada, 222
Morgenthau Plan, 298
morphine, 113
mortgages, 86. *See also* credit policies
MPs (Members of Parliament), 302
Mussolini, Benito, 22

Nafpliotis, Alexandros, 3, 8
narcissism, 187
National Can, 119
National Council of Education, 152
National Ethical Instruction, 144
National Front, 326
National Investment Bank of Industrial Development (NIBID), 107
National Regeneration, 49, 50
National Revolution, 57
National Schism, 37
National Security Action Memorandum No. 22, 105
National Security Council (NSC), 299
National Security Decision Memorandum (NSDM 34), 256
nation building, 242, 245
NATO (North Atlantic Treaty Organization), 41, 44, 167, 242, 244, 247, 254, 266, 268, 273–79, 280, 283, 286, 287, 299, 300, 304, 305, 343; attacks on, 272; Brandt, Willy, 314; burden-sharing, 307–9 (*see also* burden-sharing); Defence Planning Committee (DPC), 308; Greece's relationships with, 283–85; November Polytechnic uprising (1973), 312; role of, 274; South Eastern flank, 277; West Germany, 306–7
Nazis: invasion of Greece, 111; liberal resistance to, 166; occupation of Greece, 154
Nea Demokratia, 206
Nea Estia, 168
Nea Politeia, 39, 185
Near East Foundation, 298
Nea Techni, 168
Nenni, Pietro, 273
neo-Nazi Golden Dawn, 345
Netherlands, the, 313
the Netherlands, 269, 271
New Democracy government, 158, 344
New Left, 166, 302

New York City (USA), 231
New York Times, 173, 232
nihilism, 148
Nixon, Richard M., 255, 256, 257, 258, 308, 320, 330
noncommissioned officers (NCOs), 41
Norway, 269, 271, 279, 311
November Polytechnic uprising (1973), 312
Nutricia, 127–30

Oder-Neisse border, 305
Officers Save Fatherland Ideals Democracy Meritocracy, 46
Ohnesorg, Benno, 302
oil shocks, 90
Onassis, Aristotle, 123
Onassis industrial complex (Megara, Greece), 85
Oncken, Dirk, 311
Organization for Economic Co-operation and Development (OECD), 74
Orthodox Observer, 226
Ostpolitik (West Germany), 310
Othon I (King), 15
Othonaios, Alexandros, 24
Otto (King), 198
"Our Belief" speech (Papadopoulos), 200
output, 75. *See also* economic policies

Pagoulatos, George, 108
Pakistanis, Gregorios, 224
Panagoulis, Alexandros, 313
Panayotakos, Constantine, 233
Pangalos, Theodoros, 38, 52, 178, 199
Papadimitriou, G., 153
Papadopoulos, Georgios, 5, 7, 34, 36, 37, 39, 42, 45, 47, 49, 50, 51, 54, 58, 59, 79, 86, 115, 116, 141, 204, 205, 224, 225, 250, 281, 284; Clergy-Laity Congress (1968), 234, 235; Cyprus crisis (1973–74), 328–31;

liberalization and, 283; "Our Belief" speech, 200; removing Cyprus from foreign policy, 324; speeches (1967), 52–53; unified Hellenism, 227
Papagos, Alexander, 20, 23, 26, 27, 42, 243, 244
Papakonstantinou, Theofylaktos, 141, 176
Papandreou, Andreas, 46, 48, 56, 79, 117, 241, 249, 251, 252, 304, 344
Papandreou, George, 4, 44, 79, 145, 146, 158, 246, 251; opposition to partition of Cyprus, 322; relationship with United States, 247
Papanoutsos, Evangelos, 145
Paparrigopoulos, Konstantinos, 150, 175, 176
Papathanasopoulos, Charalambos, 28
Pappas, Tom A., 123, 124, 125, 127, 222
PASOK (Πανελλήνιο Σοσιαλιστικό Κίνημα, Panhellenic Socialist Movement), 157, 158, 331, 343, 344
Patriarchal and Synodical Act of 1928, 203
Patrinacos, Nicon, 226
Pattakos, Stylianos, 37, 47, 151, 204, 225, 230, 231, 256, 284
Paul (Apostle), 227
Paul (King), 27, 202, 218, 246, 247, 249, 250
Pechiney conglomerate, 106, 114
Pedaliou, Effie G. H., 298
Pelt, Mogens, 5, 112, 297
Pepsi-Cola, 122–27
Pesmazoglou, Ioannis, 282
Pesmazoglu, John, 109
Phantom case, 309
Phokas, Nikolaos, 19
Piel, Gerard, 112, 113
Pipinelis, Panagiotis, 277
Piraiki-Patraiki Cotton Manufacturing Company, 116

Plan Percicles, 45, 47
Plan Prometheus, 49
Plastiras, Nikolaos, 19, 24, 38
Plytas, Amvrosios, 223
Plytzanopoulos, Ioannis, 28
Podlesski, Nick, 123, 124, 125
poetry, 164, 190; artistic integrity, 189; Heaney, Seamus, 188, 189; ideology of revolution, 166–69; "Ithaca" (Cavafy), 179, 180, 181, 182; "Thermopylae" (Cavafy), 179, 181, 182; "Waiting for the Barbarians" (Cavafy), 172; "Walls" (Cavafy), 170, 173; "The Windows" (Cavafy), 170, 171, 173. *See also* Cavafy, C. P.
Political Education (Papakonstantinou), 151
politics: Cold War, 24; Greek Army in, 15; left-wing, 3; military involvement in, 2
Politis 2, 153, 158
Polytechnic uprising (1973), 156
populism, 81
Populist Party, 19
Portugal, 342
post-World War II Greece, 3, 216
Poulantzas, Nicos, 91
power, centralizing, 140. *See also* dictatorships
Pravda, 331
prices, 83*f*
primary education, 145. *See also* education
private sector lending, 87
pro-enosis statements, 325
propaganda, 148, 150–51, 158; anticommunism, 169–74; Cold War, 164–65 (*see also* Cold War); Colonels, the, 184; Metaxas, Ioannis, 54
property rights, 78, 80
Protopapadakis, Petros, 17
provincialisms, 187

pseudo-ideology, 200. *See also* ideologies
pseudointellectuals, 143
Psichari, Jean, 178
Ptolemais Project, 112
public investments, 84
public opinion, 301–4
Public Power Corporation (Greece), 106

Rallis, Dimitrios, 15, 28, 37
Rallis, Ioannis, 23
real credit growth, 85*f*
recessions, 90
The Redress of Poetry (Heaney), 188
Red totalitarianism, 50
reforms, 144–48
religion, 198–99; Cavafy, C. P., 174–79; Iakovos, Archbishop, 215–16 (*see also* Iakovos, Archbishop); laws and, 199. *See also* Christianity; Greek Orthodox Church
revolts, 15
Revolutionary Council, 47
Revolutionary Group, 48
revolutions, 28, 232; the Colonels and, 51; ideologies, 166–69
Reynolds Metal Company, 114
Ritsos, Giannis, 166
Rodgers, William P., 232
Rodinos-Orlandos, John, 123, 125
Rostow, Walt W., 253
Royal Crown Cola, 124
Royal Decree 322/69, 152
Royal Decree 702/69, 151
Royal Greek Navy, 311
Royal Hellenic Navy, 301
royalist-dominated officer corps, 20, 21, 24
Rusk, Dean, 240, 247, 253, 301

Sakkas, John, 321
Savidis, G. P., 169, 174, 175
Scheel, Walter, 308, 310
Schmidt, Helmut, 310
Schmitt, Hans O., 121, 122

school leaving certificate *(Akadimaiko Apolytirio)*, 146
secondary education, 145. *See also* education
Second Balkan Pact (1953), 243
secret associations, 28
Security Battalions, 23, 25, 28
Seferis, George, 169, 177
shipping, 84–86
Sifnaios, Panagiotis, 142
Simpson, Nicos, 233
Sioris, Nikitas, 141
Sisco, Joseph, 330
Six, the, 17, 18
Six-Day War (1967), 273
Social Democrats (SPD), 302, 305, 309, 310, 312
Socialists (Belgium), 272
social security (IKA) payments, 130
soft propaganda, 164. *See also* propaganda
Sorokos, Ioannis A., 272
South Africa, 274
Southern Flank, 254
Soviet Bloc, 301
Soviet Union, 242, 257; containment of, 298–99; and Cyprus, 321, 322 (*see also* Cyprus); Cyprus crisis (1973–74) and, 328–31; Makarios, Archbishop, 325, 326
Spain, 342
Spais, Leonidas, 17
Spandidakis, Gregory, 47, 55, 56
Special Disciplinary Council, 158
Special Operations Executive (SOE), 22
SS Alesia, 112
stability, 4; economic development and, 76–78; and economic policies, 80–81
Statistical Yearbook, 93
Stefanopoulos, Stefanos, 251
Stewart, Michael, 270, 284
Stratos, Nikolaos, 17
subversive ideas, punishment for, 150

Sulzberger, Cyrus L., 170, 171, 172, 173, 187
Supreme Administrative Court, 204
Supreme Military Council, 26
Swarts, Jonathon, 282, 320
Sweden, 269, 271

Talbot, Phillips, 46, 54, 57, 223, 240, 251, 252, 277
Tasca, Henry, 230, 257, 270
Tasca Report, 256
taxes, 84, 130, 131
TEA (Τάγματα Εθνοφυλακής Αμύνης, National Defense Battalions), 42
Teachers' Training College, 146
TEIs (Τεχνολογικό Εκπαιδευτικό Ίδρυμα, Technological Higher Education Institutions), 159
Tel Aviv, Israel, 123
textiles, 155
Theologitis, John, 125
Theotokas, George, 177
Theotokis, Nikolaos, 17
"Thermopylae" (Cavafy), 179, 181, 182
Thessaloniki, Greece, 230, 231
Third Greek Civilization, 53
Third Hellenic Civilization, 175, 199
Time magazine, 123
Tom Pappas Decree (1968), 125, 126
Topika Somateia fraternities, 222
Tories (Great Britain), 268
totalitarianism, 142
tourism, 84–86, 118, 119
trade: alliances, 88*f*; balances, 88*f*; bilateral, 267; partners and Greece, 268
trademark policies, 84–86
transterritorial Hellenism, 215, 216
Treaties of Alliance, Establishment, and Guarantee, 322
Truman, Harry, 218, 242
Truman Doctrine, 298
Tsakas, Christos, 91
Tsellos, Epaminondas, 21

Turkey, 9, 44, 112, 219, 233, 234, 273, 277; Cyprus and, 321 (*see also* Cyprus); Cyprus crisis (1973–74), 328–31; invasion of Cyprus, 323; United States support of, 242
Tying Greece to the West: US–West German–Greek Relations 1949–74 (Pelt), 297

unification, 244
unified Hellenism, 227
Union Carbide, 131
unions, 77
United Democratic Left (EDA), 245, 246, 249
United Kingdom (UK), 267, 287; expulsion of Greece from CoE, 270; policies toward Greece, 282; support of the junta, 274. *See also* Great Britain
United Nations (UN), 219, 247, 269
United States Drug Enforcement Administration, 112, 113
United States of America: aid to Greece, 4; burden-sharing, 308 (*see also* burden-sharing); capitulation, 252–54; CIA (Central Intelligence Agency), 27, 41; Clergy-Laity Congress (1967), 220, 221; common objectives of, 241; control of Greek military, 26; and the coup d'état (1967), 240–41; and Cyprus, 325 (*see also* Cyprus); Cyprus and, 320 (*see also* Cyprus); Cyprus crisis (1973–74), 328–31; economic aid, 241, 243; economic assistance to Greece, 104–6; economic imperialism, 103; European Economic Community (EEC), 279–83; expulsion of Greece from CoE, 270; gaining trust of Greek people, 340; Greece's relationships with, 283–85; Greek America policies and, 216; Greek anger against, 333; Greek Orthodox

Church in the, 217, 232, 233, 234; interventions, 252–54; involvement in coup, 8; limits of power and, 241–44; Makarios, Archbishop, 328; Marshall Plan, 103 (*see also* Marshall Plan); military aid and, 279; NATO (North Atlantic Treaty Organization), 273–79; Papandreou, George, 247 (*see also* Papandreou, George); policies toward Greece, 320; policies toward West Germany, 299; reaction to coup d'état (1967), 300–301; reconstruction of Greece, 298–99; relationship with Great Britain, 272; returning Greece to constitutional government, 255–58; soft propaganda, 164 (*see also* propaganda); training of Greek officers, 40
University of Athens, 152, 230
University of Crete, 156
University of Cyprus, 320
University of Ioannina, 146
University of Patras, 146
University of Thessaloniki, 142
University of Thrace, 156
U.S. Development Loan Fund (DLF), 105
U.S. Orthodox Church, 255
USS Franklin D. Roosevelt, 255
U.S. Sixth Fleet, 252, 253, 255
USSR. *See* Soviet Union

Varkiza Agreement, 25
Vekris, Socrates, 126
Venizelists, 16, 17, 22, 23, 27, 37, 186
Venizelos, Eleftherios, 16, 17, 37
Venizelos, Sophokles, 246
Vidalis, Orestis, 225, 230
Vietnam, 258
von Bohlen Krupp, Bertold, 112

wages, 80, 83*f*
"Waiting for the Barbarians" (Cavafy), 172

"Walls" (Cavafy), 170, 173
Wassman, William P., 131
Western Alliance, 300
Western Peloponnesus, 121
West Germany, 8, 106, 112, 254, 285, 287; Brandt, Willy, 312–14 (*see also* Brandt, Willy); Bundestag, 309; burden-sharing, 296, 299–300, 305; expulsion of Greece from CoE, 270; Free Democratic Party (FPD), 310; NATO (North Atlantic Treaty Organization), 306–7; November Polytechnic uprising (1973), 312; Ostpolitik, 310; policies toward Greece (junta period), 295–98; public opinion and, 301–4; reaction to coup d'état (1967), 300–301; reactivating burden-sharing, 307–9; reconstruction of Greece, 298–99; relationship with the junta, 311–12; rising opposition, 309–10; Social Democrats (SPD), 309, 310; as trade partners, 268; United States of America policies toward, 299
Wilson, Harold, 266, 267, 276, 277
"The Windows" (Cavafy), 170, 171, 173
World Bank, 155
World War I, 16, 35, 295
World War II, 3, 111, 145; anticommunist propaganda, 175; dictatorships after, 266; Greece's entrance into, 217; Greek Army prior to, 15; and the occupation, 21–24; post-World War II Greece, 216

Xanthopoulos-Palamas, Christos, 273, 278

youth demobilization, 148–50
youth movements, 142. *See also* education

Zambelios, Spyridon, 175
Zepos, D., 129
Zoitakis, Georgios, 231

www.ingramcontent.com/pod-product-compliance
Lightning Source LLC
Chambersburg PA
CBHW071331080526
44587CB00017B/2794